SECOND EDITION

HRM REALITY

PUTTING COMPETENCE IN CONTEXT

Peter J. Frost

University of British Columbia

Walter R. Nord

University of South Florida

Linda A. Krefting

Texas Tech University

Prentice Hall

UPPER SADDLE RIVER, NEW JERSEY 07458

Library of Congress Cataloging-in-Publication Data

HRM reality: putting competence in context / [compiled] by Peter J. Frost, Walter R. Nord,
  Linda A. Krefting.—2nd ed.
      p.   cm.
    Previously published: Cincinnati, Ohio: College Division, South-Western Pub. Co., c1992.
    Includes bibliographical references.
    ISBN 0-201-43390-7
    1. Personnel management—United States. I. Frost, Peter J. II. Nord, Walter R. III. Krefting,
  Linda A.

  HF5549.2.U5 H75 2002
  658.3—dc21   2001036278

Acquisitions Editor: Melissa Steffens
Editor-in-Chief: Jeff Shelstad
Senior Managing Editor (Editorial): Jennifer Glennon
Assistant Editor: Jessica Sabloff
Editorial Assistant: Kevin Glynn
Media Project Manager: Michele Faranda
Marketing Manager: Shannon Moore
Marketing Assistant: Christine Genneken
Managing Editor (Production): John Roberts
Production Editor: Maureen Wilson
Permissions Coordinator: Suzanne Grappi
Associate Director, Manufacturing: Vincent Scelta
Production Manager: Arnold Vila
Manufacturing Buyer: Diane Peirano
Cover Design: Jayne Conte, Art Director
Cover Illustration/Photo: Diana Ong/ SuperStock, Inc.
Full-Service Project Management and Composition: Impressions Book and Journal Services, Inc.
Printer/Binder: Hamilton Printing Co.

Credits and acknowledgments borrowed from other sources and reproduced, with permission, in this textbook
appear on appropriate page within text.

Prentice
Hall

10 9 8 7 6 5 4 3 2 1

ISBN 0-201-43390-7

**For Tom Mahoney, Vance Mitchell,
and Larry Williams**

CONTENTS

PART IV: IMPLEMENTING COMPENSATION AND BENEFITS   147

PART V: DEALING WITH DIVERSITY AND DISCRIMINATION   183

PREFACE

For more than 20 years we have been concerned with helping business students connect the descriptive and normative dimensions they study in their textbooks with their experiences. The success of our first effort in this direction, *Organizational Reality: Reports From the Firing Line* (now in its 4th edition) suggested other instructors had the same concern. That book's reception in the market went far beyond our original intention as it attracted attention from instructors of communication and creative writing. Our second attempt, *Managerial Reality*, had similar aims but was directed to students of management; it was also well received as a supplement to traditional, more normative approaches to the subject. Accordingly, when we were asked to prepare the first edition of this book, we welcomed the opportunity to provide a teaching tool that contained vivid illustrations of human resource management's past, present, and future.[1] In that book as well as in this second edition, we emphasized the context within which the practice of HRM takes place. Indeed, it is the changing context that has required us to produce the current edition so that we can offer materials that reflect contemporary reality. These changes have been so great that there are no selections in this edition that were also in the first edition. However, the structure and, for the most part, the headings of the first edition remained useful. As before, we believe our approach provides students with materials that center on reality rather than primarily conceptual aspects of HRM, thereby providing students with an interesting and relevant perspective that conventional textbooks do not.

We are indebted to the many authors whose reporting and insights shaped this book. As the reader will note, we have drawn from a broad spectrum of sources in our effort to portray the reality of human resource management. We also acknowledge with sincere thanks the administrative support of Melissa Steffens, David Shafer, and Michael Campbell of Prentice Hall. We are grateful to Cynthia Rée and Graham Brown of the Faculty of Commerce and Business Administration at UBC and Norma Walker at USF for their excellent secretarial services. We want to give special thanks to Cynthia Cohen and Charles Michaels for preparing original articles for this volume.

Finally, we owe a very special debt to three scholars: Thomas Mahoney, Vance Mitchell, and Lawrence K. Williams to whom we dedicate this book. Professors Mahoney and Williams were instructors of one or more of us when we first began our graduate studies. Their scholarship and teaching skills were a major reason we continued to work in this area. Professor Mitchell is a long-time colleague whose intellect and enthusiasm for learning and teaching played a central role in shaping our work along the reality-centered course that is reflected in this and the related books we have published. Indeed we have been most fortunate to have had these people in our lives.

Note

1. In this preface, the words *we* and *our* in the first paragraph refer to Frost, Mitchell, and Nord. In the subsequent paragraphs, *we* and *our* refer to the current editors—Frost, Nord, and Krefting. Vance Mitchell has retired, but is working so hard in his retirement that he decided not to work on this second edition. Fortunately, Linda Krefting was interested in joining Frost and Nord on this edition.

SEPTEMBER 11 AND THE ENDURING VALUE OF HRM

We were awaiting page proofs for this edition of *HRM Reality* when the two towers of the World Trade Center and the Pentagon were attacked by hijacked planes and a fourth hijacked plane crashed in Pennsylvania on September 11, 2001. With millions of others across the globe, we felt shock, horror, and grief at the senseless loss of life. Most of those who died were in harm's way for work-related reasons—airline flight crews, business travelers, employees working in the doomed buildings, and rescue workers. Mass media and business press coverage in the days following September 11 made clear that this event and the aftermath have much significance for the reality and future of HRM.

HRM policies and practices played a prominent role in many aspects of this story. Employment records have been crucial in establishing who would have been at work at the time the buildings were attacked and to the issuance of death certificates that survivors need for insurance and legal purposes. Concerns have been raised about the adequacy of records kept for temporary assignments and whether missing temp workers have all been identified. The high quality of on-site day care centers at both the World Trade Center and the Pentagon has been credited for the orderly and safe evacuation of children. Counseling available through medical plans and employee assistance programs has helped many throughout the nation, not just in the target areas, handle their grief and fears. Staffing plans and selection procedures in place before the tragedy have eased the very difficult task of hiring replacement workers. Regulations provide protection both to those who face harassment at work because of perceived ethnic or religious similarity to the hijackers and to employees now called up to active military duty.

The centrality of HRM in the wake of September 11 is consistent with the themes and selections in this book. Those organizations that had "put people first for organizational success," as Pfeffer and Veiga advocate (Selection I-3), seemed best positioned to deal with the tragedy. Managers and executives who understood HRM and its role were able to mobilize the available HR infrastructure to address both human and business dimensions. Public acts of grief and compassion, perhaps most visibly those of New York Mayor Giuliani, helped engage both healing processes and commitment to work (see Dutton et al., 2002). Even the most mundane HR elements often regarded as irritants, records and regulations, have been significant.

"September 11 changed everything" is now oft repeated. In the aftermath many have reconsidered their priorities. The meaningfulness of their work helped rescue workers through the long, difficult days of rescue and recovery efforts while lack of meaning made it difficult for others to concentrate on work in the days after the tragedy. However meaningful work might be, there is evidence of renewed commitment to personal relationships beyond work and, for some, to faith. The complex interfaces between work and life, the subject of Part VII, have renewed importance as we seek, in Annie Dillard's terms (Selection VII-I), not just good days but good lives.

At the organizational level, the events of September 11 have also led to reconsideration of HRM policies and practices for the future. Safety has become a major issue. How should HRM concerns be incorporated in the selection and design of the workplace—from high-occupancy buildings to airplane cockpits? Are employees adequately informed about and practiced in emergency evacuation procedures? The individual confined to a wheelchair who was carried heroically from the sixty-ninth floor down to the first floor of the World Trade Center raises particular questions about the effectiveness of evacuation procedures for persons whose mobility is impaired. How should flight crews, and others who might face terrorists willing to die, be trained and equipped to deal with them? When can other methods of communication and collaboration adequately substitute for business travel? Beyond physical safety, questions have been raised about economic security: the adequacy of insurance coverage and benefits for affected workers, including lower-level workers and temps, and whether they understand and have access to services.

Perhaps the reconsideration of basic values has the greatest potential for significantly changing the future of HRM. The "inglorious" past of HRM discussed in the introduction to this book stems, in part, from its lack of success in advancing employee interests. Shareholder and management concerns have most often taken precedence over those of workers, particularly lower-level workers. Discussions currently taking place have questioned these values and, in so doing, opened up possibilities for those concerned with HRM to advocate change. In an essay titled "Real Masters of the Universe," Business Week editor Bruce Nussbaum (2001) suggests our real heroes are working class, the "men and women making 40 grand working for the city" who risked and lost their lives. The "self-sacrifice by civil servants in uniform" endeavoring to rescue "the investment bankers and traders making 10 times" as much "was simply breathtaking" (55).

We add that the wave of letters in October delivering infectious agents such as anthrax to media and political offices again put lower-level employees at risk: mail room workers and others who handle mail.

"Tragedy has the power to transform us," Nussbaum goes on, "but rarely is the transformation permanent" (55). These words note both an opportunity and a challenge for HRM. The transformation from this tragedy is more likely to be permanent if those of us concerned with HRM keep the issues alive. Through our conversations as well as the policies and practices we propose, we can reassert the importance of all employees—from blue-collar heroes and mail handlers to investment bankers and CEOs—as organizational stakeholders. Lingering images from the tragedy and rescue support our efforts.

Peter J. Frost, Walter R. Nord, Linda A. Krefting
October 11, 2001

References

Dutton, Jane E., Frost, Peter J., Worline, Monica C., Lilius, Jacoba M., & Kanov, Jason M. (2002). Leading in time of trauma. *Harvard Business Review,* 80(1).

Nussbaum, Bruce. (October 1, 2001). Real masters of the universe. *Business Week,* 55.

INTRODUCTION

"Putting people first" is crucial "for organizational success," a case Jeffrey Pfeffer and John F. Veiga make convincingly in their article in Part I of this collection. However, it takes more than a catchy slogan for organizations to realize the competitive advantages of treating employees as assets. Evidence suggests it takes a consistent management philosophy and a coherent set of human resource (HR) practices, but the payoff in terms of profits, quality, and productivity can be substantial. Several readings in this volume provide details of organizations that have successfully implemented this approach. Other readings address the significant challenges organizations face in implementing consistent and coherent human resource policies and the costs—organizational, human, and societal—of failing to do so. What becomes clear in these readings is that for the potential advantages to be realized, good human resource management must be both a priority and a collective responsibility in organizations. As important as human resource specialists are to developing the human resource practices of high performance management, such practices are successful only if implemented as intended by managers throughout the organization.

There are no magic bullets or quick fixes. The promise of human resource management (HRM) can only be fulfilled through systematic efforts. Success at putting people first requires Getting Human Resource Management into Focus (Part I), developing perspective on the role and importance of systematic, collaborative HRM. The vision of how HRM practices that treat employees as assets contribute to the organization must be understood by employees as well as managers and human resource professionals. The challenge of Meeting Human Resource Requirements (Part II) requires understanding both organizational needs and the HR options available for addressing those needs. Day-to-day organizational life provides the evidence on which employees decide whether they are valued as assets. The links between HR policies, employee voice and experience, and organizational outcomes are explored in Creating a Productive Work Environment (Part III). Pay policies are arguably the most visible among HRM policies with tangible financial impact on both employees and employers. The prosperity gap between Old and New Economies and changing expectations are prominent factors in our section on Implementing Compensation and Benefits (Part IV). Although articles on diversity appear in many of the parts of the book, the complexities and significance of this topic to HRM now and in the foreseeable future merit further consideration in Dealing with Diversity and Discrimination (Part V). The "wild new workforce" (see the article by Michele Conlin and Peter Coy), technology, and the changing nature of employee–employer relationships are highlighted in Grappling with Issues (Part VI). The Interfaces of Work and Life (Part VII) put employment in the broader context of life and explores the resulting tensions which HRM must address. Finally, as we move into the twenty-first century, the implications for employers, employees, and HRM are the subject of Anticipating the Future (Part VIII)

Despite impressive evidence to support "putting people first for organizational success," there is also good evidence that many organizations overlook and fail to capitalize on the advantages of systematic HRM. To understand why organizations routinely miss the easily apparent benefits of HRM, a historical context is helpful.

HISTORICAL ROOTS OF HRM

Human resource management (the modern term for what had been called personnel management and before that industrial welfare work) as a separate field of management has had a short and not very glorious history. Why has its history been so brief and inglorious?

Widespread recognition of the need for a specialized personnel function awaited both the growth of large organizations in the late 1800s and early 1900s and the human and social problems associated with them. This is not to say that human resources were well managed before. In fact, the writings of Frederick Taylor and his followers from early in the twentieth century and the work of modern scholars (e.g., Jacoby, 1985) indicate that problems were rampant. However, the times were not conducive to attending to them, for many reasons. First, there were few large organizations, and small organizations (even today) do not sense the need for an HRM department. Moreover, back then, the professionalization of management was barely spoken of. Daniel Nelson (1975), a leading historian on this period, suggested that to improve organizational performance the people who controlled these organizations focused almost exclusively on more and better machinery. Nelson observed that these people viewed the factory primarily as a place to house machinery and thought it unnecessary to provide even drinking water and toilets in the workplace.

Another factor associated with low concern for people in the factories was that the workforce included a very high number of immigrants and many uneducated and seemingly recalcitrant workers. Further, the combination of violent strikes; concerns over a potential, working-class revolt; and the dominant ideology of social Darwinism gave managers of the time a rather dim and unsympathetic view of their employees. At the time, most of these matters were seen more as social and less as managerial problems, although they eventually did contribute to the beginnings of personnel administration. Thus, the history of HRM is short, its origins appearing in fragmented form in the mid to late 1800s. (The readings from Sanford Jacoby in Part I will explore this development more fully.)

Answering the second question, "Why has HRM's history been so inglorious?", is more difficult. Fortunately, Jacoby's excellent book *Employing Bureaucracy* provides us with some revealing insights about HRM's low status. Specifically, the field of personnel administration grew out of social work and industrial welfare. Foremen (who had much more power in the late 1800s and early 1900s than they typically do today) frequently perceived the early HR practitioners as a constraint on their authority. Moreover, many of the positions taken by personnel appeared to be very similar to the positions taken by the trade unions, and unions were often perceived as bitter rivals by the foremen and other managers. Further, personnel practitioners often advocated expenditures on things that were not clearly linked to such widely accepted goals as improving efficiency and productivity. To make matters worse, they often had little knowledge of the industries in which they worked. In short, personnel departments did not seem to be well aligned with the organizations in which they functioned.

To a degree, modern HRM managers suffer from a similar lack of alignment. For example, they frequently have primary responsibility for implementing affirmative action programs and other policies mandated by law that are perceived negatively by many managers. Moreover, HRM is plagued by the belief (perhaps partially grounded in fact) that members of HRM departments were recruited from the ranks of those who "couldn't cut it elsewhere." Students seeking jobs in HRM often contribute unwittingly to the problem. Frequently, they are asked, "Why do you want to work in human resources?" Many managers recoil when they hear the common answer "I like working with people."

Then too, even sophisticated HRM professionals have contributed to the low status of their field. For one thing, over time they mindlessly introduced a series of innovations (e.g., sensitivity training, job enrichment, quality of work life, quality circles, etc.), advancing one fad after another without establishing the relationship of any given innovation to the fabric and goals of their particular organizations. *Please note, that we are not saying that these ideas lack merit.* We are, however, suggesting that HRM professionals have contributed to their being adopted without carefully evaluating their fit with particular circumstances. As a result, there has been increased cynicism about new programs and decreased respect for the field in general. Closely related is the failure of HRM specialists to understand and relate to the strategies and missions of their organizations. For these and other reasons, they have missed opportunities to make important contributions and have failed to frame their messages in ways that effectively communicate to key decision makers.

In a similar vein, HRM departments have often operated in ways that lead them to be perceived as obstacles to getting things done. In this context, consider the observations of two leading economists writing in a major academic journal:

> In every organization with which we have been associated, and in most of those of which we have heard, the Personnel Department is viewed by line managers and employees as unresponsive, rule-bound, and bureaucratic. It takes forever to get a decision from Personnel, and the decisions seem aimed more at maintaining the Personnel Department's precious rules, procedures, and job classification/earnings curves than in attracting, rewarding, and retaining the best people for the organization. Moreover, protests fall on deaf ears. Personnel people are always in meetings when you try to reach them, and they do not return your calls. (Milgrom and Roberts, 1988, p. S176.)

While this portrayal may be as much a caricature as a valid description, the fact such a stereotype often exists is important because it is a salient element of the reality in which HRM professionals exist. However, as we will see in the pages that follow, HRM's image may be improving. In the last decade or so, it has come to be perceived by many high-ranking executives as an increasingly vital element for high levels of organizational performance.

To summarize so far, modern HRM has a short and not very glorious history. In the distant past as well as more recently, HRM managers have often lacked the context and the means to convey their expertise in ways that will induce other managers to use it.

In our view, the reality of most modern HRM managers has placed them in a struggle to be heard. However, the recent turbulence of the business and social worlds may provide the means to a more glorious future for HRM. However, success will depend on the ability of HRM professionals to respond to the realities of dynamic business environments. We believe that the materials we have included in this book provide key elements to help HRM professionals make such responses. Several features should be especially helpful: (1) the materials are as current as the print medium permits, (2) the readings emphasize what organizations and people are actually doing, and (3) the materials emphasize the context in which HRM operates.

LESSONS FOR THE PRESENT

The historical process reviewed above helps to put the modern HRM function in context. In particular, it reveals two enduring characteristics of HRM tasks that make them extremely difficult.

First, HRM managers deal with many matters that often, at first glance, appear to be peripheral to the mission of their organizations. In other words, most people seem to believe that the primary reasons for the existence of most organizations are to increase the wealth of their owners and to provide goods and services. While it might be asserted that some organizations can, do, and should serve other ends (e.g., providing jobs for people or promoting the physical and psychological welfare of their members), at least in our culture these other purposes are usually viewed as secondary. Consequently, HRM managers often find themselves advocating programs that serve goals that other managers see as less central than profits and efficiency.

Second, and closely related, the problems that HRM practitioners confront are ones generated by rapidly changing social, political, and moral environments that impact organizations. These problems tend to defy clear, simple answers. They are rife with issues that entail considerable conflict and are not easily resolved. For example, justice, equality, due process, and equal opportunity for all individuals are typically seen in our culture as characteristics of the Good Society. Typically we turn to governments to address these concerns. While governments have played important roles, it is also true that how work organizations select, reward, and govern their employees may have even more frequent and direct effects on the extent to which many members of society are treated justly and equitably on a day-to-day basis. In fact, some political scientists refer to modern business organizations as private governments.

In short, HRM often deals with matters that are central to human welfare in modern society. Most methods for selecting, rewarding, and governing employees entail conflicts about what constitute fundamental human rights. For instance, procedures that on the one hand protect workers from arbitrary dismissal or discriminatory hiring, on the other hand can be interpreted as restricting employers' rights to use their private property and make sound business decisions. Similarly, efforts of an organization to protect information that might compromise its competitive position can lead to actions that seemingly violate employees' rights to free speech and privacy.

Many of the issues HRM professionals address reflect such hard-to-resolve conflicts. In complex, pluralistic societies such matters can be especially intractable. Moreover, when these societies are experiencing rapid demographic changes, fluctuating economic circumstances, changing technologies, and changing values, even conceptualizing appropriate resolutions is difficult. In our society, many of these issues are addressed by "private governments" operating under the scrutiny of federal and state governments. HRM plays a key function in these "private governmental roles."

All of this is not to excuse poor performance by HRM professionals or to suggest they face impossible obstacles to performing well. Rather, it is to point to the context that shapes the reality in which HRM professionals function and to suggest that the criteria defining what constitutes good performance of the HRM profession are by no means obvious.

The remainder of this book is designed to provide a richer understanding of these issues and their context. To do so, we have selected a diverse set of materials, drawn from traditional business publications. However, we have gone beyond these, especially to newspapers and popular magazines, and we requested two selections be written specifically for this volume. In our view, these sources provide a richer, more grounded understanding of the reality facing contemporary and future HRM professionals than do most traditional textbooks. As a result, we feel this book is a valuable complement to more formal and technical treatments provided in most existing textbooks on personnel and human resource management.

IMPLICATIONS FOR DEVELOPING HRM PROFESSIONALS

One interpretation of what we have said so far might be that the problems of HRM are so complex and value driven that the technical knowledge at the core of HRM training is of little value. That is not what we intend to convey. Rather, we believe that the technical knowledge provides essential tools and concepts for envisioning and implementing better approaches to the complex problems we have noted. However, we also feel that often knowledge of the technical issues falls short because it is a bit abstract and not employed with a sensitivity to existing realities and contexts. In other words, the technical knowledge is presented in ways that do not link it effectively to the complex settings in which HRM professionals must function. We believe that recognizing the complexity and comprehending the richness and inherent conflict of this context are necessary steps for understanding HRM work. Technically competent and contextually informed HRM professionals are needed. Many other books have attempted to develop the first dimension. Our effort in this book is to provide a set of materials that complements these by developing the latter.

IMPLICATIONS FOR *ALL* MANAGERS

For organizations to reap the benefits of "putting people first for organizational success," effective HRM must truly become *everyone's* responsibility. Compartmentalizing HRM as the province of a separate HRM department or HRM professionals undercuts HRM's potential contribution. *All* managers must understand the vision of HRM and have detailed familiarity with the package of HRM practices through which that vision is implemented in their own organization. Beyond understanding, they must incorporate HRM practices as part of their management and, when problems arise, work with HRM professionals to resolve them. Managers must resist persistent pressures toward short-term focus and norms that confuse analytic, cost-cutting management with good management if a successful collaboration is to emerge. The high-performance management practices that treat employees as assets must be taken to heart. Actions of immediate managers have the greatest impact on the lived experience of employees. It is at this point of contact that employee competencies and contributions are nurtured and engaged—or not—with important consequences for organizational productivity and financial returns. For the promise of HRM to be fulfilled, everyday interactions must reflect the view that employees are assets.

HRM REALITY

Finally, by understanding the deeper levels of HRM reality, both managers and HRM professionals may be more able to appreciate not only their current roles but also the potential of their work. In many ways, the work of HRM is far more important than simply helping individual organizations to be more effective. This work has major implications for the quality of the society in which we live—its justice, humaneness, and utilization of its people.

References

Jacoby, Sanford M. (1985). *Employing bureaucracy*. New York: Columbia University Press.

Milgrom, P. & Roberts, J. (1985). An economic approach to influence activities in organizations. *American Journal of Sociology, 94* (Supplement): S154–S179.

Nelson, Daniel. (1975). *Managers and workers*. Madison: University of Wisconsin Press.

Pfeffer, Jeffrey & Veiga, John F. (1999). Putting people first for organizational success. *Academy of Management Executive, 13*(2): 37–48.

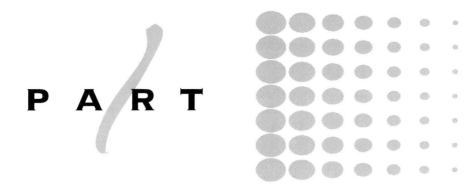

PART

GETTING HUMAN RESOURCE MANAGEMENT INTO FOCUS

Some things old,
some things new,
many things doubted are
now coming true.

This little jingle (modeled after the traditional advice to the bride) captures the major themes we advance throughout this book. Specifically, when we focus on human resources management (HRM), we see (1) a number of things that are part of HRM's history (i.e., old things), (2) many things that are quite new, and (3) that many of these recent bold developments, which had seemed questionable when they were first suggested, have become almost mainstream. These recent developments reflect how HRM practitioners must work if they are to help their organizations meet the challenges of today's complex and dynamic world. New challenges are changing the essence of HRM in dramatic ways.

To get these dynamics into focus we must understand HRM's history as part of a complex social process that has been driven by more than changes in technical knowledge—the "technicist" treatments portrayed in most HRM textbooks. These treatments usually center almost exclusively on endogenous developments to explain developments in the field. Such treatments, unfortunately, lead students to see the field primarily as a chronological flow of research and ideas that at one time or another were accepted, used, and then made obsolete by new research revealing new ideas superior to the earlier ones. This leads students to overlook the dynamic social and political context that has shaped the practice of HRM, continues to affect it today, and will continue to shape it in the future.

True, technical and academic changes have played a role, but their impact is dwarfed by the social and political/economic changes. Examining HRM in terms of the larger social context helps us to better comprehend recent developments as well as those of the more distant past that formed the field's foundation. We begin by exploring the history of HRM.

To present a contextually informed history we have included excerpts from two recent books by the leading scholar, Sanford M. Jacoby. While we heartily recommend careful study of both of these books in their entirety, for present purposes brief summaries must suffice. While you read these selections, keep in mind that in the United States, HRM has been shaped by the joint effects of two competing ideological concerns: (1) preserving economic liberalism (i.e, free enterprise), and (2) protecting the welfare of people. These two concerns pulled in different directions as industrialism unfolded. As organizations pursued profit in the spirit of a free enterprise system, desired standards of well being for individuals (both at work and in general) were threatened.

In response to the social tensions, some businesses pursued limited welfare objectives, often by employing units of social workers. Over time welfare departments, as these units became known, evolved into personnel departments, which in turn evolved into what we now call human resource departments. While evolving, these departments competed with engineers and foremen for influence. Often in the short run, the macro-economic conditions of supply and demand in the labor market affected who won these contests. Tight labor markets usually favor HRM's interests.

In short, human resource departments are rooted in social value conflicts that have never been fully resolved and have been heavily influenced by the economic conditions and political agendas of the times. HRM must be understood in the context of political economy. In the introduction to his first book on this topic, *Employing Bureaucracy,* Jacoby documents how beginning in the mid-1800s, personnel management emerged to manage these tensions.

In the introduction to his second book, *Modern Manors,* Jacoby shows how early in the twentieth century, the responses corporations made to these tensions produced the particular social form he termed "welfare capitalism." Welfare capitalism was an outgrowth of the efforts of a few somewhat atypical firms to manage the social tensions in their local settings. Although these programs differed in detail, they had one thing in common—they were private (i.e., nongovernmental) attempts to attend sufficiently to welfare concerns in order to stave off public outrage and the associated intrusions of unions and even, perhaps, socialist governments. To reiterate, HRM's development has been heavily influenced by ideological, political, economic, and value concerns—all operating in a dynamic political economic context.

In the next selection, Jeffrey Pfeffer and John F. Veiga provide a persuasive evidence for the value organizations gain from doing HRM well, or in their words, "Putting People First for Organizational Success." In the next selection, Philip H. Mirvis provides additional support to Pfeffer and Veiga's paper by reporting results of a survey of over 400 corporations. The results show that an organization's philosophy concerning human resources predicted the organization's ability to respond to contemporary challenges successfully. Following this, the article by Dave Ulrich explains how and why HR is more important now than it was before.

The last paper gives HR managers advice about how they can be effective. In Chapter I-6, Bill Leonard answers the important question "What do CEOs Want from HR?" Using data collected from CEOs, Leonard reveals some of the special things that human resources practitioners should consider as they enter inner circles of strategic management.

Much of the rest of the book is intended to help HRM practitioners meet the new challenges firms face today. Although we must be aware of continuity with the past, we influence HRM in the future. All of this is not to suggest that developments in knowledge or technical skills have not and will not be important. However, the nature of the knowledge and the ability to bring this knowledge to bear will enable complex and dynamic organizations to function in even more complex and equally dynamic political economies.

I-1: Employing Bureaucracy
Managers, Unions, and the Transformation of Work in American Industry, 1900–1945

SANFORD M. JACOBY

INTRODUCTION

In 1972, a dramatic strike took place at a General Motors assembly plant in Lordstown, Ohio. The strikers, many of whom were young and well-educated, walked out in protest over working conditions at the plant. They said they were seeking something more from their labor than high wages, pensions, and job security. One young worker wanted "a chance to use my brain," a job "where my high school education counts for something."[1]

The strike received national attention and unleashed a torrent of books and articles about job satisfaction, the work ethic, and the quality of working life. Their authors sounded a common theme: that workers were dissatisfied because their jobs were uninteresting, meaningless, and lacking in opportunities for personal growth. This view was shared by a diverse group, ranging from liberal corporate managers to Marxist students of the labor process. But there was little agreement over what should be done to improve the situation. Work reform experts prescribed remedies such as job enrichment and more participative forms of management;[2] radical scholars argued that these were Band-Aids at best, that employers had intentionally drained most jobs of their conceptual content and would never willingly restore it.[3]

But hindsight and national survey data suggest that the Lordstown experience was not typical and that researchers in the 1970s gave insufficient attention to the so-called "extrinsic" features of the work environment—pay and other economic benefits, job security, and opportunities for promotion. Attitude surveys show that these are still very important to blue-collar workers. For example, workers who regard their income as adequate and their job security as good are five times more likely to be very satisfied with their jobs than are those who think that their income is inadequate and their job insecure.[4] Dissatisfied workers complain more about extrinsic factors like hours, earnings, job insecurity, and company policy than they do about intrinsic factors such as "the work itself."[5]

The point is not that intrinsic rewards are unimportant or job enrichment unwelcome. Rather, these findings demonstrate that the blue-collar worker's definition of a "good job" turns on matters that are relatively mundane: A good job is one that pays well, offers stability and promotion opportunities, and protects against arbitrary discipline and dismissal.

We tend to take these things for granted, in part because a sizable proportion of today's jobs fit this definition. Yet industrial employment conditions were much different as recently as fifty years ago: Workers had little protection from the vagaries of the labor market. Wages and employment levels were unstable and tenure insecure. Foremen meted out rough and arbitrary discipline. Most employers looked upon their workers as indolent children or beasts of burden and treated them accordingly.[6] Good jobs, as they are defined today, were scarce and hard to come by.

The present work is an attempt to understand how industrial labor was transformed and to identify the historical process by which good jobs were created. It is, therefore, an account of the bureaucratization of employment, since many of the features that define good jobs—stability, internal promotion, and impersonal, rule-bound procedures—are characteristic of bureaucratic organization.

Bureaucracy is a loaded word; it carries a host of connotations. To modern organization theorists, the bureaucratic features of employment are an inevitable and automatic result of the technical imperatives imposed by large and complex organizations. As Talcott Parsons put it, "Smaller and simpler organizations are typically managed with a high degree of particularism. . . . But when the "distance" between points of decision and operation increases, uniformity and coordination can be obtained only by a high degree of formalization."[7] Recent radical accounts of the evolution of the labor process take issue with this view, seeing bureaucratic devices such as calculable rules and career ladders as mechanisms of employer control over the workforce. From this perspective, bureaucracy is not neutral; it is rationality shaped to serve the employer's interests.[8]

When I began this study, I had to consider both of these points of view. Eventually I discovered that neither of them provides a satisfactory guide to historical developments in the United States. Thus, I found that size mattered but that, contrary to modern organization theory, there was no lockstep relation between how big a company was and how its employment system was organized. Giant manufacturing

establishments were a common feature of the industrial environment by 1890, yet in many of them, blue-collar employment did not acquire bureaucratic characteristics until four or five decades later. Moreover, medium-sized firms (those with fewer than a thousand workers) were often among the first to get rid of the traditional system of factory labor administration. Management in these firms employed bureaucracy to solve a variety of problems, many of them unrelated to size.

But management was not the only group to use bureaucracy and to derive benefit from it. Through their unions, workers sought to bureaucratize employment in order to enhance their bargaining power, shield themselves from turbulent competition, and ensure managerial consistency and fairness. In fact, managers in some companies resisted or delayed bureaucratization even as their employees promoted it. These managers were concerned that structure and rules would hinder their discretion, although they were sometimes willing to impose these things on themselves in order to forestall what they regarded as a greater evil—unionization. This situation differs considerably from the view of radical theorists that bureaucracy was "systematically and consciously" designed by employers to increase their control.[9]

Thus, a problem shared by both schools is their tendency to view bureaucracy as an expressive totality,[10] all of whose features are prevaded by a dominant principle: for organization theorists, the imperatives of size and efficiency; for radicals, the logic of control. A related problem is that both theories portray management as the agent of all organizational change, rationally adjusting employment structures either to shifts in technology and market forces or to new forms of worker resistance.

This study takes a different approach. It treats bureaucratic employment practices as the outcome of a prolonged struggle to overcome the insecurity and inequities produced by a market-oriented employment system. The struggle was played out both within management and between management and other groups; its result was by no means inevitable. At a broader level, this struggle was part of what Karl Polanyi called "the double movement" of two great organizing principles in society. One was the principle of economic liberalism, which used laissez-faire and contract as its methods; the other was the principle of social protection, which relied on protective legislation, restrictive associations, and other methods of market intervention.[11]

Each of the world's major industrial nations experienced this struggle as part of its transition to modernity, a passage marked by several dramatic shifts: from the entrepreneurial firm to the large corporation; from the old to the new middle class; and from local protests to national unions and labor parties. These transitions all occurred within the century after 1850, although nations modernized at different times and at different speeds during this period. They differed as well in the timing and sequence of the various shifts that constituted the transition. England, for example, had powerful trade unions very early in its passage to modernity, something that was not true of Japan. As a result of these dissimilarities, each nation varied considerably with respect to the constellation of forces—economic, social, and political—that played out Polanyi's double movement.[12]

In most nations, regulation and stabilization of the labor market were achieved through bargaining by workers organized into trade unions, and through legislation supported by middle-class reformers and labor parties. To some extent this was also true of the United States, except that the absence of an effective labor party made middle-class reform activity especially important. In addition, American manage-ment manifested a comparatively strong strain toward self-regulation, given the relative weakness prior to the 1930s both of government regulation and of trade unionism. The relationships are, however, complex: Unionism's limited scope gave American managers room to act preemptively whenever they felt threatened by an increase in labor's bargaining power, as during World War I. The result, as John R. Commons observed at the time, was that in the United States, "the restraints which laborers place on free competition in the interests of fair competition [are being] taken over by employers and administered by their own labor managers."[13]

The differences between the United States and other nations are to some extent attributable to the large proportion of immigrants in America's industrial labor force. Language barriers, tensions inherent in ethnic heterogeneity, and the high mobility of immigrant workers militated against the formation of workplace and other organizations. The newcomers' lack of roots, their frequent moves from one place to another, made for instability in America's cities and workplaces and at the same time permitted the persistence of a market-oriented employment system that was equally unstable.

For economic liberals, the creation of a free labor market was one of the great achievements of the nineteenth century. The employment contract allowed workers and employers to enter, design, and terminate their relationship at will, without interference from the state or traditional moral authority. Hence it facilitated the movement away from the eighteenth century's highly personal employment relationship, constrained by mutual obligations, to an impersonal and freer relationship of contractual equality. But the liberal formula had numerous defects; and Commons, like other critics of his day, pointed out several of them. First, a large corporation and a single employee could hardly be regarded as equal in bargaining power when it came to forming the contract, especially when the latter could find no alternative employment. Second, in accepting the contract, the employee agreed to submit to the authority of the employer (or his agent, the foreman), causing the relationship to revert to one of domination and subordination. Third, the employer's power to terminate the contract at will, and to control the supply of jobs, had far graver consequences for the worker than the worker's mutual right to quit had for the employer.[14]

Commons thought that, in the United States, protective legislation and trade unionism were bringing some measure of equality and fairness to the labor exchange. But he thought that this also was occurring through the restraints or "working rules" that American employers were taking over from regulative bodies and placing upon themselves. These rules filled in the contract's empty spaces with procedures and regulations specifying how employers, foremen, and workers should conduct themselves; hence they made the contract more an agreement than a command. From this, said Commons, came a movement away from "coercion" and toward the establishment of legality, of "rights, duties, and liberties." Moreover, these working rules signified that the employee was part of a "going concern," a relatively permanent relationship. Rules governing layoff and dismissal, for example, reduced some of the transience associated with the labor contract; they established "a new equity" that protected the worker's job. In the familiar legal formula, employment was shifting back from contract to status, as the industrial worker's job became a "position" with circumscribed rights and duties, including safeguards against its loss.[15]

Between 1900 and 1945, two forces—one supporting the status quo and the other pressing for change—contended within the American manufacturing firm. On the one side were foremen, production managers, and plant superintendents—persons committed to the existing employment system for both economic and philosophical reasons. These men had a manufacturing orientation: Their overriding concern was to get the product out as quickly and cheaply as possible. In administering employment, they looked for quick results and maximum flexibility; the workforce was to be adjusted to changes in technology and to fluctuations in output, never the other way around. Hence they favored strict discipline for the worker and freedom from the restraint of rules and commitments for themselves. They also shared an ideology, a set of beliefs, about the industrial worker—that he was lazy, grasping, and untrustworthy—and about their responsibility to him—which was that they had none, beyond paying the going wage rate. Liberality and security would, they thought, corrode the work ethic. This ideology meshed with their production orientation and with the policies that flowed from it, forming a structure of mutually reinforcing ideas, a world view.

On the other side was a disparate group of trade unionists, social reformers, and personnel managers. Each was trying to make the employment relationship more orderly and stable, but for different reasons. Unions sought to give industrial labor some of the security, dignity, and status rights associated with white-collar occupations; that is, they wanted to create new social norms for manual employment. Social reformers were sympathetic to these goals (if not always to organized labor) both because of humanitarian impulses and fears of more radical change from below. They criticized industry's employment practices as backward, crude, and wasteful. They were not, however, antagonistic to industrial capitalism; rather, they wanted to make it more rational and viable. Yet these middle-class professionals also had interests of their own; they were more than mere servants of power. They encouraged the proliferation of bureaucracy and top-down reform because these were likely to give them a greater directive role in public and private affairs.

Within management, the conflict between the traditional and the bureaucratic approach to employment was epitomized by clashes between the production division and the new personnel departments that began to appear after 1910. The personnel manager's point of view differed from that of most line managers, in part because of the personnel department's function in the managerial hierarchy. The creation of a personnel department signalled that employment policy would now be treated as an end in itself rather than as a means to the production division's ends. One of the personnel manager's chief responsibilities was to stabilize labor relations, a task that required trading off short-term efficiency in the interests of achieving high employee morale over the long run. In practice, this meant preempting many of the union's employment policies and placing stringent checks on line managers, especially foremen. Production officials were not happy about this turn of events. They were especially skeptical of the personnel manager's claim that good employee relations contributed to high productivity, since most of them believed just the opposite.

But personnel management was more than a new slot in the corporate hierarchy. Unlike marketing or finance, it was deeply affected by developments external to the firm, such as changes in social attitudes and norms regarding industrial employment. Because it had its roots in various Progressive reform movements, personnel management attracted to its ranks educators, social workers, and even former socialists. It was influenced by new middle-class beliefs in the necessity of market intervention, the

beneficial effects of rational administration, and the power of the educated expert to mediate and mitigate social conflict. Many early personnel managers thought of themselves as neutral professionals, whose job was to reconcile opposing industrial interests and make employment practices more scientific and humane.

Personnel management and the new bureaucratic approach to employment did not gradually take hold in an ever-growing number of firms. Instead they were adopted during two periods of crisis for the traditional system of employment—World War I and the Great Depression. These were periods when the unions gained strength, when social experimentation was popular, and when the government intervened in the labor market. As this uneven growth suggests, many companies did not immediately see much value in a bureaucratic employment system. Normally, top management in these firms either paid little attention to employment (which they regarded as relatively unimportant) or were ideologically committed to the production manager's world view. Shedding traditional employment practices required a change in managerial values as well as external pressure from government and unions.

This view is somewhat different from that favored by modern business historians. For example, Alfred D. Chandler, Jr., argues that the rise of managerial capitalism was almost entirely an economic phenomenon, and that "neither the labor unions nor the government has taken part in carrying out the basic functions of modern business enterprise."[16] Chandler's claim is correct with respect to those functions that top management considered essential to the enterprise, such as marketing or production. But it does not hold true for the employment sphere: here, although market forces mattered, they were not all that mattered. Chandler misses this point because he accepts the American manager's bias that employment is a distinctly secondary corporate function. Hence, despite the comprehensiveness of his work, he omits any discussion of personnel and labor relations. This omission gives a misleading picture of the modern business enterprise as something that was not, and very likely cannot be, greatly affected by social norms and restraints.

Notes

1. Stanley Aronowitz, *False Promises: The Shaping of American Working Class Consciousness* (New York, 1973), p. 26.
2. See, for example, Richard E. Walton, "Innovative Restructuring of Work," in Jerome M. Rosow, ed., *The Worker and the Job: Coping with Change* (Engelwood Cliffs, NJ, 1974); David A. Whitsett, "Where Are Your Unenriched Jobs?" *Harvard Business Review* (January–February 1975), vol. 53; J.R. Hackman and G.R. Oldham, *Work Redesign* (Reading Mass., 1980).
3. See, for example, Harry Braverman, *Labor and Monopoly Capital: The Degredation of Work in the Twentieth Century* (New York, 1974); Dan Clawson, *Bureaucracy and the Labor Process: The Transformation of U.S. Industry, 1860–1920* (New York, 1980).
4. Ivar Berg, Marcia Freedman, and Michael Freeman, *Managers and Work Reform: A Limited Engagement* (New York, 1978), pp. 64–74. Also see George Strauss, "Workers: Attitudes and Adjustments," in Rosow, ed., *Worker and the Job*, pp. 73–98; Patricia Voydanoff, "The Relationship Between Perceived Job Characteristics and Job Satisfaction Among Occupational Status Groups," *Sociology of Work and Occupations* (May 1978), 5: 179–182; Robert P. Quinn, Graham L. Staines, and Margaret R. McCullough, "Job Satisfaction: Is There a Trend?" Manpower Research Monograph No. 30, U.S. Department of Labor (Washington D.C. 1974).
5. Paul Andrisani, Eileen Appelbaum, Ross Koppel, and Robert Miljus, "Work Attitudes and Work Experience," R&D Monograph No. 60, U.S. Department of Labor (Washington D.C. 1979), pp. 32–35.
6. Reinhard Bendix, *Work and Authority in Industry: Ideologies of Management in the Course of Industrialization* (New York, 1956), pp. 288–289.
7. Talcott Parsons, *The Social System* (Glencoe, Ill., 1951), p. 508. Also see William H. Starbuck, "Organizational Growth and Development," in J.G. March, ed., *Handbook of Organizations* (Chicago, 1965), pp. 477–479; D.S. Pugh et al., "The Context of Organization Structures," *Administrative Science Quarterly* (March 1969), 14: 115–126; Clark Kerr, John Dunlop, Frederick Harbison, and Charles Myers, *Industrialism and Industrial Man* (Cambridge Mass., 1960).
8. See, for example, Richard Edwards, *Contested Terrain: The Transformation of the Workplace in the Twentieth Century* (New York, 1979); David M. Gordon, Richard Edwards, and Michael Reich, *Segmented Work, Divided Workers: The Historical Transformation of Labor in the United States* (Cambridge, 1982).

   These perspectives have analogues in two historical models of the period covered by this book: the organizational synthesis, with its focus on the imperatives of bureaucracy; and corporate liberalism, which argues that reform was conceived and directed by large corporations to benefit themselves. Louis Galambos, "The Emerging Organizational Synthesis in Modern American History," *Business History Review* (Autumn 1970), 44: 279–290; James Weinstein, *The Corporate Ideal in the Liberal State, 1900–1918* (Boston, 1968).
9. Richard C. Edwards, "The Social Relations of Production in the Firm and Labor Market Structure," in Edwards, Reich, and Gordon eds., *Labor Market Segmentation* (Lexington, Mass., 1975), p. 8.
10. Michael Burawoy, "Contemporary Currents in Marxist Theory," *The American Sociologist* (February 1978), 13: 50–64.
11. Karl Polanyi, *The Great Transformation: The Political and Economic Origins of Our Time* (1944; reprint Boston, 1957), p. 132.

12. For a discussion of some consequences of these differences, see Ronald Dore, *British Factory—Japanese Factory: The Origins of National Diversity in Industrial Relations* (Berkeley, Calif., 1973).
13. John R. Commons, *The Legal Foundations of Capitalism* (New York, 1924), p. 311.
14. Commons, *Legal Foundations*, 72. Commons noted that "if the corporation has 10,000 employees it loses only one ten-thousandth part of its working force if it chooses to not-employ the man, and cannot find an alternative man. But the man loses 100 percent of his job if he chooses to not-work and cannot find an alternative employer . . . from the quantitative concept of the will as a choosing between actual alternatives in a world of limited opportunities, the right of the one is greater—or perhaps 10,000 times greater—than the right of the other."
15. *Ibid.*, pp. 59, 303–304, 307. Also see Philip Selznick, *Law, Society and Industrial Justice* (New York, 1969); and Sanford Jacoby, "The Duration of Indefinite Employment Contracts in the United States and England: An Historical Analysis," *Comparative Labor Law* (Winter 1982), 5: 85–128.
16. Alfred D. Chandler, Jr., *The Visible Hand: The Managerial Revolution in American Business* (Cambridge Mass., 1977), p. 497. One notable exception to the business history approach is Daniel Nelson, *Workers and Managers: Origins of the New Factory System in the United States, 1880–1920* (Madison, Wis., 1975).

I-2: Modern Manors
Welfare Capitalism Since the New Deal
SANFORD M. JACOBY

INTRODUCTION

During the early twentieth century, one of America's leading employers was S. C. Johnson & Son of Racine, Wisconsin, makers of floor wax and other household products. Samuel C. Johnson, who founded the company in 1886, plied his employees with recreational facilities, a profit sharing plan, paid vacations, group life insurance, and myriad other benefits. Samuel's son, Herbert, followed in his father's footsteps. During the First World War, he stabilized the company's erratic employment levels by

hiring more full-time workers and then training them to perform several jobs, so they could be rotated around the company. Then, in 1922, he started what was to become a highly publicized private unemployment insurance plan. As Herbert Johnson told Congress in 1929, he felt "there should be something more permanent and more definite for the average working man." To reformers concerned about the "labor question" of the early twentieth century, companies like S. C. Johnson offered a distinctively American answer: the business corporation, rather than government or trade unions, would ~~be~~ a source of security and sta~~bility~~ society. This appr~~oach~~ capitalis~~m~~

Reprinted from the Introduction to *Modern Manors*, Sanford M. Jacoby, (Princeton N.J., Princeton University Press, 1997): 3–10.

Today, S. C. Johnson continues to win accolades for its progressive employment policies. A leader in the corporate child-care movement, it has day care facilities for children from infancy to adolescence and a summer camp for older children. JoAnne Brandes, a company manager and founder of the child-care program, says, "This isn't a benefit—it's a good business decision because we want to attract the best." Although innovative, S. C. Johnson has a strong sense of tradition. In a recent interview at Johnson headquarters, an impressive building designed by Frank Lloyd Wright, the firm's chairman recalled that his great-grandfather Samuel Johnson "laid the first building block for the first Y.M.C.A. in Racine. Our company's social involvement grew out of this early sense of local community involvement. My great-grandfather had a sense that there had to be a fair way to do things." The company currently provides profit sharing, child care, an aquatic center, and other benefits because, says the chairman, they create "a family atmosphere within the company. We all sit on the same side of the table, so to speak, so we don't have a confrontational environment between the various groups of people who work here. As a result, we have very low employee turnover and no unions," the same desiderata sought by welfare capitalism since its inception.[1]

The origins of welfare capitalism lie in the nineteenth century, when people began moving in large numbers from rural to urban areas. This transformation forced people to seek new ways of dealing with the uncertainties of life. City-dwelling workers could not rely on home-grown food to get them through a spell of joblessness. The elderly, who were an important part of rural family life, found that industrial corporations were reluctant to employ them. for unmarried women began to work factor home, raising parental concern 's Meanwhile, dangerous d cities brought on occupational injuries and other health problems.

One response to these problems was a recrudescence of market individualism: workers saved as best they could while taking fierce pride in the independence and employability that came from having a well-rounded set of skills. Another strategy was to form mutual benefit associations to provide savings funds, health plans, and burial benefits. The associations sometimes grew into trade unions that negotiated risk-sharing arrangements with employers. An alternative to individualism and mutualism was government, which increasingly sought to minimize risk through protective legislation or to redistribute it via mandatory social insurance. The latter approach reflected the logic of the European welfare state: to pool risks by providing all citizens with unemployment, sickness, and old-age security. A fourth option was to have corporations reduce risk or indemnify their employees against it. This, essentially, was welfare capitalism.

By the end of the nineteenth century, welfare capitalism could be found throughout the industrialized world, but it was especially popular in the United States. Not only did American employers favor welfare capitalism because they thought it would inhibit the growth of unions and government, they also saw it as an efficient alternative to market individualism: training would be cheaper and productivity higher if employees spent their work lives with a single firm instead of seeking their fortunes on the open market. Also impelling welfare capitalism was a moral impulse: self-made business owners felt a sense of stewardship and paternal obligation to their employees. But virtue was conveniently conflated with strategic considerations, as when American employers convinced themselves that welfare capitalism constituted the best defense of freedom against laborism and statism. In short, welfare capitalism was a good fit for a distinctive American environment composed of large firms, weak unions, and small government.

Welfare capitalism was an influential movement for the first three decades of this century. It was embraced by employers as well as by intellectuals, social reformers, and political leaders, all of whom shared the belief that industrial unrest and other problems could best be alleviated by this distinctively American approach: private, not governmental; managerial, not laborist. To put its ideas into practice, employers cleaned up their factories, constructed elaborate recreational facilities, launched "company" unions, and even built housing for their employees. Like S. C. Johnson, they turned casual positions into career jobs offering health, pension, and other benefits. By the 1920s, welfare capitalism reached millions of workers at thousands of firms. It was an impressive if imperfect system, one whose notions of order, community, and paternal responsibility recalled the preindustrial household economy. The firms pursuing welfare capitalism were, in effect, industrial manors.

But the edifice crumbled during the Great Depression. Companies cut wages, instituted massive layoffs, and discontinued most of their welfare programs. Economist William Leiserson, who earlier had been dazzled by welfare capitalism, wrote pessimistically in 1933 that the Depression had "undone fifteen or so years of good personnel work." In its wake, workers searched for alternatives to safeguard their security. They voted for the Democratic party, supported the New Deal, and enthusiastically joined unions. Welfare capitalism appeared to be dead and gone.[2]

Or was it? In fact, welfare capitalism did not die in the 1930s but instead went underground—out of the public eye and beyond academic scrutiny—where it would reshape itself. Without doubt, welfare capitalism *had* to change if it were to survive what was

becoming a hostile climate, one in which company unions were unlawful, collective bargaining was public policy, and a nascent welfare state promised to shield workers from the uncertainties of industrial life. In response to these challenges, welfare capitalism gradually was modernized by a group of firms that had been spared unionization and the ravages of the Depression. Studies of three of these companies—Kodak, Sears Roebuck, and Thompson Products—form the core of this book. The three companies were exceptions to the "rise and fall" story of welfare capitalism: each one made major contributions to welfare capitalism's modernization between the 1930s and 1960s, the high point of labor and government activism in the United States.

In their attempts to build "modern manors," these companies retained many of the elements of earlier welfare capitalism. Kodak, Sears, and Thompson still provided generous welfare plans, though now the benefits were cast as supplements to Social Security and other public programs. And each company still asserted that it was a corporate community whose cohesion stood in opposition to the occupational and industrial solidarity of the labor movement. But the events of the 1930s forced employers to do a better job of bolstering words with deeds. Workers took seriously the idea that they were part of the corporate community and demanded more of the privileges that previously had been reserved for salaried employees. Modern welfare capitalism responded by becoming less tolerant than its predecessor of the foreman's coercive "drive" system. And paternalism itself was redefined during the era. Companies still drew attention to their lord of the manor—the CEO—but they also tried to routinize paternalism by offering insur~~ instead of discretionary benefi~~ educating managers about ~~ to~~

With modern w~~

the emphasis ~~

this was a kinder, gentler sort of paternalism. One reason for the change was the Wagner Act, which, along with labor's newfound strength, made it more difficult for employers to resort to force majeure when threatened by an organizing campaign. Coercion did not disappear, but large nonunion companies had to rely on persuasion to carry more of the load. The emphasis on persuasion mirrored changes occurring in the realm of production, where the "carrot" of a career job system was displacing the "stick" of close supervision. Thus, modern welfare capitalism was controlling yet consensual, coldly efficient yet cozily humane.

Mixed motives like those represented in modern welfare capitalism have never been handled well by social critics and historians. Liberals focus on workplace conflict, while conservatives emphasize the harmony between labor and capital. But in reality, workers and managers simultaneously have opposing *and* shared interests. They disagree over issues such as the split between profits and wages while at the same time they depend on each other for their livelihoods, a point that Emile Durkheim made a century ago when he observed that the division of labor creates a shared interest in the enterprise as an economic commonweal.[3]

Within the industrial community, workers not only relied on management for their livelihoods but shared skills and technical expertise with their employers. Hence they tolerated, even respected, managerial authority. As for managers, they depended on workers' expertise, intelligence, and discretion—whether in service industries, where managers sought but could not command consummate performance, or in mass-production manufacturing industries, where labor ostensibly no longer needed to ʰskilled. Mutual dependence between reg⸍ and managers created a consensus work, ʰʰhts and responsibilities at ⸍lict occurred—as it often

did—the dispute was likely to be over the specific terms of agreement rather than its fundamental axioms.

Managers and workers also shared cultural aspirations. Even the lowliest manual laborer had middle-class yearnings: to own a home, be comfortable, and obtain respect in the community. Even if people did not personally identify with successful businessmen, a sizable portion of the population hoped that they would someday have their own businesses or that their children would. Workers held fast to the idea that it was within their power to succeed and, in fact, it was not unrealistic for them to expect some amount of advancement in the career-type jobs offered by welfare capitalism. Here in the realm where hope and reality mingled lay the "reefs of roastbeef" that, according to Werner Sombart, had beached American socialism. None of this is to deny the truth that social class constituted a cultural divide. But class barriers could be bridged by bonds of shared belief, ethnicity, and gender, as often they were in America's modern manors.

More than a few workers were indifferent or opposed to unions even before they entered the workplace. During and after the 1930s industry was filled with cantankerous individualists, Black Legionnaires, and skilled workers who "boasted of their superior experience, dedication, and loyalty." Not all anti-union workers were ideologues, though; some were merely fearful, or caught up in the economic anxieties of daily life. Others, like African-American workers, were skeptical of both sides but willing to give management the benefit of the doubt so long as it kept its promises, especially about employment security, a critical issue for all workers who lived through the Great Depression.[4]

Workers who were indifferent or unresponsive to unions are invisible in much of the scholarship on American labor history, which frequently ends with a surge of solidarity in the 1930s and 1940s. But even then, labor's victory was neither stable nor complete. At its peak after World War II, the labor movement represented less than a third of nonagricultural workers and its strength was concentrated in only a few regions and industries. Just three sectors—construction, manufacturing, and regulated transport and energy utilities—accounted for more than 80 percent of organized labor at its peak. Although much has been written recently about union losses in representation elections, this trend actually started during World War II.

What stopped labor's rise? First, by the mid-1940s the most easily organized workers had already been signed up. Second, problems festered inside the house of labor, ranging from factional schisms to an inability to broaden unionism's appeal beyond certain well-defined types of workers. Finally, welfare capitalism killed unions with kindness and occasional ferocity. Even the most progressive nonunion employers were willing to spend enormous sums both in the factory and in Congress to stave off unions. Costs aside, it was simply an article of faith that unions were anathema. Employers who acknowledged that collective bargaining might be beneficial—either as a stabilizing force in competitive industries like apparel or as a prop to oligopolistic pricing practices in industries such as steel—were a distinct minority. In steel, Myron C. Taylor of U.S. Steel failed in the late 1930s to convince fellow steelmakers Tom Girdler, Ernest Weir, and Eugene Grace that the virtues of price stabilization outweighed the vice of recognizing unions. Each of these men saw their companies organized against their wishes during World War II, along with holdouts from many other industries. That left a small group of sophisticated nonunion companies to develop the strategies that checked labor's growth in the postwar decades.

In contrast to employers in other industrialized nations, these modern manors preserved an American tradition of vehement employer opposition to organized labor. With its roots in America's distinctive social and economic history, employer exceptionalism remains a relatively unexamined counterpart to the labor exceptionalism about which scholars have written so much. Explanations of labor's weakness in the United States often fail to mention that employer policies as well as worker attitudes were a key determinant of union strength. These policies set a ceiling on unionization during labor upswings (the early 1900s, late 1910s, and the 1930s and 1940s) and hastened the erosion of unionism during downswings (the 1920s and today). While this book is about management, in its reverse image one can trace the fortunes of the American labor movement.

Although there is a sizable literature on welfare capitalism during the first three decades of this century and an abundance of articles about today's progressive nonunion employers, the pickings get slim when one seeks information on such companies during the intervening decades, the heyday of organized labor in America. Explanations for this gap are not hard to find. Industrial relations experts were preoccupied during the 1940s and 1950s with forging a new labor relations system based on collective bargaining. Dedicated pluralists, they saw organized labor as a vital challenge to management's power in the economy, the polity, and the workplace. They thought collective bargaining would protect individuals from the political power of business and from the psychological demands of bureaucratic work organizations, and thereby preserve freedom in the modern world. By investing the labor movement with such an important historical function, liberal academics inevitably treated nonunion companies as socially retrograde and thus undeserving of scrutiny.

A result of this scholarly blind spot was the erroneous impression that organized labor had achieved greater stability and acceptability than was actually the case. Thus a distinguished group of economists asserted in 1956 that American business-men had "come to accept the legitimacy and respectability of labor unions." The claim was not entirely without justification, since managers from unionized companies often sounded as if they had agreed. John E. Rovensky, a prominent industrialist, said in 1952 that "All sound-thinking businessmen today recognize the right of labor to collec-tive bargaining. Unions are an absolute necessity." But Rovensky's words masked a disjunction between management's public pronouncements and its private beliefs. Plu-ralism did not have deep roots in manage-ment circles, even during the period of its purported hegemony, from the 1940s through the 1960s. Two speakers made this exceptionally clear at a 1957 meeting of the Industrial Relations Research Association, when they cautioned that "if American management upon retiring for the night, were assured that by the next morning the unions with which they dealt would have disappeared, more management people than not would experience the happiest sleep of their lives."[5]

There was, however, one group of man-agers who would not have slept well if unions had disappeared: the thousands of new personnel and labor relations special-ists whose expertise lay in administering the increasingly abstruse world of collective bar-gaining. For if organized labor had vanished overnight, most of these managers would have been jobless the next morning. As a group they had a vested interest in collective bargaining, even in preserving its technical complexity. Those who strongly felt this way were likely to attend professional events where they rubbed shoulders with, and molded the perceptions of, labor economists and other industrial relations experts.

But the vast majority of managers, although demoralized by the New Deal, eventually regained their self-confidence and took aggressive steps to contain union inroads. The effort to get the Taft-Hartley Act passed was one example; another was seen by the actions of General Electric. The firm had ostensibly accepted industrial unionism in the mid-1930s, but began to move plants to the South in the 1950s while taking a more combative stance toward its remaining unions. GE managers, and others following them, looked for inspiration to those progressive employers who had never been organized by unions, firms like Du Pont, Eli Lilly, IBM, Procter & Gamble, S. C. Johnson, Standard Oil, and the companies examined in this book.

Until the 1960s, modern welfare capital-ism was confined to a minority of large nonunion companies. Though the practi-tioners were well known in their regions and industries, their practices spread at a slow pace. Organized employers such as General Motors found that their unions either resisted the introduction of modern welfare capitalism or sought to control it and take credit for it. Smaller nonunion employers were skeptical of welfare capital-ism or else lacked the necessary resources to pursue it; hence they stuck to traditional approaches. But in the 1960s and 1970s modern welfare capitalism began to spread rapidly, not so much because managers modified their views of it, but because of changes in the economy and society that supported it, such as the shift away from mass production, the growing importance of educated workers, and the decline of orga-nized labor. Labor's fading strength encour-aged employers to deploy the anti-union tactics developed by welfare capitalist com-panies after World War II. Put more posi-tively, modern welfare capitalism's empha-sis on commitment proved well suited to managing college-educated workers, who were fast becoming dominant in the labor force, and it meshed neatly with the partici-pative principles that were supplanting tra-ditional Taylorist approaches to work orga-

nization. Thus was modern welfare capitalism transformed into the "new" nonunion
model of today.

Magazines and academic journals lately
are filled with articles about "the modern
American workplace." Few of them, however, can tell us what makes the workplace
"modern" or "American." We are all familiar with the latest crop of model employers,
companies like Microsoft and Motorola,
Nucor and Nordstrom, yet we have little
idea how these "new" companies came to
be what they are today. Some managers
even think they invented the world as it is.
Thus the history of welfare capitalism, while
fascinating in its own right, can also be read
as a cautionary tale about the present.[6]

Pundits tell us we are living in a post-
modern age in which the institutions that
fueled America's postwar prosperity—mass
production, labor unions, and the Keynesian
welfare state—have been replaced by a new
set of sensibilities: postindustrial, decentralized, and privatized. If one measures present circumstances against the activism of
the New Deal or the optimism of the 1960s,
it is easy to conclude that we have entered a
new age that breaks with the past. But if one
looks back beyond the Great Depression,
other interpretive possibilities arise, and the
present seems less like a break than a rerun.
Immigration restriction is again a national
obsession; entrepreneurs are lionized by the
media; and creationist biology is back in the
schools. The labor market also looks like an
atavism. The United States once again has
one of the lowest unionization rates and
one of the most miserly social insurance
programs in the industrialized world. As in
the 1920s, the workforce increasingly is split
between the "have-nots" and the "haves,"
who will spend most of their careers working in modern manors like S. C. Johnson or
Microsoft.[7]

Yet things are not exactly the same this
time around, and too much can be made of
the parallels. Public confidence in business
is not as strong now as it was in the 1920s,
nor are major corporations as stable as they
used to be. Indeed, welfare capitalism today
is undergoing its first major crisis since the
Great Depression, reflected in "downsizing" at blue-ribbon firms like IBM, a pervasive sense of insecurity among American
workers, and a growing national debate
about corporate responsibility. Clearly,
employers are reluctant to shoulder as
much risk as they once did. On the other
hand, many Americans still look first to corporations to meet their needs, rather than to
government or organized labor.

Notes

1. Samuel C. Johnson, *The Essence of a Family Enterprise: Doing Business the Johnson Way* (Indianapolis, Ind., 1988), 24–31, 113–20; S.C. Johnson and Son, Inc., *Jonwax Journal: 75th Anniversary Issue* (Racine, Wisc., 1961), 47–50; Herbert Johnson quoted in Daniel Nelson, *Unemployment Insurance: The American Experience, 1915–1935* (Madison, Wisc., 1969), 54–55; "What Price Child Care?" *Business Week*, February 8, 1993, 104; Joel Kurtzman, "Managing when It's All in the Family," *New York Times*, April 9, 1989.
2. William S. Leiserson, "Personnel Problems Raised by the Current Crisis," *Management Review* 22 (April 1933), 114.
3. Emile Durkheim, *The Division of Labor in Society* (New York, 1933), first published in French in 1893, Durkheim thought that small-scale firms were more harmonious than large-scale because the latter's exces-sive division of labor weakened norms of solidarity. These norms were supplied by the employer, his employees, and by the social milieu, a mixture that today is somewhat mushily called "corporate culture." The con-cept has received less attention from histori-ans than it deserves, although see Charles Dellheim, "Business in Time: The Historian and Corporate Culture," *Public Historian* 8 (Spring 1986), 9–25.
4. Daniel Nelson, "The Great Goodyear Strike of 1936," *Ohio History* 92 (1983), 14. Also see Morris Janowitz, "Black Legions on the

March" in Daniel Aaron, ed., *America in Crisis* (New York, 1952), 305–26, and, for an insightful overview, Robert Zieger, *The CIO, 1935–1955* (Chapel Hill, NC, 1995).

5. Francis X. Sutton, Seymour E. Harris, Carl Kaysen, and James Tobin, *The American Business Creed* (Cambridge, Mass., 1956), 247; Rovensky quoted in Herman E. Krooss, *Executive Opinion: What Business Leaders Said and Thought on Economic Issues* (Garden City, 1970), 397; Douglass V. Brown and Charles A. Myers, "The Changing Industrial Relations Philosophy of American Management." *Proceedings of the Ninth Annual Meeting of the Industrial Relations Research Association* (Madison, Wisc., 1957), 84–99.

6. Gavin Wright, "Labor History and Labor Economics" in Alexander J. Field, ed., *The Future of Economic History* (Boston, 1987). Although it is erroneous to believe that everything in the present is seamlessly connected to the past, the opposite and prevailing tendency (especially in the United States) is to see the present constantly reinventing itself. Here I try to remedy our historical amnesia while at the same time avoiding what might be called, following David Hackett Fischer, the "fallacy of continuity."

7. Stephen A. Marglin and Juliet Schor, eds., *The Golden Age of Capitalism* (Oxford, 1990). On the rebirth of conservatism, see Alan Brinkley, "The Problem of American Conservatism" and Leo P. Ribuffo, "Why Is There so Much Conservatism in the United States and Why Do so Few Historians Know Anything about It?" *American Historical Review* 99 (April 1994), 409–29, 438–49; and Charles W. Romney, "The Business of Unionism: Race, Politics, Capitalism, and the West Coast Teamsters, 1940–1952." Ph.D. dissertation. University of California, Los Angeles, 1996.

I-3: Putting People First for Organizational Success

JEFFREY PFEFFER AND JOHN F. VEIGA

Over the past decade or so, numerous rigorous studies conducted both within specific industries and in samples of organizations that cross industries have demonstrated the enormous economic returns obtained through the implementation of what are variously called high involvement, high performance, or high commitment management practices. Furthermore, much of this research serves to validate earlier writing on participative

Academy of Management Executive by Pfeffer J. and Veiga J. F. Copyright 1999 by Academy of Management. Reproduced with permission of Academy of Management in the format Textbook via Copyright Clearance Center.

management and employee involvement. But even as these research results pile up, trends in actual management practice are, in many instances, moving in a direction exactly opposite to what this growing body of evidence prescribes. Moreover, this disjuncture between knowledge and management practice is occurring at the same time that organizations, confronted with a very competitive environment, are frantically looking for some magic elixir that will provide sustained success, at least over some reasonable period of time.

Rather than putting their people first, numerous firms have sought solutions to competitive challenges in places and means that have not been very productive—treating their businesses as portfolios of assets to be bought and sold in an effort to find the right competitive niche, downsizing and outsourcing in a futile attempt to shrink or transact their way to profit, and doing a myriad other things that weaken or destroy their organizational culture in efforts to minimize labor costs.

SHOW ME THE EVIDENCE

Though we could go on at length about a company like Apple as a case in point, executives frequently say, "Don't just give me anecdotes specifically selected to make some point. Show me the evidence!" Fortunately, there is a substantial and rapidly expanding body of evidence, some of it quite methodologically sophisticated, that speaks to the strong connection between how firms manage their people and the economic results achieved. This evidence is drawn from studies of the five-year survival rates of initial public offerings; studies of profitability and stock price in large samples of companies from multiple industries; and detailed research on the automobile, apparel, semiconductor, steel manufacturing, oil refining, and service industries. It shows that substantial gains, on the order of 40 percent, can be obtained by implementing high performance management practices.[1]

According to an award-winning study of the high performance work practices of 968 firms representing all major industries, "a one standard deviation increase in use of such practices is associated with a . . . 7.05 percent decrease in turnover and, on a per employee basis, $27,044 more in sales and $18,641 and $3,814 more in market value and profits, respectively."[2] Yes, you read those results correctly. That's an $18,000 increase in stock market value *per employee!* A subsequent study conducted on 702 firms in 1996 found even larger economic benefits: "A one standard deviation improvement in the human resources system was associated with an increase in shareholder wealth of $41,000 per employee"[3]—about a 14 percent market value premium.

Are these results unique to firms operating in the United States? No. Similar results were obtained in a study of more than one hundred German companies operating in ten industrial sectors. The study found "a strong link between investing in employees and stock market performance. Companies which place workers at the core of their strategies produce higher long-term returns to shareholders than their industry peers."[4]

One of the clearest demonstrations of the causal effect of management practices on performance comes from a study of the five-year survival rate of 136 non-financial companies that initiated their public offering in the U.S. stock market in 1988.[5] By 1993, some five years later, only 60 percent of these companies were still in existence. The empirical analysis demonstrated that with other factors such as size, industry, and even profits statistically controlled, both the value the firm placed on human resources—such as whether the company cited employees as a source of competitive advantage—and how the organization rewarded people—such as stock options for all employees and profit sharing—were significantly related to the probability of survival. Moreover, the results were substantively important. As shown in Figure 1, the difference in survival probability for firms one standard deviation above and one standard deviation below the mean (in the upper 16 percent and the lower 16 percent of all firms in the sample) on valuing human resource was almost 20 percent. The difference in survival depending on where the firm scored on rewards was even more

FIGURE 1 Probability of an Initial Public Offering Firm's Surviving Five Years

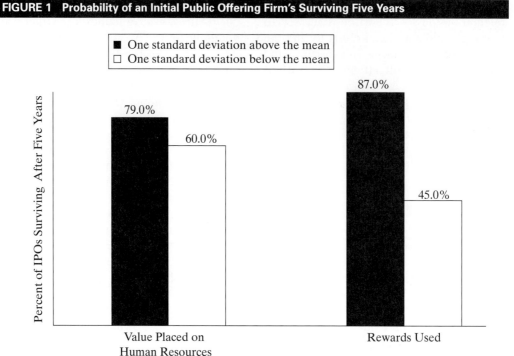

Source: Based on information from Theresa Welbourne and Alice Andrews, 1996. "Predicting Performance of Initial Public Offering Firms: Should HRM Be in the Equation?" *Academy of Management Journal,* 39: 910–911.

dramatic, with a difference in five-year survival probability of 42 percent between firms in the upper and lower tails of the distribution.

How can such substantial benefits in profits, quality, and productivity occur? Essentially, these tremendous gains come about because high performance management practices provide a number of important sources for enhanced organizational performance. Simply put, people work harder because of the increased involvement and commitment that comes from having more control and say in their work; people work smarter because they are encouraged to build skills and competence; and people work more responsibly because more responsibility is placed in hands of employees farther down in the organiza-

tion. These practices work not because of some mystical process, but because they are grounded in sound social science principles that have been shown to be effective by a great deal of evidence. And, they make sense.

● ● ● ● ● ● ● ● ● ● ● ● ● ● ●
SEVEN PRACTICES OF SUCCESSFUL ORGANIZATIONS

Based on these various studies, related literature, and personal observation and experience, a set of seven dimensions emerge that seem to characterize most, if not all, of the systems producing profits through people emerge. Let's take a look at each one briefly.

EMPLOYMENT SECURITY

Most research on the effects of high performance management systems has incorporated employment security as an important dimension. Indeed, "one of the most widely accepted propositions . . . is that innovations in work practices or other forms of worker-management cooperation or productivity improvement are not likely to be sustained over time when workers fear that by increasing productivity they will work themselves out of their jobs."[6]

The idea of providing employment security in today's competitive world seems somehow anachronistic or impossible and very much at odds with what most firms seem to be doing. But employment security is fundamental to the implementation of most other high performance management practices. For example, when General Motors wanted to implement new work arrangements in its innovative Saturn plant in the 1990s, it guaranteed its people job security except in the most extreme circumstances. When New United Motors Manufacturing, Inc. (NUMMI) was formed to operate the Fremont automobile assembly plant, it offered its people job security. How else could it ask for flexibility and cooperation in becoming more efficient and productive?

Many additional benefits follow from employment assurances besides workers' free contribution of knowledge and their efforts to enhance productivity. One advantage to firms is the decreased likelihood that they will lay off employees during downturns. How is this a benefit to the firm? In the absence of some way of building commitment to retaining the work force—either through pledges about employment security or through employment obligations contractually negotiated with a union—firms may lay off employees too quickly and too readily at the first sign of financial difficulty. This constitutes a cost for firms that have done a good job selecting, training, and developing their work force, because layoffs put important strategic assets on the street for the competition to employ. Herb Kelleher, the CEO of Southwest Airlines, summarized this argument best when he wrote:

> Our most important tools for building employee partnership are job security and a stimulating work environment. . . . Certainly there were times when we could have made substantially more profits in the short-term if we had furloughed people, but we didn't. We were looking at our employees' and our company's longer-term interests. . . . [A]s it turns out, providing job security imposes additional discipline, because if your goal is to avoid layoffs, then you hire very sparingly. So our commitment to job security has actually helped us keep our labor force smaller and more productive than our competitors'.[7]

SELECTIVE HIRING

Companies serious about obtaining profits through people will expend the effort needed to ensure that they recruit the right people in the first place. This requires several things. First, the organization needs to have a large applicant pool from which to select. In 1993, for example, Southwest Airlines received about 98,000 job applications, interviewed 16,000 people, and hired 2,700. In 1994, applications increased to more than 125,000 for 4,000 hires. Some organizations see processing this many job inquiries as an unnecessary expense. Southwest sees it as a necessary first step.

Second, the organization needs to be clear about what are the most critical skills and attributes needed in its applicant pool. At Southwest, applicants for flight attendant positions are evaluated on the basis of initiative, judgment, adaptability, and their ability to learn. These attributes are assessed in part from interview questions that evoke specific instances of these attributes. For instance, to assess adaptability, interviewers ask, "Give an example of working with a difficult co-worker. How did you handle it?"[8] To measure initiative, one question asks, "Describe a time when a co-worker failed to pull their weight and what you did about it."

Third, the skills and abilities sought need to be carefully considered and consistent with the particular job requirements and the organization's approach to its market. Enterprise Rent-A-Car is today the largest car rental company in the United States, and it has expanded at a rate of between 25 and 30 percent a year for the past 11 years. It has grown by pursuing a high customer service strategy and emphasizing sales of rental car services to repair garage customers. In a low-wage, often unionized, and seemingly low-employee-skill industry, virtually all of Enterprise's people are college graduates. But these people are hired primarily for their sales skills and personality and for their willingness to provide good service, not for their academic performance. Brian O'Reilly interpolates Enterprise's reasoning:

> The social directors make good sales people, able to chat up service managers and calm down someone who has just been in a car wreck.... The Enterprise employees hired from the caboose end of the class have something else going for them ... a chilling realization of how unforgiving the job market can be.[9]

Fourth, organizations should screen primarily on important attributes that are difficult to change through training and should emphasize qualities that actually differentiate among those in the applicant pool. Southwest rejected a top pilot from another airline who did stunt work for movie studios because he was rude to a receptionist. Southwest believes that technical skills are easier to acquire than a teamwork and service attitude. Ironically, many firms select for specific, job-relevant skills that, while important, are easily acquired. Meanwhile, they fail to find people with the right attitudes, values, and cultural fit—attributes that are harder to train or change and that are quite predictive of turnover and performance.

One MBA job applicant reported that interviewers at PeopleSoft, a producer of human resource management software, asked very little about personal or academic background, except about learning experiences from school and work. Rather, the interviews focused mostly on whether she saw herself as team-oriented or as an individual achiever, what she liked to do outside school and work, and her philosophy on life. The specific question was "Do you have a personal mission statement? If you don't, what would it be if you were to write it today?" Moreover, the people interviewing the applicant presented a consistent picture of the values that were shared among employees at PeopleSoft. Such a selection process is more likely to produce cultural fit. A great deal of research evidence shows that the degree of cultural fit and value congruence between job applicants and their organizations significantly predicts both subsequent turnover and job performance.[10]

SELF-MANAGED TEAMS AND DECENTRALIZATION AS BASIC ELEMENTS OF ORGANIZATIONAL DESIGN

Numerous articles and case examples, as well as rigorous, systematic studies, attest to the effectiveness of teams as a principle of organization design. For example, Honeywell's defense avionics plant credits improved on-time delivery—reaching 99 percent in the first quarter of 1996 as compared with below 40 percent in the late 1980s—to the implementation of teams.[11] Perhaps one of the greatest payoffs from team-based organizations is that teams substitute peer-based control for hierarchical control of work. Team-based organizations also are largely successful in having all of the people in the firm feel accountable and responsible for the operation and success of the enterprise, not just a few people in senior management positions. This increased sense of responsibility stimulates more initiative and effort on the part of everyone involved. In addition, and perhaps most importantly, by substituting peer for hierarchical control, teams permit removal of layers of hierarchy and absorption of administrative tasks previously performed by specialists, avoiding the enormous costs of having people whose sole job it is to watch people who watch other people do the work.

The tremendously successful natural foods grocery store chain, Whole Foods Markets, organized on the basis of teams, attributes much of its success to that arrangement. Between 1991 and 1996, the company enjoyed sales growth of 864 percent and net income growth of 438 percent as it expanded, in part through acquisitions as well as through internal growth, from 10 to 68 stores. In its 1995 annual report, the company's team-oriented philosophy is clearly stated.

> Our growing information systems capability is fully aligned with our goal of creating a more intelligent organization—one which is less bureaucratic, elitist, hierarchical, and authoritarian and more communicative, participatory, and empowered. The ultimate goal is to have all team members contributing their full intelligence, creativity, and skills to continuously improving the company.... Everyone who works at Whole Foods Market is a team member. This reflects our philosophy that we are all partners in the shared mission of giving our customers the very best in products and services. We invest in and believe in the collective wisdom of our team members. The stores are organized into self-managing work teams that are responsible and accountable for their own performance.[12]

Teams also permit employees to pool their ideas to come up with better and more creative solutions to problems. Teams at Saturn and at the Chrysler Corporation's Jefferson North plant, for example, "provide a framework in which workers more readily help one another and more freely share their production knowledge—the innumerable 'tricks of the trade' that are vital in any manufacturing process."[13]

Team-based organizations are not simply a made-only-in-America phenomenon. Consider, for example, Vancom Zuid-Limburg, a joint venture in the Netherlands that operates a public bus company. This company has enjoyed very rapid growth in ridership and has been able to win transport concessions by offering more services at the same price as its competitors. The key to this success lies in its use of self-managed teams and the consequent savings in management overhead.

> Vancom is able to [win transport contracts] mainly because of its very low overhead costs. ... [O]ne manager supervises around forty bus drivers. ... This management-driver ratio of 1 in 40 substantially differs from the norm in this sector. At best, competitors achieve a ratio of 1 in 8. Most of this difference can be attributed to the self-managed teams. Vancom ... has two teams of around twenty drivers. Each team has its own bus lines and budgeting responsibilities. ... Vancom also expects each individual driver to assume more responsibilities when on the road. This includes customer service (e.g., helping elderly persons board the bus), identifying problems (e.g., reporting damage to a bus stop), and active contributions (e.g., making suggestions for improvement of the services).[14]

COMPARATIVELY HIGH COMPENSATION CONTINGENT ON ORGANIZATIONAL PERFORMANCE

It is often argued that high compensation is a consequence of organizational success, rather than its progenitor, and that high compensation (compared with the average) is possible only in certain industries that either face less competition or have particularly highly educated employees. But neither of these statements is correct. Obviously, successful firms can afford to pay more, and frequently do so, but high pay can also produce economic success.

When John Whitney assumed the leadership of Pathmark, a large grocery store chain in the eastern United States in 1972, the company had about 90 days to live, according to its banks, and was in desperate financial shape. Whitney looked at the situation and discovered that 120 store managers in the chain were paid terribly. Many of them made less than the butchers, who were unionized. He decided that the store managers were vital to the chain's success and its ability to accomplish a turnaround. Consequently, he gave the store managers a substantial raise—about 40 to 50 percent. Whitney attributes the subsequent success of the chain to the store managers' focusing on improving performance instead of worrying and complaining about their pay.

The idea that only certain jobs or industries can or should pay high wages is belied by the example of many firms. Home Depot has been successful and profitable, and its stock price has shown exceptional returns. Even though the chain emphasizes everyday low pricing as an important part of its business strategy and operates in a highly competitive environment, it pays its staff comparatively well for the retail industry, hires more experienced people with building industry experience, and expects its sales associates to provide a higher level of individual customer service.

Contingent compensation also figures importantly in most high performance work systems. Such compensation can take a number of different forms, including gain sharing, profit sharing, stock ownership, pay for skill, or various forms of individual or team incentives. Wal-Mart, AES Corporation, Southwest Airlines, Whole Foods Markets, Microsoft, and many other successful organizations encourage share ownership. When employees are owners, they act and think like owners. However, little evidence suggests that employee ownership, by itself, affects organizational performance. Rather, employee ownership works best as part of a broader philosophy or culture that incorporates other practices. Merely putting in ownership schemes without providing training, information sharing, and delegation of responsibility will have little effect on performance. Even if people are more motivated by their share ownership, they don't necessarily have the skills, information, or power to do anything with that motivation.

EXTENSIVE TRAINING

Training is often seen as a frill in many U.S. organizations, something to be reduced to make profit goals in times of economic stringency. Studies of firms in the United States and the United Kingdom consistently provide evidence of inadequate levels of training and training focused on the wrong things: specialist skills rather than generalist competence and organizational culture. This is the case in a world in which we are constantly told that knowledge and intellectual capital are critical for success. Knowledge and skill are critical—and too few organizations act on this insight. Training is an essential component of high performance work systems because these systems rely on frontline employee skill and initiative to identify and resolve problems, to initiate changes in work methods, and to take responsibility for quality. All of this requires a skilled and motivated work force that has the knowledge and capability to perform the requisite tasks.

Training can be a source of competitive advantage in numerous industries for firms with the wisdom to use it. The Men's Wear-house, an off-price specialty retailer of men's tailored business attire and accessories, went public in 1991. Its 1995 annual report noted that it had achieved compounded annual growth rates in revenues and net earnings of 32 and 41 percent, respectively, and that the value of its stock had increased by approximately 400 percent. The company attributes its success to how it treats its people and particularly to the emphasis it has placed on training, an approach that separates it from many of its competitors. The company built a 35,000 square foot training center in Fremont, California, its headquarters. In 1994, some 600 "clothing consultants" went through Suits University, and that year the company added Suits High and Selling Accessories U.[15] During the winter, experienced store personnel come back to headquarters in groups of about 30 for a three- or four-day retraining program.

While training is an investment in the organization's staff, in the current business milieu it virtually begs for some sort of return-on-investment calculations. But such analyses are difficult, if not impossible, to carry out. Successful firms that emphasize training do so almost as a matter of faith and because of their belief in the connection between people and profits. Even Motorola does a poor job of measuring its return on training. Although the company has been mentioned as reporting a $3 return for every $1 invested in training, an official from Motorola's training group said that she did not know where these numbers came from and that the company is notoriously poor at evaluating its $170 million investment in training. The firm mandates forty hours of training per employee per year, and believes that the effects of training are both difficult to measure and expensive to evaluate. Training is part and parcel of an overall management process and is evaluated in that light.

REDUCTION OF STATUS DIFFERENCES

The fundamental premise of high performance management systems is that organizations perform at a higher level when they are able to tap the ideas, skill, and effort of all of their people. In order to help make all organizational members feel important and committed, most high commitment management systems attempt to reduce the status distinctions that separate individuals and groups and cause some to feel less valued. This is accomplished in two principle ways—symbolically, through the use of language and labels, physical space, and dress, and substantively, in the reduction of the organization's degree of wage inequality, particularly across levels.

At NUMMI, everyone wears the same colored smock; executive dining rooms and reserved parking don't exist. At Kingston Technology, a private firm manufacturing add-on memory modules for personal computers, the two cofounders sit in open cubicles and do not have private secretaries.[16] Status differences are also reduced, and a sense of common fate developed, by limiting the difference in compensation between senior management and other employees. Herb Kelleher, who earns about $500,000 per year as the CEO of Southwest, including base and bonus, has been on the cover of *Fortune* magazine with the headline, "Is he America's best CEO?" In 1995, when Southwest negotiated a five-year wage freeze with its pilots in exchange for stock options and occasional profitability bonuses, Kelleher agreed to freeze his base salary at $395,000 for four years. Sam Walton, the founder and chairman of Wal-Mart, was one of the most underpaid CEOs in the U.S. Kelleher and Walton weren't poor; each owned stock in his company. But stock ownership was also encouraged for their employees. Having an executive's fortune rise and fall together with those of the other employees differs dramatically from providing large bonuses and substantial salaries for executives even as the stock price languishes and people are being laid off.

SHARING INFORMATION

Information sharing is an essential component of high performance work systems. The sharing of information on such things as financial performance, strategy, and operational measures conveys to the organization's people that they are trusted. John Mackey, the chief executive of Whole Foods Markets, states, "If you're trying to create a high-trust organization, . . . an organization where people are all-for-one and one-for-all, you can't have secrets."[17] Whole Foods shares detailed financial and performance information with every employee, including individual salary information. Every Whole Foods store has a book that lists the previous year's salary and bonus of all 6,500 employees.[18]

Even motivated and trained people cannot contribute to enhancing organizational performance if they don't have information on important dimensions of performance and training on how to use and interpret that information. The now famous case of Springfield ReManufacturing Corporation (SRC) illustrates this point. On February 1, 1983, SRC was created when the plant's management and employees purchased an old International Harvester plant in a financial transaction that consisted of about $100,000 in equity and $8.9 million in debt, an 89-1 debt to equity ratio that has to make this one of the most leveraged of all buyouts. Jack Stack, the former plant manager and now chief executive, knew that if the plant was to succeed, all employees had to do their best, and had to share all their wisdom and ideas for enhancing the plant's performance. Stack came up with a system called "open-book management," that has become so popular that

SRC now makes money by running seminars on it. When General Motors canceled an order in 1986 that represented about 40 percent of Springfield's business for the coming year, the firm averted a layoff by providing its people with information on what had happened and letting them figure out how to grow the company and achieve the productivity improvements that would obviate layoffs. SRC has since enjoyed tremendous financial success. In 1983, its first year of operation, sales were about $13 million. By 1992, sales had increased to $70 million and the number of employees had grown from 119 to 700. The original equity investment of $100,000 was worth more than $23 million by 1993. No one who knows the company, and certainly not Jack Stack or the other managers, believes this economic performance could have been achieved without a set of practices that enlisted the cooperation and ingenuity of all of the firm's people. The system and philosophy of open-book management took a failing International Harvester plant and transformed it into a highly successful, growing business.

IT ALL SEEMS SO EASY

How difficult can it be to increase the level of training, to share information and plans with people, to reorganize work into teams, to upgrade hiring practices, and to do all the other things described above? It is easy to form the ideas that are the foundation for people-centered management. But, if it were actually easy to implement those ideas, other airlines would have been able to copy Southwest, other grocery stores would be as successful as Whole Foods Markets, other power producers would be as profitable and efficient as AES, other retailers would have achieved the same record of growth and profitability as the Men's Wearhouse. Implementing these ideas in a systematic, consistent fashion remains rare enough to be an important source of competitive advantage for firms in a number of industries. Why is this so?

MANAGERS ARE ENSLAVED BY SHORT-TERM PRESSURES

Because achieving profits through people takes time to accomplish, an emphasis on short-term financial results will not be helpful in getting organizations to do the right thing. Short-term financial pressures and measurements abound. Many organizations provide raises and bonuses based on annual results. Ask senior managers how long it takes to change an organization's culture, and it's extremely unlikely that you will hear, "a year or less." But that is the time horizon of the evaluation process. Taking actions with payoffs that will occur beyond the time for which you will be measured on your performance is difficult and risky.

A second pressure occurs when organizations seek to create shareholder value by increasing stock price. The time horizon for evaluating stock market returns is again often quite short, often a year or less. Mutual fund and other institutional money managers are themselves frequently evaluated on a quarterly or at most an annual basis; they often invest in stocks for only a short time and have high portfolio turnover, so it is little surprise that they, in turn, put pressure on organizations for short-term, quick results.

A third pressure is that the immediate drives out the long-term. Today's pressing problems make it difficult to focus on actions aimed at building a better organization for the future. Managerial career processes contribute to this short-term pressure. When and where managers are hired for an indefinite period and careers are embedded in a single organization, it makes sense for those individuals to take a long-term view. But movements by managers across organizations have increased dramatically at nearly all organizational levels. Individuals trying to build a track record that will look good on the external labor market aren't likely to take a longer-term view of building organizational competence and capabilities. Stephen Smith has argued that the typical career system facing managers today encourages "managerial opportunism." He suggests that "managers are rewarded . . . for appropriating the ideas of their subordinates or for improving the bottom line in the short run and then moving on to other positions before the long-term implications of the strategies they have adopted make themselves felt."[19]

ORGANIZATIONS TEND TO DESTROY COMPETENCE

Organizations often inadvertently destroy wisdom and competence or make it impossible for wisdom, knowledge, and experience to benefit the firm. Management practices that require programs and ideas to be explained and reviewed in groups are a major culprit.

That formal planning and evaluation, and particularly the use of financial criteria, destroy competence is consistent with the results of research on innovation. Experts on organizational management have acquired the ability to see and understand things that are not evident to novices. An expert advertising executive moves quickly and creatively to come up with a good advertising campaign; an expert in production management understands the dynamics of both the human and mechanical elements of the production system and can accurately and quickly diagnose problems and figure out appropriate action; an expert in management or leadership has a good grasp of the principles of human motivation, great intuition, and the ability to read people and situations. But in any domain of expertise, by definition, some portion of the expert's knowledge and competence must be tacit, not readily articulated or explainable, irreducible to a formula or recipe. If that were not the case, then the expert knowledge would be codified and novices could do about as well as experts at the task in question, given access to the same formulas or insights.

But if expert knowledge has a substantial component of tacit knowledge, it will be impossible for experts to present the real basis of their judgments and decisions. Experts are more likely to rely on those factors and evidence that are available and accessible to all. In so doing, they lose virtually all the benefits of their expertise. Forced to explain decisions to a wider audience, the experts will have to rely on the same data and decision processes as anyone else. Thus, the organization will have created a decision process in which its experts behave like novices, and will have lost the benefits of the experts' wisdom and competence.

Consider the following example. Bob Scott, associate director of the Center for Advanced Study in the Behavioral Sciences at Stanford, had to give a talk about the Center's management to an outside group interested in establishing an interdisciplinary, social-science research center. As he was giving the talk, he recalled thinking, "If we actually managed the center this way, it would be a disaster." It was not possible for him to articulate his expertise, to explain his tacit knowledge. Suppose that instead of a group of curious outsiders, his audience had been a governing board or oversight body that would hold Scott and his colleagues accountable for following and implementing the ideas he expressed? They might have been forced to manage in ways that could seriously degrade the organization's operations.

MANAGERS DON'T DELEGATE ENOUGH

Relying on the tacit knowledge and expertise of others requires trust and the willingness to let them do what they know how to do. Using self-managing teams as an organizing principle requires permitting the teams to actually manage themselves. At NUMMI, teams were given real responsibility and were listened to, while at the General Motors Van Nuys, California, plant, a culture of hierarchical control meant that team members were frequently told to be quiet and supervisors exercised the same control they had before the institution of teams.

Even though employee participation is associated with enhanced economic performance, organizations frequently fail to introduce it, and it remains fragile even when it is implemented. At least some of this resistance derives from two social psychological processes: first, belief in the efficacy of leadership, that is, the "faith in supervision" effect; and second, a self-enhancement bias. The faith in supervision effect means that observers tend to believe that the greater the degree of supervisor involvement and control, the better the work produced. In one study, for instance, identical company performance was evaluated more positively when the leadership factors accounting for the performance were made more apparent.[20] The self-enhancement bias is a pervasive social psychological phenomenon. Researchers have found that "one of the most widely documented effects in social psychology is the preference of most people to see themselves in a self-enhancing fashion. As a consequence, they regard themselves as more intelligent, skilled, ethical, honest, persistent, original, friendly, reliable, attractive, and fair-minded than their peers or the average person. . . . On the job, approximately 90 percent of managers and workers rate their performances as superior to their peers."[21] It is no wonder then that such a bias would lead supervisors to evaluate more positively the work they have been involved in creating.

Both of these processes contribute to the same prediction: work performed under more oversight and control will be perceived as better than the identical work performed with less oversight. This effect will be particularly strong for the person doing the supervision. In a real work setting, these social psychological processes would, of course, be counterbalanced by pressures to achieve results and by the knowledge that participation and empowerment may be helpful in improving performance. Nonetheless, these beliefs may be significant factors hindering the use of high performance work practices and the participation and delegation they imply.

PERVERSE NORMS ABOUT WHAT CONSTITUTES GOOD MANAGEMENT

Two norms about what constitutes good management are simultaneously growing in acceptance and are enormously perverse in their implications. The first is the idea that good managers are mean or tough, able to make such difficult choices as laying off thousands of people and acting decisively. The second is that good management is mostly a matter of good analysis, a confusion between math and management. The two views are actually related, since an emphasis on analysis takes one away from such issues as motivation, commitment, and morale, and makes it more likely that one can and will act in a tough fashion.

An article in *Newsweek* stated that "firing people has gotten to be trendy in corporate America.... Now you fire workers—especially white collar workers—to make your corporate bones.... Wall Street and Big Business have been in perfect harmony about how in-your-face capitalism is making America great."[22] *Fortune* magazine regularly runs an article entitled "America's Toughest Bosses." Does one want to appear on that list, especially since many of those on it do not last very long in their jobs, having been "fired—in part, for being too mean"?[23] Little evidence exists that being a mean or tough boss is necessarily associated with business success. "Financial results from these bosses' companies vary from superb to pathetic. The median return on shareholder's equity over the past five years for seven of the ten companies for which data are available ranged from 7.3 percent ... to 18.1 percent.... That compares with the median for the *Fortune* 500 of 13.8 percent."[24] Nonetheless, *Fortune* predicts that "toughness ... will probably become more prevalent. Most nominees for this list rose to prominence in industries shaken by rapid change.... As global competition heats up and turmoil rocks more industries, tough management should spread. So look for more bosses who are steely, super demanding, unrelenting, sometimes abusive, sometimes unreasonable, impatient, driven, stubborn, and combative."[25]

The belief that the good manager is a skilled analyst also has questionable merit and validity. The belief first arose after World War II with the emergence of Robert McNamara and systems analysis in the Defense Department. It spread to operations research and mathematical analysis in such business schools as Carnegie Mellon and such businesses as the Ford Motor Company. The emphasis on mathematical elegance and analysis as cornerstones for effective management implicitly derogates the importance of emotion, leadership, and building a vision. It represents an attempt to substitute data and analytical methods for judgment and common sense. Emphasizing analytical skills over interpersonal, negotiating, political, and leadership skills inevitably leads to errors in selection, development, and emphasis on what is important to an organization.

● ● ● ● ● ● ● ● ● ● ● ● ●
A ONE-IN-EIGHT CHANCE

Firms often attempt piecemeal innovations. It is difficult enough to change some aspect of the compensation system without having to also be concerned about training, recruitment and selection, and how work is organized. Implementing practices in isolation may not have much effect, however, and, can actually be counterproductive. Increasing the firm's commitment to training activities won't accomplish much unless changes in work organization permit these more skilled people to actually implement their knowledge. If wages are comparatively low and incentives are lacking, the better-trained people may simply depart for the competition. Employment security can be counterproductive unless the firm hires people who fit the culture and unless incentives reward outstanding performance. Implementing work teams will not accomplish much unless the teams receive training in specific technical skills and team processes, and are given financial and operating performance goals and information

Implementing and seeing results from many of these practices takes time. It takes time to train and upgrade workers' skills and even more time to see the economic benefits of this training in reduced turnover and enhanced performance. It takes time to share operating and financial information with people, and to be sure that they understand and know how to use it. Even more time is needed before suggestions and insights can provide business results. It cer-

tainly requires time for employees to believe in employment security and for that belief to generate trust and produce higher levels of innovation and effort. Consequently, a long-term view of a company's development and growth is at least useful, if not absolutely essential, to implementation of high performance organizational arrangements.

One must bear in mind that one-half of organizations won't believe the connection between how they manage their people and the profits they earn. One-half of those who do see the connection will do what many organizations have done—try to make a single change to solve their problems, not realizing that the effective management of people requires a more comprehensive and systematic approach. Of the firms that make comprehensive changes, probably only about one-half will persist with their practices long enough to actually derive economic benefits. Since one-half times one-half times one-half equals one-eighth, at best 12 percent of organizations will actually do what is required to build profits by putting people first. Don't like these odds? Well, consider this: almost every other source of organizational success—technology, financial structure, competitive strategy—can be initiated in a short period of time. How many other sources of competitive advantage have a one-in-eight chance of success?

In the end, the key to managing people in ways that lead to profits, productivity, innovation, and real organizational learning ultimately lies in the manager's perspective. When managers look at their people, do they see costs to be reduced? Do they see recalcitrant employees prone to opportunism, shirking, and free riding, who can't be trusted and who need to be closely controlled through monitoring, rewards, and sanctions? Do they see people performing activities that can and should be contracted out to save on labor costs? Or, do they see intelligent, motivated, trustworthy individuals—the most critical and valuable strategic assets their organizations can have? When they look at their people, do they see them as the fundamental resources on which their success rests and the primary means of differentiating themselves from the competition? With the right perspective, anything is possible. With the wrong one, change efforts and new programs become gimmicks, and no army of consultants, seminars, and slogans will help.

Notes

1. Pfeffer, J. *The Human Equation: Building Profits by Putting People First,* Harvard Business School Press: Boston, MA, 1998, Chapter 2.
2. Huselid, M. A. 1995. The impact of human resource management practices on turnover, productivity, and corporate financial performance. *Academy of Management Journal,* 38:647.
3. Huselid, M. A., & Becker, B. E. 1997. The impact of high performance work systems, implementation effectiveness, and alignment with strategy on shareholder wealth. Unpublished paper, Rutgers University, New Brunswick, NJ: 18–19.
4. Blimes, L., Wetzker, K., & Xhonneux, P. 1997. Value in human resources. *Financial Times,* February: 10.
5. Welbourne, T., & Andrews, A. 1996. Predicting performance of initial public offering firms: Should HRM be in the equation? *Academy of Management Journal,* 39:891–919.
6. Locke, R. M. 1995. The transformation of industrial relations? A cross-national review, in *The Comparative Political Economy of Industrial Relations,* eds. Kirsten S. Wever and Lowell Turner, Madison, WI: Industrial Relations Research Association: 18–19.
7. Kelleher, H. 1997. A culture of commitment. *Leader to Leader,* 1:23.
8. Southwest Airlines. 1994. Case S-OB-28, Palo Alto, CA: Graduate School of Business, Stanford University: 29.
9. O'Reilly, B. 1996. The rent-a-car jocks who made Enterprise #1. *Fortune,* 28:128.
10. See, for instance, O'Reilly, C. A., Chatman, J. A., & Caldwell, D. F. 1991. People and organizational culture: A profile comparison approach to assessing person-organization fit. *Academy of Management Journal,* 34:487–516; and Chatman, J. A. 1991. Managing people and organizations: Selection and socialization in public accounting firms. *Administrative Science Quarterly,* 36:459–484.
11. Work Week. 1996. *The Wall Street Journal,* 28 May: A1.
12. Whole Foods Market, Inc. *1995 Annual Report,* Austin, TX: 3, 17.
13. Shaiken, H., Lopez, S., & Mankita, I. 1997. Two routes to team production: Saturn and Chrysler compared. *Industrial Relations,* 36:31.
14. Van Beusekom, Mark. 1996. *Participation Pays! Cases of Successful Companies with Employee Participation,* The Hague: Netherlands Participation Institute: 7.
15. Men's Wearhouse, *1994 Annual Report,* Fremont, CA: 3.
16. Doing the right thing. 1995. *The Economist,* 20:64.
17. Fishman, C. 1996. Whole Foods teams. *Fast Company,* April–May: 106.
18. Ibid., 105.
19. Appelbaum, E., & Batt, R. 1994. *The New American Workplace.* Ithaca, NY: ILR Press: 147.
20. Meindl, J. R., & Ehrlich, S. B. 1987. The romance of leadership and the evaluation of organizational performance. *Academy of Management Journal,* 30:91–109.
21. Ibid.
22. Sloan, A. 1996. The hit men. *Newsweek,* 28:44–45.
23. Dumaine, B. 1993. America's toughest bosses. *Fortune,* 18:39.
24. Flax, S. 1984. The toughest bosses in America. *Fortune,* 6:19.
25. Nulty, P. 1989. America's toughest bosses. *Fortune,* 27:54.

I-4: Human Resource Management: Leaders, Laggards, and Followers

PHILIP H. MIRVIS

● ● ● ● ● ● ● ● ● ● ● ● ● ● ● ● ● ●

EXECUTIVE OVERVIEW

Most American companies face intense competition, have had to cut costs, and see a continuing need to improve quality and customer service. In response, they have trimmed their workforces and expanded operations overseas. Those companies that rank as human resource leaders have combined downsizing with restructuring, reengineering, employee involvement programs, and team-based work redesigns. They have retrained and redeployed twice as many workers as the human resource laggards, are more apt to sponsor private-public partnerships with schools, offer employees flexible work arrangements, and conduct diversity training and mentoring programs. Neither leaders nor laggards, HR followers are hampered by short-term pressures, indifferent middle management, and other barriers to change; such companies wait for innovations to take hold in their industries. Because HR executives are generally not well positioned to promote innovation in their companies, the gap between leaders, followers, and laggards may widen in the years ahead.

Intense global competition, pressures to cut costs and improve performance, declines in the nation's skill bank, growing diversity in the workforce, an aging population—all of these factors make competing claims on the resources and imagination of all businesses.

To assess how companies respond to them, a team of researchers analyzed results of the Louis Harris Laborforce 2000 survey of over 400 American-based corporations.[1] The findings highlight the extent to which a company's size, industry, workforce composition, and management philosophies influence that response.

Among the issues the researchers examined:

- Most firms surveyed downsized in the decade past. What have been the consequences? What differentiates firms that have redesigned their organizations and retrained employees from those that have simply cut back? Will periodic downsizing become a fact of life in years ahead?

- Higher skill jobs require higher skill workers. Which companies have taken the most innovative steps to reduce the skills gap? What kinds lag behind?

- The skills of entry workers are suspect. Which firms are providing the needed basic and remedial skill training? Which ones have partnerships with public schools?

- Demography could be density. How many companies are trying to capital ize on diversity in their workforces? Responding to work/family issues? What distinguishes leaders from firms that just "muddle through?"

- The population is aging. Are more workers over age 55 destined to be "deadwood" or can they find a meaningful place in corporations? Are companies responding to this growing issue?

The need for systematic knowledge about how businesses manage these issues is urgent. Anecdotal accounts of top performing companies portray them in glowing terms. By contrast, daily news stories about cutbacks in staffing, training, and health insurance, coupled with indifference to the needs of their workforce and society, show firms to be short-sighted and self-serving. Both pictures are misleading. This study of companies large and small, public and private, across the breadth of industry (see box on sample) presents a clearer picture of corporate conduct today. It shows where human resource (HR) management in companies is pacing the demands of change, following along, and where, in some cases, it is seriously behind.

STRATEGIC PRIORITIES OF BUSINESS

The Laborforce 2000 survey began with a simple question: "What are the dominant strategic issues—of any kind—that are of most concern or interest to your top management?" Three issues were rated as most significant:

- Global competitiveness, cited by one-third of the companies, especially those with more than $1 billion in sales, with substantial overseas operations, and those in the manufacturing sector.

- Economic concerns. One-third of the companies identified a need to cut costs or improve profitability.

- Quality, productivity, and customer service concerns.

Also cited with some frequency were the need to modernize marketing, to improve R&D, and to undertake mergers and acquisitions.

Given these strategic priorities, what has been the most prominent response in industry? Five of six firms surveyed undertook some form of downsizing—shutting down plants and facilities (64 percent of companies), selling off business units (51 percent), eliminating one or more layers of management (38 percent)—and over half laid off a

---

Data Base and Sample

The Laborforce 2000 data come from face-to-face interviews conducted by Louis Harris & Associates with top human resource executives in a sample of 406 randomly selected Conference Board member companies. Most of the firms are in manufacturing (35 percent), financial services (27 percent), or other service industries (27 percent). Two-thirds are publicly owned companies.

The sampled companies are generally larger than the norm in the U.S. (28 percent have more than 10,000 employees; 23 percent have 1,000 or less; with the median being 4,050 domestic workers). They also have more total sales (43 percent have sales over $1 billion), and are more likely to have international plants and offices (one third have substantial overseas sales, marketing, or production facilities). Roughly half of the employees in these companies are white-collar workers (technical, professional, or clerical) and 17 percent are managers. The great majority of employees hold high school diplomas and more than two-fifths have college degrees.

Interviewees were all experienced human resource professionals with 57 percent carrying the title of vice-president or above and another quarter holding the office of director or manager of human resources. Two-thirds reported to a CEO, executive vice-president, or senior vice president in their firms. The average length of time interviewees have been working in HR was 19.4 years.

substantial number of their workers. These measures eliminated 12.4 percent of the jobs in these firms from the late 1980s through the early 1990s. Large manufacturers shed the greatest proportion of jobs, with financial services close behind. Controlling for size and industry sector, public companies, subject to earnings pressures from Wall Street, made bigger cuts than privately owned firms.

What is the outlook on future downsizing? Over 70 percent of the manufacturers and financial service companies expected to continue downsizing through the mid-1990s, along with 60 percent of the nonfinancial service businesses—a trend currently in evidence.[2] When asked whether periodic downsizing was necessary to maintain a competitive organization, over half of the HR heads surveyed reported that it had become essential. This perception was strongest in large, publicly held companies and in firms with more unionized employees. Companies with a large proportion of contingent workers on staff were least likely to agree with this proposition.

DOWNSIZING: REASONS AND REPERCUSSIONS

When asked the single most important reason for downsizing, the majority of companies surveyed cited a need for cost control (27 percent) or a lack of profitability (25 percent). By comparison, roughly two-in-five cited a need to improve productivity (22 percent), counter competition (12 percent), or implement a change in their business strategy (8 percent). As for consequences, over 60 percent of the interviewees cited lower morale among the remaining workforce as the chief downside of their downsizing. Other reported problems cited by over one-third of the downsizing companies included an unexpected increase in the use of temporary workers and consultants,

overtime, and the need to retrain the remaining workforce. One-in-five firms found that they lost the wrong people in their downsizings and 16 percent absorbed severance costs greater than expected.

The study team looked into the relationship between downsizing motives and the consequences. Firms were classified into two groups: those who downsized for reasons of cost-containment and profitability (cost-control) versus those who did so to improve productivity, deal with competitors, or implement a new business strategy (productivity). We found that firms that cut back for the sake of cost control experienced many more post-downsizing problems than those that downsized for purposes of increased productivity.

Working backward, we then looked at factors predicting whether a company would cite cost-control or productivity as its chief reason for downsizing. Size, industry, and workforce composition did not prove to be significant predictors of a company's downsizing motivations in statistical analyses.[3] Indeed, far and away the best predictor proved to be what we characterize as a company's human resource philosophy.

HUMAN RESOURCE PHILOSOPHY

Interviewees were asked several questions about factors influencing HR management in their firms and about barriers they encountered when proposing change. Among the most significant factors influencing HR policies and attitudes were (1) demands from customers or the marketplace; (2) changes in the job mix; (3) new technology; and (4) actions of competitors. All were rated as having a "great deal of influence" by roughly a third of the interviewees and as having some influence by three-fourths of the interviewees. On the other side of the ledger, interviewees cited as major barriers to change (1) the costs of making change; (2) the need to address other priorities; (3) their company's focus on short-term goals; and (4) trouble getting the attention of top management. Another barrier noted by over half of the HR heads was a corporate culture that did not "emphasize human resource issues."

Finally, interviewees were asked to rate their company's approach to adopting new HR practices. Eleven percent said they usually tried to be in the lead with HR innovations; 39 percent adopted policies to stay ahead of other companies; 39 percent introduced them when a consensus developed in their industry; and 11 percent adopted policies only after they were proven effective in other companies. This yields the familiar "diffusion of innovation curve" (see Figure 1) that represents the sampled companies' position as leading, following, and lagging in adopting new HR policies.[4]

We found a consistent pattern between companies' innovative orientations and ratings of the influences on HR and barriers to change. For instance, at leading edge corporations, far more interviewees saw customers, changes in workforce demographics, and new technology as having a "great deal" of impact on HR management than in other firms sampled. They were also less constrained by competing priorities, costs, and an unresponsive culture when proposing change. The next group along the diffusion curve, fast followers, were not as influenced by customers and demographics as the leaders, and were more limited in innovation by prevailing attitudes in their companies. The slow followers, waiting for a consensus to develop in their industries, were somewhat less influenced by external forces and more hampered in making change by the costs and their company cultures. At the back of the pack, laggards had

FIGURE 1 Position of Company in Adopting New Human Resources Policies

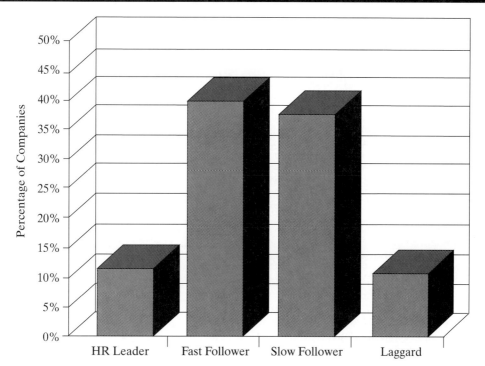

the most trouble getting the attention of top management and reported their corporate cultures to be a substantial barrier to change (see Table 1).

There were some interesting differences in these ratings across companies. For instance, HR management in larger companies was more influenced by customers and competitors, and by changes in the educational and demographic mix of their workforce, than in smaller ones. Larger firms also encountered more opposition to change from middle management and unions. There were, however, no consistent differences between firms based on size, sales, workforce composition, or industry in ratings of the barriers posed by the costs of making change, top management attitudes, or corporation culture. The key differentiator between companies in these regards was their relative emphasis on HR innovation. In leading edge companies, for example, interviewees found top executives, middle managers, unions, and employees to be much less resistant to change than in firms characterized as followers. Laggards were

twice as likely as leaders to say that competing crises, their company's focus on short-term goals, and the costs of making change were significant barriers to adopting new approaches to human resource management.

● ● ● ● ● ● ● ● ● ● ●
PHILOSOPHY IN ACTION: RESTRUCTURE, REDESIGN, REBUILD

The primacy of HR philosophy as a predictor of innovative action becomes apparent when we look at how companies respond to the strategic priorities identified by interviewees. With regard to downsizing, for example, human resource leaders were far more likely than laggards or followers to cite improved competitiveness and productivity as key reasons for reducing staff (see Figure 2). In turn, these firms were also more apt to be resized because of mergers or acquisitions, or when spinning off businesses. One interpretation is that HR lead-

TABLE 1 Characteristics of HR Innovators: Influences on HR and Barriers to Change	Leader n = 44	Fast Follower n = 157	Slow Follower n = 151	Laggard n = 43
Influences on HR Management (% a great deal of influence . . .)				
Customers or Marketplace	52%	36%	28%	40%
Changes in Corporate Culture	45	34	31	30
Changes in Technology	41	25	25	21
Actions of Competitors	27	25	24	30
Changes in Demographics	23	8	7	5
Perceived Barriers to Change (% a major barrier . . .)				
Trouble Getting Attention of Top Management	37%	48%	47%	58%
Costs of Making Change	16	27	37	49
Need to Address Crises and More Immediate Issues	16	32	28	35
Focus on Short-term Goals	11	25	31	40
Culture Doesn't Emphasize Human Resource Issues	7	16	22	37

FIGURE 2 Corporate Downsizing and Human Resource Philosophy

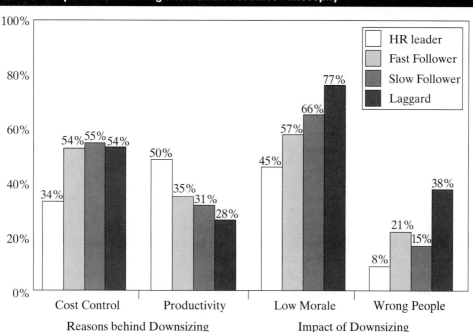

ers took a more strategic approach to their cutbacks and were restructuring their organizations in light of future needs.

The consequences of downsizing also differed across the sample. Firms that are typically slowest to make HR innovations were far more likely to incur higher-than-expected severance costs, to increase their use of costly overtime and consultants, and to lose more of the "wrong kind of people" than were HR leaders. Laggards experienced more post-downsizing morale problems than followers, and followers more than leaders. A possible explanation is that some slow-to-innovate firms find themselves in a downward spiral, continuing to lay off people without the critical mass of skills and motivation to right the business.[5] As one interviewee put it, his company first went through downsizing, then through "rightsizing," and is now at risk of "capsizing" because of continued cost-cutting. Another philosophized: "We used to be fat and dumb; now we're lean and dumb."

While cutting back has been the most widespread competitive response of American companies, three of four firms in this study also made "substantial investments" in advanced computing systems for factories and offices and introduced all manner of telecommunications technology. Although some firms used automation primarily to replace direct labor, clerical staff, and supervision, nearly 45 percent said that they upgraded technology as part of a reengineering or work redesign effort. In many of these cases, companies created work teams where, for example, production workers manufacture or assemble a whole product or clerical and service workers team up to manage customer accounts.

Two of five firms surveyed had formal programs to promote employee involvement in work planning, problem solving, and decision making or introduced Total Quality Management (TQM).

U.S. firms have also been expanding globally. One-in-four companies in this sample have over 20 percent of their work-force located outside the United States, and over half report that they are likely to expand their overseas operations in the near future. The chief reasons companies give for overseas expansion are to be global competitors and to be closer to markets. Lower labor and transportation costs are a consideration for some firms, as well. By comparison, taxes, government regulation, and the skills and work ethic of foreign versus U.S. employees are not considered very important criteria in global expansion.

The strategic challenge for companies has been to increase their global reach and enhance productivity, quality, and service, while still controlling costs. The common formula involves downsizing coupled with substantial investments in advanced technology and a search for opportunities in the global marketplace.

What is missing from this overall competitive response are innovative ways of managing people. Here is where HR philosophy becomes an important ingredient. In the Laborforce 2000 study, leaders and fast followers invested somewhat more on high tech than companies that were slow-to-innovate or laggards. But they were two and three times more apt to invest substantially in "high touch" workplace improvements—work redesign, TQM, and employee involvement programs. HR leaders downsized as much as other firms in the sample, yet they retrained over 84 percent of their workforce in the aftermath as compared with laggards, who retrained only 39 percent. And, as we shall see, leaders also regularly train workers in new technologies, take innovative steps to attract and prepare newcomers, and have specialized programs to respond to changes in workforce demographics.

What's behind this human capital strategy? We found that HR leaders were consistently more likely than followers and laggards to rate selected HR issues—the education of workers, their family responsibilities, increasing workforce diversity—as having a major impact on company competitiveness. Having projected human resource issues more forcefully into their overall strategic outlook, they in turn made investments in people a prime source of competitive advantage. Their example yields a new version of the three R's for businesses: restructure, redesign, and rebuild.

INVESTING IN PEOPLE

Based on these data, it seems that Johnston and Packard's "Workforce 2000" projection of labor shortages in the mid-1990s has been forestalled by a combination of slow growth and downsizing.[6] Nevertheless, a skills gap threatens industries of all types and sizes. Three-fourths of the firms studied anticipated problems in recruiting qualified scientists and technologists and over half foresaw problems getting highly skilled blue-collar workers. The most immediate skills gap concerns the supply of entry-level college and high school graduates. Over 50 percent of entry-level job applicants lack the skills to be hired.

Several national studies have documented the declining academic performance of America's high schoolers, who score two-to-three years behind their Japanese counterparts on standardized tests and rank lower on math-and-science achievement than students in most other developed countries.[7] As a result, U.S. employers have had to take on the job of the nation's high schools to the point that roughly half in this sample offer entry-level workers a mix of remedial education and basic skills training. Interestingly, smaller, manufacturing firms, with a larger proportion of blue-collar workers, take the lead in this regard. HR leaders are not especially innovative in this way, but with good reason; they have less difficulty attracting qualified people and less to do in the way of remedial education.

HR leaders were almost twice as likely as laggards to encourage their employees to do volunteer work in public schools and seven times more likely to provide them with paid leaves-of-absence for this purpose. They also gave schools significantly more money and equipment, and several had formed partnerships with local school districts to provide part-time and summer employment to students and job placement for them upon graduation.[8] These programs may contribute to their success in attracting qualified people.

HR leaders retrain more of their employees and more often than followers and laggards. But general HR innovativeness is not the sole predictor here. Leaders that redesigned their workplaces, introduced TQM, and launched employee involvement programs were even more committed to retraining. They put the lion's share of their training monies into technical skill development (40 percent) and general management training (20 percent). HR leaders and fast followers spend twice as much as other companies to improve employees' problem-solving and communication skills. Again, this distinction is even more pronounced in the subset of leading companies that have redesigned their workplaces. The competitive message here is that leaders invest in both the workforce and the workplace.

● ● ● ● ● ● ● ● ● ● ● ● ● ● ● ●
FLEXIBILITY AND WORK/FAMILY ISSUES

Most companies in this sample are experiencing changes in the makeup of their workforce and are at least cognizant of future demographic trends. And many are sensitive to the conflicting demands of work and family life that their employees encounter. Yet these labor force issues are

rated as far less urgent than, say, the training needs of entry workers and current employees. One explanation is that many of the interviewees saw work/family programs as "benefits" for employees rather than as means of increasing the flexibility and productivity of their organizations.[9]

There were some quantitative differences in what companies do to increase workplace flexibility. For instance, four out of five firms in this sample offer flextime and provide hourly personnel with the option of part-time employment. Large, multinational companies are most innovative in this regard. But an even more significant predictor of the use of flextime was the proportion of women in a company's workforce. This may have to do with the preponderance of clerical and data processing work in these firms as compared to others. Another factor to consider is the clout women have as they move up the ranks in greater numbers in companies. Indeed, another important predictor of flexibility was the proportion of women in management positions in the firms studied.

HR innovativeness is a factor in uncommon work/family programs. HR leaders, for example, are far more likely to offer employees the option of job sharing or of working at home. And, although the absolute numbers are small, HR leaders are also more apt to directly assist their employees with eldercare, to organize parent support groups, and to provide on-site childcare services.

Even more notable are qualitative differences in ways companies approach such programs. Laggards and those who have been slow to innovate report that the primary advantage of flextime and other work/family innovations is an "enhanced corporate image." Fast followers, in turn, are most apt to say it helps in "recruiting and retention." By contrast, leaders see increased productivity as an advantage of flexibility. Once again, they perceive a clear link between investing in people and reaping better performance.

HR leaders are also more apt to offer executive sabbaticals, giving upper level managers time and space to rethink their careers and retool themselves, and to offer mid-level managers and professionals part-time work options. Leaders also make more use of the contingent workforce—part-time seasonal employees and consulting services. At the leading edge, the flex-firm is taking shape.[10]

VALUING DIVERSITY

There were notable differences, too, in ways that companies dealt with the increasing racial, ethnic, and gender diversity of their workforce. Human resource leaders are more likely to have issued a statement from senior management that they value diversity, to offer diversity training for managers and employees, and to operate mentoring programs for women and minorities. Workforce composition is also important here: Firms with more women and especially more minorities are more apt to have specialized training and mentoring programs aimed at capitalizing on diversity.

Qualitative differences among leaders, followers, and laggards are most apparent when it comes to management's outlook on workforce diversity. Interviewees in lagging companies saw attention to diversity as primarily a matter of federal Equal Employment Opportunity compliance. Followers, interestingly enough, believed that "good management" is the best solution to problems posed by diversity. By contrast, interviewees in HR leaders reported that workforce diversity requires specialized and concerted attention. In turn, they were more apt to say that workforce diversity provides companies with "unique" competitive opportunities.[11] This may explain why they have so many more initiatives underway in this regard.

THE AGING WORKFORCE

The age group 50 years and older is the fastest-growing age segment in the workforce today and will increase substantially as baby boomers mature and life spans increase. Furthermore, many more older workers will delay full retirement in the future and desire to work in part-time or rescaled jobs. Indeed, many may have to work in order to provide for themselves and cover the costs of health care.

Many companies (41 percent) use early retirement incentive programs (ERIPs) to remove older workers. Companies with a larger proportion of employees over age 50—chiefly large manufacturers with more unionized employees—have eliminated many more jobs and a larger percentage of their workforce than employers with a younger workforce. To compound matters, many of these firms retired a disproportionate number of their older workers through ERIPs and job elimination.

The core issue here is the gap between attitudes and practices.[12] Although the human resource executives interviewed professed to see older workers as having better work attitudes and job skills than younger workers, only one in five provided workers the option of phased retirement that allowed them to work part-time prior to their full retirement from a company. And just one in three provided opportunities for mature employees to transfer to jobs with reduced pay and responsibilities. Furthermore, companies spend less on retraining older workers than they do younger ones and few adapt their training to the learning styles and needs of older people.

HR leaders, although somewhat more innovative than followers and laggards, have not kept pace with the changing demographics. Since the bulk of baby boomers will reach age 55 in the twenty-first century, it may be that the implications of an aging labor force are simply too far off on the corporate horizon to yet register attention. Indeed, firms with the largest proportion of older workers are doing more to respond to this issue than other companies.

Current inattention to the issues posed by aging does not necessarily mean that older workers will be seen as useless in the future. For instance, older workers may help to fill the skill gap that is projected to expand over the rest of the decade. This would, of course, require massive retraining and substantial corporate and public investment.[13] It is noteworthy that three in four companies say that problems in recruiting qualified, skilled people would cause them to reassess their current programs or start new ones to hire and use more older workers.

Older workers may also fill new and expanding roles in the service sector and make up a larger share of the contingent workforce. Firms like McDonald's, Day's Inn, and Walmart have already capitalized on the interpersonal skills and work ethic of older people. Finally, it is foreseeable that older workers will be folded under the umbrella of diversity in leading-edge corporations.[14] Having a different outlook and mirroring a growing segment of the consumer marketplace, they could indeed prove a valuable and flexible resource for innovative companies.

. . . .
PROGRESS AND PROBLEMS

Most of the companies surveyed recognize an urgent need to build and capitalize on a more competitive workforce. This is important because through the 1970s, many U.S. corporations downplayed the relationship between innovative human resource management and productivity.[15] Executives were unreceptive, even hostile, to the heightened aspirations and nonconformist values of massive numbers of baby boomers then entering their companies and were at a loss to respond to the demands for equal opportunity and upward mobility expressed by women and minorities.[16] Furthermore, the nascent threat posed by Japanese auto, tool, and electronics manufacturers was largely discounted, and Pacific Rim and European competitors were scarcely blips on the strategic screen.

Our study found companies keenly aware of foreign and domestic competition and striving to increase productivity, enhance quality, improve service, and control costs. Companies seem now to understand that many people want to apply their knowledge and skills at work, thrive with more freedom and flexibility on their jobs, and have much to contribute to work decisions. Indeed, when asked to rate the relative importance of several job-related factors in attracting, motivating, and retaining the kinds of employees that their companies need, interviewees cited "interesting work" as the most important factor and "opportunities to participate in decisions" near the top of the list. Companies also recognize that new entrants to their workforce require extensive training to catch up to foreign counterparts and that employees at all levels have to be retrained regularly to keep pace with rapid change and the challenge of high technology jobs.

A second encouraging finding is that select firms in this sample are getting the job done. Companies at the leading edge or following fast in the arena of HR management, roughly half of the sample, invest heavily in innovative work redesign, employee involvement, and total quality management programs—boosting their bank of human capital and applying it to turn out better product and services. They do more in the way of retraining and involving themselves in public education. They are more apt to help their employees balance the stressful demands of their jobs and family lives. And they have more commitment and programs aimed at capitalizing on increased racial, ethnic, and gender diversity in their workforce (see Table 2).

What is most notable about this table is that leaders have been consistently more innovative than followers, and followers more so than laggards, in every aspect of human resource management measured here. It can, of course, be argued that some firms opt for investing in people while others put their monies into technology, advertising, or physical assets as a means of gaining competitive advantage. Statistical analyses throughout this data base showed, however, that neither company size (as measured by the number of workers or by sales) nor industry nor workforce composition were consistent predictors of this broad range of human resource activity. This means that some manufacturers, financial service firms, and other service-sector organizations have invested a great deal in innovative HR management and others not; and the same is true of firms of equal size and comparable work-force populations. One hypothesis, then, is that a company's emphasis on human capital investment is a function of strategic choice rather than of the particular characteristics of its markets or workforce.

HR management in innovative firms is more influenced by customers, new technologies, and changes in the demographics of the workforce than in companies that follow and lag with innovation. Innovators, in turn, are more apt to have the attention of top management and to have a company culture that values HR management. The combination of these influences seems to create a cultural mind-set in leading companies that investing in people is essential to their success. Interviewees in leading and fast-following firms were two and three times as likely as their peers to see worker education, family responsibilities, and growing diversity in the workforce as having a significant impact on their competitiveness. This mind-set engages a virtuous cycle that stimulates and reinforces innovation on many HR fronts.

TABLE 2 Characteristics of HR Innovators: Investments in Human Capital				
	Leader *n = 44*	*Fast Follower* *n = 157*	*Slow Follower* *n = 151*	*Laggard* *n = 43*
Workplace Improvement				
Redesign Jobs for Teamwork	61%	51%	37%	28%
Employee Involvement Program	61	45	30	26
Percentage of Workforce Retrained after Downsizing	84	69	51	39
Education and Training				
Involved in Public Schools	70	58	52	39
Annually Retrain Workers	52	33	34	28
Workplace Flexibility				
Job-Sharing Option	66	53	39	33
Work-at-Home Option	45	31	24	16
On-site Child Care	27	10	7	5
Managing Diversity				
Senior Management Commitment	75	57	40	37
Management Training in Diversity	80	69	56	49
Mentoring Programs	50	33	19	12
Programs for Older Workers				
Phased Retirement	32	25	16	12

Speaking to this point, Lawler argues that while advances in technology can be acquired and business strategies copied, innovative investments in people are harder to duplicate and provide firms with a unique and sustainable competitive advantage.[17] The Laborforce 2000 survey found some evidence that HR management is moving up on the agenda of companies currently classified as slow-to-innovate and lagging behind. Over 50 percent of the interviewees in these companies said that their top management is devoting substantially more "time and energy" to HR issues than the five years previous. Another third registered at least some increased interest.

Does this mean, in turn, that the ideas and human resource management practices of pacesetting companies will inevitably spread to less innovative and culturally attuned organizations? Our final conclusion of this study is cautionary: Building a world-class workforce and putting it to effective use takes considerably more investment, imagination, and stick-to-itiveness than many companies, even some leaders, have mustered to this point. Heightened competition can drain, as well as energize, and this study suggests that the perceived need for constant cost-cutting can create a "vicious cycle," focusing companies on short-term measures and making HR innovation seem too costly. Regular restructuring and downsizing can, in turn, sap morale—from top to bottom—and deflect attention from investing in human resources and long-range productivity.

Longitudinal research by Lawler, Mohrman, and Ledford confirms that more companies today are beginning or expanding efforts at work redesign, employee involvement, and total quality management compared with five years ago.[18] This adds weight to the notion that human resource innovations follow a diffusion curve from leaders to followers to laggards. But there could be problems in the packaging of the full battery of HR innovations adopted by leaders. New methods diffuse from leading edge firms to the mainstream once they become fully coherent and attain scientific status. At present, however, there are myriad ideas on effecting change in corporate cultures but no standard body of knowledge or tested protocol.[19] Furthermore, there is scant empirical evidence on, say, the rate of return on training production workers in interpersonal communication skills, on the merits of flextime, or even the payoff of valuing diversity. Without keenly interested top management, able and outspoken human resource leadership, and a congenial corporate culture, an innovative and integrative approach to human resource management may never reach firms that are slow to innovate or laggards.

Research on the spread of seemingly more digestible TQM practices in *Fortune* 1000 companies reinforces the point: top management's inattention and resistance on the part of middle-managers, employees, and unions can doom human resource innovations.[20] The new practices being proposed require large investments of time, energy, and will in corporations and depend on strong leadership, open-minded organization members, and a high degree of readiness for change within the corporate culture. Hence there is no guarantee that firms that are not prone to innovative human resource management will embrace them in a fit of competitive zeal.

As a result, certain hothouses of innovative thinking—and companies with the money and imagination to invest in the human resource frontier—may continue to enhance their leading-edge status and gain a competitive edge from these new human resource innovations. But fast followers, who would next be expected to try out these ideas and practices, may not adopt them so easily or capitalize as readily on their potential. And firms that are slow to innovate or that wait for these practices to prove themselves may be left behind at a crucial competitive disadvantage and have neither the resources nor the residual talent needed to undertake a corporate transformation. The risk is that the innovators will get richer and more responsive to change while the rest will at best muddle through or simply wither away.

Notes

1. For details on findings of the Laborforce 2000 survey, see Mirvis, P.H. (Ed.). 1993. *Building a Competitive Workforce: Investing in Human Capital for Corporate Success.* New York: Wiley. The survey was developed by a team drawn from Louis Harris & Associates, The Commonwealth Fund, ICF, and included the author. Members of the team included Elwore E. Lawler, Susan Cohen, Lei Chang, Mitchell Lee Marks, Michael Useem, Victoria Parker, Douglas Hall, Michael Barth, William McNaught, Phillip Rizzi, and Karen Davis.

2. For up-to-date statistics in the United States, see the 1995 annual report on downsizing by the American Management Association, New York, New York.

3. Regression analyses were applied to data reported throughout this article.

4. Research on the "diffusion of innovations" was pioneered by E.M. Rogers. 1962. *Diffusion of Innovation.* New York: Free Press.

5. For recent data on the consequences of downsizing see "Downsizing," published by consulting firm Wm. Mercer & Co., Los Angeles, California, 1995. Also see W.F. Cascio. 1993. Downsizing: What do we know? What have we learned? *Academy of Management Executive,* 7(1):95–104.

6. Johnston, W.B. & Packer, D.T. 1987. *Workforce 2000.* Indianapolis: Hudson Institute.

7. Useem, M. 1993. Company policies on education and training. In P.H. Mirvis (Ed.), *Building the Competitive Work Force.* New York: Wiley.

8. Marshall, R. & Tucker, M. 1992. *Thinking for a Living: Education and the Wealth of Nations.* New York: Basic Books. Also see D.T. Hall and V.A. Parker. 1993. The Role of Workplace Flexibility in Managing Diversity. *Organizational Dynamics,* Summer, 4–18.

9. Mirvis, P.H. and Hall, D.T. 1996. In D.T. Hall and Associates (Eds.), *The career is dead— Long live the career: A relational approach.* San Francisco: Jossey-Bass.

10. Several leading companies offer diversity training and mentoring programs and ensure that project and work groups have a multicultural makeup. Our belief is that racial and gender diversity in work groups enhances creativity and encourages people to take a close look at their assumptions, inferences, and logic. It is also argued that increased diversity in idea-generating and problem-solving forums is akin to market research—it provides companies with an inside look at distinct market segments and their more diverse customer base. For a description of the latest research on diversity, see T. Cox, 1993. *Cultural diversity in organizations: Theory, research & practice.* San Francisco: Berrett-Koehler.

11. Hall, D.T., and Mirvis, P.H. 1993. The new workplace: A place for older workers? *Perspective on Aging.* October–December: 15–17.

12. Bass, A. and Barth, M. 1994. The next educational opportunity: Career training for older adults. In *Americans over 55 at Work Program.* New York: The Commonwealth Fund.

13. Hall, D.T. and Mirvis, P.H. 1996. Increasing the Value of Older Workers. In Auerbach, J.A. (Ed.) *Through a Glass Darkly: Building the New Workplace for the 21st Century.* Washington, D.C.: National Planning Association.

14. *Report of a Special Task Force to the Secretary: Work in America.* 1972. U.S. Department of Health, Education, and Welfare, Washington, D.C.: US Government Printing Office.

15. Yankelovich, D. 1979. Work, Values, and the New Breed. In Kerr, C. and Rosow, J.M. (Eds.) *Work in America: The Decade Ahead.* New York: Van Nostrand Reinhold.

16. Lawler, E.E. 1994. *The Ultimate Advantage.* San Francisco: Jossey-Bass.

17. Lawler, E.E., Mohrman, S.A., and Ledford, G.E. 1992. *Employee involvement and total quality management: Practices and results in Fortune 1000 companies.* San Francisco: Jossey-Bass.

When new management practices move through the mainstream and reach less innovative firms, they are typically translated into products, such as schematics on new work designs or how-to manuals on how to introduce principles of TQM. At this point, models on how to conduct organization-wide change do not lend themselves to neat packaging and standardized delivery. The closest thing may be the "Handbook for Revolutionaries" in N.M. Tichy and S. Sherman. 1993. *Control your own density or someone else will.* New York: Doubleday/Currency, 1993.

18. *Employee Involvement and Total Quality Management,* op. cit.

I-5: A New Mandate for Human Resources
HR Should Be Defined Not by What It Does but by What It Delivers

DAVE ULRICH

Should we do away with HR? In recent years, a number of people who study and write about business—along with many who run businesses—have been debating that question. The debate arises out of serious and widespread doubts about HR's contribution to organizational performance. And as much as I like HR people— I have been working in the field as a researcher, professor, and consultant for 20 years—I must agree that there is good reason for HR's beleaguered reputation. It is often ineffective, incompetent, and costly; in a phrase, it is value sapping. Indeed, if HR were to remain configured as it is today in many companies, I would have to answer the question above with a resounding "Yes—abolish the thing!"

But the truth is, HR has never been more necessary. The competitive forces that managers face today and will continue to confront in the future demand organizational excellence. The efforts to achieve such excellence—through a focus on learning, quality, teamwork, and reengineering— are driven by the way organizations get things done and how they treat their people. Those are fundamental HR issues. To state it plainly: achieving organizational excellence must be the work of HR.

The question for senior managers, then, is not Should we do away with HR? but What should we do with HR? The answer is: create an entirely new role and agenda for the field that focuses it not on traditional HR activities, such as staffing and compensation, but on outcomes. HR should not be defined by what it does but by what it delivers—results that enrich the organization's value to customers, investors, and employees.

More specifically, HR can help deliver organizational excellence in the following four ways:

- First, HR should become a partner with senior and line managers in strategy execution, helping to move planning from the conference room to the marketplace.

- Second, it should become an expert in the way work is organized and executed, delivering administrative efficiency to ensure that costs are reduced while quality is maintained.

- Third, it should become a champion for employees, vigorously representing their

Reprinted from *Harvard Business Review* (January–February 1998): 125–134.

concerns to senior management and at the same time working to increase employee contribution; that is, employees' commitment to the organization and their ability to deliver results.

- And finally, HR should become an agent of continuous transformation, shaping processes and a culture that together improve an organization's capacity for change.

Make no mistake: this new agenda for HR is a radical departure from the status quo. In most companies today, HR is sanctioned mainly to play policy police and regulatory watchdog. It handles the paperwork involved in hiring and firing, manages the bureaucratic aspects of benefits, and administers compensation decisions made by others. When it is more empowered by senior management, it might oversee recruiting, manage training and development programs, or design initiatives to increase workplace diversity. But the fact remains: the activities of HR appear to be—and often are—disconnected from the real work of the organization. The new agenda, however, would mean that every one of HR's activities would in some concrete way help the company better serve its customers or otherwise increase shareholder value.

Can HR transform itself alone? Absolutely not. In fact, the primary responsibility for transforming the role of HR belongs to the CEO and to every line manager who must achieve business goals. The reason? Line managers have ultimate responsibility for both the processes and the outcomes of the company. They are answerable to shareholders for creating economic value, to customers for creating product or service value, and to employees for creating workplace value. It follows that they should lead the way in fully integrating HR into the company's real work. Indeed, to do so, they must become HR champions themselves. They must acknowledge that competitive

success is a function of organizational excellence. More important, they must hold HR accountable for delivering it.

Of course, the line should not *impose* the new agenda on the HR staff. Rather, operating managers and HR managers must form a partnership to quickly and completely reconceive and reconfigure the function—to overhaul it from one devoted to activities to one committed to outcomes. The process will be different in every organization, but the result will be the same: a business era in which the question Should we do away with HR? will be considered utterly ridiculous.

WHY HR MATTERS NOW MORE THAN EVER

Regardless of their industry, size, or location, companies today face five critical business challenges. Collectively, these challenges require organizations to build new capabilities. Who is currently responsible for developing those capabilities? Everyone—and no one. That vacuum is HR's opportunity to play a leadership role in enabling organizations to meet the following competitive challenges:

GLOBALIZATION

Gone are the days when companies created products at home and shipped them abroad "as is." With the rapid expansion of global markets, managers are struggling to balance the paradoxical demand to think globally and act locally. That imperative requires them to move people, ideas, products, and information around the world to meet local needs. They must add new and important ingredients to the mix when making strategy: volatile political situations, contentious global trade issues, fluctuating exchange rates, and unfamiliar cultures. They must be more literate in the ways of international customers, commerce, and competition than ever before. In short, globalization requires that organizations increase their ability to learn and collaborate and to manage diversity, complexity, and ambiguity.

PROFITABILITY THROUGH GROWTH

During the past decade, most Western companies have been clearing debris, using downsizing, reengineering, delayering, and consolidation to increase efficiency and cut costs. The gains of such yard work, however, have largely been realized, and executives will now have to pay attention to the other part of the profitability equation: revenue growth.

The drive for revenue growth, needless to say, puts unique demands on an organization. Companies seeking to acquire new customers and develop new products must be creative and innovative, and must encourage the free flow of information and shared learning among employees. They must also become more market focused—more in touch with the fast-changing and disparate needs of their customers. And companies seeking growth through mergers, acquisitions, or joint ventures require other capabilities, such as the finely honed skills needed to integrate different organizations' work processes and cultures.

TECHNOLOGY

From videoconferencing to the Internet, technology has made our world smaller and faster. Ideas and massive amounts of information are in constant movement. The challenge for managers is to make sense and good use of what technology offers. Not all technology adds value. But technology can

and will affect how and where work gets done. In the coming years, managers will need to figure out how to make technology a viable, productive part of the work setting. They will need to stay ahead of the information curve and learn to leverage information for business results. Otherwise, they risk being swallowed by a tidal wave of data—not ideas.

INTELLECTUAL CAPITAL

Knowledge has become a direct competitive advantage for companies selling ideas and relationships (think of professional service, software, and technology-driven companies) and an indirect competitive advantage for all companies attempting to differentiate themselves by how they serve customers. From now on, successful companies will be the ones that are the most adept at attracting, developing, and retaining individuals who can drive a global organization that is responsive to both its customers and the burgeoning opportunities of technology. Thus the challenge for organizations is making sure they have the capability to find, assimilate, develop, compensate, and retain such talented individuals.

CHANGE, CHANGE, AND MORE CHANGE

Perhaps the greatest competitive challenge companies face is adjusting to—indeed, embracing—nonstop change. They must be able to learn rapidly and continuously, innovate ceaselessly, and take on new strategic imperatives faster and more comfortably. Constant change means organizations must create a healthy discomfort with the status quo, an ability to detect emerging trends quicker than the competition, an ability to make rapid decisions, and the agility to seek new ways of doing business. To thrive, in other words, companies will need to be in a never-ending state of transformation, perpetually creating fundamental, enduring change.

●●●●●●●●●●●●●●●

HR'S NEW ROLE

The five challenges described above have one overarching implication for business: the only competitive weapon left is organization. Sooner or later, traditional forms of competitiveness—cost, technology, distribution, manufacturing, and product features—can be copied. They have become table stakes. You must have them to be a player, but they do not guarantee you will be a winner.

In the new economy, winning will spring from organizational capabilities such as speed, responsiveness, agility, learning capacity, and employee competence. Successful organizations will be those that are able to quickly turn strategy into action; to manage processes intelligently and efficiently; to maximize employee contribution and commitment; and to create the conditions for seamless change. The need to develop those capabilities brings us back to the mandate for HR set forth at the beginning of this article. Let's take a closer look at each HR imperative in turn.

BECOMING A PARTNER IN STRATEGY EXECUTION

I'm not going to argue that HR should make strategy. Strategy is the responsibility of a company's executive team—of which HR is a member. To be full-fledged strategic partners with senior management, however, HR executives should impel and guide serious discussion of how the company should be organized to carry out its strategy. Creating the conditions for this discussion involves four steps.

First, HR should be held responsible for defining an organizational architecture. In other words, it should identify the underlying model of the company's way of doing business. Several well-established frameworks can be used in this process. Jay Galbraith's star model, for example, identifies five essential organizational components: strategy, structure, rewards, processes, and people. The well-known 7-S framework created by McKinsey & Company distinguishes seven components in a company's architecture: strategy, structure, systems, staff, style, skills, and shared values.

It's relatively unimportant which framework the HR staff uses to define the company's architecture, as long as it's robust. What matters more is that an architecture be articulated explicitly. Without such clarity, managers can become myopic about how the company runs—and thus about what drives strategy implementation and what stands in its way. They might think only of structure as the driving force behind actions and decisions, and neglect systems or skills. Or they might understand the company primarily in terms of its values and pay inadequate attention to the influence of systems on how work—that is, strategy execution—actually gets accomplished.

Senior management should ask HR to play the role of an architect called into an already-constructed building to draw up its plans. The architect makes measurements; calculates dimensions; notes windows, doors, and staircases; and examines the plumbing and heating infrastructures. The result is a comprehensive set of blueprints that contains all the building's parts and shows how they work together.

Next, HR must be accountable for conducting an organizational audit. Blueprints can illuminate the places in a house that require immediate improvement; organizational-architecture plans can be similarly useful. They are critical in helping managers identify which components of the company must change in order to facilitate strategy execution. Again, HR's role is to shepherd the dialogue about the company's blueprints.

Consider a company in which HR defined the organization's architecture in terms of its culture, competencies, rewards, governance, work processes, and leadership. The HR staff was able to use that model to guide management through a rigorous discussion of "fit"—did the company's culture fit its strategic goals, did its competencies, and so forth. When the answer was no, HR was able to guide a discussion of how to obtain or develop what was missing. (For an example of the questions asked in this discussion, see the chart "From Architecture to Audit.")

The third role for HR as a strategic partner is to identify methods for renovating the parts of the organizational architecture that need it. In other words, HR managers should be assigned to take the lead in proposing, creating, and debating best practices in culture change programs, for example, or in appraisal and reward systems. Similarly, if strategy implementation requires, say, a team-based organizational structure, HR would be responsible for bringing state-of-the-art approaches for creating this structure to senior management's attention.

Fourth and finally, HR must take stock of its own work and set clear priorities. At any given moment, the HR staff might have a dozen initiatives in its sights, such as pay-for-performance, global teamwork, and

---

TABLE 1   From Architecture to Audit

After HR has determined the company's underlying architecture, it can use a framework like the one below to guide the organization through the discussion and debate of the audit process.

	Question	*Rating (1–10)*	*Description of best practice*	*Gap between company's current practice and best practice*
Shared mind-set	To what extent does our company have the right culture to reach its goals?			
Competence	To what extent does our company have the required knowledge, skills, and abilities?			
Consequence	To what extent does our company have the appropriate measures, rewards, and incentives?			
Governance	To what extent does our company have the right organizational structure, communications systems, and policies?			
Capacity for change	To what extent does our company have the ability to improve work processes, to change, and to learn?			
Leadership	To what extent does our company have the leadership to achieve its goals?			

action-learning development experiences. But to be truly tied to business outcomes, HR needs to join forces with operating managers to systematically assess the impact and importance of each one of these initiatives. Which ones are really aligned with strategy implementation? Which ones should receive attention immediately, and which can wait? Which ones, in short, are truly linked to business results?

Because becoming a strategic partner means an entirely new role for HR, it may have to acquire new skills and capabilities. Its staff may need more education in order to perform the kind of in-depth analysis an organizational audit involves, for example. Ultimately, such new knowledge will allow HR to add value to the executive team with confidence. In time, the concept of HR as a strategic partner will make business sense.

BECOMING AN ADMINISTRATIVE EXPERT

For decades, HR professionals have been tagged as administrators. In their new role as administrative experts, however, they will need to shed their traditional image of rule-making policy police, while still making sure that all the required routine work in companies is done well. In order to move from their old role as administrators into their new role, HR staff will have to improve the efficiency of both their own function and the entire organization.

Within the HR function are dozens of processes that can be done better, faster, and cheaper. Finding and fixing those processes is part of the work of the new HR. Some companies have already embraced these tasks, and the results are impressive. One company has created a fully automated and flexible benefits program that employees can manage without paperwork; another has used technology to screen résumés and reduce the cycle time for hiring new candidates; and a third has created an electronic

bulletin board that allows employees to communicate with senior executives. In all three cases, the quality of HR work improved and costs were lowered, generally by removing steps or leveraging technology.

But decreased costs aren't the only benefit of HR's becoming the organization's administrative expert. Improving efficiency will build HR's credibility, which, in turn, will open the door for it to become a partner in executing strategy. Consider the case of a CEO who held a very low opinion of the company's HR staff after they sent a letter to a job candidate offering a salary figure with the decimal point in the wrong place. (The candidate called the CEO and joked that she didn't realize the job would make her a millionaire.) It was only after the HR staff proved they could streamline the organization's systems and procedures and deliver flawless administrative service that the CEO finally felt comfortable giving HR a seat at the strategy table.

HR executives can also prove their value as administrative experts by rethinking how work is done throughout the organization. For example, they can design and implement a system that allows departments to share administrative services. At Amoco, for instance, HR helped create a shared-service organization that encompassed 14 business units. HR can also create centers of expertise that gather, coordinate, and disseminate vital information about market trends, for instance, or organizational processes. Such groups can act as internal consultants, not only saving the company money but also improving its competitive situation.

BECOMING AN EMPLOYEE CHAMPION

Work today is more demanding than ever—employees are continually being asked to do more with less. And as companies withdraw the old employment contract, which was based on security and predictable promotions, and replace it with faint promises of trust, employees respond in kind. Their relationship with the organization becomes transactional. They give their time but not much more.

That kind of curtailed contribution is a recipe for organizational failure. Companies cannot thrive unless their employees are engaged fully. Engaged employees—that is, employees who believe they are valued—share ideas, work harder than the necessary minimum, and relate better to customers, to name just three benefits.

In their new role, HR professionals must be held accountable for ensuring that employees are engaged—that they feel committed to the organization and contribute fully. In the past, HR sought that commitment by attending to the social needs of employees—picnics, parties, United Way campaigns, and so on. While those activities must still be organized, HR's new agenda supersedes them. HR must now take responsibility for orienting and training line management about the importance of high employee morale and how to achieve it. In addition, the new HR should be the employees' voice in management discussions; offer employees opportunities for personal and professional growth; and provide resources that help employees meet the demands put on them.

Orienting and training line management about how to achieve high employee morale can be accomplished using several tools, such as workshops, written reports, and employee surveys. Such tools can help managers understand the sources of low morale within the organization—not just specifically, but conceptually. For instance, HR might inform the line that 82% of employees feel demoralized because of a recent downsizing. That's useful. But more than that, HR should be responsible for educating the line about the *causes* of low employee morale. For instance, it is generally agreed by organizational behavior experts that employee morale decreases when people believe the demands put upon them exceed the resources available to meet those demands. Morale also drops when goals are unclear, priorities are unfocused, or performance measurement is ambiguous. HR serves an important role in holding a mirror in front of senior executives.

HR can play a critical role in recommending ways to ameliorate morale problems. Recommendations can be as simple as urging the hiring of additional support staff or as complex as suggesting that reengineering be considered for certain tasks. The new role for HR might also involve suggesting that more teams be used on some projects or that employees be given more control over their own work schedules. It may mean suggesting that line executives pay attention to the possibility that some employees are being asked to do boring or repetitive work. HR at Baxter Healthcare, for example, identified boring work as a problem and then helped to solve it by redesigning work processes to connect employees more directly with customers.

Along with educating operating managers about morale, HR staff must also be an advocate for employees—they must represent the employees to management and be their voice in management discussions. Employees should have confidence that when decisions are made that affect them (such as a plant closing), HR's involvement in the decision-making process clearly represents employees' views and supports their rights. Such advocacy cannot be invisible. Employees must know that HR is their voice before they will communicate their opinions to HR managers.

BECOMING A CHANGE AGENT

To adapt a phrase, Change happens. And the pace of change today, because of globalization, technological innovation, and information access, is both dizzying and dazzling. That said, the primary difference between winners and losers in business will be the ability to respond to the pace of change. Winners will be able to adapt, learn, and act quickly. Losers will spend time trying to control and master change.

The new HR has as its fourth responsibility the job of building the organization's capacity to embrace and capitalize on change. It will make sure that change initiatives that are focused on creating high-performing teams, reducing cycle time for innovation, or implementing new technology are defined, developed, and delivered in a timely way. The new HR can also make sure that broad vision statements (such as, We will be the global leader in our markets) get transformed into specific behaviors by helping employees figure out what work they can stop, start, and keep doing to make the vision real. At Hewlett-Packard, HR has helped make sure that the company's value of treating employees with trust, dignity, and respect translates into practices that, for example, give employees more control over when and where they work.

Change has a way of scaring people—scaring them into inaction. HR's role as a change agent is to replace resistance with resolve, planning with results, and fear of change with excitement about its possibilities. How? The answer lies in the creation and use of a change model. (For an example of a very effective change model, developed with and used extensively by GE, see the chart "Change Begins by Asking Who, Why, What, and How.") HR professionals must introduce such a model to their organizations and guide executive teams through it—that is, steer the conversation and debate that answers the multitude of questions it raises. The model, in short, must be a managerial tool championed by HR. It helps an organization identify the key success factors for change and assess the organization's strengths and weaknesses regard-

ing each factor. The process can be arduous, but it is one of the most valuable roles HR can play. As change agents, HR professionals do not themselves execute change—but they make sure that it is carried out.

Consider the case of a company whose senior management team announced that "valuing diversity" was a top priority in 1996. Six months into the year, the team acknowledged that the diversity initiative had received more rhetoric than action. The company's HR professionals asked the team to spend several hours profiling the diversity initiative using a change model. (See the graph "Profile of a Change Initiative in Distress.") The resulting analysis revealed that the diversity initiative would fail unless the senior management team explored several critical questions, among them: Why are we seeking diversity? What will be the benefit to the business and its customers? What is the ideal form of diversity for this organization? Who needs to be supportive and involved to make the initiative come to life?

HR leaders spent several more hours with the management team guiding a conversation that answered those questions. Shortly afterward, they were able to present the team with an action plan for moving the diversity initiative forward. Thus HR did not decide what changes the organization was going to embrace, but it did lead the process to make them explicit.

Perhaps the hardest and most important challenge facing many companies in this era of flux is changing their culture. In helping to bring about a new culture, HR must follow a four-step process:

- First, it must define and clarify the concept of culture change.
- Second, it must articulate why culture change is central to business success.
- Third, it must define a process for assessing the current culture and the desired new culture, as well as for measuring the gap between the two.

TABLE 2   Change Begins by Asking Who, Why, What, and How

HR staff at GE used this change model to guide a transformation process at the company.

Key Success Factors for Change	Questions to Assess and Accomplish The Key Success Factors for Change
Leading change (Who is responsible?)	Do we have a leader ... who owns and champions the change? who publicly commits to making it happen? who will garner the resources necessary to sustain it? who will put in the personal time and attention needed to follow through?
Creating a shared need (Why do it?)	Do employees ... see the reason for the change? understand why it is important? see how it will help them and the business in the short term and long term?
Shaping a vision (What will it look like when we are done?)	Do employees ... see the outcomes of the change in behavioral terms (that is, in terms of what they will do differently as a result of the change)? get excited about the results of accomplishing the change? understand how it will benefit customers and other stakeholders?
Mobilizing commitment (Who else needs to be involved?)	Do the sponsors of the change ... recognize who else needs to be committed to the change to make it happen? know how to build a coalition of support for the change? have the ability to enlist support of key individuals in the organization? have the ability to build a responsibility matrix to make the change happen?
Modifying systems and structures (How will it be institutionalized?)	Do the sponsors of the change ... understand how to link it to other HR systems such as staffing, training, appraisal, rewards, structure, and communication? recognize the systems implications of the change?
Monitoring progress (How will it be measured?)	Do the sponsors of the change ... have a means of measuring its success? plan to benchmark progress against both the results of the change and the process of implementing it?
Making it last (How will it get started and last?)	Do the sponsors of the change ... recognize the first steps in getting started? have a short-term and long-term plan to keep attention focused on the change? have a plan to adapt the change over time?

• And fourth, it must identify alternative approaches to creating culture change.

HR played an important part in changing the culture at Sears, which underwent a transformation of its business beginning in 1994. In facilitating that change, HR first took on the task of getting the organization to define and clarify the concept of culture. It helped lead the top 100 managers through discussions and debates of the questions, What are the top three things we want to be known for by our customers? and What do we do that is world class in those things? Ultimately, those conversations led to a consensus that Sears would

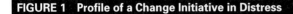

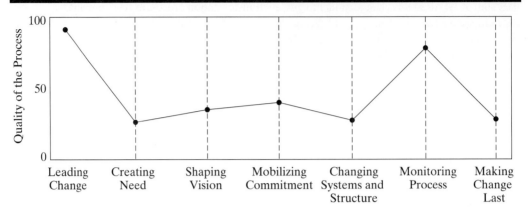

FIGURE 1 Profile of a Change Initiative in Distress

One company's HR professionals used this chart to help senior management understand why a high-profile diversity initiative was going nowhere.

define its culture as "the identity of the company in the minds of the best customers." In addition, HR at Sears took on the responsibility of making the business case for a transformation of the company's culture. It compiled data showing that even a small increase in employee commitment led to a measurable increase in customer commitment and store profitability. The data illustrate conclusively that Sears's transformation affected employees, customers, and investors.

HR at Sears guided the company's culture change in numerous other ways.[1] The specific details, however, are not nearly as important as their implications. HR can be the architect of new cultures, but to do so, its purpose must be redefined. Virtually every imperative of the new mandate for HR requires such a redefinition. And for it to happen, senior managers must lead the way.

● ● ● ● ● ● ● ● ● ● ● ● ● ● ●

FOUR CHANGES FOR THE LINE

The new mandate for HR requires dramatic changes in how HR professionals think and behave. But perhaps more important, it also requires that senior executives change what

they expect from HR and how they behave toward the HR staff. The following are four ways senior operating managers can create an era in which HR is focused on outcomes instead of activities:

COMMUNICATE TO THE ORGANIZATION THAT THE "SOFT STUFF" MATTERS

At Hewlett-Packard, managing people was one of the two *hoshin* (major objectives) of the CEO for 1997. At General Electric, CEO Jack Welch claims he spends 40% of this time on people issues. At Southern Company, senior managers are working to create an empowered organization to ensure faster and better decision making. The point? For HR to be taken seriously, senior managers must demonstrate that they believe typical HR issues—the soft stuff like culture change and intellectual capital—are critical to business success.

Operating managers can signal this belief in several ways. They can talk seriously about how organizational capabilities create value for investors, customers, and employees. They can invest the time needed to make sure organizational changes are debated and implemented. They can include HR professionals in strategy discussions and state explicitly that without the collaboration of HR, strategies are more hopes than realities, promises than acts, and concepts than results.

Explicitly Define the Deliverables from HR and Hold HR Accountable for Results

It is one thing to tell HR that it is responsible for employee contribution and quite another to set a specific goal—say, a 10% increase in employee morale as measured by a survey. And once such specific goals are set, consequences must follow if they are missed.

The new mandate for HR is like any other business initiative in this way. A company has a much better chance of achieving its goals if senior managers state specifically what they expect from HR and then track, measure, and reward performance.

Invest in Innovative HR Practices

Like every other area of business, HR gets its share of new technologies and practices, and senior line executives should be always on the lookout for such practices. Conferences and management literature are always good places to hear of new ways of approaching HR, but senior managers should also be aware of innovative HR practices going on at other companies and of new practices that are being advocated by respected consultants.

Investing in new HR practices is another way to signal to the organization that HR is worthy of the company's money and attention. It is also a way to make sure that HR has the tools, information, and processes that it needs to execute its new mandate.

As new practices are identified, line managers should expect HR to adapt to them, not adopt them. Too often, after learning about an innovative idea, HR immediately tries to

copy it wholesale. Such efforts often fail, and at a high emotional cost. Instead, investment in new HR practices should focus on learning not only what works elsewhere but also how a new practice should work in the company's unique competitive situation.

Upgrade HR Professionals

Finally, the hardest but perhaps most important thing senior managers can do to drive forward the new mandate for HR is to improve the quality of the HR staff itself. Too often, HR departments are like computers made up of used parts. While the individual parts may work, they don't work well together. When more is expected of HR, a higher quality of HR professional must be found. Companies need people who know the business, understand the theory and practice of HR, can manage culture and make change happen, and have personal credibility. Sometimes, such individuals already exist within the HR function but need additional training. Other times, they have to be brought in from other parts of the company. In still other cases, they must be hired from outside.

Regardless, HR cannot expand its role in an organization without the requisite expertise. Becoming a strategic partner demands a degree of knowledge about strategy, markets, and the economy. Becoming an administrative expert demands some knowledge of reengineering, as well as the intricacies of what the line actually docs. If HR is to effect real change, it must be made up of people who have the skills they need to work from a base of confidence and earn what too often it lacks—respect.

. . . .
HARD WORK AHEAD

To meet the increased expectations of their organizations, HR professionals must begin to act professionally. They must focus more on the deliverables of their work and less on just getting their work done. They must articulate their role in terms of the value they create. They must create mechanisms so that business results quickly follow. They must measure their effectiveness in terms of business competitiveness rather than employee comfort and lead cultural transformation rather than consolidate, reengineer, or downsize in order to turn a company around.

Senior executives who recognize the economic value and the benefit to their customers of intellectual capital and organizational capability need to demand more of the HR function. They need to invest in HR as if it were a business. And they must get beyond the stereotype of HR professionals as incompetent, value-sapping support staff. It's time to destroy that stereotype and unleash HR's full potential.

Note

1. For more on the transformation of Sears, see *The Employee-Customer-Profit Chain at Sears,* by Anthony J. Rucci, Steven P. Kirn, and Richard T. Quinn, in *Harvard Business Review* 76(1): 82–97.

I-6: What Do CEOs Want from HR?

BILL LEONARD

What do chief executive officers really think of the human resource profession? And how do CEOs think HR should change to meet the growing needs of their organizations?

To find out, *HR Magazine* recently interviewed five CEOs who represent a broad spectrum of industries, company sizes, and geographic locations. One CEO spent many years working in HR; the others have less experience with human resource management.

Despite these varied backgrounds, the comments from all five CEOs reveal common themes—and common areas where HR can stand to improve.

● ●

A UNIQUE RELATIONSHIP

As HR professionals increasingly strive to become strategic partners with top manage-ment, their relationship with CEOs takes on new significance. All the CEOs interviewed for this article agree that—of all the members of their management teams—their relationship with the top HR professional may be the most important.

The amount of time CEOs spend with HR executives underlines the importance of this relationship.

"I'm probably speaking with our senior V.P. of human resources about 40 percent of my time at work," says Robert McDonald, CEO of the North American division of Standard Chartered Bank in New York. "It seems that I am always talking to her and seeking her advice and input."

Likewise, Mike R. Bowlin, chairman and CEO of ARCO, the Los Angeles–based oil and energy giant, constantly consults his top HR executive.

"I believe that I spend as much time with John Kelly (senior vice president of HR) as anyone else who works for me," he says. "There is no major decision that takes place in the company that John is not involved with, and I fully expect him to have an opinion on business decisions. As

CEO, I use John as a personal consultant and sounding board for ideas and problem solving. Many times, he and I go to lunch and just bounce ideas off each other, which works well for us."

All five CEOs say that as HR has gained more access to their offices, the head of HR has assumed a unique relationship with the CEO. But how can HR make sure that relationship remains solid?

"The key to a good relationship between the CEO and the head of HR is honesty," believes Craig Sturken, chief executive officer of Farmer Jack Supermarkets in Detroit. "For the relationship to really work well, there has to be a trust, closeness, and almost intuitive understanding between the CEO and the head of HR. The last thing that you want to do as CEO is stifle that relationship; it's crucial to the success of your business."

Girard Miller, president and CEO of ICMA Retirement Corp. in Washington, D.C., says HR must relate well to both employees and top management. "It's a hard role to play, I believe. A good HR professional must have the ability to thoroughly develop a trusting relationship with the employees, while at the same time be something of a collaborator and serve as a confidant to the CEO."

Miller adds that HR must work closely with CEOs. "I'm a firm believer that the HR function must be a direct report to the CEO," he says. "I think that there are just too many opportunities for mischief, if it is not."

THE STRATEGIC ROLE OF HR

Why do these CEOs place such emphasis on the strategic role of HR in their organizations? The answer lies in the evolving and strategic role of the profession.

"HR has become a very important component in our strategic planning processes," says Mike Goodrich, president and CEO of BE&K Inc., an engineering and construction company based in Birmingham, Alabama. "We need to anticipate where our company is going to be five to six years down the road, and HR is crucial to understanding the changing demographics and expectations of our workforce."

The other CEOs agree that HR executives must understand and embrace their evolving strategic role, which includes helping track the skills of the workforce and matching them up with the organization's needs.

"HR management is one of the critical resources that we have to carry on our business plan," says Bowlin. "Our people are what will truly build a sustainable competitive advantage. In the long run, everyone has the same access to capital and technology, so a company's human resources is what makes the difference and makes it successful. It is the key resource."

McDonald fully expects "HR to be the guardian of information as to where your best people are in the organization and what their talents are."

Miller adds that "HR needs to know how the personnel talent of the organization can make a difference to the short-term business plans as well as the long-term strategy."

THE BOTTOM-LINE APPROACH

As HR's role as a strategic partner has evolved, the focus and knowledge necessary to be a successful HR executive have also changed. For example, the CEOs interviewed for this article emphasized that—although HR has improved its understanding of financial issues—more work needs to be done.

"When it comes to the bottom line, I would say that HR generally has been a bit out to lunch," says McDonald. "But their understanding of the bottom line has improved over the past few years, and I do believe most HR executives are striving to better understand how their decisions and actions can truly affect the bottom line."

Miller goes so far as to characterize HR's comprehension of financial issues as "soft." "HR professionals are not as far along as I, as a CEO, would like to see them," he says. "I believe they get the idea when it comes to their own budget but have a tough time understanding concepts such as variable costs versus fixed costs."

Miller says this is true with his current vice president of HR but adds that she has been a willing student. "And her willingness to learn is really the key here and clearly shows that she is interested and committed to improving the bottom line of this organization," he adds.

Sturken's experience mirrors that of McDonald and Miller; a solid financial orientation has not been a strength of most of the HR professionals he has worked with.

"I believe there has been a lack of concentration on the bottom line among many of the HR people I have known," Sturken says. But, like Miller, he sees improvement.

"I will hand it to my current vice president of HR," he says. "She is trying hard to learn and improve her knowledge and skills, and I believe that her efforts will pay off for both her and our company in the long run."

Sturken encourages HR professionals to strengthen their financial knowledge by taking advantage of educational opportunities. "I always advise my HR staff to take courses in business finance and financial planning," he says. "There are a lot of seminars and workshops on the fundamentals in accounting for nonfinancial managers. I have had managers come back from these courses and give suggestions and ideas to our accounting department on streamlining and improving some systems."

● ● ● ● ● ● ● ● ● ● ● ● ● ●
OTHER SKILLS

Besides a strong bottom-line orientation, several of the CEOs say their HR executives and managers need to be more aggressive and work on their powers of persuasion.

"At my company, we have a saying that you need to push the envelope," says Goodrich. "And HR has never really pushed the envelope with me. I have no problem saying 'no' if I think it's too much. I have said 'no' plenty of times to our information technology department. But HR has never pushed hard enough or far enough for me to say 'no' yet."

Bowlin says that HR has moved into the role of internal consultants at ARCO, but he is quick to point out that the term "consultants" does not mean he wants a bunch of "yes men or women" on his staff. He wants people who will challenge and question decisions that they believe are flawed.

"The people who acquiesce too quickly are usually gone quickly," he says. "But then if you have someone who tries to be too controlling, that's not good either. What we want is a team player who is knowledgeable, bright, and aggressive and has good consulting skills," Bowlin says.

Part of being a good consultant, says Bowlin, is being persuasive. "This is a skill that HR needs to work on, I believe," he says. "To succeed, you must have the ability to be persuasive and move the organization forward and to influence key business decisions."

To be more persuasive, however, many HR professionals need more education in business fundamentals.

"Clearly, HR professionals today are better trained than I was when I began my career 30 years ago [in HR]. But they do need sufficient and fundamental business training to participate and contribute to the company."

Miller goes a step further, saying that HR managers seem to lack some business training that is necessary to perform in today's workplace.

"I find generally that many HR professionals' business math skills and dimensions are fairly weak," Miller says. "I believe that the skill level is slowly improving and that's largely due, in part, to the fact that it is changing from the personnel function to the HR function."

Miller also believes that HR professionals have a "lack of vision" when it comes to the big picture of the organization.

"HR professionals have been getting by focusing on the day-to-day. They need to develop a broader and farther-reaching vision and understand where their organization is headed and how they can help steer the company in that direction," Miller adds.

McDonald says that HR is "being a bit insular." He says that one of the major problems with HR is that the profession's executives and managers have tended to focus solely on their HR departments.

"Their primary focus was HR, and the company was secondary to that. All the company did was provide them a paycheck, and that was the prevailing attitude 20 years ago," says McDonald. "It has improved, but I think because of that attitude, HR's reputation among other departments was a bit tainted. That reputation has improved vastly in recent years, but there's always room for improvement."

McDonald believes that improvement comes when HR sees itself as an internal consultant. "It really makes my job easier if I'm working with people who see themselves as working with internal clients rather than seeing themselves as just a part of the HR group," says McDonald. "Those who think outside the four dots and believe

that they are serving internal clients get my vote."

BEYOND SKILLS

The CEOs interviewed for this article tend to agree that the best and most successful HR professionals have a real passion for their jobs.

"The better HR professionals that I have worked with have been compassionate and have deep feelings for our employees," says Goodrich. "They have a burning desire to see our employees succeed and build better lives for themselves. It's a trait that I have truly admired among most of the really good and successful HR professionals that I have known."

Bowlin agrees that true success comes from a passion for your job. "To really truly succeed, you have to be passionate about your work. You have to feel that you can make a difference," he says. "And if you are really good and passionate about your job, and you work in HR, you can really make one of the most positive impacts of any group within a company."

THE FUTURE OF HR

All five of the CEOs have to think strategically about the short- and long-term issues that confront their organizations. Two of the key issues they identified for their organizations—and, consequently, for HR—are recruiting and diversity.

Sturken says that the primary problem his company faces is a drastic labor shortage. The tight labor market has made recruiting and retention top priorities at his company.

"Retail is really tough right now." Sturken says. "It's a quality of life issue. The question that we face is How can we improve our employees' lifestyle? People don't want to work weekends and evenings, and that's the lifeblood of retail. None of the old rules work when it comes to recruiting and hiring people. HR has to be very creative and market and merchandize our company and the advantages of working here. It's a very different ball game now."

Goodrich agrees that the labor market's rules have changed but attributes many of the changes to a dramatic shift in demographics.

"We really have been paying close attention to the changing demographics of our workforce," Goodrich says. "We have more women and more Latinos working in the construction industry today, and we must be prepared to respond to these changes."

He adds that the aging of the workforce will present some interesting challenges to the workplace. That is a trend that will also profoundly affect Miller's organization, which manages retirement funds for local governments.

"As the baby boom generation ages, we will have a powerful growth curve over the next five to six years in this organization," Miller says. "The demand for more retirement benefits and retiree medical care will be tremendous and will affect all businesses.

We have to begin considering how we are going to pay for those benefits."

Bowlin believes that effectively managing multicultural diversity is the primary challenge that faces HR and corporate America.

"ARCO has to design HR systems that recognize cultural differences and help the company be more effective in those cultures. It's a high priority for us," Bowlin says. "As this company becomes more global, how we manage diversity will be key to our success."

The workplace challenges of multicultural diversity only emphasize the importance of developing a global focus when dealing with HR issues, according to McDonald.

"The challenge of HR is cross-cultural. It is a huge job to make that cultural bridge," he says. "HR professionals can prepare to meet these challenges by making themselves available for international assignments, and by that I mean living outside the country for three to four years. International mobility is key. Today's economy is a global economy, and HR has to be ready to accept the roles and challenges that the global marketplace brings."

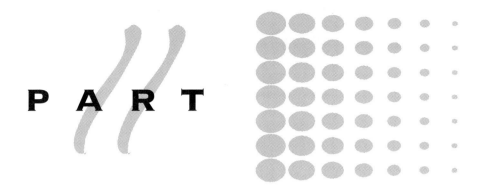

PART II

MEETING HUMAN RESOURCE REQUIREMENTS

The never-easy task of meeting and maintaining human resource requirements has become vastly more complicated in recent years. Several things
have contributed to the increased difficulty and importance of this task. Among
these forces are the necessity for organizations to compete more effectively in
the marketplace, the globalization of this marketplace, the changed expectations
of potential and present employees, their diversity in and across national boundaries, and the growing numbers of ambitious and capable women in the labor
force. As a consequence, managers at all levels increasingly are finding it necessary to change the ways through which they manage and even the way in which
work is organized.

Further, the body of employment law has expanded exponentially in the last
decade leading to increased litigation and grievances. In a large number of
instances, lawsuits and litigation have severely circumscribed the discretion of
employers in the interests of fair and equitable treatment of both applicants and
employees.

When the topic is gender inequality and the focus is on improving the representation of women in senior management positions, the persistence of what has
been termed the "glass ceiling" makes the challenge of promoting women formi-
dable. In their article ("A Modest Manifesto for Shattering the Glass Ceiling"),
Debra E. Myerson and Joyce K. Fletcher propose an evolutionary, persistent
strategy of incremental changes (small wins) to create dialogue and experimentation within the organization. They argue this approach will benefit both women
and men in the management ranks.

Knowing how to effectively hire people is rarely a cut-and-dried affair. How
does the organization get a useful and representative picture of how an applicant
responds to pressure, how well they can listen (if this is a prerequisite for effectiveness), or how they are around subordinates as well as peers? Lee Clifford
describes a recent trend: the group interview ("Group Interviews among New

Ways to Case Hires"). These can involve either formally interviewing a set of interviewers concurrently or observing how candidates behave in informal groups and gatherings.

The next reading focuses on a growing segment of the workforce, one many readers may have experienced personally—the temporary worker. Daniel C. Feldman, Helen I. Doerpinghaus, and William H. Turnley point out that the nature of the psychological contract between temporary workers and their employers has changed considerably over time ("Managing Temporary Workers: A Permanent HRM Challenge"). Many of today's temporary workers would rather be permanently employed. The reading describes the benefits of temporary work, the key concerns of temporary workers, and ideas for improving management practice.

The dramatic rise in the number of temps in the past decade has made this an attractive group for organizing. Is this good or bad for workers? In the next brief article, Nicholas Kulish and Carlos Tejada raise some issues pertaining to this question ("Labor Board Allows Organizing of Temps").

Most Human Resource research and practice tend *not* to focus attention on family-owned business. However, as Carolyn Hirschman in "All in the Family" points out, experts estimate between 80 percent and 90 percent of all businesses are family owned. It will become increasingly important for Human Resource management to understand this facet of business. The leadership of these businesses will increasingly be in transition as their baby-boomer founders age and hand over their companies to the next generation. The reading provides a description of some of the nuances, advantages, and disadvantages of practicing HR in the family-owned organization. A short and humorous insert, "Ladha and Ladha" by Abdul Ladha chronicles the arrival of a new member of a family and the responsibilities of *this* "family-owned organization."

Finally, HR requirements must now be understood outside North America. The globalization of work offers Human Resource managers new challenges and opportunities that will escalate in the twenty-first century. The reading "Managing the Global Workforce: Challenges and Strategies" by Karen Roberts, Ellen Ernst Kossek, and Cynthia Ozeki identifies practical challenges to managers of global workforces and suggests strategies for resolving them.

II-1: A Modest Manifesto for Shattering the Glass Ceiling

DEBRA E. MEYERSON AND JOYCE K. FLETCHER

The new millennium provides an occasion to celebrate the remarkable progress made by women. That women now hold seats on corporate boards, run major companies, and are regularly featured on the covers of business magazines as prominent leaders and power brokers would have been unimaginable even a half century ago.

But the truth is, women at the highest levels of business are still rare. They comprise only 10% of senior managers in *Fortune* 500 companies; less than 4% of the uppermost ranks of CEO, president, executive vice president, and COO; and less than 3% of top corporate earners.[1] Statistics also suggest that as women approach the top of the corporate ladder, many jump off, frustrated or disillusioned with the business world. Clearly, there have been gains, but as we enter the year 2000, the glass ceiling remains. What will it take to finally shatter it?

Not a revolution. Not this time. In 1962, 1977, and even 1985, the women's movement used radical rhetoric and legal action to drive out overt discrimination, but most of the barriers that persist today are insidious—a revolution couldn't find them to blast away. Rather, gender discrimination now is so deeply embedded in organizational life as to be virtually indiscernible. Even the women who feel its impact are often hard-pressed to know what hit them.

That is why we believe that the glass ceiling will be shattered in the new millennium only through a strategy that uses *small wins*[2]—incremental changes aimed at biases so entrenched in the system that they're not

Reprinted from *Harvard Business Review* 78(1) (2000): 126–136.

even noticed until they're gone. Our research shows that the small-wins strategy is a powerful way of chipping away the barriers that hold women back without sparking the kind of sound and fury that scares people into resistance. And because the small-wins strategy creates change through diagnosis, dialogue, and experimentation, it usually improves overall efficiency and performance. The strategy benefits not just women but also men and the organization as a whole.

● ● ● ● ● ● ● ● ● ● ● ●
THE PROBLEM WITH NO NAME

Time was, it was easy to spot gender discrimination in the corporate world. A respected female executive would lose a promotion to a male colleague with less experience, for instance, or a talented female manager would find herself demoted after her maternity leave. Today such blatant cases are rare; they've been wiped out by laws and by organizations' increased awareness that they have nothing to gain, and much to lose, by keeping women out of positions of authority.

That doesn't mean, however, that gender inequity has vanished. It has just gone underground. Today discrimination against women lingers in a plethora of work practices and cultural norms that only appear unbiased. They are common and mundane—and woven into the fabric of an organization's status quo—which is why most people don't notice them, let alone question them. But they create a subtle pattern of *systemic* disadvantage, which blocks all but a few women from career advancement.

For an example of this modern-day gender inequity, take the case of a global retail company based in Europe that couldn't figure out why it had so few women in senior positions and such high turnover among women in its middle-manager ranks. The problem was particularly vexing because the company's executives publicly touted their respect for women and insisted they wanted the company to be "a great place for women to work."

Despite its size, the company had a strong entrepreneurial culture. Rules and authority were informal; people were as casual about their schedules as they were about the dress code. Meetings were routinely canceled and regularly ran late. Deadlines were ignored because they constantly shifted, and new initiatives arose so frequently that people thought nothing of interrupting one another or declaring crises that demanded immediate attention.

The company's cultural norms grew from its manner of conducting business. For instance, managers were expected to be available at all times to attend delayed or emergency meetings. And these meetings themselves followed certain norms. Because roles and authority at the company were ambiguous, people felt free to make suggestions—even decisions—about any area of the company that interested them. A manager in charge of window displays, for example, might very well recommend a change in merchandising, or vice versa. To prevent changes in their own area from being made without their input, managers scrambled to attend as many meetings as possible. They had to in order to protect their turf.

The company's norms made it extraordinarily difficult for everyone—women and men—to work effectively. But they were particularly pernicious for women for two reasons. First, women typically bear a disproportionate amount of responsibility for home and family and thus have more demands on their time outside the office.

Women who worked set hours—even if they spanned ten hours a day—ended up missing essential conversations and important plans for new products. Their circumscribed schedules also made them appear less committed than their male counterparts. In most instances, that was not the case, but the way the company operated day to day—its very system—made it impossible to prove otherwise.

The meetings themselves were run in a way that put women in a double bind. People often had to speak up to defend their turf, but when women did so, they were vilified. They were labeled "control freaks"; men acting the same way were called "passionate." As one female executive told us, "If you stick your neck out, you're dead."

A major investment firm provides another example of how invisible—even unintentional—gender discrimination thrives in today's companies. The firm sincerely wanted to increase the number of women it was hiring from business schools. It reasoned it would be able to hire more women if it screened more women, so it increased the number of women interviewed during recruiting visits to business school campuses. The change, however, had no impact. Why? Because, the 30 minutes allotted for each interview—the standard practice at most business schools—was not long enough for middle-aged male managers, who were conducting the vast majority of the interviews, to connect with young female candidates sufficiently to see beyond their directly relevant technical abilities. Therefore, most women were disqualified from the running. They hadn't had enough time to impress their interviewer.

● ●
THE ROOTS OF INEQUITY

The barriers to women's advancement in organizations today have a relatively straightforward cause. Most organizations have been created by and for men and are based on male experiences. Even though women have entered the workforce in droves in the past generation, and it is generally agreed that they add enormous value, organizational definitions of competence and leadership are still predicated on traits stereotypically associated with men: tough, aggressive, decisive. And even though many households today have working fathers and mothers, most organizations act as if the historical division of household labor still holds—with women primarily responsible for matters of the hearth. Outdated or not, those realities drive organizational life. Therefore, the global retail company was able to develop a practice of late and last-minute meetings because most men can be available 15 hours a day. The investment firm developed a practice of screening out women candidates because men, who were doing most of the interviewing, *naturally* bond with other men. In other words, organizational practices mirror societal norms.

That the "problem with no name" arises from a male-based culture does not mean that men are to blame. In fact, our perspective on gender discrimination does not presume intent, and it certainly does not assume that all men benefit from the way work is currently organized. Lots of companies run by men are working hard to create a fair environment for both sexes. And many men do not embrace the traditional division of labor; some men surely wish the conventions of a *Father Knows Best* world would vanish.

Men, then, are not to blame for the pervasive gender inequity in organizations today—but neither are women. And yet our research shows that ever since gender inequity came onto the scene as one of business's big problems, women have blamed themselves. That feeling has been reinforced by managers who have tried to solve the problem by fixing women. Indeed, over the past 30-odd years, organizations have used three approaches to rout gender dis-

crimination, each one implying that women are somehow to blame because they "just don't fit in."

TALL PEOPLE IN A SHORT WORLD

To describe the three approaches, we like to use a metaphor that replaces gender with height. Imagine, therefore, a world made by and for short people. In this world, everyone in power is under five-foot-five, and the most powerful are rarely taller than five-foot-three. Now imagine that after years of discrimination, tall people finally call for change—and short people agree that the current world is unfair and amends should be made.

Short people first try to right things by teaching tall people to act like short people—to minimize their differences by stooping to fit in the doorways, for example, or by hunching over to fit in the small chairs in the conference room. Once tall people learn these behaviors, short people insist, they will fit right in.

Some short people take another approach to routing discrimination: they make their world more accommodating to tall people by fixing some of the structural barriers that get in their way. They build six-foot-high doors in the back of the building and purchase desks that don't knock tall people's knees. They even go so far as to create some less demanding career paths—tall-people tracks—for those who are unwilling or unable to put up with the many realities of the short world that just can't be changed.

Other short people take a third approach: they celebrate the differences of their tall associates. Tall people stand out in a crowd, short people say, and they can reach things on high shelves. Let's recognize the worth of those skills and put them to good use! And so the short people "create equity" by putting tall people in jobs where their height is an advantage, like working in a warehouse or designing brand extensions targeted to tall people.

Those three approaches should sound familiar to anyone who has been involved in the many gender initiatives proliferating in the corporate world. Companies that take the first approach encourage women to assimilate—to adopt more masculine attributes and learn the "games their mothers never taught them." Thus, HR departments train women in assertive leadership, decision making, and even golf. Male colleagues take women to their lunch clubs, coach them on speaking up more in meetings, and suggest they take "tough guy" assignments in factories or abroad.

Companies that take the second approach accommodate the unique needs and situations of women. Many offer formal mentoring programs to compensate for women's exclusion from informal networks. Others add alternative career tracks or an extra year on the tenure clock to help women in their childbearing years. Still others offer extended maternity leave, flexible work arrangements, even rooms for nursing infants.

In the third approach, companies forgo assimilation and accommodation and instead emphasize the differences that women bring to the workplace. They institute sensitivity training to help male managers appreciate traditionally "feminine" activities or styles, such as listening and collaborating. And they eagerly put women's assumed differences to work by channeling them into jobs where they market products to women or head up HR initiatives.

All of these approaches have helped advance women's equity in the corporate world. But by now they have gone about as far as they can. Why? Because they proffer solutions that deal with the *symptoms* of gender inequity rather than the sources of inequity itself. Take the first approach. While many female executives can now play golf and have used relationships formed on the fairways to

move into positions of greater power, these new skills will never eradicate the deeply entrenched, systemic factors within corporations that hold many women back.

The same is true of the second approach of accommodation through special policies and benefits. It gives women stilts to play on an uneven playing field, but it doesn't flatten out the field itself. So, for example, mentoring programs may help women meet key people in a company's hierarchy, but they don't change the fact that informal networks, to which few women are privy, determine who really gets resources, information, and opportunities. Launching family-friendly programs doesn't challenge the belief that balancing home and work is fundamentally a woman's problem. And adding time to a tenure clock or providing alternative career tracks does little to change the expectation that truly committed employees put work first—they need no accommodation.

The limits of the third approach are also clear. Telling people to "value differences" doesn't mean they will. That is why so many women who are encouraged to use "feminine" skills and styles find their efforts valued only in the most marginal sense. For example, women are applauded for holding teams together and are even told, "we couldn't have succeeded without you," but when promotions and rewards are distributed, they are awarded to the "rugged individuals" who assertively promoted their own ideas or came up with a onetime technical fix. Ultimately, the celebration approach may actually channel women into dead-end jobs and reinforce unhelpful stereotypes.

• • • • • • • • • • • • • • • • • • • •

A FOURTH APPROACH: LINKING EQUITY AND EFFECTIVENESS

Since 1992, we have helped organizations implement a fourth approach to eradicating gender inequity. This approach starts with the premise—to continue the metaphor—that the world of short people cannot be repaired with piecemeal fixes aimed at how tall people act and what work they do. Because the short world has been in the making for hundreds, if not thousands, of years, its assumptions and practices—such as job descriptions that conflate the physical characteristics of short people with the requirements of the job—will not be undone by assimilation or accommodation or even celebration. It will be undone by a persistent campaign of incremental changes that discover and destroy the deeply embedded roots of discrimination. These changes will be driven by short and tall people together—because both will ultimately benefit from a world where height is irrelevant to the way work is designed and distributed.

Returning to the real world of men and women, the fourth approach starts with the belief that gender inequity is rooted in our cultural patterns and therefore in our organizational systems. Although its goals are revolutionary, it doesn't advocate revolution. Instead, it emphasizes that existing systems can be reinvented by altering the raw materials of organizing—concrete, everyday practices in which biases are expressed.

The fourth approach begins when someone, somewhere in the organization realizes that the business is grappling with a gender inequity problem. Usually, the problem makes itself known through several traditional indicators. For example, recruiting efforts fail to get women to join the company in meaningful numbers; many women are stalled just before they reach leadership positions or are not rising at the same rate as their male colleagues; women tend to hold low-visibility jobs or jobs in classic "women's" departments, such as HR; senior women are waiting longer or opting to have fewer (or no) children; women have fewer resources to accomplish comparable tasks; women's pay and pay raises are not on par

with men's; and women are leaving the organization at above average rates.

After recognizing that there is a problem, the next step is diagnosis. (For a description of the diagnosis stage of the small-wins strategy, see "How to Begin Small Wins.") Then people must get together to talk about the work culture and determine which everyday practices are undermining effectiveness. Next, experimentation begins. Managers can launch a small initiative—or several at one time—to try to eradicate the practices that produce inequity and replace them with practices that work better for everyone. Often the experiment works—and more quickly than people would suspect. Sometimes it fixes only the symptom and loses its link to the underlying cause. When that happens, other incremental changes must be tried before a real win occurs.

Small wins are not formulaic. Each organization is unique, and its expressions of gender inequity are, too. Consider, then, how the following companies used incremental change to bring about systemic change.

Let's begin with the European retail company that was having trouble keeping its women employees. When the problem finally became impossible to ignore, the president invited us to help the organization understand what was going on. The answer wasn't immediately obvious, of course, but as we began talking to people, it became clear that it had something to do with the lack of clarity and discipline around time. Then the question was raised, Did that lack of clarity affect men and women differently? The answer was a resounding yes.

After discussing and testing the idea further, executives started using the phrase "unbounded time" to refer to meeting overruns, last-minute schedule changes, and tardiness. The term struck a chord; it quickly circulated throughout the company and sparked widespread conversation about

How to Begin Small Wins

Once an organization determines that it has a problem—female employees won't join the company, say, or women are leaving in alarming numbers—it is time to start searching for causes. Such diagnosis involves senior managers probing an organization's practices and beliefs to uncover its deeply embedded sources of inequity. But how?

An effective first step is often one-on-one interviews with employees to uncover practices and beliefs in the company's culture—how work gets done, for instance, what activities are valued, and what the assumptions are about competence. After that, focus groups can more closely examine questionable practices. Some companies have found it useful to have women and men meet separately for these initial discussions, as long as the outcomes of these meetings are shared.

Diagnosis isn't always straightforward. After all, the group is looking for the source of a relatively invisible problem. Yet we have found a collection of questions that help keep the process on track:

- How do people in this organization accomplish their work? What, if anything, gets in the way?
- Who succeeds in this organization? Who doesn't?
- How and when do we interact with one another? Who participates? Who doesn't?
- What kinds of work and work styles are valued in this organization? What kinds are invisible?

- What is expected of leaders in this company?
- What are the norms about time in this organization?
- What aspects of individual performance are discussed the most in evaluations?
- How is competence identified during hiring and performance evaluations?

After the initial diagnosis, managers should identify cultural patterns and their consequences. For example, Which practices affect men differently than women, and why? Which ones have unintended consequences for the business? Following this analysis, change agents can discuss these patterns with different people. We call this stage "holding up the mirror," and it represents the first part of developing a new shared narrative in the organization.

The next step, of course, is designing the small wins. We have found that by this point in the process, groups usually have little trouble identifying ways to make concrete changes. It is critical, however, that the managers guiding the process keep the number and scope of initiatives relatively limited and strategically targeted. Managers and other change agents should remind the organization that a single experiment should not be seen as an end in itself. Each small win is a trial intervention and a probe for learning, intended not to overturn the system but to slowly and surely make it better.

how meeting overload and lax scheduling damaged everyone's productivity and creativity.

At that point, the president could have asked the company's female managers to become more available (assimilation). He could have mandated that all meetings take place between nine and five (accommodation). Or he could have suggested that female employees work together in projects

and at times that played to their unique strengths (celebration). Instead, he and a few other senior managers quietly began to model a more disciplined use of time, and even discouraged people who suggested last-minute or late-night meetings.

Soon people began to catch on, and a new narrative started to spread through the company. The phrase "unbounded time" was used more and more often when people wanted to signal that they thought others were contributing to ineffectiveness and inequity by being late or allowing meetings to run overtime. People realized that the lack of clarity and discipline in the company had negative consequences not just for people but also for the quality of work. Over a nine-month period, norms began to shift, and as new people were hired, senior managers made sure that they understood the company was "informal *and* disciplined." To this day, the concept of "unboundedness" pops up whenever people feel the organization is slipping back into norms that silently support gender inequity.

The small-wins strategy also worked at the investment firm that tried—unsuccessfully—to hire more women by increasing the number of interviews. After executives realized that their 30-minute interviewing approach was backfiring, they began to investigate their entire recruiting practice. They examined how the questions they asked candidates, their interview procedures, and even the places in which they were recruiting might be giving traditional people—that is, male MBAs—an advantage.

And so a series of small initiatives was launched. First, the firm lengthened its interviews to 45 minutes. Partners acknowledged that shorter interviews might have been forcing them to rely on first impressions, which are so often a function of perceived similarity. Although comfort level may make an interview go smoothly, it doesn't tell you if a candidate has valuable skills, ideas, and experience. Second, and perhaps more important, the firm revised its interviewing protocol. In the past, partners questioned candidates primarily about their previous "deal experience," which allowed only those who had worked on Wall Street to shine. Again, that practice favored men, as most investment bank associates are men. In their new approach, managers followed a set protocol and began asking candidates to talk about how they would con-

tribute to the firm's mission. The interviews shifted radically in tone and substance. Instead of boasting from former Wall Street stars, they heard many nontraditional candidates—both women and men—describe a panoply of managerial skills, creative experiences, and diverse work styles. And indeed, these people are bringing new energy and talent into the firm. (As an added bonus, the following year the firm arrived at one prominent business school to find it was earning a reputation as a great place to work, making its recruiting efforts even more fruitful.)

Both the retail company and investment firm saw their equity and performance improve after implementing changes in their systems that could hardly be called radical. The same kind of success story can be told about an international scientific research institute. The institute, which produces new agricultural technologies for farmers, had a strong cultural norm of rewarding individual achievement. When a breakthrough was reached, a new product was developed, or a grant was won, individual scientists usually got the credit and rewards. The norm meant that support work by secretaries and technicians, as well as by scientists and professionals in departments like biotechnology and economics, was often ignored.

Paradoxically, top-level managers at the institute spoke enthusiastically about the value of teamwork and asserted that success was a group, not an individual, product. In fact, the organization planned to move to a team-based structure because senior managers considered it an imperative for addressing complex cross-functional challenges. But in the everyday workings of the organization, no one paid much heed to supporting contributors. The stars were individual "heroes."

The undervaluation of support work was an issue that affected many women because they were more likely to be in staff positions or scientific roles that were perceived as support disciplines. In addition, women more often took on support work because they were expected to do so or because they felt it was critical to a project's success. They connected people with one another, for instance, smoothed disagreements, facilitated teamwork, and taught employees new skills.

Many women expressed frustration with this type of work because it simply wasn't recognized or rewarded. Yet they were reluctant to stop because the costs of not doing it were clear to them. Without it, information would flow less easily, people would miss deadlines, more crises would erupt, and teams would break down. As we talked with them, women began to recognize the value of their efforts, and they gave them a name: "invisible work."

As in the European retail company, naming the problem had a striking effect. It turned out that invisible work wasn't just a problem for women. Men and women started talking about how the lack of value placed on invisible work was related to much larger systemic patterns. For example, people noted that the company tended to give sole credit for projects to the lead scientists, even when others had contributed or had helped spare the projects from major crises. People, especially women, admitted that mentors and bosses had advised them—and they had often advised one another—to avoid taking on invisible work to focus on work that would afford more recognition. Stemming from these informal discussions, a narrative about the importance of invisible work began to spread throughout the organization.

For senior managers who saw the link between invisible work and their goal of moving to a team-based structure, the challenge was to find ways to make invisible work visible—and to ensure it was valued and more widely shared by men and women. A task force on the topic proposed a new organizationwide evaluation system that would gather input from peers and direct reports—people to whom an employee's invisible work is visible. Although that step seemed insignificant to many, it was approved and launched.

Several years later, people say that the institute is a different place. The first small win—the new evaluation process—gave way to others, such as a new process to increase information flow up, down, and sideways; new criteria for team leaders that emphasize facilitation rather than direction; and new norms about tapping expertise, no matter where it resides in the hierarchy. Implicitly, these changes challenged the prevailing masculine, individualist image of competence and leadership and opened the way for alternatives more conducive to teamwork. Today both men and women say there is a stronger sense of fairness. And senior managers say that the systemic changes brought about by the small-wins strategy were central to the institute's successful move to a team-based structure.

● ● ● ● ● ● ● ● ● ●
SMALL WINS CAN MAKE BIG GAINS

It's surprising how quickly people can come up with ideas for small wins—and how quickly they can be put into action. Take, for example, the case of the finance department at a large manufacturing company. The department had a strong norm of *overdoing* work. Whenever senior managers asked for information, the department's analysts would generate multiple scenarios complete with sophisticated graphs and charts.

The fact was, however, senior managers often only wanted an analyst's back-of-the-envelope estimates. People in the finance department even suspected as much, but there was an unspoken policy of never asking the question. The reasons? First, they worried that questions would indicate that they couldn't figure out the scope of the request themselves and hence were not competent. Second, many of the requests came in at the end of the day. Analysts feared that asking, "How much detail do you want?" might look like a way to avoid working late. To show their commitment, they felt they had to stay and give every request the full treatment.

The norm of devoting hours on end to each request hit women in the department especially hard. As women in an industry dominated by men, they felt they had to work extra hard to demonstrate their competence and commitment, especially when commitment was measured, at least in part, by time spent at work. However, the norm negatively affected men, too. The extra work, simply put, was a waste of time; it lowered productivity and dampened enthusiasm. The organization suffered: talented people avoided the department because of its reputation for overtime.

The small-wins process at this company began when we met with a group of analysts and managers in the finance department. We presented our diagnosis of the root causes of the overwork problem and asked if they could come up with small, concrete solutions to counteract it. It didn't take them long. Within an hour, the analysts had designed a one-page form that asked senior managers to describe the parameters of each request. How much detail was required? What was the desired output? The form very simply took the onus off individuals to ask taboo questions, relieving women of the fear that they might appear less than committed and allowing all analysts—not just women—to use their time more productively.

Interestingly, after only a short time, the form was dropped. Analysts reported that simply having a conversation with their managers about the company's norms and taboos changed the department's dynamics. By establishing an open dialogue, analysts could now ask clarifying questions without fearing that they were signaling incompetence or lack of commitment.

Small wins make sense even at companies that already have programs designed to combat gender inequity. Consider the case of a New York advertising agency that was particularly proud of its mentoring program aimed at developing high-potential female leaders. Although that program got women's names into the mix, the jobs that women were ultimately offered tended to be in human resource–type positions—positions women were thought to be particularly well suited for. These jobs often required a high level of skill, but their lack of rainmaking potential resulted in career disadvantages that accumulated over time.

The situation was compounded by an unspoken rule at the company of never saying no to developmental opportunities. This norm, like so many others, seems gender neutral. It appears to be a risk for both men and women to pass up opportunities, particularly those offered in the name of developing leadership potential. Yet because of the different types of opportunities offered, women stood to lose whether they said yes or no. Saying no signaled lack of commitment. But saying yes meant they would spend valuable time and energy doing a job that was unlikely to yield the same career benefits that men were deriving from the opportunities offered to them. What made the situation particularly problematic for the organization was that the HR-type jobs that women were reluctant to accept were often critical to overall functioning.

The women in the mentoring programs were the first to realize the negative impact of the company's informal policy of channeling women into these critical HR positions. So they got together to brainstorm about ways to extricate themselves from their double bind. (Like many small-wins campaigns, this one was launched with the

knowledge and approval of senior management. For ideas on how to start the change
process without official sanction, see
"Going It Alone.") The women coached
one another on how to respond to the HR-
type job offers in ways that would do minimal damage to their careers. For instance,
they came up with the solution of accepting
the job with the stipulation that senior managers assign its year-end objectives a "rainmaking equivalency quotient." The group
pushed senior managers to think about the
underlying assumptions of putting women
in HR jobs. Did they really believe men
could not manage people? If so, didn't that
mean that men should be given the developmental opportunities in HR? These questions led senior managers to several revela-
tions, which were especially important since
the organization had recently decided to

sell itself to potential clients as the relation-
ship-oriented alternative to other agencies.
The full effect of this small-win effort,
launched recently, will likely be seen over
the course of the next few years.

THE POWER OF SMALL WINS

Small wins are not silver bullets; anyone
familiar with real organizational change
knows that there is no such thing. Rather,
the reason small wins work so effectively is
that they are not random efforts. They
unearth and upend systemic barriers to
women's progress. Consider how:

First, small wins tied to the fourth
approach help organizations give a name to
practices and assumptions that are so subtle

Going It Alone

One of the most important virtues of the
fourth approach is that it helps people realize
that they are not alone: the problems are systemic, not individual. That said, individuals or
small groups may still have to "go it alone"
without the support of an organizational
mandate or formal change program.
Although first efforts are aimed at subverting
the status quo, over time they may, in fact, be
embraced by the organization because they
create the impetus for learning and positive
change.

Individuals can adopt one of two methods. First, they can simply operate solo. They
can conduct a diagnosis, identify sources of
gender discrimination, and design small wins
themselves. That approach is hard, as the
process depends so heavily on frank discussion and testing of ideas. That is why we suggest that individuals use a second method:
finding like minds to join them in the exercise. The group can be internal to the organization or it can include people from various

organizations. It can include only women or it
can include women and men. The point is to
hear one another's stories about workplace
practices and their consequences in order to
discover common themes and underlying factors. Small groups can generate small wins on
their own and experiment with them quietly
but persistently.

So often, the "problem with no name" is
experienced by women as a situation that
affects them alone or worse, as a problem
with them. In our executive education programs, we have seen that when women share
their experiences, they recognize that many
of the problems they experience as individuals are actually systemic and not unique to
them or to their organization. And they realize that promoting change can benefit the
organization as well as the men and women
in it. That insight motivates them to work on
their own and in collaboration with others
to create small wins that can make a big difference.

they are rarely questioned, let alone seen as the root of organizational ineffectiveness. When the retail company started using the phrase "unbounded time," people began developing a shared understanding of how the lack of discipline around time affected men and women differently and how the lack of boundaries in the culture contributed to people's inability to get work accomplished. The act of naming the "problem with no name" opens up the possibility of change.

Second, small wins combine changes in behavior with changes in understanding. When a small win works—when it makes even a minor difference in systemic practices—it helps to verify a larger theory. It says that something bigger is going on.

Third, and related, small wins tie the local to the global. That is, people involved in small wins see how their efforts affect larger, systemic change, in much the same way as people taking part in small-town recycling campaigns come to understand their impact in decreasing global warming. This big-picture outlook is both energizing and self-reinforcing, and it links seemingly unrelated small wins together.

Fourth, small wins have a way of snowballing. One small change begets another, and eventually these small changes add up to a whole new system. Consider again the investment firm that revised its recruiting processes. It realized that something as simple as lengthening interview time could begin to address its recruitment problem. But if it had stopped there, it is unlikely that fundamental changes would have occurred. Recognizing why the length of an interview was an issue—how "feeling comfortable" and "fitting the mold" had been implicit selection criteria—helped the firm make additional, more substantial changes in, for instance, the questions asked. This change is encouraging the executives to look into initiatives to revise other practices, ranging from publicity to training, that also held hidden biases, not just for women but also for other underrepresented groups.

The fifth and final source of power in the small-wins approach is that it routs discrimination by fixing the organization, not the women who work for it. In that way, it frees women from feelings of self-blame and anger that can come with invisible inequity. And it removes the label of troublemaker from women who complain that something is not right. Small wins say, "Yes, something is wrong. It is the organization itself, and when it is fixed, all will benefit."

As we enter the new millennium, we believe that it is time for new metaphors to capture the subtle, systemic forms of discrimination that still linger. It's not the ceiling that's holding women back; it's the whole structure of the organizations in which we work: the foundation, the beams, the walls, the very air. The barriers to advancement are not just above women, they are all around them. But dismantling our organizations isn't the solution. We must ferret out the hidden barriers to equity and effectiveness one by one. The fourth approach asks leaders to act as thoughtful architects and to reconstruct buildings beam by beam, room by room, rebuilding with practices that are stronger and more equitable, not just for women but for all people.

Notes

1. Statistics on women of color are even more drastic. Although women of color make up 23 percent of the U.S. women's workforce, they account for only 14 percent of women in managerial roles. African-American women comprise only 6 percent of the women in managerial roles.
2. The small-wins approach to change was developed by Karl Weick. See "Small Wins: Redefining the Scale of Social Problems," *American Psychologist*, 1984.

II-2: Group Interviews among New Ways to Case Hires
Social Gatherings Are Common Venues

LEA CLIFFORD

Picture the scene: Twenty candidates for pilot positions have been called to Southwest Airlines' Dallas headquarters. As the applicants wait in the reception area, employee "plants" surreptitiously scope them out from stairwells or pass through the room making mental notes, looking for the ones who strike up conversations with their peers or offer to help someone struggling with heavy boxes.

Then, when all applicants are called into a conference room, they are instructed to sit informally in a circle along with Southwest employees and asked, for example, to tell the group about how they defused a difficult situation. The point, one would assume, is to gauge their composure under pressure. Not entirely—Southwest also is looking to see who's a good listener.

"There will be some who hear that question and immediately begin scribbling down what they're going to say," said spokeswoman Beth Harbin. "We want someone who's interested in what everybody else has to say; we want someone who's not so me-focused that it's like they're preparing for a test."

It's the latest trend in hiring tactics: group interviews.

"I'm seeing more and more, often in casual environments outside the office," said Bradley Richardson, founder of Job-Smarts, a Dallas firm that helps businesses attract young talent. Companies are starting

©2000 by Smart Money, a joint venture of Hearst Communications, Inc. and Dow Jones & Company, Inc.

to realize that "anyone can fake it in a 20-minute interview," he said, but with group interviews, "the candidates usually don't realize what the purpose is."

That's what Colleen Aylward, president and CEO of Devon James Associates, was counting on when her Seattle search firm landed a contract to find 30 employees for a local online marketing firm. She rented a bus and took prospects on an after-work bar crawl. Why? One thing the agency wanted, she explained, was "people who loved fun, who could work hard, play hard, interact socially, and could talk coherently after a drink." What most candidates assumed was a preliminary meet-and-greet was a potential deal killer for the wallflowers.

At the college level, too, seemingly innocuous social gatherings often come with an ulterior motive. When screening undergraduate prospects. Anice Genender, who until recently was campus recruiting manager for Deloitte Consulting in Dallas, used to arrange happy hours before the formal one-on-one interviews.

"We'd get to see how they interact with the alcohol, whether they were nervous, whether they approached our analysts and partners with good questions. We'd even watch how much they were eating. Sometimes there were students who were only interviewing for the food."

Genender remembers one candidate who got nixed because, after kissing up to a partner, he was rude to a rank-and-file analyst. "The rule of thumb is be nice to everyone," Genender said. "If you're nice to everyone, everything falls into place."

II-3: Managing Temporary Workers: A Permanent HRM Challenge

DANIEL C. FELDMAN, HELEN I. DOERPINGHAUS, AND WILLIAM H. TURNLEY

The U.S. is going from just-in-time manufacturing to just-in-time employment. The employer tells us, "I want them delivered exactly when I want them, as many as I need, and when I don't need them, I don't want them here." Can I get people to work under these circumstances? Yeah. We're the ATMs of the job market.

—MITCHELL FROMSTEIN,
PRESIDENT AND CEO,
MANPOWER, INC.

I have been approached on a new assignment with "Hey you, we ordered you today," to which I replied, "My name is Wendy, but I am not a hamburger."

—WENDY PERKINS,
TEMPORARY-EMPLOYEE
ADVOCATE

These recent quotes, the first from the president of the world's largest temporary agency, the second from the country's most vocal advocate of temporary-employees' rights, highlight how entrenched temporary work has become in our economy. Indeed, 10 years ago, only 100 temporary-employment agencies existed in this country, and only about 250,000 workers were temps; today, there are close to 1,500 temporary-help services and over 1.5 million temporary workers.

Moreover, temporary employment is now a $20 billion a year business. In fact, between 1991 and 1993, more than 20 percent of all the new positions created in the U.S. economy were temporary jobs. Manpower, Inc. currently has a whopping 560,000 employees, deploying more than 100,000 of them each day. And, where the temporary workforce was once largely dominated by clerical help, today it includes large numbers of technical workers, nurses and medical personnel, hotel and restaurant workers, industrial laborers, and business executives and consultants as well.

The nature of the psychological contract between temporary workers and their employers has changed considerably over time. Ten years ago most temporary employees were individuals who worked temp jobs by choice—for example, college students working during vacations and married women with children who wanted to earn some additional income, keep their skills current, or make social contacts outside of the home. Today, however, the temporary workforce is dominated by individuals who would rather not work on temporary assignments— for example, college graduates who can't find permanent jobs, unemployed workers (and their spouses) trying to make ends meet, and laid-off workers who are waiting for positions more consistent with their education and previous work experience to open up.

In addition, more than 25 percent of temporary workers today have no medical insurance, and more than 50 percent are trying to convert their temporary jobs into permanent jobs or find permanent jobs with greater job security and advancement potential.

While some of the management literature has covered how temporary agencies can best recruit both employees and customers, very little has been written about how the employing organizations should manage temporary workers themselves. However, as management interest in just-in-time production strategies grows and the public policy debate over the plight of the working poor

Reprinted from *Organizational Dynamics* 23 (2) (1994): 49–64.

mounts, managing temporary workers in more economically rational and humane ways is likely to become a permanent HRM challenge. To address this lack of information, we recently completed a survey study of 200 temporary employees from seven employment agencies in the Southeast (see Exhibit 1). Both the quantitative results of our survey data and the qualitative comments of our respondents highlight the pros and cons of temporary work from the employee's perspective. They also provide some suggestions on how organizations can more effectively manage their temporary workers.

● ● ● ● ● ● ● ● ● ● ● ●

THE BENEFITS
OF TEMPORARY WORK

For some of the participants in our study, temporary work is an attractive job opportunity. Four groups, in particular, find it especially rewarding.

1. Working mothers. For many working women with young children or other major responsibilities in the home (including caring for older relatives), temporary work provides a way of balancing financial and personal demands. Our participants who fall into this group made the following comments:

> The jobs are conveniently located near home. The agency understands that I am a single parent with two children and that I prefer school-day hours . . . I will be attending vocational school this summer, and the agency will still consider me for employment on the days I am available.

> Working temp has let me spend time with my sick mother.

> If you're a housewife and want to earn some extra shopping money and have a very flexible schedule, temporary work can be a fun situation.

Another reason why many women feel good about temporary work is that it pro-

EXHIBIT 1	Characteristics of Survey Respondents	
Gender:	Male	35.3%
	Female	64.7%
Marital Status:	Married	38.8%
	Single	61.2%
Average Age:	34.5	
Education:	High School	41.7%
	Community College	25.2%
	College	24.7%
	Graduate School	8.4%
Type of Work:	Clerical	37.3%
	"Light Industrial"	40.0%
	Service/Other	22.7%
Wages:	$5 or less per hour	28.7%
	$5.01 to $6.00	32.4%
	$6.01 to $15.00	38.9%
Nature of Temporary Work:	Voluntary Temp	23.0%
	Involuntary Temp	77.0%
Career Plan:	Looking for Permanent Job	79.8%
	Planning on Remaining Temp	20.2%
Quality of Temporary Job:	Employee's job is consistent with his or her education and prior experience	41.0%
	Employee is underemployed	59.0%

vides them a way of re-entering the job market after an extended period away for childcare. Temporary work often allows these women to upgrade their skills, try out different types of jobs and companies, and discover the types of work they would ultimately like to perform:

> The best part of being a temp is working with a wide variety of organizations [and] seeing what kinds of jobs are available and what I like or don't like.

> The best part of doing temporary work has been being able to learn different types of software and getting more experience in the types of skills I already have.

> The best part of being a temp is you get to find something you like to do.

2. College students. The second group of workers who feel good about temporary jobs is college students, who are pleased with the opportunity to earn extra money during their time off from classes. For these people, scheduling flexibility is the main attraction of temporary work:

> I first began working with temporary agencies because I am in college and the agencies satisfied my short-term needs for a job—especially when we have breaks from school that would be a couple of days up to several months. In addition, this was a great way to make extra spending money for college.

> I am currently getting my Bachelor's in engineering. I'm registered with six temporary agencies, for which I work during breaks or summers or days I don't attend class, to supplement my income. The best parts: flexibility, setting my own schedule, [and the fact that] I can earn money and remain focused on school.

> Right now I'm only doing temp work [on weekends] to earn some extra money for school. What I'm doing isn't difficult or challenging—anyone could do it. However, I like what I do and get to meet a lot of interesting people. . . . Temp services are convenient.

3. Peripheral workers. The third group attracted to temporary work consists of individuals who are essentially out of the full-time workforce by choice (e.g., older workers in early retirement) and who want the opportunity to have adult companionship outside of the home, variety in their days, and additional spending money for nonessential goods:

> I am semi-retired, so I work when I want to. I have been pleased with both the company and my direct supervisors from the temporary help agency. I think it's a great way to get out of the house and meet other people.

> Temporary work is okay for people like myself [because it allows me] to have some change in my pocket and to not have so much idle time.

> I enjoy meeting new people, so I like going on many different and varied assignments. . . . The best parts for me as a temporary worker are the new people I meet and work with and the different office atmospheres I work in.

4. Short-run unemployed. The fourth group of workers for whom temporary work may be beneficial includes individuals who have been laid off from a job, have relocated geographically, or have had trouble finding a full-time job in their chosen field and need some type of stop-gap employment:

> My temporary assignment may become permanent, and with that I am both pleased and excited. The job market is tough right now.

> Temp work is great for me. . . . I just moved here. . . . As a temp I get to work at jobs that under normal circumstances I wouldn't try.

> I was laid off, and the agency continued to find me jobs until I got called back.

These four groups, then, are attracted to temporary work because of its inherent advantages—variety, flexibility, and convenience. However, it is important to recognize that even larger numbers of people work temporary jobs—despite the fact that they feel overqualified—because they are unable to find permanent full-time employment. And, as the data in Exhibit 2 so clearly demonstrate, individuals who become temporary employees out of necessity have significantly poorer attitudes towards their work than those who voluntarily assume these jobs. These "involuntarily" temporary workers feel a very strong sense of deprivation.

KEY CONCERNS
OF TEMPORARY WORKERS

Many of our respondents, regardless of their reasons for assuming temporary jobs, readily acknowledge the potential benefits of temp work. However, many also have serious reservations about temporary work, both as a short-term employment situation and as a longer-term career path. In our survey results, six key concerns emerged:

1. Temporary workers are discouraged by the dehumanizing and impersonal way that they are treated on the job. As the opening quote from Wendy Perkins illustrates, many temporary workers feel they are treated as things rather than people, and command significantly less respect and courtesy than they deserve:

> I don't like temporary work. It's degrading. It makes me feel inferior. People on these jobs have no respect for temporary workers.

> Temps should be treated with respect, too—they are also humans.

> Sometimes [being a temp] is demeaning. I cannot remember how many . . . times I have been referred to as "just a temp," and that has a permanent effect on your ego.

> I feel that most temporaries are looked down upon and are only asked to do basic work.

> Temps are just like permanent employees and want to feel their work is appreciated. . . .

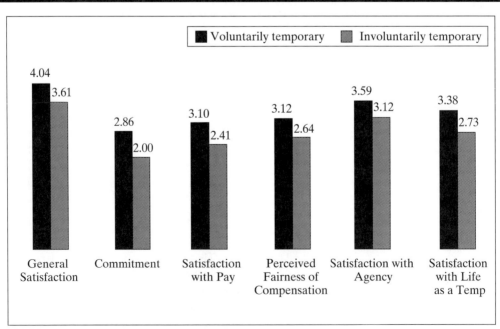

EXHIBIT 2 Employee Reaction to Temporary Work

Legend: ■ Voluntarily temporary ■ Involuntarily temporary

Category	Voluntarily temporary	Involuntarily temporary
General Satisfaction	4.04	3.61
Commitment	2.86	2.00
Satisfaction with Pay	3.10	2.41
Perceived Fairness of Compensation	3.12	2.64
Satisfaction with Agency	3.59	3.12
Satisfaction with Life as a Temp	3.38	2.73

Sometimes I think employers on an assignment are too quick to misjudge a temp.

In the company [I am assigned to], they make me feel so much like an outsider, a nobody. Whenever the whole office does something together, I am not included. It is as if I do not exist.

2. Temporary workers feel insecure about their employment and are pessimistic about the future.

Temporary jobs often seem like a dead end, particularly to individuals who are trying to find permanent work with advancement opportunities. Many temporary workers are frightened because they have no job security and are pessimistic about their chances for escaping this career path for one that offers advancement potential.

If you want a full-time job, there is no good experience as a temp worker. . . . Ninety-five percent of the people I talk with want steady work. . . . Companies get workers for nothing, don't let the agencies pay them any benefits, work us for three to six months, then get a new bunch.

The worst parts of this job: It can end at any time, there is no job security, no benefits, just the not knowing of what's ahead.

The worst parts of being a temporary worker are not feeling secure about keeping a job [and not] having a job permanently.

I could not imagine having to live solely on the salary earned from temporary work. The stress alone caused by not knowing when and if your next assignment will come would drive anyone crazy!

3. Temporary workers worry about their lack of insurance and pension benefits.

As Exhibit 3 suggests, the respondents in our survey fare poorly when it comes to fringe benefits. Only 7.5 percent receive agency contributions to medical insurance payments, and only another 13.4 percent have the option of buying medical coverage through an agency-affiliated group. Fewer than 5 percent receive life insurance, disability insurance, or paid sick leave, and none receive pension benefits.

Survey respondents complained most frequently about this lack of fringe benefits. This is understandable, since very few temporary workers can afford medical coverage on their own. Many temporary workers who have been on the same assignment for six months or more said they believe their company is not hiring them on a permanent

EXHIBIT 3 Fringe Benefits that Temporary Workers Receive

Fringe Benefit	Percentage Receiving Benefit
Life Insurance	2.2
Disability Insurance	2.7
Agency Contribution to Medical Insurance	7.5
Employee Option to Join Agency Medical Group	13.4
Paid Vacation Leave	31.7
Paid Sick Leave	2.7
Paid Holiday Leave	22.0
Merit Pay Raises	14.0
Pay Raises Based on Number of Hours Worked	19.9
Bonuses for Referring New Employees to Agency	27.4
Tuition Reimbursement for Vocational Training	1.6
Job-Search Skills Training	14.5
Career Counseling	4.8
Pension Benefits	0.0

basis in order to avoid paying fringe-benefit costs. In addition, temporary workers often said they resented the fact that temporary agencies make significant profits off their labor yet offer them few, if any, benefits.

> The only bad thing about temporary work is that you don't get benefits. You should get them if the position is going to [last] at least three months or more.

> The irony is not lost on me that I am working as a temp for one of the country's major health-care insurance providers and for no benefits. . . . What good is an economic recovery if the only concern is for the corporate bottom line, not for a good job for me and people like me? A good framework for providing health insurance [for temps] would be an excellent start, but my feeling is that it will only come about through comprehensive national reform.

> They should not hold out the promise of a permanent job if, in fact, the client just uses a succession of temporaries to avoid paying benefits. Temporary work can be a lifesaver, but it can also make you cynical.

> I worked with the same agency for nine months on one job. I had a medical problem and I had to take some days off. The organization I was assigned to had no problem with the days I needed off, but the agency did. . . . When the job ended they refused to give me any more assignments. I thought it was unfair. . . . I am about to lose everything I have, and right now even temporary work isn't helping out.

> Agencies should consider giving benefits to workers who work for a certain length of time. . . . I don't think it is fair that they receive 25 to 33 percent of our wages and we get no benefits.

4. Temporary workers claim that employers fail to provide an accurate picture of their job assignments. Respondents tend to have ambivalent feelings toward the temporary agencies they work for. On the one hand, they reported that agency personnel are generally pleasant and helpful in finding them employment quickly. But, on the other, many reported that the agencies are not honest about whether temporary assignments are likely to become full-time positions. The gratitude many temps feel toward their agencies for finding them jobs is tempered by their eventual disappointment when the job is not converted into full-time work—even though, according to many temps, the agency led them to believe it would be.

> One thing I am not happy about is the fact that I went to the temporary agency to get help in finding permanent employment. I agreed to work for them temporarily until they found me a permanent position. I have called several times inquiring about their progress. Nothing has [happened].

> Agencies lie about the jobs available just to have us in their pool.

> Sometimes companies lead the agencies to believe they want their workers for temporary assignments that will become permanent. . . . Maybe a company should be made to explain if the job is only a long-term assignment. . . . It would eliminate the uncertainty of our jobs.

> The agency can improve on its honesty to its workers. . . . The agency gave me a temporary job which they said would lead to a permanent hire at the end of the assignment. . . . The agency lied about this being a definite permanent position.

5. Temporary workers feel underemployed. This is particularly true of temporary workers trying to return to the full-time labor market. Temps are often clustered in jobs that require significantly less education, skill, and prior work experience than they have. As a result, they often find their jobs boring and unchallenging. Respondents frequently commented that they feel stranded in dead-end, low-level jobs.

> The worst part for me is doing the boring and non-challenging tasks, such as stuffing thousands of envelopes or opening and

distributing mail. I would like to have more challenging tasks to do on my assignments and less mundane work.

I work on temporary positions because I have not been able to find a permanent full-time job. I work on jobs that I am overqualified for. . . . I am not a person who likes not being able to advance. . . . I don't like doing jobs that are way below my qualifications.

Being employed at a temporary agency can be a very positive experience if you are not overly qualified . . . the type of work they have to offer can easily be performed by your average high school drop-out.

The thing I am dissatisfied with is how much work I do in a week—not enough—and I feel I'm not doing the kind of work I would like to be doing.

When I applied at my temp agency . . . I wanted to find types of jobs that I might consider as full-time, permanent, long-term, upwardly mobile possibilities. Unfortunately, the jobs I have worked were not challenging.

6. Temporary workers feel a generalized anger toward corporate America and its values. Perhaps the greatest surprise in the survey was the amount of hostility respondents expressed about the political and economic system behind their employment situation. Temporary work has made many of these workers bitter and cynical, not only about corporations' concerns for workers, but also about the government's willingness to look out for the average American laborer. Participants repeatedly expressed feelings of alienation and disenchantment:

Working three months here and two months there [expletive deleted]! This is America. It should be easy to get a good job without a middle man.

The good jobs are sent overseas for cheap labor.

We need to bring the unions back. My mother and father worked for unions, and

they had security. I was a Republican before but now I'm switching to the Democratic Party. They seem to be for the working man. Temporary services are for rich Republicans. They keep their feet on the working man's neck.

My complaint with my present job assignment is only that it is mindless and repetitive, but my complaints with temporary work in general are many. I deeply resent that I am regarded as expendable by the entire system, that once I have completed the task at hand I will be discarded like a used condom.

If you think I sound bitter you are right. I don't like what these greedy bastards are doing to my country and to its people.

● ●

IMPROVING MANAGEMENT PRACTICE

The preceding discussion suggests that the relationships between temporary workers and their employers—both the agencies that employ them and the organizations in which they work—are less productive and constructive than they might be. Considering how the temporary workforce has grown in size and diversity, and how temporary workers' job expectations have changed, organizations may want to consider alternative ways of managing these employees. Below we outline six suggestions for human resource managers.

1. Provide honest information to both temporary agencies and temporary workers about the length of the job assignment. It has long been agreed that realistic pre-employment discussions are an important ingredient of good staff relations. However, as the comments from our study make clear, miscommunications among organizations, agencies, and temporary workers about job security and job permanence are common. Organizations claim that agencies promise temps more than they can deliver in an effort to sign up new employees; agencies maintain that organizations create false hopes among temps in order to motivate them to work harder; and temporary workers say they can't get a straight story from anyone:

> I have a major complaint about the way we were lied to. We were told [by the agency] that after we completed the six-month assignment, we would become permanent employees of [the organization] at significantly more wages. But once we were here at the job, we heard—first from our immediate supervisors and then from the director—that this was not the case. [Instead, we were told that after we completed the assignment], we could . . . apply for a job that was advertised in the newspaper, but we would be on equal footing as someone applying from the outside.

> [My agency] can improve on its manners and honesty to its workers. The best thing that this agency did was to give me a temporary job which would lead to a permanent hire at the end of the temporary assignment. The worst thing was that this agency lied about this being a definite permanent position.

> [Agencies] need to not lie about the [job-security] aspects of a job. Tell the truth no matter what happens. If there is a misunderstanding between the agency and the customer, then [the agency should say it is] sorry for the misunderstanding, and not try to say that we temps are at fault.

In many cases, an organization will assume that the agency will set realistic expectations for the temp before the assignment starts, while the agency assumes the organization will take care of setting expectations once the temp arrives. Given the fact that honesty is a key concern for temporary workers, both organizations and agencies should work on setting (or correcting) employee perceptions of their long-term employment prospects.

2. Implement personnel policies that ensure fair and respectful treatment of temporary workers. Perhaps nothing is more frustrating to temporary workers than being treated as "just a temp." Temporary workers often feel like stepchildren—useful enough to do the unpleasant chores, but not really all that welcome.

Moreover, during the June 1993 U.S. Senate hearings on "the disposable workforce," many expressed concern that temporary workers may fall between the cracks of labor laws. Temporary workers testified that they are caught in a web of contractual relationships that do not protect their rights. For example, in one case, claims of sexual harassment by supervisors in the employing organization were not addressed by the organization because the temps were not its legal employees, and not addressed by the agency because the perpetrators were not employees of the agency. Along the same lines, another temporary worker testified:

> In 1986, I, [along with] most everyone else in my department, was laid off. I was devastated. . . . [I was hired back,] but was told that to take the job I would have to be a "consultant" rather than an employee. From speaking with my supervisor, I learned that this meant that I would not get any benefits and would have to pay the employer's share of Social Security taxes. . . . The company then terminated some of the consultants in January of 1988. I was one of the unlucky ones. I was quite upset, not only because I was again unemployed but also because I didn't understand how the company got rid of me while keeping younger, less experienced workers on payroll.

> My lawsuit said that the company violated ERISA by saying that I was not an employee for the sole purpose of taking away my benefits. My lawsuit also said that I was the victim of age discrimination when I was fired and younger workers were kept on the payroll. . . . The first judge said that ERISA and the Age Discrimination in Employment Act [don't] protect you unless you are a real employee. . . . My case is now on appeal . . . but even my [own] lawyer says that the Age Discrimination Act and ERISA and a lot of other federal laws don't protect workers

unless they are "employees," and that the word "employee" has a very technical legal meaning.

Policies governing the day-to-day treatment of temporary employees are not especially costly and may even decrease liability for inappropriate conduct by permanent employees. For example, it is relatively easy to extend sexual harassment policies for full-time permanent workers to temporary employees as well. As organizations increasingly rely on contingent workers to fill their staffing needs, they need to vigorously promote respectful and thoughtful treatment of their not-so-temporary visitors.

3. Use independent contractors and permanent part-time employees to complement the conventional temporary agency workforce. In their research on "externalized laborers," Alison Davis-Blake and Brian Uzzi found that organizations that required greater amounts of technical skill and were subject to extensive governmental oversight were less likely to use temporary workers. Although these firms would have paid less in wages and benefits by hiring temporary workers, training costs, along with the potential costs of errors committed by temps, were sufficiently high to argue against the use of temps. By contrast, these authors found that firms that had a cyclical labor demand and needed only low-skilled workers were more likely to use temporary workers.

For organizations that require large numbers of so-called "externalized" or "contingent" workers, the implications of Davis-Blake and Uzzi's research are clear. Organizations need to consider not only the potential savings stemming from lower wages and fringe benefits but also the potential costs of training temporary workers and fixing errors in their work. Thus, temporary workers may make excellent business sense for fast-food services and discount merchandise stores but for organizations that require a highly skilled and committed workforce, permanent part-timers and independent contractors may be a more reasonable staffing alternative.

4. Before hiring temporary workers, consider their potential impact on regular full-time employees. In her research on contract laborers, Jone Pearce looks at another important aspect of the temporary-worker situation: the impact of temporary workers on the behaviors and attitudes of their full-time colleagues. Pearce found that managers are likely to assign temporary workers tasks that require little or no organization-specific knowledge, while shifting more difficult assignments that require teamwork to regular employees. In addition, in some cases organizations ask full-time employees to take on tasks of greater complexity and responsibility for no additional pay.

Even more interesting, Pearce found that the use of temporary and leased workers can negatively impact the attitudes of regular full-time employees. Even though regular employees prefer their own positions and compensation packages to those of contract workers, they may believe that the organization is exploiting its contract workers. According to Pearce, this perception may lead them "to question the organization's fairness to the contractors today—and possibly to themselves tomorrow."

Thus, the decision to use temporary workers is more complicated than many managers realize. It raises concerns among regular employees about equity, the quality of employer-employee relationships, and the meaning of organizational loyalty. As organizations lay off workers, outsource them to employment agencies, and hire them back as temporaries, they need to realize that this employment practice may have a negative impact on their internal "observers."

5. Provide more extensive training and orientation for temporary workers. As the preceding discussion highlights, two key factors largely determine whether temporary workers will be an efficient human resource: the amount of training they will need and the speed with which they will be able to learn to perform their jobs well. While the amount of training required will certainly vary across occupations, it is clear from the responses to our survey that organizations could improve, at the minimum, their basic communication of job duties:

> If you are expected to hit the ground running, that should be specified when requesting a temp from the agency.

> [Organizations] need to be more specific in their instructions to temps. Give them the [correct] tools and materials to do their jobs.

> [The organizations and agencies] need to be more specific about the assignments, provide a brief orientation of the situation, and make work standards and work rules clear up front.

An organization can improve its training and orientation of temps in at least two major ways. First, it can work more closely with temporary agencies, making clear the types of workers it wants and the specific assignments it has. That way, the agency can do a better job of sending out the appropriate temps. Second, when the temporary workers arrive at the work site, the organization can provide a detailed, specific orientation regarding the day's assignment. This would likely result in significantly greater productivity from the temps at virtually no more cost, since in many cases it would involve no more than 10 to 15 minutes of the supervisor's time.

6. Be selective in choosing temporary agencies and systematically evaluate the performance of temporary workers. In many ways, the quality of the temporary agency has a ceiling effect on the quality of the organization-employee relationship. If the temporary agency does a poor job of recruiting, selecting, training, orienting, and placing employees, then the relationship between the organization and the temp is unlikely to be positive. Temporary agencies vary widely in terms of the loyalty and stability they engender among employees, the training and orientation they provide, and the compensation packages they offer. Choosing a temporary agency that provides the best service can be half the battle in managing temporary workers more effectively.

In choosing a temporary agency, organizations should consider the type of labor force the agency specializes in and the stability of its labor pool. The greater the agency's experience with a specific occupational group, the greater its ability to understand the nuances of job assignments and the differences in employees' skills. This helps the agency make optimal placements. Similarly, agencies with a relatively stable temporary workforce may bring two additional benefits to a client firm. First, the organization may bear less risk in hiring temps, since the temps from this agency have stood some test of time; second, the agency is more likely to be staffed with voluntarily temporary workers, who are content to be working on a contingent basis and have more realistic expectations of what temporary jobs entail.

An organization should also consider the amount of training the agency offers to temporary workers. Some agencies do little more than verify previous employment, provide drug screening, and check whether the employee has a phone and a car; others provide extensive self-paced instruction for clerical jobs and tuition reimbursement for courses taken at local vocational schools. To the extent that an agency provides relevant training, its temps will be able to "hit the floor running" when they arrive on the job.

Finally, many organizations use multiple temporary agencies over a long period of time. However, working with fewer agencies may actually be a better alternative, since some agencies try to send their best temps to organizations with which they have continuous and exclusive relationships. Thus, it makes sense for an organization to systematically evaluate each agency's ability to provide high-quality help, work with a small number of highly effective agencies, and thereby increase the quality of the temporary workers the agency sends over.

● ● ● ● ● ● ● ● ● ●
SUMMARY

In some ways, managing a temporary workforce takes considerable pressure off of supervisors. The agency does the recruiting and selection; the organization sets the cost of labor and benefits, rarely leaving this open to negotiation; most of the training and orientation is done outside the firm; and the employment relationship is readily terminated at will. In other ways, however, managing a temporary workforce presents unique challenges. For example, the supervisor does not have the same level of social control over employees, since promotions and pay raises are rarely given for work well done. In addition, the psychological contract between the organization and the employee engenders little commitment or effort on the part of the employee beyond the call of duty.

Because of the increasing size and diversity of the temporary workforce, managing temporary workers has becomes a significant HRM challenge. Organizations need to consider providing temporary workers with better training and orientation, clearer explanations of the temporary employment contract, and more consistently respectful treatment. In addition, organizations need to be more judicious in selecting well-run employment agencies to screen and train contingent workers. Per-

haps most importantly, organizations need to consider using independent contractors, leased workers, and permanent part-time workers as alternatives to temporary workers, and they need to recognize the impact that widespread use of temporary workers has on the work flow and job attitudes of their full-time employees.

In the final paragraph of his statement during the Senate hearings on contingent workers, Howard Metzenbaum (D-Ohio), chair of the Senate Committee on Labor and Human Resources, comments:

> When companies replace full-time employees with disposable workers to cut labor costs, these costs do not simply "disappear"—they are borne by workers and by taxpayers. The more "contingent" our workforce becomes, the more dependent workers will be on government programs for income assistance, health care, and retirement income. Ultimately, I am very concerned that if this trend continues, we may wake up one morning to find that the American dream has slipped away. As we will hear today, for many workers, that morning has already come.

In the months and years ahead, the public policy debate over the treatment of temporary workers will increase in intensity. The period of benign neglect of temporary workers will soon be over. It is now in an organization's best interests to manage the contingent workforce in ways that are both more humane and more economically rational.

Selected Bibliography

A fuller discussion of the theoretical arguments that underlie this paper can be found in Daniel Feldman's "Reconceptualizing the Nature and Consequences of Part-time Work," *Academy of Management Review,*15 (1990), 103–12.

The growth and characteristics of the temporary workforce have been well documented by various governmental statistical surveys. Among the most informative of these are

Harry Williams's "What Temporary Workers Earn: Findings from New BLS Survey," *Monthly Labor Review,* 112 (1989), 3–6; Max Carey and Kim Hazelbaker's "Employment Growth in the Temporary Help Industry," *Monthly Labor Review,* 109 (1986), 37–44; and Anne E. Polivka and Thomas Nardone's "On the Definition of Contingent Work," *Monthly Labor Review,* 112 (1989), 9–16.

There have been several well-researched popular press articles on the daily experiences of temporary workers. Particularly notable here are Lance Morrow's "The Temping of America," *Time,* March 29, 1993 and Clare Ansberry's "Hired Out: Workers Are Forced to Take More Jobs with Few Benefits," *Wall Street Journal,* March 11, 1993.

The use of temporary workers has received increased attention from social and governmental policy experts as well. Among the most informative of these articles are Robert Moberly's "Temporary, Part-time, and Other Atypical Employment Relationships in the United States," *Labor Law Journal,* 37 (1989), 689–96; and Sar Levitan and Elizabeth Conway's "Part-timers: Living on Half-rations,"

Challenge, 31 (1988), 9–16. Recently, the United States Senate has been conducting hearings on various aspects of temporary, part-time, and contingent employment. Particularly enlightening is the testimony presented to the United States Senate Committee on Labor and Human Resources in a hearing entitled "Toward a Disposable Workforce: The Increasing Use of Contingent Labor" on July 15, 1993, Senator Howard Metzenbaum, presiding.

Two articles on the efficiency of temporary workers relative to other types of employees are especially useful: Alison Davis-Blake and Brian Uzzi's "Determinants of Employment Externalization: A Study of Temporary Workers and Independent Contractors," *Administrative Science Quarterly,* 38 (1993), 195–223; and Paul Osterman's "Employment Structures Within Firms," *British Journal of Industrial Relations,* 20 (1982), 349–61. To better understand the impact of temporary workers on other members of the organization, please see Jone Pearce's "Toward Psychological Involvement and Effects on Employee Co-workers," *Academy of Management Journal,* 36 (1993), 1082–96.

II-4: Labor Board Allows Organizing of Temps
Ruling Is Seen As Victory for Unions, but Some Say It Is Bad for Workers

NICHOLAS KULISH AND CARLOS TEJADA

Washington—In a victory for unions and a nod to changes in the American workplace, the National Labor Relations Board eased restrictions on organizing temporary workers into collective bargaining units.

In a decision yesterday, the board overruled precedent and allowed temp workers to be included with permanent employees

in bargaining units, provided they have similar job characteristics.

The decision also allows temp workers to jointly bargain with both the so-called user employer that has engaged them and with the temp agency itself.

● ● ● ● ● ● ● ● ● ● ● ●
AN IMPORTANT DEVELOPMENT

"It closes an artificial distinction between workers," said Judith Scott, general counsel for the Service Employees International Union. "Will it open the floodgates to organizing? No. Is it an important development in some workplaces? Absolutely."

In previous cases, the board had ruled that temporary workers could only unionize with the consent of both the temp agency and the company where they are working.

The decision applies to temporary, or contingent, workers, which the NLRB defined as workers employed by both the user employer and a so-called supplier employer, such as a temp agency, which provides them with pay and benefits.

The increase in the number of temps has been a powerful labor trend during the past decade.

Temporary workers accounted for roughly 2.2% of the nation's work force in 1999, double the 1990 level, according to the American Staffing Association, a trade group representing temporary-employment agencies.

A KEY INGREDIENT

"If the decision ends up creating a significant chilling effect on the use of temporary workers, then I think it's bad for workers and bad for the economy," said Edward Lenz, general counsel at the ASA. "Flexible labor is a key ingredient in the economic growth that we've been experiencing over the past decade."

Ed Kemp, a computer technician who has worked as a temporary employee for about 3½ years with Seattle-area tech firms, said any decision that makes it easier for temporary workers to organize and bargain collectively is "a wonderful thing." Mr. Kemp, who recently took on a full-time job, said that in particular, he thinks temporary workers should have the right to know how much their agency is being paid for the hourly services of their temp workers. "Companies have a propensity to take advantage of workers," he said. "I do believe workers should have a right to organize."

The ruling covered two disputes, including a five-year-old case involving roughly a dozen temporary employees at a plant owned by M.B. Sturgis Inc. in Maryland Heights, Mo.

BARGAINING WITH TEMP WORKERS

Business groups said the decision could make using temps, which companies do to be flexible as well as cost-efficient, a lot more complicated.

While employers without unions should be unaffected, unionized employers could have to consider bargaining with temp workers on temp-related changes. Employers might also have to bargain along with temp agencies, which may have different benefits and seniority packages.

"This has really muddied the waters," said Daniel Yager, general counsel of LPA, a Washington, D.C., employer group.

Those who disagree with the decision worry about the effect that it might have on the job market.

"I think this will cause people to reassess whether they're going to use temporary help," said John Raudabaugh, former member of the NLRB and now an attorney in Chicago.

Many labor advocates feel the ruling doesn't go far enough to protect the rights of temps and contract workers. "The labor-relations board is finally recognizing and trying to expand the rights of temporary employees, but it's far short of saying that they're just like any other worker and have the same rights," said Marcus Courtney, co-founder of WashTech, a Washington-based alliance of technology workers and an affiliate of the Communications Workers of America.

ACCRETING TEMPORARY WORKERS

The board remanded a portion of the Sturgis case that would have determined whether a bargaining unit could simply absorb, or "accrete," temporary workers without a vote.

To accrete temporary workers, a unit would petition an NLRB regional director to consider whether the temporary workers have similar interests.

Charles Cohen, a former NLRB member and now an employer attorney, says: "That's where the real potentially nefarious effect of all this is."

The decision could be overturned, but the process could take months. Board decisions can be taken to a federal appeals court. Yesterday's Sturgis decision has the added step of having been remanded.

The board most likely won't see the case again until the employer refuses to recognize the bargaining unit. Then it can go to a federal appeals court.

"This is going to be the law of the land for quite a while," Mr. Yager said.

II-5: All in the Family

CAROLYN HIRSCHMAN

The boss's son is deadwood. Family members get perks that other employees don't. The owner is a control freak who often rejects your advice. Welcome to the world of human resource management at a family-owned business.

It's a stint that could be one of the most rewarding times of your career. Why? Because you'll have a unique opportunity to make an impact on the company. Odds are your predecessors were part-time family members who handled HR functions on top of other administrative duties—which means there was probably little organization or consistency to HR management.

But working in a family-owned company can also be challenging because the job may require a lot of hand-holding and justifying initially. Just ask Bruce Stec. He was hired earlier this year to start an HR department at a 300-person, family-owned construction firm in Omaha, Nebraska—and he

still isn't sure the owners understand why they hired him. "Getting owners to believe in HR overall is somewhat difficult." says Stec.

Hiring an outside, professional HR director is a big step for a family-owned business, say many consultants. For firms to successfully take that step, two factors usually have to come into play.

The first is that the company must be large enough to warrant the hire. There are no official data showing how many of the approximately 1 million family-owned businesses in the United States employ full-time HR managers, but anecdotal evidence suggests large companies use them and small ones don't. Bernard Liebowitz, a Chicago-based family business consultant, estimates that the break point happens at around $10 million in revenues for a service company and $15 million in revenues for a manufacturer.

The second factor is that family owners must be willing to yield some control for the sake of managing growth. "One of the problems in a family-owned business is the shift from an entrepreneurial company to a managerial company," explains Thomas Hubler of Hubler Family Business

HR Magazine by Carolyn Hirschman. Copyright 1998 by Society for Human Resource Management. Reprinted with permission of HR Magazine published by the Society for Human Resource Management, Alexandria, VA.

Consultants in Minneapolis. "Unless you begin to delegate, you won't grow. Unless you hire professional managers, you won't grow."

ONE BIG, HAPPY FAMILY

There are distinct advantages to working at a family-owned business. There's often a casual atmosphere, where workers are treated like extended family. Owners tend to be sympathetic to and flexible in meeting employees' personal needs. Loyal, long-time employees may result in lower turnover.

Even larger familial companies can keep their close-knit feel. "I've known my boss so long, I feel like I'm part of the family," says Debra Besch, director of HR and risk management at Lunch Inc., a 2,500-person, family-controlled nonprofit in Baton Rouge, Louisiana. Lunch Inc. monitors family day care providers' compliance with government lunch guidelines and runs two hospitals and 18 nursing homes.

"There's more of a family feel throughout the business," Besch adds. "When one of my employees has a situation, there's no stick to the black-and-white rules." For example, the company allowed an employee to work at home following surgery to avoid using up sick time, although it has no formal telecommuting policy.

At some family-owned businesses employees move up the ladder faster than in other settings, experts say. "You're able to grow very quickly," says Kimberly Wheeland, who rose rapidly from executive assistant to national sales associate at a 30-person, family-owned, computer systems vendor in Colorado Springs, Colorado.

And you may luck out by having the best of both worlds—a professional, yet relaxed working environment—like Betsy Amos.

"We have a management team in place like any corporation," says Amos, HR director at Omega World Travel Inc., a 1,000-employee travel agency based in Fairfax, Virginia. The wife-and-husband ownership team are "hands-on and very involved," she adds. But "I'm pretty much able to do my job. They've never really interfered."

Perhaps the biggest reason to work for a family-owned business is that you may not be able to avoid it. Experts estimate that between 80 percent and 90 percent of all businesses are family owned.

THE DYSFUNCTIONAL FAMILY

Of course, there are some downsides to deal with. HR experts say that handling human resources at a family-owned firm can be like walking through a minefield. HR professionals must tread carefully between family members, who are the owners and top executives, and nonfamily employees, who make up the lower managerial and staff ranks. It's a tricky act to balance both sides' demands and keep everyone happy.

What's more, HR managers can often end up in the middle of a personal family dispute that spills over to the workplace.

There are many frustrations and challenges, some more easily resolved than others. Here are three common scenarios HR professionals can face in family-owned businesses, as well tips on how to handle them.

RELATIVELY SPEAKING

Disparate treatment of family and non-family employees is one of the most common difficulties of working in family-owned firms. Family members make more money than nonrelatives; they enjoy more benefits and perks. The most talented outsiders never rise to the top echelon because these positions are reserved for relatives.

"You might as well throw salary structure out the window," says one HR manager who asked not to be identified. "Our [management] salaries are all over the board. There's no rhyme or reason. There are people in this company whose pay is based on the fact that they knew the owners before, and it has nothing to do with their skills."

There's little room to maneuver on this one, HR experts say. Their advice is to recognize from the start that inconsistency is inherent in some family-owned businesses, even when there are accepted policies and procedures that apply to everyone.

In some cases, favoritism is unethical and possibly illegal; in others, it's merely annoying.

Ray Palen ran into a sticky situation while working for a family-owned manufacturer. A male family employee was accused of sexual harassment. The owners didn't want to fire their relative, but they didn't want a discrimination lawsuit either. In the end, the man got a slap on the wrist, a pay cut, and a tarnished reputation. The alleged victim stayed on and was even promoted.

"If this had been a nonfamily member, this person would have been terminated," Palen says. No lawsuit resulted in this case.

Charles Cole, now HR manager at a Massachusetts manufacturer, had to handle an unethical situation when he worked as HR manager at a large, family-owned textile company. Before the firm went public, some—but not all—workers were given a chance to purchase company stock at a low price. Some people made fortunes overnight. Others were left out in the cold. "That led to a great deal of discontent," Cole recalls.

People complained, but "I could only say this was the owner of the company and what he decided to do," Cole says. "There was no rationale. I could not lie to them." Although the owner did not break the law, Cole resigned in protest over the incident.

Other cases may not be considered unethical but may be unfair, leading to hostility among workers. Wheeland says her former employer had a casual-dress policy that did not allow jeans. People grumbled but followed the rule—except the senior engineer—who happened to be the president's son-in-law and the chief financial officer's husband.

Some employees were upset "because of the principle of the matter," Wheeland says. In her role as informal employee relations manager, she asked for a meeting with the top managers. A shouting match ensued. The boss defended his son-in-law and nothing changed. A few employees actually quit over the matter.

Because of this and other experiences, Wheeland is not sure she'd work for another family-owned business. "I wouldn't seek it out. It's too subjective," she says.

● ● ● ● ● ● ● ● ● ● ● ● ●
THE LAZY SON

Hiring unqualified, do-nothing relatives and friends is a classic problem at family-owned businesses. Other workers must take up the slack. It hurts morale, and it damages productivity. As awful as these employees are, they are untouchable, protected by their loyalty to and relationships with family owners.

"Nepotism with family members is a given. I have a problem when a job is manufactured" for a relative who is incompetent or can't find a job elsewhere, Cole says.

What to do? HR managers often work around these problem employees as best they can. Experts say don't bad-mouth them, but don't treat them with kid gloves, either. And don't complain to the boss unless the person's behavior creates legal or financial problems.

One HR manager who asked not to be identified says he and his colleagues have heeded that advice when dealing with a do-nothing employee—a friend of the CEO's son—who is supposed to handle salary reviews. Otherwise, he says, no one would get a raise. But there's little the manager can do to console frustrated co-workers who are doing the laggard's job for him.

Some workers have quit because of this man, he adds. Others rely on a sympathetic ear from colleagues and focus on the positives of working for the company.

Marginalizing the employee may help solve part of the problem. Justin Hocker remembers a time when the owner of a small engineering consulting firm in Overland Park, Kansas, hired his wife as a secretary. She was a terrible typist. Letters with errors went out to clients and vendors, he says. To alleviate the problem, people started shifting her work to another secretary to proofread, correct, and mail.

Then the wife found out. "Behind closed doors, she was upset about it," says Hocker, who is now an HR manager at Pekin Insurance Co. in Pekin, Illinois. Getting rid of the wife was out of the question. In the end, "she made a more conscious effort," and some business and its correspondence was moved to another department with a different secretary.

THE ENTREPRENEURIAL BOSS

These bosses usually have poured blood, sweat, and tears into their businesses. They are stubborn, difficult, and resistant to change. They just can't seem to let go. They control hiring and firing, although that's supposed to be your job.

Confrontation rarely works in this situation, experts say. The best solution for an HR manager is to take the time to understand the boss and to gain his confidence. Then offer new ideas and solutions, but don't expect him to agree with you every time.

"You have to create an area of trust," says Leon Danco, who heads the Center for Family Business, a consulting firm in Cleveland. "Until the HR [manager] is accepted by the owner as his best friend, all the HR [manager] is doing is suggesting ways to spend the owner's money."

The HR manager's job is to help business owners be successful, Hubler adds. When serious problems arise, "you don't confront [CEOs], but you let them know what's going on," he says. This softer, diplomatic style may convince an owner that making a change or disciplining an employee is in the best interest of the company.

"Owners don't want to hear 'no' all the time, but they do want to know about something that could hurt the company," such as a potential legal violation, says Palen, who's worked at two family-owned manufacturers and is now an HR manager at Long Island Savings Bank.

But sometimes a situation is so emotionally charged that the HR manager can't handle it. In that case, it's best to call in an independent consultant "who can take the heat that will be generated no matter what," Liebowitz advises.

WHEN TO QUIT

Sometimes, despite an HR manager's best efforts, it's time to say goodbye to a family-owned business. A clear-cut case would be a request to do something illegal or unethical. In the latter case, the manager must ask how critical the problem is and whether it's really worth quitting over. Consultants advise picking your battles carefully and letting minor irritants go. Leaving is the best option "when you can't hold your head up"—and live with your actions—says Danco. Everyone must draw his or her line in the sand, he says.

Another time to quit is when you can't make a difference. Your advice falls on deaf ears, repeatedly. Your attempts to change policies and treatment of employees go unheeded. In short, the owners aren't committed to HR.

But sometimes it's better to stay and fight. Palen, the HR manager who had to deal with a sexual harassment complaint, did just that.

Although the incident bothered him, he didn't quit. "I couldn't do anything about what happened, but I could make sure it wouldn't happen again," Palen says. In the aftermath, he rewrote and strengthened the company's sexual harassment and other HR policies, which earned him respect.

"I thought I made a difference," he says.

II-6: Ladha and Ladha
(the "Entity")
Appointment of Sabrina Alia Ladha

Abdul Ladha and Brina (Hanifa) Ladha, the senior partners of Ladha and Ladha, formerly Ladha and Jiwa are pleased to announce the appointment of Sabrina Alia Ladha as Daughter. She will report jointly to Mr. & Mrs. Ladha.

As Daughter, Miss Sabrina Ladha's immediate responsibilities will include: immediate implementation of a sleep deprivation program for senior management, restructuring of all known habits, and extensive waste management. She will be located at head Office in Burnaby, British Columbia.

Sabrina assumed her responsibilities October 23, 1999, at 02:28 hours, weighing in at 5 pounds and 1 ounce with placement by Dr. Delisle. Formerly of the The Womb Inc., she brings 9 months of extensive production and development experience to her new position.

Ladha, Ladha and Ladha is family owned and operated with emotional support coming jointly from grandparents Gulnar and Late Akberali Ladha of Burnaby, and Sultan and Sadrudin Jiwa also of Burnaby.

By Order of the Board of Trustees
Abdul Ladha
President

Reprinted from the *Vancouver Sun* (January 1, 2000).

II-7: Managing the Global Workforce: Challenges and Strategies

KAREN ROBERTS, ELLEN ERNST KOSSEK, AND CYNTHIA OZEKI

● ● ● ● ● ● ● ● ● ● ● ● ● ● ● ●

EXECUTIVE OVERVIEW

The globalization of the workplace has become a fact of life for a substantial seg-

ment of U.S. companies, bringing a dramatic expansion of the scope of workforce management and a whole host of new organizational challenges. Using data collected from interviews with international human resource managers in eight large companies, this paper identifies three practical challenges to managing the global workforce and four strategies for meeting those challenges. The three challenges are deployment,

Academy of Management Executive by Karen Roberts, Ellen Ernst Kossek and Cynthia Ozeki. Copyright 1998 by Academy of Management. Reproduced with permission of Academy of Management in the format Textbook via Copyright Clearance Center.

knowledge and innovation dissemination, and talent identification and development. The four strategies are aspatial careers, awareness-building assignments, SWAT teams, and virtual solutions. A diagnostic framework for each challenge is provided that indicates when to use which strategy and basic implementation points are presented.

The line went dead. Steve Prestwick slowly hung up the telephone, wondering what he could possibly say to the executive committee monitoring the Singapore R&D center project. Shortly after being assigned to help staff the facility, he had attended a committee meeting that left him excited about tapping into the potential of the company's large global workforce. "Get the best people from everywhere," said one executive. "Don't just rely on information from headquarters. Try to find out what the people in Europe or Japan might know," chimed in another. And from the CEO, "Let's use this as an opportunity to develop a global mindset in some of our more promising people." The vision sounded great, and Steve's role seemed simple: put together a team with all the experts needed to get the new facility up and running smoothly in its first two years.

Right away Steve began having trouble finding out who had the right skills, and even where the choices seemed obvious, he wasn't getting anywhere. The engineer who refused the assignment over the telephone was the best the company had in her field. She told him that spending two years in Singapore wouldn't really help her career. Plus, it would be hard on her children and impossible for her husband, a veterinarian with a growing practice. Not only did he need a top engineering manager, but Steve also had to find a highly competent corps of technical researchers who knew about the company and its approach to R&D. He also needed technicians who could set up the facility. He thought he would bring in people from the United States to select and set up equip-

ment, then lead a research team of local engineers that the U.S. engineers would train in company practices and technologies. To his chagrin, most of the U.S. technical people he had talked to weren't interested in such an assignment. A European perspective might be useful, but he didn't even have records on possible candidates from the other overseas offices. Steve was on his own, and he had less than a week to come up with a plan.

● ●

WHAT CAN STEVE DO?

Although Steve is fictional, he is facing a composite of real problems for global HR managers. The need to develop a global perspective on human resource management has been part of the managerial landscape for well over a decade, but there is no consensus about what tools to use. Adler and Bartholomew noted that organizational "strategy (the what) . . . is internationalizing faster than implementation (the how) and much faster than the managers and executives themselves (the who)."[1] Steve has been given an assignment that reflects his organization's commitment to manage globally but little guidance about how to meet his goals.

The challenges, strategic approaches, and diagnostic framework we present are based on interviews with senior managers in large corporations with reputations for excellence in international operations. We chose the firms in this study using three criteria. First, we wanted firms experienced in operating internationally that could comment on the evolution of transnational HR management. Second, we wanted variation across industries to assure that we were not uncovering information idiosyncratic to certain types of industries. Third, we selected firms whose recruitment policies indicated a commitment to the strategic use of HRM in global management.

We sent the most senior international HR professional in each firm a letter describing our study and requesting an interview. We asked that they identify any other HR professionals in their organization whom we might also interview. Based on this process, we interviewed 24 professionals at eight firms.[2] The letter listed four questions that we wanted to cover during the interview:

1. What are the key global pressures affecting human resource management practices in your firm currently and for the projected future?
2. What is the level and substance of knowledge about human resource issues that human resource professionals should possess?
3. What are examples of leading edge international human resource practices in your organization?
4. To what extent is international knowledge needed by entry-level professionals in human resource management at your organization?

The questions were deliberately broad, reflecting our exploratory approach. Each interview lasted 1½ to 2 hours. During the interviews, we asked for any additional materials the HR managers thought would be valuable to our study. Once we had begun to analyze our interview information, we used follow-up phone calls both to those we interviewed as well as to other professional contacts to supplement or clarify the data from the interviews.

The information from these interviews was distilled into a two-dimensional framework. One dimension was the set of challenges these executives saw confronting global managers. The second was a set of four prototypical strategies to address these challenges.

THE CHALLENGES

In the course of each interview, we asked these executives to describe their vision of the ideal global internal labor market. Three broad features emerged from their responses:

1. Deployment: easily getting the right skills to where they are needed in the organization regardless of geographical location
2. Knowledge and innovation dissemination: spreading state-of-the-art knowledge and practices throughout the organization regardless of where they originate
3. Identifying and developing talent on a global basis: identifying who has the ability to function effectively in a global organization and developing those abilities

Although skill deployment, information dissemination, and talent identification have long been basic HR challenges, in the global environment, these issues are overlaid with the complexities of distance, language, and cultural differences. Part of the challenge to global management is to reinterpret successful past practices in terms of these complexities.

DEPLOYMENT

All the organizations had a history of operating internationally, but had relied on a headquarters-subsidiary structure and the traditional expatriate model of human resource staffing where U.S. nationals held most positions of authority. This arrangement was adequate in yesterday's international organization because leadership, decision-making authority, and organizational power flowed from the parent site to the foreign subsidiaries. Today, however, new technologies, new markets, innovation, and new talent no longer solely emanate from headquarters but are found cross-nationally, making the expatriate model obsolete.[3] Further, the cost of deploying an expatriate has become excessive. One Merck and Co., Inc., executive estimated that it was three times more expensive to have an expatriate than a local national in any given job.

All of the organizations were developing alternative ways to get the right people to where the work is on an as-needed basis. The key innovation is that organizations are making distinctions between when it is necessary to physically move a person to a particular location and when the person's skills can be delivered through other means. Permanent transfers are no longer seen as the only method for delivering certain services to parts of the organization, giving way to short-term assignments and virtual deployment. Getting managers to stop relying on physical transfers and to think globally about resources is not easy.

Managers will use company-wide job postings when there is a formal job opening, but will not think outside their units, let alone countries, when it comes to finding the expertise to solve a specific problem, such as poor market response to a new consumer product or dysfunctional work relationships that are due to cross-cultural ignorance.

KNOWLEDGE DISSEMINATION AND INNOVATION TRANSFER

The HR executives cited two global information flow blockages: disseminating knowledge from one location to another and spreading innovation. Under earlier expatriate structures, information flowed from the center out. Current global organizations need structures where all units concurrently receive and provide information. Valuable market and production technology information is being produced outside the parent location. One example of the perils of not using local expertise in collecting market information is Marks & Spencer, Britain's largest retailer. The company failed routinely overseas until it found its niche by selling M&S branded clothes in Hong Kong, a former British colony.[4]

The executives at both Dow Chemical Co. and Merck saw this challenge as being one of cross-functional communication, where the greatest opportunities for growth and innovation are at hand-off points between functions. These executives saw hand-off opportunities as easily lost in a global environment, primarily because of the difficulties of establishing cross-cultural trust. As one manager noted:

> As long as diversity is not valued, trust of people from different backgrounds is not developed. There is a tendency to duplicate functions so one does not have to rely on people one does not trust. As a result, rather than having a single global enterprise, many international companies are operating more like a collection of lots of smaller companies.

All of the executives we interviewed noted that language compounded the trust problem. Although English was the business language in all of these organizations, halting speech, misused words, strange grammar, and mispronounced words can subtly undermine the perception that the speaker is competent.

TALENT IDENTIFICATION AND DEVELOPMENT

One executive at General Motors Corp. began his interview with us by noting that:

> . . . the key global issue [for GM] is how to transform the organization internally to become globally competitive. Even for employees who may never go overseas, it is necessary to constantly sensitize everyone to the fact that they are in a global business.

All the executives reiterated this theme in one way or another. But, eventually, each interview came to the reality that not everyone in the organization is going to thrive and prevail in a global environment. Therefore, one of the larger challenges of managing the global labor force is identifying who is most likely to grasp the complexities of the transnational operations and function well in that sort of environment. As one Merck executive described it:

> In the 1940s, transactions were the basis for determining the types of skills managers needed. The [new] challenge to [global human resource management] is to learn to

talk in terms of "stories." Organizations need people who understand the business and who are able to see where the business is going globally and the cultures that need to be bridged, people able to manage conflict and change.

One aspect of this challenge is that the scope of the transnational organization is so large that just collecting information about employees is difficult. Also, all of the executives we interviewed acknowledged that there were cultural biases in the selection process that probably caused talented people to be overlooked. One Amoco Corp. executive gave the example of their operations in Norway. Norwegian work-family values differ from those in the United States, and it is common for men who are senior in their organizations to leave work at 3 P.M. to pick up their children after school. While U.S. norms are beginning to tilt somewhat more toward family in the work balance, leaving early still signals a lack of commitment to the job in most U.S. workplaces.[5] The Amoco executive noted that it was very difficult for U.S. managers to trust that their Norwegian employees would get the job done in a crisis and thus had trouble seeing them as potential global managers. Duplicative staffing was sometimes the result.

A final component of this challenge was motivating employees to want to spend time overseas. Most of the executives considered overseas experience a *sine qua non* for promotion to top jobs in their organizations. But, for a variety of reasons, many talented employees do not want to move overseas. One executive noted that, "talent marries other talent," and that spousal careers are increasingly an obstacle to overseas assignments.[6] Another point, made by both Merck and Amoco, was that the expected growth in their industries was in locations that were not viewed as desirable by employees from developed countries. An Amoco executive noted that in some West African countries where Amoco had opera-

tions, 30 to 35 percent of the population was thought to be HIV positive, dramatically undermining the appeal of those countries to potential expatriates.

· · · · · · · · · · · · · · · · · ·

FOUR STRATEGIES FOR MANAGING THE GLOBAL WORKFORCE

The managers we interviewed described how their organizations had moved away from the traditional expatriate assignment and the new arrangements they were using to meet the three challenges above. Tables 1 through 4 summarize the key points of each of the strategies.

ASPATIAL CAREERS

Aspatial careerists have borderless careers, typically working in multiple countries over the course of their work lives. The chief difference between the aspatial career and the expatriate assignment is that these careers exist in an environment where authority and expertise are no longer thought to reside exclusively at the parent company. Aspatial careerists can come from any part of the globe.

Aspatial careers can take several forms. An employee may live and work overseas with frequent moves; others may have a geographically stationary home base but are required to travel and to have the ability to think about the organization in ways that are spatially neutral. If they relocate, their families go with them.

The aspatial careers model does not overcome the high costs associated with the traditional expatriate model. As a result, only a small percent of most organizations' employees follow aspatial career paths. GM estimates that only about 900 of its employees pursue aspatial careers. Merck has approximately 250 employees on this path out of a workforce of 37,000.[7]

Aspatial careerists are usually managers, not technicians. Over the course of their several moves, they accumulate rich contextual knowledge, also known as tacit or implicit knowledge. Successful aspatial careerists develop an in-depth understanding of global organizations because they have managed across cultures and know how culture affects work.

They have also developed extensive global networks that help them identify and draw on expertise throughout their organizations. These managers' global insights tend to filter through the organization rather than be distributed by means of explicit training or the introduction of new technology. One exception is when companies use aspatial careers to develop technical personnel below the top management level. A plant manager at Dow described cross-national rotation of engineers as part of a strategy for cross-training and to assure comparability of engineering skill level across Dow plants in all countries.

Through long rotations with in-depth experience, aspatial careerists acquire globally applicable skills. One company had a manager who had begun his career as a health care expert in France. He then spent four years in London, three in Tokyo, and three in Switzerland, at each point deepening his health care expertise and expanding his network. He had become a repository of cross-cultural health care information as well as someone who knew the players across these different sites. His gradually accumulated information made him an insightful manager and valuable to the company.

The talent identification potential of aspatial careers is not yet fully realized. Several companies noted that they are beginning to explicitly view their aspatial careerists as a recruiting pool for the highest level of corporate management. The underlying logic is that those who have rotated across different countries have the global perspective needed at the top of the organization. However, none of the companies we interviewed had fully committed to

TABLE 1 Aspatial Careers	
Who	*What*
Globally oriented, highly mobile people, with proven ability and company loyalty	Corps of experts with borderless careers on long-term overseas assignment

How		
Deployment	*Knowledge Dissemination*	*Talent Identification and Development*
Geographically relocate employees with high-level skills and rich cross-cultural perspective	Employees with in-depth global experiences and networks in leadership positions across sites	Rotation as development

Implementation Points

- Encourage company over country culture.
- Assign within culturally homogeneous regions.
- Use pan-region selection meetings.
- Evolve selection criteria that are shared across countries.
- Provide cross-cultural training for families.
- Recognize family life-cycle realities.

reliance on aspatial career experience as an indicator of top management potential. Rather, several admitted that their companies still had difficulties with recognizing the value added by overseas experience when reintegrating those who have been overseas into home country operations.

AWARENESS-BUILDING ASSIGNMENTS

The primary purpose of awareness-building assignments is to develop cross-country sensitivity in high-potential employees in a short time. These assignments last anywhere from three months to one year. Families are not expected to relocate, so that depending on assignment length, regular home visits might be part of this strategy. Usually this assignment is made early in one's career and typically an employee will only have one such assignment.[8]

At the end of an awareness-building assignment, a high-potential employee is expected to have a broadened cultural perspective and an appreciation of the diversity in the organization. One of the Dow executives summarized the purpose of these assignments:

Overseas assignments are no longer used just to get the "overseas stamp." ... We may transfer them to acquire knowledge available only overseas, or perhaps as a way to export a leading-edge practice to an overseas location. Often, though, an overseas assignment is not specifically a technical transfer—we are going more for [developing an employee with an] "open mind."

GM also incorporates a training component in the form of short-term cross-function transfers and cross-plant training. This can be a mechanism for innovation dissemination. GM has found that rotated employees must demonstrate technical competence to be accepted at the overseas site. As one GM executive described it:

If the need is to cultivate openness and develop cross-cultural awareness, it has to be done early in one's career. However, the reality is that those who go overseas first have to demonstrate technical competence to be accepted in a different location, and this is more necessary than cultural awareness.

Several firms use these assignments to aculturate local nationals who after the rotation will spend most of their careers in their home countries. These assignments

TABLE 2   Awareness-Building Assignments

Who	What
High-potential employees early in their careers	3- to 12-month assignments

How		
Deployment	Knowledge Dissemination	Talent Identification and Development
Technically competent, high-potential employees	Cross-cultural immersion to produce global perspective	• Screening for ability to function out of own culture • Develop globally aware future performers

Implementation Points
• Use to bridge geofunctional disconnects. • Rotate employees with demonstrable competence. • Manage the adjustment cycle. • Use to develop local nationals.

serve as screens for global awareness potential. Awareness-building assignments are not long enough to develop in-depth cultural knowledge. However, an employee who can shed provincialism and learn that value can be added from any location in the company is one who is likely to function effectively in the global organization.

SWAT TEAMS

SWAT teams are highly mobile teams of experts, deployed on a short-term basis, to troubleshoot, solve a very specific problem, or complete a clearly defined project. (The name derives from the special weapons and tactics units used by many police departments.) SWAT teams play a role like that of the technical troubleshooter, an individual sent to a foreign location to analyze and solve a particular operational problem.[9]

SWAT teams comprise nomadic experts who are identified internationally and deployed as internal consultants on an as-needed basis. As a Dow executive described the objective of this approach, the company does not "expect to move people across areas but does want to leverage resources across our different businesses." At GM, the SWAT team takes the form of an expert network, internal consultants deployed throughout the organization. The actual amount of time spent overseas varies with the purpose or project but in general is under three months.

The primary strength of this approach is that it permits the organization to cultivate highly specialized knowledge and expertise on a limited basis, and to apply that expertise wherever it is needed within the organization. One difference between SWAT teams and awareness-building assignments is that there is no explicit developmental component to the SWAT team model other than to complete whatever project is defined. Development of cross-cultural awareness on the part of SWAT team members may be a by-product of the job, but it is not its intention.

Once a SWAT team has been assembled, it can be redeployed each time a situation requiring its skillset emerges. Frequent opportunities to apply their skills in different settings can add significantly to the existing skill accumulation of team members, providing the developmental component to the SWAT team strategy.

VIRTUAL SOLUTIONS

Virtual solutions are a collection of practices that exploit the rapidly evolving electronic communication technologies. These

TABLE 3 SWAT Teams		
Who		*What*
Technical specialists		Short-term, project-length assignments
	How	
Deployment	*Knowledge Dissemination*	*Talent Identification and Development*
Specialized skills on an as-needed basis	Transfer of technical processes and systems	Specialized skills honed through varied and frequent applications
	Implementation Points	

- Best SWAT team member has single contributor mindset.
- Use to spread acultural innovation.
- Good at smaller locations or at start-up.
- Recognize clear limitations.

include use of all forms of the Internet and intranets, videoconferencing, electronic expert systems, and electronic databases coupled with user-friendly front-end systems. The chief advantages to this strategy are the low cost of communication and the uncoupling of real time from virtual time. Awareness-building and virtual solutions are the strategies with which most of the firms we interviewed had had the least experience, but also were the approaches they saw as having the most potential for managing and developing the global workforce.

Internet and intranets, including E-mail, are the most democratic form of overseas deployment, allowing communication among employees regardless of organizational level. Videoconferencing has a similar advantage; however, videoconferencing facilities are a scarce resource compared with E-mail in most organizations. Both Dow and Merck managers said that their videoconferencing rooms were in constant use.

Virtual international teams design software at IBM Corp. Communication through intranets allows for 24-hour product devel-

opment. One team includes software developers from the United States, several former Soviet Union states, and India. The work is usually initiated in the United States. At the end of the day, the U.S. team transmits its files via the intranet to the Soviet team, which works on the project until the end of the workday. The Soviet team then sends its work on to the Indian team whose workday ends at the start of business for the U.S. team, which picks up the files and continues the production cycle.

A more sophisticated virtual deployment tool is the use of virtual reality. NASA uses virtual reality to train international teams of astronauts.[10] These teams need to perform complex tasks requiring lengthy training. Actually convening these teams of astronauts from different countries at a single geographical location for months at a time is prohibitively expensive and disrupts family life. A virtual simulation of a repair of the Hubble telescope was constructed for training purposes and allowed team members to simulate the repair as though in the same room. One Russian and one U.S. member virtually shook hands at the end of

TABLE 4 Virtual Solutions		
Who	**What**	
Nonrotating employees who need overseas connections	Electronic communications	
How		
Deployment	**Knowledge Dissemination**	**Talent Identification and Development**
Videoconferencing and E-mail allow virtual deployment.	Web pages, bulletin boards, intranets, distance learning, and interactive training disperse information across locations.	GHRIS, electronic job posting, video, and virtual interviews identify and screen for assignments.
Implementation Points		

- Encourage virtual friendships.
- Couple with cross-culture awareness training.
- GHRIS works best with standardized information.
- GHRIS trade-off between standardized information and universal access.
- Use global job posting for clearly defined jobs.
- Don't expect instant results.

the repair exercise. However, this simulation took months to develop. While virtual reality is almost as good as being there, it is also almost as expensive.

All the companies have web pages on the Internet with company background and product information, as well as public information about new developments. E-mail is in common use and electronic bulletin boards to solve technical problems were becoming more common. At the time of our interviews, comparable intranet systems with proprietary information were in development. This sort of communication is one mechanism to break down some of the barriers to information flow erected by technical chauvinism. Reiterating the theme of cross-cultural distrust, one GM executive noted that "technically skilled people in one country feel their training and skills are superior [to those of employees from other countries] and they have little to learn from their international counterparts." He noted this was a substantial problem in motivating technical employees to rotate overseas and that use of E-mail and electronic bulletin boards is expected to ameliorate this problem as technical solutions are offered cross-nationally and recognized as valid.

One solution not yet widely implemented is distance learning. Ford Motor Co. uses this commonly to continuously update the skills of its engineers, videotaping classes that employees can play individually or as a group. The students can then hold discussion groups and interact with the instructor who holds electronic office hours at a predetermined time. Another version is a highly interactive broadcast class where students can interact with the instructor across networks that permit student questions and discussion, even pop quizzes. However, distance learning is still in its infancy and was not cited as a commonly used tool.

All the firms had Global Human Resource Information Systems (GHRIS),

which allowed for global job posting. The companies stressed that talent identification below the highest level on a global basis was key to the success of the company. Amoco Corp., Dow, and Merck used their GHRIS to store career data about their employees useful for selection and, on a more limited basis, for job posting. Amoco has implemented a worldwide job posting system that allows all employees to use electronic systems to learn about and apply for jobs.[11]

DIAGNOSING THE CHALLENGES

We developed a diagnostic framework for evaluating each of the challenges and deciding among the four strategies.

DIAGNOSING THE DEPLOYMENT CHALLENGE

The challenge of global deployment is getting the needed skills from one part of the organization to another inexpensively. Not all of the tools associated with each of the strategic solutions were equally effective in all situations. There are two components to deciding among the deployment strategies: contact time required and extent to which the skills can be applied out of cultural context.

If the need is for ongoing on-site leadership, in-depth cultural understanding, or skills that can only be successfully applied if culturally embedded, use aspatial careers. To provide short-term training or skills application that requires cultural sensitivity, use awareness-building assignments. SWAT teams offer on-site technical skills, knowledge of production process, operations, and systems that need to be implemented, with little cultural content. Virtual solutions provide frequent, brief iterative interactions, with only a little cultural component to the interaction, or a wide sweep of the organization to search for or communicate technical details or information.

DIAGNOSING THE KNOWLEDGE AND INNOVATION DISSEMINATION CHALLENGE

The information organizations need to stay competitive ranges from highly technical to informally communicated background information. The effectiveness of each of the four strategies depends on the type of knowledge or innovation being disseminated. Choosing among the four strategies depends on the technical complexity of the information that is to be shared and the extent to which it must be culturally embedded. If the knowledge or innovations to be disseminated can be successfully shared only when communicated in a cultural context, use aspatial careers. Awareness-building assignments succeed when the knowledge is primarily cultural awareness and cross-cultural sensitivity training. If the knowledge is defined technology or practices with minimal cultural content, use SWAT teams. If the knowledge requires ongoing and frequent information exchanges among dispersed employees, use virtual solutions.

DIAGNOSING TALENT IDENTIFICATION AND DEVELOPMENT CHALLENGES

Development of a global mindset is essential to operating globally. Executives are looking for a similar set of characteristics among their global managers.[12] Merck looks for people who have a broad perspective and can intelligently apply practical leadership skills to guide change in the organization. Baxter International looks for "patience, flexibility, communication skills, intellectual curiosity about the rest of the world." GM looks for a skillset that includes, "communication skills, the ability to value diversity, and the ability to be objective."

Cultural training notwithstanding, a manager from Merck noted the difficulty of finding people with this skillset:

> Merck uses two-thirds selection and one-third development . . . [We rely more on selection than development in our selection criteria because] it is difficult to impart needed skills, and people don't get that much out of classroom training—they are more likely to remember what they had for dinner than what went on in the training session. . . . We are looking for people with curiosity and a mix of skills.

This suggests that organizations should select well, then develop. Companies that need to identify and develop leaders with in-depth cultural knowledge and proven cross-cultural abilities and are willing to spend time and money to have those people, should use aspatial careers. To identify and develop high-potential performers with an understanding that they are functioning in a global organization and an appreciation of cultural diversity, companies should use awareness-building assignments. SWAT teams provide mobile and technically competent specialists whose skills tend to be needed on a short-term basis. Virtual solutions identify employees using shared selection criteria to fill vacancies with well-understood job requirements.

● ● ● ● ● ● ● ● ● ● ● ● ●

IMPLEMENTING THE STRATEGIES

Following are examples of how companies implemented each of the strategies, including some of the obstacles they have encountered.

IMPLEMENTING THE ASPATIAL CAREER STRATEGY

All the companies encourage the development of a culture of company over country. Baxter has deployed leadership throughout the organization regardless of national origin: the VP for the European region is of U.S. origin located in Germany; the VP for the Diagnostics division is an Italian located in Switzerland; the VP of Cardiovascular is Irish and located in France; the Hospital group is led by a French person in Belgium. This is not just a happy accident but the result of an explicit strategy on Baxter's part to develop a company-over-country identity, where the managers focus on the competitive strategies of the entire company, not only for the region in which they reside. Baxter has eliminated country-based organization and reorganized by product group or business function. Also, the position of country general manager has been eliminated to encourage a business-over-country orientation.

These geographically fluid careers are more successful if rotations occur within culturally homogeneous regions. Both Baxter and GM have divided their global operations into regions, and Baxter is deliberate about rotating employees within rather than across regions as much as possible. This policy is consistent with results from a study of Singaporean managers showing that the cultural similarity between origin and destination locations positively affected employee and spouse willingness to relocate.[13] GM also uses a regional basis for determining benefit plans, distinguishing between intracontinental (policies reflecting continent-wide norms) and intercontinental policies (policies applied at GM sites worldwide). This distinction simplifies within-region rotations.

Schlumberger uses a "borderlands career track" version of aspatial careers in which rotating employees move often across adjoining borders. The cultural homogeneity of border areas allows the company to move people quickly with minimal adjustment.[14]

One identification mechanism used by several companies is the pan-regional meet-

ing. This meeting takes place regularly, three to four times a year, where higher- (but not just the highest-) level managers and sometimes technical people within a geographical region meet to exchange information and network. The meetings last several days to a week and are used to showcase potential aspatial careerists. HR people are included and charged with identifying potential talent for global reassignment. Dow holds four annual meetings, one in each region, where managers are asked to recommend, review, and present the top 1.5 percent of the employees in terms of high management potential. Because it is important for managers to present very talented people, these annual meetings are high-pressure events. These meetings are used also to identify candidates for awareness-building assignments.

An informal outcome from Dow's meetings is the evolution of a shared understanding of what is meant by global competencies. This evolves out of formal identification and presentation of high-potential talent at the pan-regional meetings. Each meeting serves as an iteration in the development of global selection criteria. This evolving understanding of the managerial traits required by the global organization is used to identify candidates for both aspatial careers and awareness-building assignments.

A key component to motivating talented employees to go overseas, even for a short time, is their belief that the organization values overseas experience. This will be especially true for aspatial careerists, but also true to a lesser extent for awareness-building assignments and SWAT team employees. Most organizations send a mixed message to employees about the value of overseas experience.[15]

There is often a sharp decline in authority, responsibility, and autonomy for the employee returning to the parent company. Most aspatial careerists are at or near the top of the overseas organization and in many cases behave like CEOs. Their jobs at the parent site are of necessity of lower status. The more hierarchical an organization, the more difficult this problem will be. Structuring jobs of returning aspatial employees to allow sufficient autonomy and identifying explicit ways to fully utilize their overseas expertise is important. GM does this by using returned overseas employees in the first-round selection process for aspatial careers and awareness-building assignment candidates.

The firms varied in how they valued overseas experience. At one firm it was impossible to receive more than 1000 Hay points (from the Hay Group's method of evaluating jobs based on technical skills, problem-solving, and accountability) without an international experience, so employees were willing to relocate to avoid that career ceiling. At another extreme, one executive candidly described his organization as having a top management that stressed overseas experience; below top management, however, was a headquarter-centered culture, where overseas experience was viewed as inferior.

GM sets up home-based mentor relationships between each overseas employee and what they call a repatriation facilitator. This provides a support system for the overseas employee but also helps home-based employees value what the overseas employee can contribute upon return. GM also uses home leave where rotated employees present their overseas projects and show how they will contribute to home operations. GM has found that repatriated employees are more successful when brought back into a unit where the manager has had some overseas experience.

Recognizing family needs is key to successful aspatial career deployment. According to numerous studies, family circumstances are the leading cause of overseas assignment failures.[16] Spousal careers and child care are important family considerations and cited in one survey as the top family reasons to refuse an overseas assignment.[17] Cultural awareness training for family members was just beginning at several of the companies we studied and held promise for smoothing family transitions. GM uses relocation facilitators and assigns mentor families to aspatial career families early in their assignments. Job-seeking assistance and/or partial remuneration for loss of job income for spouses were provided by most of the companies we studied, but these were considered feasible only if the family was staying overseas at least two years.

It is also important to recognize that all aspatial careerists may not stay aspatial forever. Although some individuals will spend their entire careers outside of their native countries, most eventually return to the parent site. One driver of this decision is family life-cycle change, which pushes an employee to move the family back home. For example, executives wanting their children to go to U.S. high schools so they can get into U.S. colleges was a factor noted by GM.

IMPLEMENTING THE AWARENESS-BUILDING ASSIGNMENT STRATEGY

The missed opportunities at hand-off points described earlier by a Merck executive are often the result of geofunctional disconnects. These are points where functional and geographical boundaries are coterminous, compounding cross-functional cooperation problems. Awareness-building assignments can effectively bridge these gaps when they are used to collect consumer market information. Amoco uses awareness-building assignments to develop product preference sensitivity in employees who design products used or sold overseas. Two examples of the need to develop intimate knowledge of local markets are Proctor & Gamble's faulty start selling all-temperature detergents to

Japanese housewives who wash clothes only in cold water and GM's attempt to sell two-door trucks to Chinese with a strong preference for four-door vehicles.[18] Baxter learned this lesson after medical equipment intended for Japan was designed and sized using U.S. patients as the standard. The firm now has a cross-cultural training program, often in the form of awareness-building assignments, for engineers who design products for global markets.

Awareness-building assignments blur the traditional distinction between learning and contributing jobs. Most of the executives we interviewed noted that these assignments should be used judiciously. The awareness-building benefit will be lost if the rotated employee is perceived as having nothing to offer the overseas site. The challenge is to select people early enough in their careers that the assignments serve as screens for future potential but not so early that they have few skills to offer.

Merck gives awareness-building assignments to more mature employees, believing that generating a global mindset is more a selection than a developmental issue, and that mature workers can develop a global awareness if the predisposition is there. Both Merck and Baxter note, however, that language ability limits the candidate pool. At Merck, this has meant that more overseas employees are rotated for awareness-building assignments in the United States than the other way around.

Awareness-building assignments must avoid the negative effects of what is termed the "intercultural adjustment cycle."[19] A Dow executive described a cycle on long-term overseas assignments. During the first three months, employees are euphoric about the new country, soak up the culture, and enjoy the superficial differences between the overseas post and the home country. Because most rotated employees are top performers in their home country, however, by the third month they become discour-

aged by the drop in their productivity and by their lack of linguistic or cultural fluency. During the next three to six months, relocated employees and their families begin to miss their home countries and find fault with the overseas sites. At about nine months, the employees regain the confidence they had before being sent overseas and function as competent members of the overseas society.

Most aspatial careerists will pass through the cycle to regain their sense of competence, but an awareness-building assignment may not last through the entire adjustment cycle. An assignment that ends during the euphoric period will leave the employee with a superficial understanding of the overseas location. An assignment ending during the trough of the cycle may leave the employee soured about overseas experiences and negative about the global scope of the organization. Rather than trying to avoid the adjustment cycle, organizations should use training to prepare employees for it. The virtue of the adjustment cycle is that its low point prompts individuals to reconceptualize their mental frames and begin to develop in-depth understanding of the new cultures.

Since a solution to the problem of motivating aspatials to go to unattractive locations is to develop indigenous talent, Amoco, Baxter, and Merck give awareness-building assignments to local nationals. Rotations to headquarters familiarize them with the company mission and culture, while rotations to various worldwide production locations familiarize them with operations. Local nationals must be given challenging assignments in the United States or the rotation may be demotivating.

IMPLEMENTING THE SWAT TEAM STRATEGY

Two factors seemed to help optimize the staffing of SWAT teams. First, despite the likelihood that work will be done on a team basis, individual contributor employees with a technical orientation are the best candidates. Second, because technical challenges are what motivates them, mechanisms such as outside training are needed to keep SWAT team members on the leading edge.

SWAT teams are best used to export clearly defined technologies or practices. While some training may have to take place at the overseas site to allow those employees to become users, knowledge or innovations conveyed by a SWAT team do not usually have a developmental or cross-cultural component. The SWAT team approach is most easily applied in a manufacturing setting where production processes are less dependent on cultural idiosyncrasies. For example, GM uses what they refer to as internal consulting teams to collect information about best manufacturing processes and to disseminate them to other plants worldwide.

In some cases, SWAT assignments are used at sites that are too small to have a sustained need for certain skills, especially in developing countries. In Pakistan, for example, where the human resource relations function is a part-time job, a traveling unit of negotiators travels from site to site at contract negotiation time, completes the negotiations, secures a contract, and leaves. Both GM and Merck use teams of internal experts and external consultants to do global benefit planning. These teams immerse themselves in local government regulations and set up the benefit plan for each site.

SWAT team assignments can be useful in setting up new operations where start-up skills are needed for a brief period. Amoco uses SWAT teams when it is deciding whether to permanently locate in a country. Because location usually depends on finding oil and securing drilling rights, Amoco may be in a country for a relatively long time before withdrawing.[20] Using SWAT teams during start-ups also requires more cultural-awareness training than the conventional SWAT team assignment.

SWAT teams have their very clear limitations, tending to draw on the manufacturing model to conceptualize deployment and information dissemination challenges, and applying that model to nonproduction situations. The pure SWAT team approach will be effective only when interpersonal relationships and cultural understanding are of minimal importance to the transfer of knowledge or innovation. The development of interpersonal relationships and cultural awareness is time consuming and the benefits are often intangible, but in many cases these are necessary prerequisites for information exchange and effective working relationships. If these are needed, the SWAT team strategy will fail.

IMPLEMENTING THE VIRTUAL SOLUTIONS STRATEGY

The virtual solutions model allows cross-national relationships to form below the level of top management. Virtual communications that are not necessarily task-oriented but that foster interpersonal exchanges enable task information to flow more smoothly. In addition, opportunities for innovation can occur at electronic hand-off points if information about production methods, problems, and solutions is shared informally.

In most cases, electronic communication is not yet a perfect substitute for direct contact. Small misunderstandings can become full-blown E-mail wars because of the absence of such communication cues as tone of voice and facial expression.

Cultural differences and differing abilities in the language of the exchange increase the likelihood of misunderstanding. Thus, virtual deployment is best used in conjunction with some other form of cultural awareness building. Recognizing this, one Dow executive encourages modest expectations for E-mail initially—to develop in employees "a different mentality, to get them to agree that there is more than one way to skin a cat."[21]

Both Dow and Baxter use employee questionnaires designed by international teams to collect information about operations, practices, and values across the firm to build cross-cultural data bases. These data bases can be retrieved by employees throughout the organization and can supplement other cultural training for virtual solution users. The Baxter survey is customized to fit local conditions and uses local terminology appropriate to each culture. The Dow instrument measures climate as well as management practices.

All of the companies had a Human Resource Information System (HRIS) in place, but varied in the degree to which it could be characterized as a global system. Merck has developed templates that vary with the employee's level in the organization. Employees lower in the organization are less likely to be relocated globally and thus fewer data are required about them for the GHRIS. Approximately one hundred pieces of data are entered into the GHRIS for lower-level employees, compared with approximately four hundred entries for higher-level employees.

Storing benefit information continues to be a GHRIS challenge. Dow has developed regional benefit models and determined that approximately 80 percent of the data needed for any given employee is standard across nations. The remaining nonstandard 20 percent is country-specific. However, some of this nonstandard information can be collapsed into a smaller number of models, each with its own data template. One example, cited by Dow, is that while there is no worldwide set of educational certifications, most countries' educational systems can be classified into one of a few models. Decisions about which information can be standardized globally and which need to reflect local custom were made after a series of global stakeholder meetings.

One Dow executive commented that to be truly valuable, a GHRIS must be a dynamic tool, evolving over time. He also said that this is easy to say, but something of a headache to implement. One significant gap between the ideal and the reality of a GHRIS is the ability to combine universal access with standardized information. Amoco uses a kiosk system to allow employees to enter information about themselves but has found that not all employees have the ability to do this. Dow has faced the same challenge and has decided to sacrifice universal access for completeness of standardized information.

Global job posting works best for those jobs with relatively well-understood skill requirements. The more subtle or idiosyncratic the skill requirements, the more difficult the job description is to translate globally. As noted earlier, employees below a certain level are not likely to rotate internationally, so clarity about skill requirements also helps screen out certain types of postings for which the company reasonably wants to recruit only locally.

There are technological hurdles to implementing the virtual solutions model, and one should not expect instant results. Even when using established technologies like video broadcasting, learning will take on new forms and periods of adjustment will be required.

WHAT CAN STEVE DO?

There is no instant solution to Steve's problem. The people he wants with the skills he needs are not going to convene in Singapore to work together for two years. But, by employing a combination of strategies, Steve can accomplish his goal. He can:

- Select a SWAT team to come in and set up the equipment, a clearly defined task that can be accomplished in a short time with minimal interpersonal contact.

Technical people from Tokyo, just a few hours away by plane, could fly in three or four times to set up the equipment and conduct inspections once the facility is running.

- Virtually connect the talented engineer with the Singapore team using E-mail, the phone, and videoconferencing, combining this with a short-term awareness-building assignment to foster personal relationships with the technical team and build cross-cultural understanding.

- Ask European, Asian, and South American regional heads to set up regular regional talent identification meetings to nominate potential people for both aspatial career and awareness-building assignments at their next regional conference. The list can be used to select people to conduct initial training sessions and handle early trouble-shooting in Singapore as well as a few who may be suited for a longer-term assignment to the new facility.

- Post jobs on an internal bulletin board or intranet web site with full details about the skills required, so that interested and qualified people can also volunteer for Singapore assignments.

- Set up a web page for the site and E-mail technically capable people throughout the organization to stay tuned for brainstorming sessions during the R&D process. Good ideas will win prizes.

- Start scouting for a local national to head up the R&D center, then begin the development with an awareness assignment to headquarters to teach about company culture.

This version of using the four strategies to manage a cross-national workforce differs from the traditional staffing mindset with which Steve initially approached the problem. These strategies allow firms operating on a global basis to make the best use of their widely dispersed internal resources and find innovative solutions to their HR problems.

Notes

1. Adler, N. and Bartholomew, S. 1992. "Managing Globally Competent People," *Academy of Management Executive,* 6(3), 52.
2. The companies included Amoco, Baxter, Dow (interviews at both U.S. and Canadian locations), General Motors, IBM, Merck, and Wyeth-Ayerst. Some information about distance learning as a knowledge dissemination–innovation transfer tool was also collected from Ford Motor Co.
3. See Taylor, S., Beechler, S., and Napier, N. 1996. "Toward an Integrative Model of Strategic International Human Resource Management," *Academy of Management Review,* 21(4), 959–85 for a description of the information flows in a globally integrated organization.
4. *Fortune.* 1995. "Retailers Go Global." February 20, 102–108.
5. *Fortune.* 1997. "Is Your Family Wrecking Your Career (And Vice Versa)?" March 3, 70–90.
6. This is consistent with the findings of a study by Brett, Stroh & Reilly of *Fortune* 500 company managers who were willing to relocate. They found that spouse willingness to move was the most significant factor in an employee's willingness to move. See Brett, J., Stroh, L., and Reilly, A. 1993. "Pulling Up Roots in the 1990s: Who's Willing to Relocate?" *Journal of Organizational Behavior,* 14(1), 49–60.
7. This total workforce number excludes employees of recent acquisitions by Merck.
8. Use of these assignments as a tool is still evolving and this aspect could easily change.
9. Schuler, R., Fulkerson, J., and Dowling, P. 1991. "Strategic Performance Measurement and Management in Multinational Corporations," *Human Resource Management,* 30(3), 365–92.
10. Loftin, R. B. 1996. "Hands Across the Atlantic," *Virtual Reality Special Report,* 3(2), 39–41.
11. See Kossek, E. E. 1993. "Globalization: What Every Human Resource Professional Should Know—Examples from Amoco Production Company," presented at the National Research Symposium of the Human Resource Planning Society, June.

12. Their list corresponds closely to that described in Tung, R. 1993. "Managing National and Intranational Diversity," *Human Resource Management,* 32(4), 461–77.

13. Ayree, S., Chay, Y. W., and Chew, J. 1996. "An Investigation of the Willingness of Managerial Employees to Accept an Expatriate Assignment," *Journal of Organizational Behavior,* 17(3), 267–83.

14. This strategy may not be for every organization, at least as it is implemented by Schlumberger. These paths require a move every three years. At the time of the move, employees are permitted to move only up to 2000 pounds of personal effects and are expected to take the next plane out once a new assignment has been made. As one employee commented, "They treat their people like cattle." See Kossek, E. E., cited above.

15. See Oddou, G. and Mendenhall, M. 1991. "Succession Planning for the 21st Century," *Business Horizons,* 34(1), 26–34 for a brief description of this problem.

16. See Arthur, W. and Bennett, W. 1995. "The International Assignee: The Relative Importance of Factors Perceived to Contribute to Success," *Personnel Psychology,* 48, 99–115, and Tung, R. 1981. "Selection and Training of Personnel for Overseas Assignments," *Columbia Journal of World Business,* Spring, 68–78.

17. Greenfield, C. 1996. *Work/Family Game.* Boston: Towers Perin.

18. An alternative way of expressing this is that companies producing overseas to sell overseas need to identify sources of customer value. See Bartness, A. and Cerny, K. 1991. "Building Competitive Advantage through a Global Network of Capabilities," *California Management Review,* 35(2), 78–103, for a full discussion of the identification process.

19. Grove, C. L. and Torbiorn, I. 1985. "A New Conceptualization of Intercultural Adjustment and the Goals of Training," *International Journal of Intercultural Relations,* 9(16), 205–33.

20. See Kossek, E. E. cited above.

21. After saying this, he noted that "more than one way to skin a cat" was precisely the type of phrase that needed to be eliminated from international communications.

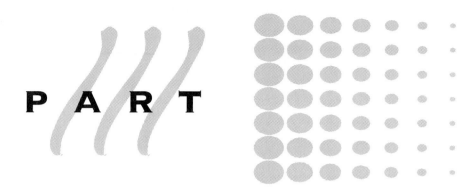

PART III

CREATING A PRODUCTIVE WORK ENVIRONMENT

Creating a productive work environment—and maintaining it—is one of the most difficult tasks confronting managers. The record shows both instances where success has been achieved and maintained and those where attempts to create such an environment have failed. Difficult as they are to build, productive relationships between management and employees are fragile and easily destroyed by miscalculations; cases chronicle how long it can take, months and even years, to repair the damage. The selections in this part recount a variety of activities—some successful and others less so—to build and maintain a culture that enhances productivity.

Fairness is essential to a productive work environment. David E. Bowen, Stephen W. Gilliland, and Roger Folger articulate the bottom-line value of equitable employee treatment in "HRM and Service Fairness: How Being Fair with Employees Spills Over to Customers." Management reluctance to jeopardize positive employee relations helps explain "Why Wages Do Not Fall in Recessions" in *The Economist's* review of Truman Bewley's book of the same name. Robert W. Thompson emphasizes the importance of respect for individuals in efforts to prevent workplace violence ("Workplace Violence Experts See Lessons from Littleton"). Leadership is particularly important to productive work environments. Based on her experience in academic medicine, Frances Conley (in an excerpt from her book *Walking Out on the Boys*) reminds us of the importance of leaders and the methods by which they are selected.

Employee interests are often distinctly different from those of management. For example, employee interests in economic security may conflict with management concern for low cost and workforce flexibility. Unless employee voice is specifically protected, management interests are likely to dominate those of workers. Unions and collective bargaining provide one mechanism to help ensure employee voice. Unfortunately, the North American system of union-management relations evolved into an adversarial process with little trust between labor and management (see excerpts from Sanford Jacoby's Employing Bureaucracy and Modern Manors included in Part I).

With the unionized portion of the labor force steadily shrinking, there are some who believe that unions have outlived their usefulness. We do not share that view. Protecting interests of the individual against potentially unfair, exploitive, and discriminatory actions by employers is necessary. Unions, together with the law and "enlightened" human resource management, are among the few institutions that facilitate such protection. However, new and more proactive methods of employment relations are important if American business is to compete successfully in the rapidly changing global business environment of the twenty-first century. Noting that interest in union representation is increasing but union membership is not, Aaron Bernstein argues that "All's Not Fair in Labor Wars." The playing field is tilted toward management's interests. To increase membership, organized labor has looked beyond their traditional base and sought to organize new groups, some of which have previously been resistant to organizing. Katherine S. Mangan describes efforts to organize a nontraditional group in "Academic Medicine Becomes a Target for Labor Organizing."

Dealing with problems that arise between employees and employers in the course of employment is important to maintaining a productive work environment. Collective bargaining agreements usually include grievance procedures to resolve problems union employees encounter during the life of the contract. Increasingly, grievance procedures have extended beyond the unionized sector. Ashlea Ebeling's "Better Safe Than Sorry" indicates increased scrutiny of such procedures and provides advice on their design. David I. Levine argues that "Reinventing Workplace Regulation" could facilitate employee-management relationships in union and nonunion contexts as well as enhance efficient compliance with law.

III-1: HRM and Service Fairness
How Being Fair with Employees Spills Over to Customers

DAVID E. BOWEN, STEPHEN W. GILLILAND, AND ROBERT FOLGER

For 20 years, Charlie, a baggage handler, was an asset to his airline. Callous rule changes and harsh supervisory treatment, however, led him to covertly retaliate. For months, he carefully evened the score by tearing off a few baggage tags each shift. Each missing tag caused the airline both service headaches and lost dollars.

Denise, a Midwestern lawyer, was new to town. She purchased new shoes from an upscale department store, but a seam split immediately. She was pleasantly surprised by the gracious return policy. The salesperson said it wasn't fair that she had to take time from her schedule to return the shoes. The salesperson also gave her a 25% discount coupon for her next purchase. Denise has been a loyal customer ever since, telling this story of quality service many times and evening the score in her own way.

—"THE FAIRNESS FACTOR"
FROM *QUALITY PROGRESS*,
JUNE 1994

We all want to be treated fairly, both as employees and customers. Aristotle, long ago, suggested that humans possess a need for justice. "Man, when perfected," he wrote, "is the best of animals, but when separated from law and justice he is the worst of all."

Fairness issues pervade organizational life in many ways; the challenge is managing to manage fairly. Fairness in the corporate world involves at least these three themes:

- Fair treatment of employees in decisions surrounding their selection, performance appraisal, and rewards.

Reprinted from *Organizational Dynamics* (Winter 1999): 7–23.

- Fair treatment of customers in both service delivery and service recovery.
- How fair treatment of employees can lead to fair treatment of customers.

Although the issue of fairness applies to most organizations, service organizations must be particularly concerned because of the impact on customers. Service businesses like banks, hotels, and doctors' offices are characterized by frequent employee-customer encounters known as "Moments of Truth." Customers are often physically present at the service facility itself, gaining first-hand exposure to the individuals responsible for the outcomes they receive and getting a close look at the processes and procedures leading to these outcomes. There are, then, many Moments of Truth in which customers gather evidence useful for judging whether they have been fairly treated.

Fairness is especially exposed in service industries because of a specific characteristic of this industry: "The *intangibility* of services heightens customers' sensitivity to fairness issues," as Leonard Berry, Parsu Parasuraman, and Valerie Zeithanel note in their article "Improved Service Quality in America: Lessons Learned" (*Academy of Management Executive*). Because services are performances rather than objects, they are difficult for customers to evaluate prior to purchase. Customers cannot try on services for fit and feel; there are no tires to kick like when buying an automobile. Customers usually must buy the service to actually experience it. Thus, they must trust a service company to deliver on its promises and conduct itself honorably.

And because many service businesses are labor-intensive, employees are the principal focus for customers as they perceive fairness. The critical role of employees to service delivery highlights the importance of treating *them* fairly. It is therefore essential to determine what factors make employees feel that their firm's staffing, performance appraisal, and reward decisions are fair. In other words, what does "fair HR" look like to employees?

Research done in a variety of service firms, such as banks, car rental agencies, and department stores, shows that employee satisfaction correlates significantly with customer satisfaction. It appears that a service firm's HR practices not only affect employees but also have a "spillover effect" on to customers.

We believe that, in service firms, if employees are treated fairly, they will, in turn, treat their customers more fairly. Fairness issues arise as a reflection of three different types of justice (distributive, procedural, and interactional) and corresponding "justice principles."

FAIRNESS: THE EMPLOYEE VIEW OF HRM PRACTICES

Employees expect human resource decisions to be made fairly and they judge the fairness of an organization by HR decisions in staffing, performance appraisal, and reward systems. Employees judge the fairness of their performance appraisal ratings, the rewards tied to those ratings, the consistency and appropriateness of the appraisal process, and the explanations and feedback that accompany the communication of performance ratings. In particular, employees make judgments in answer to question like "Was the selection procedure a fair test of whether or not I could fulfill the requirements of the job?" and "Am I paid fairly for what I feel I contribute to this organiza-

tion?" Their sense of fairness is offended by evidence of old-boy networking or pay inequality.

Perceived fairness is also one of the only ways that employees can evaluate HRM practices. Although HRM practices are often guided by technical, financial, legal, and strategic concerns, most employees do not have the information or expertise to evaluate practices from these perspectives. Employees evaluate HRM practices from the users' perspective that is largely driven by desires for fair and equitable treatment.

THE CONSEQUENCES OF "FAIR" HRM

Considerable evidence shows a strong correlation between employee perceptions of HRM fairness and employee acceptance of and satisfaction with HRM decisions. For example, managerial and nonmanagerial government employees were more likely to accept their performance appraisals, even negative evaluations, when the performance evaluation process was seen as fair; bank employees were more likely to be satisfied with their pay level and with their job in general when they perceived their rewards and performance evaluations to be fair.

Fair treatment of employees can also foster employee commitment to the organization. For example, a medium-sized government agency introduced a new performance appraisal system designed to maximize users' perceptions of fairness through new appraisal forms and extensive training. Compared with a control group of employees who continued to use the old system, those evaluated with the new "fair" performance appraisal system indicated that they were more likely to keep working at the agency for at least the next three years. Research has repeatedly demonstrated the association between perceived fairness of HRM practices and employees' emotional attachment to their organization.

Fairness perceptions also are associated with employees' demonstrating commitment to their employer through their willingness to exert extra effort, to go above and beyond the call of duty. Examples include helping coworkers who have heavy workloads, taking steps to prevent problems with others, and keeping up with new developments in the organization. These "good citizen" behaviors also include not spending a lot of time complaining and not taking excessive breaks. In companies as diverse as manufacturing and movie theaters, employee fair treatment has been associated with "good citizen" behaviors by employees.

THE CONSEQUENCES OF "FAIR" SERVICE

Customers base how much they trust a service provider, in large measure, on how fairly they have been treated. They are most likely to form enduring relationships with firms who they believe "play fair." The significant relationships between customers' perceptions of "fair" service delivery, customer satisfaction, and customer intentions to return for additional service, are clear. Interestingly, then, managing to be fair builds organizational commitment for both employees *and* customers.

As fairness helps build customer retention, positive consequences also accrue to the bottom line. A large and impressive body of evidence—from organizations such as MBNA, BancOne, Southwest Airlines, and Taco Bell—now shows that small gains in customer retention (e.g., 5% increases) can lead to 75 to 100% gains in profitability. Fairness reaps profits.

Fairness in service is particularly salient for customers in service recovery situations. Research on the consequences of handling complaints fairly shows a positive relation-ship between fairness perceptions and satisfaction with complaint handling, in turn leading to customer trust and commitment. Research also shows, however, that most customers are not impressed with firms' recovery efforts. Service firms typically fail to recover from their service failures.

THE INDIRECT EFFECTS

Treating customers unfairly can also reduce *employee* motivation. Why would employees stay energized for the hard work of satisfying customers if they feel that what their company actually does for customers, and how it goes about doing it, is unfair? When employees see management charging inflated prices or applying customer-insensitive procedures, it becomes difficult for employees to take service quality seriously.

MANAGING TO BE FAIR: THE PROPER MIX OF JUSTICE PRINCIPLES

The many aspects of fair treatment that matter to employees and customers are essentially variations on only three underlying types of justice. One type involves each party's evaluation of the outcomes received (distributive fairness). Employees and customers also judge procedures that determine outcomes (procedural fairness). In addition, they judge how such procedures are implemented and the way in which the procedures and final outcomes are explained (interactional fairness).

It also appears that procedural justice and interactional justice can make an otherwise unfair negative decision (distributive fairness) seem fair. That is, procedural and interactional justice can facilitate, if not substitute for, distributive justice.

How can one manage to be fair—delivering all three types of justice to both employees and customers? There are now separate streams of "fairness" research in services and organizational behavior/industrial-organizational psychology that can provide some answers. Table 1 draws on this research to address what we call the "justice principles," underlying employee and customer perceptions of distributive, procedural, and interactional justice. Managing to be fair requires that organizations "do right" by these principles in relationships with employees and customers.

"JUSTICE PRINCIPLES" ASSOCIATED WITH "FAIR" HRM

Although fairness and justice can be associated with every HRM practice, from recruiting, hiring, and training to labor relations, compensating, and terminating, three of the most important HRM areas in terms of fairness are hiring, performance appraisal, and compensation/reward systems.

TABLE 1 Justice Principles

| Types of Justice | Employees' Sense of "Fair HRM" | | Customers' Sense of "Fair Service" | | |
	Hiring	Performance Appraisal	Compensation Rewards	Service Delivery	Service Recovery
Distributive	Accuracy Appropriateness of hiring decision	Ratings meet expectations Outcomes based on ratings Outcomes meet expectations	External equity Internal equity Individual equity	Cost Amount of service Correctness Excellence	Compensation Apology Resolution
Procedural	Job-relatedness Opportunity Consistency Bias suppression	Consistent standards Input from employees Rater is familiar Personal bias suppression Opportunity for reconsideration	Consistency Bias suppression Accuracy Correctability Representation	Responding to unusual requests Efficiency Waiting time Helpful	Assuming responsibility Timing/speed Convenience Follow-up Process control Flexibility
Interactional	Information on schedule Feedback informativeness Feedback timeliness Honesty Two-way communication Interpersonal treatment	Performance standards communicated Adequate notice Timely performance feedback Informative performance feedback Treating employees with respect	Explain inequity Explaining changes Open communication	Friendliness Unbiased Honesty Expression of interest Politeness	Honesty Empathy Politeness Attitude Effort Explanation/Information

Hiring. The hiring process represents the first contact a future employee has with an organization. Initial impressions of the organization and the way it treats employees are formed during this stage. We are all familiar with the concept of "getting started on the wrong foot" or creating a bad first impression. This same concept applies to organizations and the fairness with which they treat job applicants. Recent research suggests that applicants' perceptions of how fairly they were treated in the hiring process are related to their initial commitment to the organization.

Drawing upon extensive interviews with job applicants, a recent program of research conducted by Stephen Gilliland (discussed in his article "The Perceived Fairness of Selection Systems: An Organizational Justice Perspective," *Academy of Management Review*) has established a set of "justice principles" associated with fairness in the hiring and selection process, as summarized in Table 1.

Distributive justice has two basic principles: accuracy of evaluation and appropriateness of the hiring decision. Applicants judge whether their skills and abilities were assessed accurately by the selection procedures. This evaluation reflects applicants' self-perceived qualifications. Distributive justice also arises from an evaluation of the hiring decision and whether the most qualified person was hired. With this principle, applicants compare their qualifications with the perceived competition.

Even successful applicants can feel they were unfairly treated by hiring decisions. One successful job applicant was incensed to discover that she had just barely passed the company's integrity test.

Consider also the reactions of the following applicant:

"There was no relationship between my credentials and how they made the decision. Another person was hired who has no experi-ence while I only received a later offer when a second position opened up. And I have great experience."

Procedural justice is determined by four principles. Job relatedness reflects the extent to which selection procedures seem job-relevant. Some selection procedures may seem unrelated to any job (e.g., personality test composed of abstract preferences and beliefs), while others may seem related to some jobs but not others (e.g., a physical ability test is related to a firefighter's job but not a bank teller's job). Applicants also prefer selection procedures that allow an opportunity to perform or to demonstrate their abilities and experiences. A selection process for a customer service job that is based purely on written tests may not provide applicants the opportunity to demonstrate their interpersonal skills. Consistency, defined in terms of standardization of the selection process as well as equal treatment for different job applicants, provides a greater sense of procedural justice. Finally, procedural justice is undermined by the existence of personal biases or prejudices on the part of interviewers (e.g., using a "similar to me" decision rule). To the extent to which these biases are suppressed, procedural justice is enhanced.

Interactional justice is associated with communication and interpersonal treatment. The hiring process creates considerable uncertainty, and applicants are looking for information to try to reduce this uncertainty. If information on the selection process is provided in advance, this can help reduce initial uncertainty.

Communication is also important after the selection process as applicants want to know how they did and why (feedback informativeness), and they want this feedback in a timely manner. Applicants are less likely to accept a job offer as the time lag between interviewing and the extension of an offer increases. Also, along the lines of communication, applicants expect honesty from the recruiting organization (e.g., candidness impresses applicants, while deception clearly violates interactional justice), and they appreciate the opportunity for two-way communication (e.g., they want to be able to ask questions). These principles of interactional justice (as well as procedural justice) are a concern at AT&T, where the selection group regularly surveys applicants to assess their reactions to the entire selection process (e.g., was it timely, convenient).

Interactional justice also involves how applicants are generally treated. This interpersonal treatment principle reflects the need for professionalism and respect in all interactions with the applicant. For example, Disney ensures interactional justice from the time applicants walk into the recruiting center. Instead of the usual windowless, subbasement recruiting office found in the hospitality industry, Disney applicants enter a "Disney-character-themed" casting center that sends a message about the importance the company places on applicants and employees.

Performance Appraisal. The fairness problems with many performance appraisal systems have led some to question whether appraisals can ever work. W.E. Deming even suggested that a typical performance evaluation creates fear and rivalry, ruins teamwork, and basically makes people bitter. Justice researchers, however, have identified specific distributive, procedural, and interactional justice principles that foster perceived fairness in performance appraisal systems.

Distributive justice has three related principles: Ratings should meet employees' expectations, outcomes should be based on ratings (e.g., merit increases or disciplinary action), and outcomes should meet employees' expectations. The third principle follows from the first two. If employees know what ratings to expect and outcomes are

systematically linked to those ratings, then employees will know what outcomes to expect. At the FINOVA Group, a provider of corporate financial services, employees and supervisors set objectives and performance standards for the year, thereby establishing realistic expectations. At the end of the year, objectives and standards are reviewed, and incentives are tied directly to evaluations of met objectives. This system satisfies the three distributive justice principles.

Procedural justice principles include consistent application of standards and soliciting input from employees. Consistency can be promoted through standardized performance appraisal procedures and formal training of supervisors. Soliciting input is important in all stages of the performance appraisal process, from the development of evaluation standards to the information-gathering and rating process itself, to providing feedback. Additional procedural justice principles include making sure the rater is familiar with the employee being evaluated and making sure raters' personal biases are suppressed and do not enter into the evaluation process. In addition to standardizing procedures and training supervisors, familiarity can be enhanced by having supervisors regularly observe and keep performance diaries on their employees. Finally, the opportunity for reconsideration or the chance to appeal an evaluation or decision is an important procedural justice principle.

Interactional justice of performance appraisal involves communication and interpersonal treatment. It is important that performance standards are communicated to employees and adequate notice is given of the performance appraisal process. These two principles suggest that it is important for employees to know *how* and *when* they will be evaluated. Similarly, timely and informative performance feedback is critical to the appraisal process. For example,

Microsoft conducts formal performance feedback sessions every six months. But between these formal reviews, employees receive monthly informal feedback sessions with their supervisors. The frequency of this feedback helps to create a "no surprises" performance appraisal process. The final interactional justice principle is treating employees with respect. As with the application process, the performance appraisal process is perceived to be more fair if employees are treated with courtesy and civility, especially when feedback is being delivered. This interpersonal treatment is a foundation of an employee's trust in his or her supervisor.

Compensation/Reward Systems. Table 1 outlines justice principles underlying perceived fairness and satisfaction with compensation and reward systems. A common theme is that these fairness perceptions involve employee unmet expectations—on pay level or how pay level is set.

Distributive justice principles define what pay outcome is seen as fair. This outcome could be a pay level, a pay range, a merit increase, or any other compensation or reward outcome. The chief distributive justice principle is equity, which can be further divided into three types. *External equity* involves comparing with those in a similar job at different companies. *Internal equity* is based on comparing one's pay with the pay of different jobs (or jobs at different levels) in the same company. With *individual equity,* individuals compare pay with coworkers' performance of the same job at the same level in their organization. It is difficult or impossible to maintain all three types of equity, and employees will often perceive some violation of distributive justice.

As suggested earlier, however, adequate procedural and interactional justice can offset distributive injustice. For example, fair reward allocation procedures were more important than distributive justice when it came to maintaining bank employees' organizational commitment. Despite low distributive justice, high procedural justice sustained organizational commitment.

Procedural justice in rewards involves a number of principles. The consistency principle suggests that allocation procedures should be consistent across people and time (at least over the short term). Related to this, the bias suppression principle dictates that self-interests and personal biases be kept out of the reward allocation process. Accuracy suggests that the reward allocation decision should be based on accurate and factual information. Salary surveys and other compensation-benchmark information, as well as careful job evaluations, can help promote perceptions of accuracy. In the event that pay problems are uncovered, employees like to see that the system is correctable. As with performance appraisal, the opportunity to appeal a compensation decision can help promote procedural justice and pay satisfaction. In other HRM practices, we have discussed the importance of offering employees that chance to impact the decision process. With compensation and rewards, this input can be accomplished through employee representation (e.g., through unions) or participation on compensation committees. For example, when the California electronics distributor Marshall Industries revamped its compensation system, it talked with every employee in the company. Although the new system resulted in higher compensation costs, company sales and stock prices soared.

Interactional justice can also promote a "fair" compensation system—in part, by ensuring that distributive and procedural justice are intact. Communication by company officials can explain why certain pay differentials exist (explain inequities) or explain why changes (e.g., reductions) must be made in compensation rates. This emphasis on communication stands in contrast to conventional policies of pay secrecy.

Pay secrecy may be important if the company is trying to hide an unjust compensation system, but existing research suggests that, in the long run, open communication is key to ensuring justice. At Competitive Engineering, Inc., employee wages, from the president on down, are posted on the wall for all to see. As a result, employees trust the fairness and integrity of the compensation system.

FAIR HRM SUPPORTS FAIR SERVICE: THE SPILLOVER EFFECT

There now is abundant evidence that shows a significant relationship between service employee attitudes and customer attitudes. Research done at Sears, Allstate, Ryder Truck, NCR, and in numerous financial institutions has found a significant statistical correlation between employee satisfaction and customer attitudes such as their satisfaction and their intentions to keep doing business with those firms or go elsewhere. An example of this type of research is a banking study that found that when tellers favorably rated their branches' practices in training, supervision, and rewards, branch customers also viewed branch service quality as high.

This dynamic, by which service employee attitudes have a significant influence upon customer attitudes, has been termed the "spillover effect." Employee attitudes seem to spill over onto customers in service encounters. Since employee attitudes strongly mirror employee reactions to HRM practices like performance appraisal and rewards, it is clear that, in service firms, HRM practices affect employees, directly, and then customers, indirectly.

This same "spillover effect" strongly suggests that "if you treat employees fairly, they will treat their customers fairly." Fair HRM can be expected to lead directly to satisfied, committed employees willing to exert extra effort, which increases the likelihood that they will deliver the fair outcomes, procedures, and interpersonal treatment that customers expect (i.e., fair service). The indirect results of fair HRM are satisfied and customers and bottom-line returns.

Employee actions called Organizational Citizenship Behaviors (OCBs) are the key variable in fair HRM leading to fair service (see Figure 1). OCBs are positive actions taken by employees, even though they are not formally specified in job descriptions and performance appraisals, nor even formally stated as a basis for rewards. OCBs can be displayed on a number of dimensions; Figure 1 lists five that have been typically identified in OCB studies. These five behaviors certainly have a strong service-oriented flavor. OCBs, then, are the behaviors by which the positive attitudes of fairly treated employees spill over on to customers.

OCBs can also be thought of as "discretionary behavior" that employees do volun-

FIGURE 1 "Fair HRM Leads To Fair Service"

Fair HRM	→	*Employees Display Organizational*	→	*Fair Service*
HRM practices, e.g., hiring performance appraisal and rewards that honor the "justice principles" Altruism		Altruism Courtesy Sportsmanship Conscientiousness Civic virtue		Service is "fair," honoring "justice principles" in service delivery and service recovery

tarily. Such behavior is critical in service encounters because no one can specify in advance the full range of things that a service employee might have to do in response to unpredictable customer requests. When such circumstances arise, an employee might exert the least amount of additional imagination and energy needed to get by (i.e., "That's not my job; I really can't"); or engage in OCBs and go the extra mile (i.e., "I'll see if I can take care of this when I'm free on my lunch hour"). The magic necessary to really delight customers seems to require a strong mix of OCBs.

What does it take to get employees to display OCBs? OCBs are strongly correlated with employee perceptions of fairness in the workplace. However, it turns out that each type of justice is not equally important. Across a number of studies with different organizations and industries, it appears that procedural and interactional justice are more important than distributive justice when it comes to developing good organizational citizens. The evidence indicates that these types of justice help develop employees' trust in their organization and their supervisors. Relatedly, there emerges a heightened sense of loyalty to the business that encourages the employee to do the extra things that can help the organization—and its customers—succeed.

MANAGING TO BE FAIR: FINAL THOUGHTS

There are four basic lessons to be drawn from the myriad of justice principles. We offer them as general managerial guidelines in which to enact the more specific principles.

- Realistically preview, then honor, your business's "psychological contract" with its employees—and customers.

A psychological contract is an implicit agreement between parties concerning what each party gives and gets in a relationship. It embodies the parties' assumptions regarding the "rules of the game" by which they will fulfill obligations to one another. It is common for organizations to think about how employees view the psychological contract. It is less typical for organizations to realize that customers also identify a psychological contract. Too often businesses see customers as parties only to an economic transaction, not parties to a psychological contract.

Because psychological contracts are implicit and unwritten, employees or customers might have unrealistic expectations of what outcomes the organization owes them and how they are to be delivered. Employees might believe that years of faithful service should lead to job security; auto insurance customers might believe that years of never filing a claim will mean that their premiums won't go up if someday they do have to file. In both cases, subsequent actions taken by the organization may show these to have been unrealistic expectations. Employees and customers then feel the psychological contract was violated and feel unjustly treated as a consequence.

For employees, HRM practices should be designed to communicate the terms of psychological contracts with clarity and internal consistency. Practices in hiring, performance appraisal, and rewards should send messages about what employee contributions the firm desires and what it will give employees in return. The practice of using "realistic job previews" in hiring is an example of how to shape accurate terms for the psychological contract.

For customers, organizations must not only shape expectations through practices such as a "realistic service preview" but also fully accept that customers do view the relation as a psychological contract. Customers expect the contract to be honored and are likely lost to the business forever if the contract is violated. Scott Cook, CEO of Intuit, is one who clearly gets this when he is quoted as saying, "We have their [customers] money. We owe them success."

- Train managers and customer contact employees in how to honor the "justice principles."

Training programs in supervision and customer service are needed in which the fair treatment of both employees and customers is the central focus. As Table 1 indicates, there are many pieces of evidence, many MOTs, that the firm must manage in its endless encounters with employees and customers if those parties are to feel they have been treated fairly. And even one unjust MOT is likely to diminish one's sense of fair treatment. In this vein, Disney has offered the 1/74 Rule. It says that each theme park guest has at least 74 MOTs each visit and a single negative moment can significantly lower the guest's feelings about his or her visit.

- Balance flexibility and consistency in the design and implementation of procedures.

Both employees and customers seem to simultaneously embrace the principle that everyone should be treated equally (i.e., "equal justice under the law"), and the belief that the application of policies should, nonetheless, take their own special circumstances into account. Efforts to ensure fairness for one employee or customer through flexibility and responding to unusual requests must be considered carefully to ensure that these efforts do not create unfairness for other employees and customers. Companies such as Hampton Inn have empowered their service employees to respond to customers' needs and problems. Although empowerment is designed to ensure satisfaction among customers, it may create feelings of inequity among those who observe others receiving special treatment. It can also slow down the speed and efficiency of the service delivery process for those waiting to be served.

To determine when consistent application of formal, standardized rules and procedures is more desirable than flexibility and individualized attention, companies must consider the degree of complexity and change in their internal and external environments. With low complexity and stable environments (e.g., fast-food restaurants), formalized procedures are probably the key to ensuring fair treatment. However, as the environment becomes more complex and more unpredictable (e.g., health care, education), flexibility will be more important in maintaining fairness.

An additional step with regard to balancing fairness when providing special treatment is carefully explaining to employees and customers why exceptions to rules are made. Or, if exceptions cannot be made and individualized treatment cannot be offered (such as when distributing company-wide profit sharing or when considering a loan application), then the reasons for the existing rules should be explained. This importance and value of communication is emphasized in our final guideline.

- Share lots of justice-relevant information with employees and customers.

Explaining the reasoning behind decisions is important with any decision and becomes critical when the decision is negative. If an employee does not receive the raise anticipated or if a customer does not receive the refund requested, they are going to want to know why. This explanation is often essential for maintaining feelings of fairness.

Openness will be helpful only when procedural and distributive justice have also been maintained. Detailed explanations of a performance appraisal that really was biased or of a service offering that was clearly poor will not likely buy the company any good will. In order for the sharing of lots of justice-related information to be effective, there first has to be justice in the actual content of what is being shared. The summary lesson is that managing to be fair to service employees and their customers requires more than "looking fair"; it requires "being fair."

Selected Bibliography

For more of a description of the "user reactions" and "service" perspective on HRM, see D. E. Bowen, "Market-Focused HRM in Service Organizations: Satisfying Internal and External Customers" *Journal of Market-Focused Management* 1 (1996), 31–49; and D. E. Bowen and L. E. Greiner, "Moving from Production to Service in Human Resources Management," *Organizational Dynamics,* 15 (1986), 35–53.

To read more about services marketing and management (e.g., dimensions of service quality, customer expectations, and some early thoughts on service fairness), see Leonard Berry, *On Great Service* (New York: Free Press, 1995); Christian Gronoos, *Services Marketing and Management* (Lanham, Md.: Lexington Books, 1990); Ben Schneider and David Bowen, *Winning the Service Game* (Boston: Harvard Business School Press, 1995); and Valerie Zeithanal and Mary Jo Bitner, *Services Marketing* (New York: McGraw Hill/Irwin 1999). The quotation about "keeping promises" is from M.J. Bitner "Building Service Relationships: It's All About Promises," *Journal of the Academy of Marketing Science,* 23(4), 1995, p. 246.

More complete descriptions of the different types of justice, their antecedents, and consequences can be found in R. Folger, "Distributive and Procedural Justice in the Workplace," *Social Justice Research,* 1 (1987), 143–59; J. Greenberg, "A Taxonomy of Organizational Justice Theories," *Academy of Management Review,* 12, (1987), 9–12; E. A. Lind and T. Tyler, *The Social Psychology of Procedural Justice* (New York: Plenum, 1988); B. H. Sheppard, R. I. Lewicki, and J. W. Minton; *Organizational Justice* (Lexington, Mass: Lexington Books, 1992); and D. B. McFarlin and P. D. Sweeney, "Distributive and Procedural Justice as Predictors of Satisfaction with Personal and Organizational Outcomes" *Academy of Management Journal,* 35 (1992), 626–37.

Works that specifically address fairness in HRM practices of hiring, performance appraisal, and compensation include R. Folger and J. Greenberg, "Procedural Analysis: An Interpretative Analysis of Personnel Systems." In K. Rowland and G. Ferrs (Eds.) *Research in Personnel and Human Resources Management,* Vol 3 (Greenwich, Conn: JAI Press); Stephen Gilliland, "The Perceived Fairness of Selection Systems: An Organizational Justice Perspective," *Academy of Management Review,* 13 (1993), 694–734; and Stephen Gilliland, "Fairness from the Applicant's Perspective: Reactions to Employee Selection Procedures," *International Journal of Selection and Assessment,* 3, (1995), 11–19. For a summary of justice principles in performance appraisal, see S. W. Gilliland and J. C. Langdon, "Creating Performance Management Systems That Promote Perceptions of Fairness" in *Performance Appraisal: State-of-the-Art Methods for Performance Management,* J. W. Smither (ed.), (San Francisco: Jossey-Bass, 1998). For more information on justice in reward systems, see M. P. Miceli, "Justice and Pay System Satisfaction," in *Justice in the Workplace,* R. Cropanzaro (ed.) (Hillsdale, N.J.: Erlbaum, 1993). For a more educative overview of fairness in HRM, see Robert Folger and Russell Cropanzano, *Organizational Justice and Human Resource Management* (Newbury Park, Calif.: Sage, 1998).

The study of fairness in service delivery was conducted by Elizabeth Clemmer and Ben Schneider and is reported in "Fair Service," in T. A. Swartz, D. E. Bowen, and S. W. Brown (eds.), *Advances in Services Marketing and Management,* Vol. 3 (Greenwich, Conn.: JAI Press, 1996). The Tax et al. Paper is the source for the majority of the results reported. The quote that presents the customer seeking service recovery as a litigant in a civil case appeared in Cathy Goodwin and I. Roes, "Consumer Responses to Service Failures: Influence of Procedural and Interactional Fairness Perceptions" *Journal of Business Research,* (1991). Also see K. Seiders and L.L. Berry, "Service Fairness: What It Is and Why

It Matters," *Academy of Management Executive,* Vol. 12 (2) (1998), 8–20.

Insights and data on the relationship between service employee attitudes and behaviors and customer attitudes and behaviors (expressed here as the "spillover effect") can be found in B. Schneider and David Bowen, "The Service Organization: Human Resource Management is Crucial," *Organizational Dynamics,* (1993), 39–52. This article also overviews the research done in bank settings that is mentioned in the discussion of service fairness. How the relationships between employee and customer data are associated with profits is developed in James Heskett, Earl Sesser, and Leonard Schlesinger, *The Service Profit Chain* (New York: Free Press, 1997); as well as Frederick Reichheld, *The Loyalty Effect* (Boston: Harvard Business School Press, 1996).

The role that fairness plays in "organizational citizenship behaviors" is documented in two articles by Robert Moorman: "The Relationship Between Organizational Justice and Organizational Citizenship Behaviors: Do Fairness Perceptions Influence Employee Citizenship?" *Journal of Applied Psychology,* 76 (1991), 845–95, and "Justice as a Mediator of the Relationship Between Methods of Monitoring and Organizational Citizenship Behavior," *Academy of Management Journal,* 36 (1993), 526–56. The relationship between OCBs and service-oriented behavior is discussed in David Bowen's *Journal of Market-Focused Management,* (1996); and Lance Bettencourt and Stephen Brown, "Contact Employees: Relationship Among Workplace Fairness, Job Satisfaction, and Prosocial Service Behaviors," *Journal of Retailing,* 73 (1997), 39–62; Donna Blancero, Scott. A. Johnson, and C. Lakshman, "Psychological Contracts and Fairness: The Effect of Violations on Customer Service Behavior," *Journal of Market-Focused Management,* 1 (1), 49–64.

A good source for learning more about psychological contracts is a special issue that *Human Resource Management* did on the subject in Fall 1994. The idea of "realistic *service* previews for customers" can be found in Bowen, "Managing Customers as Human Resources," *Human Resource Management,* 1986, and William Firanda, "Customer Participation in Service Production: An Empirical Assessment of the Influence of Realistic Service Previews" (unpublished doctoral dissertation, Arizona State University, Department of Marketing, 1994).

A discussion of how procedurally driven versus flexible service employees should be, under different circumstances, can be found in David Bowen and E. E. Lawler, "The Empowerment of Service Workers: What, Why, How, and When," *Sloan Management Review,* (Summer 1995), 73–84.

Finally, the two examples of unfair treatment that open the paper appeared in K. Myers, "The Fairness Factor" *Quality Progress,* (June 1994), 77. The quote about the role of intangibility in fairness comes from Leonard Berry, Parsu Parasuraman, and Valerie Zeithanal, "Improving Service Quality in America: Lessons Learned" *Academy of Management Executive,* 3 (2), 1994, 40.

III-2: Why Wages Do Not Fall in Recessions

Economists dislike talking to people. They prefer a more "scientific" approach to research, such as number-crunching or abstract theorizing. But that can be a weak-

Reprinted from *The Economist* (February 26, 2000): 90.

ness, as a new book by Truman Bewley, an economist at Yale University, makes clear. In *Why Wages Don't Fall During a Recession*, published by Harvard University Press, he tackles one of the oldest, and most controversial, puzzles in economics: why nominal wages rarely fall (and real wages do not fall enough) when unemployment is high. But he does so in a novel way, through interviews with over 300 businessmen, union leaders, job recruiters, and unemployment counselors in the northeastern United States during the early 1990s recession.

Explanations for why wages are sticky abound, but they are often unconvincing. Neoclassical economists, who have a starry-eyed faith in the efficiency of markets, think wage rigidity is an illusion. In their view, workers quit their jobs when pay starts to fall in a downturn. This stops wages falling much and makes them appear inflexible. But their theory implies that unemployment in a recession is voluntary—a view at which reasonable people might rightly scoff.

Keynesians, who accept that markets are often imperfect, think wages are sticky, but cannot agree why. Some blame unions or established employees ("insiders") for blocking pay cuts. Keynes himself thought that workers were so concerned about their wages relative to those at other firms that no company dared to cut pay. Others argue that firms pay high "efficiency wages" in order to make the threat of job loss more costly for workers and so spur them to work harder. (Wages might still fall in a recession, though, since workers are more afraid of not finding another job when unemployment rises.) Still others claim that firms implicitly insure workers against a fall in income in exchange for lower long-term average wages. And so on.

One or more of these theories may be true. Or perhaps none is. Economists do not really know, because the labor-market data with which they test their theories is inadequate. So Mr. Bewley tried asking people who should be in the know. He is aware of the pitfalls: interviewees may be unrepresentative, lie, or obfuscate. They may not understand their own motives. Still, since economists are ultimately trying to describe human behavior, meeting real people ought sometimes to help.

Mr. Bewley finds scant evidence to support the various wage-stickiness theories. His interviewees say unions are not to blame for wage rigidity: few American firms are unionised, and in those where unions are important "the first line of resistance to pay reduction was almost always management." Nor are "insiders" blocking pay cuts: few nonunion workers bargain over wages with their employers, and no employer remarked on a sharp division of opinion over layoffs among workers, who more typically thought that pay cuts would not save jobs.

Keynes's theory gets short shrift too. Mr. Bewley finds that, although pay rates across nonunion companies are connected by supply and demand, firms still have plenty of latitude in setting pay because workers have scant knowledge of pay rates elsewhere. Nor is much credence given to the efficiency-wage model. "People do work harder during a recession because they are concerned about their jobs . . . however, the logic does not imply that companies pay well for reasons of discipline. They do so in order to attract and retain employees," says a typical personnel officer in a middling manufacturer. The implicit insurance model fares little better. Employers do not think such a bargain exists and believe that it would be unenforceable in any case, since long-term pay is determined by competitive conditions.

ALL IN A DAY'S WORK

Why, then, are wages sticky? Mr. Bewley concludes that employers resist pay cuts largely because the savings from lower wages are usually outweighed by the cost of denting workers morale: pay cuts hit workers' standard of living and lower their self-esteem. Falling morale raises staff turnover and reduces productivity. Cheerier workers are more productive workers, not only because they work better, but also because they identify more closely with the company's interests. This last point is crucial. Mr. Bewley argues that monitoring workers' performance is usually so tricky that firms rarely rely on coercion and financial carrots alone as motivators. In particular, high morale fosters teamwork and information-sharing, which are otherwise difficult to encourage.

Firms typically prefer layoffs to pay cuts because they harm morale less, says Mr. Bewley. Pay cuts hurt everybody and can cause festering resentment; layoffs hit morale only for a while, since the aggrieved have, after all, left. And whereas a generalized pay cut might make the best workers leave, and a selective one damage morale because it is seen as unfair, firms can often lay off their least competent staff.

Mr. Bewley's theory has some interesting implications. Pay cuts are more likely at firms whose demand for labor is price-sensitive, such as those in highly competitive industries. Since many markets are becoming more competitive, wages may also be getting more flexible—and unemployment may rise less in recessions. Wages are also likely to be less rigid in short-term jobs, where workers do not become attached to their firm. On the other hand, since more workers now do jobs that are hard to monitor, or in which they need to co-operate, share information, be creative, or be nice to customers, wages may becomes stickier.

Mr. Bewley's book is not the last word on sticky wages. Some of his findings are probably specific to the northeastern United States in the early 1990s. But his theory has a ring of truth to it. And if his example spurs other economists to venture out of their ivory towers, so much the better.

III-3: Workplace Violence Experts See Lessons from Littleton

ROBERT W. THOMPSON

Employers everywhere—in towns large and small, with workforces both stable and rapidly changing—have reason to be concerned by the recent tragedy at Columbine High School in Littleton, Colorado, experts on workplace violence say.

It's not just because working parents may be distracted and less productive as they worry about their children being in peril at schools once regarded as safe havens.

Since Eric Harris and Dylan Klebold fatally shot 12 students and a teacher before

HR News by Robert W. Thompson. Copyright 1998 by Society for Human Resource Management. Reprinted with permission of HR News published by the Society for Human Resource Management, Alexandria, VA, in the format Textbook via Copyright Clearance Center.

taking their own lives on April 20, the world, it seems, has been consumed with the gruesome task of trying to figure out why the tragedy occurred.

Violent popular culture, neglectful parents, a resistant gun lobby, and lax school officials have all come in for their share of blame. But relatively little has been written or said about the psychological conditions that led to the Littleton shootings.

Several experts on workplace bullying told *HR News* they hope the debate ultimately will address the taunts, cliquishness, and other types of bullying that Littleton students say Harris and Klebold both endured and committed. Such bullying also occurs frequently in the workplace, where—if unchecked—it can lead to both physical violence and psychological damage, they said.

People who have been subjected to bullying, including British author Tim Field, know how devastating its effects can be.

Field had worked happily for 15 years in computer systems and support until he was transferred to a new department with a new boss. Soon, he became the target of constant criticism—sometimes aggressive and impatient—and was forced to seek approval for even the smallest actions.

The new boss piled work on him and, when he protested, responded with implied threats.

His contributions dismissed, requests ignored, and decisions overruled, Field suffered a stress breakdown in 1994. By early 1996, he had recovered enough to found the U.K. National Workplace Bullying Advice Line—a hot line to which employers, students, spouses, and others have brought more than 2,000 complaints.

Field detailed his experiences in a book, *Bully in Sight,* and created a World Wide Web site (www.successunlimited .co.uk) with the motto "Those who can, do. Those who can't, bully."

Field said he wouldn't hazard a guess as to the role that bullying may have played in Littleton. However, he said employers would do well to increase their awareness of the types of bullying, signs of the malady, and ways of reducing and coping with bullying.

∙ ∙ ∙ ∙ ∙ ∙ ∙ ∙ ∙ ∙ ∙ ∙ ∙ ∙ ∙ ∙ ∙ ●
BULLYING DEFINED

Like many people who have studied bullying, Field draws a distinction between harassment, which can be manifested by a single incident, and bullying, which by definition involves repeated incidents and sometimes a pattern of behavior.

Richard V. Denenberg, co-director of Workplace Solutions, a Red Hook, New York–based consortium of conflict management and crisis management professionals,

said officials in Europe sometimes refer to the malady as "mobbing."

Denenberg, co-author with Mark Braverman of *The Violence-Prone Workplace: A New Approach to Dealing With Hostile, Threatening, and Uncivil Behavior,* said bullying often occurs when a clique forms and those who aren't invited into the exclusive circle are picked on. "It's almost like you've run into organized crime," he said.

The Littleton tragedy, according to Denenberg, involved a "garden-variety, intergroup dispute spiraling into violence." He said the shootings appeared to be strongly linked to "bullying and taunting and harassment. You had a sort of group dispute that never was taken seriously. No one seemed to believe that bullying could escalate to that level of violence."

One dilemma with bullying, in both schools and the workplace, is that those in charge often fail to realize the seriousness of the problems until much too late, experts say.

"One of the key problems is that employers tend to get dismissive," particularly if they realize that the inappropriate behavior does not rise to the level of a contract dispute or legal action, Denenberg said.

Loraleigh Keashly, an associate professor of urban and labor studies at Wayne State University in Detroit, called bullying "very much a part of the workplace experience" despite the misperception—especially popular in the United States—that it is a problem largely for schools.

∙ ∙ ∙ ∙ ∙ ∙ ∙ ∙ ∙ ∙ ∙ ∙ ∙ ∙ ∙ ∙ ∙ ●
PHYSICAL VIOLENCE IS NOT THE NORM

Psychological aggression in the workplace, she said, can have "devastating" effects leading to physical, mental, and emotional illnesses, as well as reduced productivity and increased absenteeism by employees.

"Media reports give the impression that physical violence is the norm, but it's not," Keashly said. Bullying involves more subtle types of aggression, including ignoring a person's contributions, flaunting status, pulling rank, making unwanted eye contact, and openly belittling individuals, she explained.

"You should never berate someone publicly," said Keashly.

Other types of bullying include vandalism, gestures, withholding of important information, and making faces—"even smiling the wrong way," said Denenberg. "It can be very subtle."

Much bullying seems designed, either expressly or subconsciously, to undermine the target employee's self-confidence and to cause the worker to perform poorly, he said.

One reason employers have tended to dismiss psychologically aggressive behavior, experts say, is that it is much more difficult to define and diagnose than physical violence, which causes damage that is often clearly visible.

And some of the symptoms of bullying—substance abuse, declines in productivity, and increased absenteeism—may be caused by other factors or a combination of factors.

Another reason for bullying being overlooked is that employees may be hesitant to report it.

Often, Denenberg said, these workers don't like to admit that they have been victimized, and they are fearful of retribution from both bullies and employers. He said employees who have borne the brunt of bullying may worry that their managers will consider them either chronic complainers or "shirkers" looking for an excuse to avoid work.

Most people on the receiving end of aggressive behavior, when asked what they did about it, say they did nothing, according to Keashly. That's because they assume—sometimes correctly—that their organizations will be unresponsive, she said.

However, employers should remember that organizations can be "very influential" in affecting the amount of aggressive behavior, Keashly said.

A third explanation for the under-emphasis on bullying, Field said, is that employers who admit that the problem exists among their workers also might have to bear responsibility for some of the conditions causing it to flourish.

Field said most people who call his advice line work at organizations where bullying is "rife" and is used to hide managerial inadequacies. If employers were to take the problem of bullying seriously, he said, they might have to stare their own shortcomings in the face.

Keashly said employers often focus on the individual as the source of a problem when, in the case of bullying, they should cast a wider net. "We tend to have a bias toward fixing the individual, when the organization also has a responsibility," she said

Denenberg said that while bullying of subordinates by bosses occurs, peer-on-peer bullying is more of a problem for employers because there are fewer means of redress. If an employee is bullied by his or her manager, for example, the worker could sue under anti-harassment laws or file a grievance through a labor union, he said.

In contrast, Denenberg said, employees often have nowhere to turn when they are being harassed by a co-worker. "What happens when the source of the harassment is another employee?" he asked rhetorically.

Organizations that may be prone to bullying include those that are adversarial or unusually competitive, Keashly said. Also, European studies have pointed to organizations that are autocratic or rigidly hierarchical, she added.

THE SERIAL BULLY

The most dangerous type of bully, Field explained, is the "serial bully," who is not merely reacting to stressful or unhealthy workplace conditions but engages in psychological aggression regardless of the circumstances.

The serial bully, he said, is very aggressive and dysfunctional and often is an introvert, which would make him that much more difficult to detect and deal with. Field said introverted bullies tend to be very intelligent and "very subtle," leaving little, if any, evidence of their handiwork.

Some countries have addressed the workplace bully, including Sweden, which enacted a "dignity at work" law. Field said the British Parliament, under pressure from organized labor, considered a similar bill several years ago. He said the Manufacturing, Science and Finance Union, the bill's staunchest supporter, has indicated it may renew its push for the legislation.

Keashly said the United States lags behind many western European nations in addressing workplace bullying. U.S. government officials and employers place relatively more emphasis on physical attacks and on racial and sexual harassment, she said, compared with "generalized workplace harassment."

Denenberg recommended that employers concerned about bullying watch for it on a continuing basis and, if they spot a problem, establish a mediation process. He said one model might be the community mediation programs that San Francisco and other municipalities have used for years in addressing problems related to gang violence, ethnic conflicts, and sexual orientation differences.

He also said some school systems have had great success with peer mediation programs in which students are taught to be alert to bullying and other problem behaviors.

A positive policy on bullying would go beyond prohibiting certain behaviors, Keashly said, to describe what a healthy work relationship is. A good start is to "focus people on what respectful relationships are like," she said.

Denenberg said a good source of information about workplace bullying is the National Institute for Dispute Resolution (NIDR) in Washington, D.C. (The institute provides what it calls "timely and focused information on effective applications of conflict resolution in our society" and, through its clearinghouse operation, offers books and other resources. For more information about NIDR, go to the web site: www.continent.com/nidr/.)

The Workplace Solutions web site can be found at www.wps.org. Other sources of information include the Workplace Violence Research Institute and the Campaign Against Workplace Bullying, a nonprofit organization directed by Ruth and Gary Namie. The web addresses for those organizations are noworkviolence.com and www.bullybusters.org.

III-4: Walking Out on the Boys
An Excerpt

FRANCES K. CONLEY

The way leaders are selected in academic medicine is wrong. It favors those who have built their careers by intimidation and fear.

Candidates for department chairs and deans submit a curriculum vita, give a seminar or grand rounds, interview with a few faculty, and are promoted on the basis of a written record of academic achievement, one or two days of sociability, and on the basis of who knows whom. No one bothers

Reprinted from *Walking Out on the Boys*, Frances K. Conley (New York: Farrar, Straus & Giroux, 1998).

to call the head nurse of the operating room or the other "little people" at the candidate's present institution to inquire whether or not the staff enjoys working with him or her, whether or not he or she treats subordinates fairly, whether or not a passion for developing the careers of others has been evident.

We tend to forget that love and respect can also confer immense power. When it comes to academic medicine, emotion, warmth, demonstrable humanity often are equated with weakness. Because these are so-called feminine traits, why should they be used as criteria when choosing a leader in a masculine-dominated culture?

III-5: All's Not Fair in Labor Wars

AARON BERNSTEIN

This week's puzzler: How is it that more and more workers are saying they want to join unions, while at the same time the percentage of unionized employees in the workforce continues to decline?

In the midst of the best real wage gains and job opportunities in years, 43% of employees surveyed nationally this spring say that they would vote for a union at their workplace, according to Washington-based pollsters Peter D. Hart Research Associates. That's up from 39% in the mid-1990s and 30% in 1984. The reasons vary. Some workers believe that while executives and managers have been richly rewarded, they themselves have not received a large enough share of the wealth generated over the last decade. Others would want a union to fight for better health and pension benefits.

● ● ● ● ● ●

"WAR"

But whatever the motivations may be, some 40 million workers say they want a union today, compared with only 19 million in 1984. Management argues that whatever these workers tell pollsters, they end up changing their minds when an actual union

vote occurs. But can so many people change their minds so consistently?

Certainly, labor leaders are partly to blame for the disconnect between pro-union sentiment and dwindling membership. For decades, they have focused on preserving jobs rather than organizing the fastest-growing parts of the economy, such as services and high tech. So, many workers who say they favor a union may never have been offered the opportunity to join one. Only recently, prodded by AFL-CIO President John J. Sweeney, have unions shifted back to organizing.

Still, this doesn't explain why unions only win half the elections held at private companies, but are voted in 85% of the time by public-sector employees. What is the probable cause? The increasing use of anti-union tactics by private employers. According to analyses of data from the National Labor Relations Board (NLRB) by labor researcher Kate Bronfenbrenner of Cornell University, companies are increasingly using every weapon—legal or not—to thwart attempts to organize their workers.

A third of the companies in the NLRB study illegally fired union supporters during elections, Bronfenbrenner found. That was up from a mere 8% in the 1960s. Half threatened to close facilities if the union won, and 91% required workers to meet one-on-one

Reprinted from *Business Week* (July 19, 1999): 43. ©1999 The McGraw-Hill Companies, Inc.

with supervisors on the issue. Sweeney calls these tactics a "secret war in our workplaces."

To see how influential management can be, just look at the quarter-century effort to organize textile employees at Fieldcrest Cannon Inc. plants in Kannapolis, North Carolina. On June 24, a slim majority of 5,200 workers voted in the Union of Needletrades, Industrial & Textile Employees (UNITE) after five previous votes failed. In the prior elections, the NLRB intervened because Fieldcrest Cannon had harassed and fired pro-union workers.

The difference this time: a change of management. In 1997, Dallas-based Pillowtex Corp. bought the company. Its CEO, Charles M. Hansen Jr., is no fan of unions—he even sent a video of himself to workers arguing against the union. But Hansen also ordered his supervisors not to break any labor laws. "I made sure managers didn't make any threats, even implied ones," he notes. Says UNITE Secretary-Treasurer Bruce S. Raynor: Hansen simply "accepted the fact that workers have a right to vote for a union."

Such a laissez-faire attitude is unusual. Managements, according to National Association of Manufacturers Vice-President Patrick J. Cleary, are merely "exercising their First Amendment rights to give [workers] facts about unions" when they campaign against unions. But the reality is, there is a disturbing trend of management coercion that inhibits workers.

Failing to restrain anti-union campaigns has also allowed management to limit labor's overall power. If even half of the employees who say they favor union representation had been allowed to vote for unions, organized labor would represent as much as 35% of the American workforce today—the same share it held at the peak of its power in 1945. Instead, owing in part to a relatively toothless NLRB since the Reagan Administration, labor's ranks have plunged to 14%.

The United States wouldn't tolerate companies that intimidated employees who supported a politician management disliked. The standard of fairness should be no less democratic for workplace elections.

III-6: Academic Medicine Becomes a Target for Labor Organizing
Physicians and Residents Seek Union Help on Both Economic and Professional Issues

KATHERINE S. MANGAN

As a podiatric resident, Hassan Kobaissi never dreamed that he would be living in a cramped apartment, relying on food stamps and the occasional construction job to keep his family afloat.

Dr. Kobaissi, who is a resident at the California College of Podiatric Medicine, worked 60 to 80 hours a week at a Los Angeles County hospital last year and earned just $10,000. He expressed his frustration by joining a union, the Joint Council of Interns and Residents.

Neither the college nor the county has recognized the union as a bargaining agent for the medical staff members, but Mr. Kobaissi feels that the residents' complaints are being taken more seriously now. "The other players in the health-care arena are big and powerful, and it's impossible for a doctor working on his own to negotiate for a reasonable deal," he says. "Once we unionized, things started rolling. People who didn't return my calls before started to listen."

The idea that a physician, even one in training, would join a labor union used to be unheard of. Not anymore. In a move that shocked many medical educators, the American Medical Association in June voted to form a union that would represent physicians and medical residents.

A.M.A. members say they are fed up with the ways in which large managed-care companies are controlling the professional lives of doctors and interfering with their efforts to deliver high-quality medical care.

"TAKING A STAND"

"Many physicians have decried the necessity of taking a stand that 10 years ago would have been unfathomable," says Nancy W. Dickey, former president of the A.M.A. and director of the Family Practice Residency Program at Texas A&M University's College of Medicine. "But changes in the health-care market have so heavily tipped the balance of power into systems of care and big insurers that physicians have had to take steps to preserve their ability to care for patients."

It remains to be seen how the angry outcry that produced the A.M.A. vote will reverberate at medical colleges, where professors have shown little interest in unionizing. But if the predictions of many experts are correct, more and more academic physicians and residents will, like their blue-collar counterparts, be at the negotiating table and even the picket lines.

Physicians and medical residents typically form separate unions. So far, medical professors have unionized on only a handful of campuses. But medical residents—doctors who have already received their medical degrees but are undergoing the required clinical training—have shown fewer qualms about collective bargaining.

The medical association estimates that about 108,000 physicians—one in seven—will be eligible to join its union. Of those, about 37,000 are academic physicians. Antitrust laws prevent self-employed physicians from joining unions, but that's not the case for those who are employed by institutions, such as hospitals, universities, and government agencies.

In addition, about a third of the nation's 96,000 medical residents—those who work at public institutions—are expected to be eligible for the A.M.A. union on a state-by-state basis. Depending on the outcome of a long-awaited ruling from the National Labor Relations Board, the other two-thirds, who work at private institutions, might also become eligible. The pending case involves interns and residents at the Boston Medical Center who want to unionize.

Some medical educators cringe at the thought of opening up the grueling process of educating physicians to outside arbitration. They worry that allowing an arbitrator to determine, for instance, whether a resident is working too many hours without a break or spending too much time taking blood pressure could interfere with the relationship between teachers and their students. Medical professors fear that they could no longer drop a poorly performing resident from a program without worrying that their judgment would be overruled.

"What worries me is that some arbitrator will be second-guessing faculty members' judgments on a resident's academic performance," says Jordan J. Cohen, president of the Association of American Medical Colleges, which includes all 125 accredited U.S. medical schools and 400 teaching hospitals and health systems. "That opens the door to all kinds of mayhem."

It also sends the wrong message to the next generation of physicians, he says. "Residency should be a time to encourage professionalism—the idea of putting one's self-interest second to that of the patients. This whole issue of unionization drives them in the opposite direction."

Not so, argues Bruce Elwell, an organizer for the New York–based Committee of Interns and Residents, a national union with nearly 10,000 members in California, the District of Columbia, Florida, Massachusetts, New Jersey, and New York.

Mr. Elwell says medical schools and teaching hospitals often justify marathon schedules and mundane duties as "educational" when, in fact, such policies exploit the residents. "People will argue that being on call every other night and working 100 hours a week is a great educational experience," he says. "Seventy-five percent of what they do is what we call scut—drawing blood, transporting patients. By the third time you draw blood from a patient, it ceases to be educational."

QUALITY OF CARE

What's more, he and others say, exhausted, unsupervised residents in inadequately staffed hospitals may be pressured to perform procedures for which they are not trained.

The distinction between work and education is at the crux of the debate over the right of medical interns to bargain collectively. Unions argue that medical residents are employees, and so are entitled to the same protections that other workers get. Groups like the Association of American Medical Colleges, on the other hand, insist that medical residents are, in essence, students. The conflict mirrors the continuing disagreements on some campuses over whether graduate teaching assistants are students or employees.

Both sides in the medical conflict are awaiting the N.L.R.B.'s ruling in the case involving interns and residents at the Boston Medical Center, the principal teaching hospital for Boston University's medical school. The ruling, which is expected this year, will establish whether private-sector residents have the right to unionize. In a 1976 case, the labor-relations board determined that residents in private hospitals were primarily students, not employees. That ruling was challenged two years ago by interns and residents at the Boston center. If the board reverses its earlier position, many experts predict that unions like Mr. Elwell's will swoop in on disgruntled residents and find plenty of recruits.

Mr. Elwell doesn't buy the argument that medical residents are students. "The reality of medical education is that it's continuous," he says. "If, 20 years from now, you're not still engaged in education, you're a bad doctor."

Just because someone is in the process of learning doesn't mean that the person isn't an employee, he argues.

"THEY HAVE US OVER A BARREL"

In the case of Dr. Kobaissi, one of 12 podiatric residents employed by the California College of Podiatric Medicine, the union is the Los Angeles chapter of the Committee of Interns and Residents.

Because they are employed by the college, medical residents and interns are not entitled to the higher salaries paid to employees of the L.A. County + U.S.C. Medical Center, a teaching hospital for the University of Southern California.

As a result, he and his wife and their infant son live in a tiny apartment behind his parents' house. After an 80-hour workweek, he sometimes helps a friend fix a car or repair a roof to make enough money to pay the rent. "If it were anyone but my parents, we would have been evicted by now, " he says.

When the podiatric residents asked administrators for a raise, they were told that the college couldn't afford it. "They essentially said, 'If you don't like it, you're free to go.'" Dr. Kobaissi said. "They know they can get away with it, because podiatry is very competitive, and they can always find someone to work free. They have us over a barrel."

The college's dean for clinical affairs, Joel R. Clark, acknowledges that the pay is inadequate. But without any government support for the residents' salaries, a raise is unrealistic, he says. "I feel horrible about the salaries they're earning. But given the resources of our small, private college, raising the salary to a respectable level would bankrupt the college."

Medical professors, many of whom divide their time among clinical, research, and teaching duties, are becoming increasingly frustrated by the changing health-care climate. But relatively few have turned to collective bargaining—in part because of its blue-collar image, and in part because they tend to be more isolated within their specialties.

Campuses where medical professors have joined unions include the four medical schools within the State University of New York System; the University of Cincinnati, and the University of Medicine and Dentistry of New Jersey. Among the hot issues: faculty layoffs and the increased pressure on medical professors to bring in a large part of their income through outside grants.

At SUNY's Health Science Center at Syracuse, for instance, medical professors wanted an assurance that their clinical earnings wouldn't disappear into the ledger books when the university took over managing those accounts from the clinical department itself. Some professors feared that their hard-earned money would be siphoned off to other parts of the medical center.

"Five percent of the clinical revenues go into a 'dean's fund,' but it's not clear what really happens with the money," says Phillip H. Smith, a professor of medicine who heads the local chapter of United University Professions, a faculty union. The administration has agreed to report how that money is spent.

Critics of unionization say physicians who organize are compromising their responsibilities to patients. "My worry is that most people will use it as a device for physicians to try to protect their economic well-being rather than protect patients," says Dr. Cohen, of the medical-colleges association.

But a medical ethicist at the University of Michigan argues that it's morally acceptable for doctors to unionize, and even to strike, as long as they're acting in their patients' best interests.

"Doctors already act collectively and can do so morally," writes Susan D. Goold in a paper that will appear next year in the *Cambridge Quarterly of Healthcare Ethics*. "But the goal of collective action must be completely consistent with their commitment to the patient and respectful of the trust patients place in them."

For example, she says, if a health-maintenance organization added more patients to its system without hiring more physicians, the patients would be hurt by having less time with their doctors. In that case, both the physician and the patient would suffer, and a grievance would be easy to justify.

● ●
REJECTING UNIONIZATION

Medical-faculty members on some campuses have considered unionizing and decided against it. In June, professors at the University of Connecticut Health Center voted 250 to 169 against joining a union. Those who favored unionizing said it would protect them from potential layoffs. But Richard Garibaldi, chairman of the university's department of medicine, says the majority felt that the problems they were facing had to be resolved within the institution. "Faculty feel very vulnerable, and rightly so, but most of them felt that a union wouldn't provide the kinds of answers we're looking for."

While the impact of the American Medical Association's vote in support of a union remains to be seen, some observers predict that the effects won't be limited to residents and interns.

"I wonder whether the A.M.A. vote sanctioning unionization by doctors puts a cloak of legitimacy on organizing and collective bargaining that will wind up not only embracing elements of the medical-academic community, but extend beyond that," says Sheldon E. Steinbach, vice-president and general counsel of the American Council on Education.

Because doctors are regarded as "the pinnacle of professionalism," he says, if they start organizing, other professors who once dismissed unions as beneath them might have a change of heart.

III-7: Better Safe Than Sorry

ASHLEA EBELING

When Annette Phillips was bartending at a Hooters restaurant in Myrtle Beach, South Carolina, she claims the chief executive's brother slapped her buttocks. Phillips threatened to sue her employer for sexual discrimination.

Not so fast, said Hooters. Corporate policy required her to use binding arbitration. A private arbitrator would hear and decide her claim. She couldn't bring a suit and her right to appeal to the courts was limited.

Mandatory arbitration programs like Hooters' proliferated after the Supreme Court essentially endorsed the concept in 1991. The basic idea was a good one: Arbitrating employment disputes would help unclog the court system. It costs less and is speedier for both parties. About the only losers are the trial lawyers.

In just five years the number of major companies with employment dispute resolution plans has jumped from about 30 to more than 400, covering at least 4 million employees.

But the Supreme Court was careful to say that arbitration should look and feel just like a judicial case. An employer could require employees to arbitrate disputes as a term of their employment, but it had to be done fairly, with due process.

More recently there has been a backlash against enforced arbitration. Even the National Academy of Arbitrators opposes mandatory plans, and now the courts are finding that some company plans are unfair. Last March in the Hooters case, a Federal judge in Florence, South Carolina called Hooters' policy "sham arbitration" and concluded it was unenforceable. The judge cited a multitude of what she considered one-sided provisions.

In a federal appellate case in Washington, D.C., Burns International Security Services had a provision requiring employees to pay all or part of the arbitrator's fee (which can average $2,500). The court struck that provision down, reasoning that an employee doesn't have to pay for a judge in court.

In *Duffield v. Robertson, Stephens & Co.*, the Ninth Circuit Court of Appeals earlier this year declared the very notion of

Reprinted from *Forbes* (November 30, 1998): 162–163.

mandatory arbitration illegal in disputes involving racial discrimination and sexual harassment. The Supreme Court let that decision stand this month, and it recently heard arguments in another arbitration case.

In a suit in U.S. District Court in Ohio, a company buried its mandatory arbitration provision in an employee handbook. The judge said that was insufficient notice.

With many arbitration plans failing to hold up in court, some businesses are either revising—or giving up—mandatory policies. The National Association of Securities Dealers recently abandoned long-standing requirements that member companies use arbitration to resolve discrimination claims. The New York Stock Exchange will no longer provide an arbitrator for mandatory plans.

Now many brokerages are designing their own plans. In May Merrill Lynch agreed to replace its mandatory policy with a voluntary one as part of a settlement of a class action sex discrimination suit. Under the new policy, an employee with a discrimination complaint can choose between arbitration and the courts. In the last six months, eight major corporations have installed voluntary plans, according to Robert Meade, of the American Arbitration Association.

Also in May, United Parcel Service implemented a voluntary program for roughly 65,000 employees after a year-long pilot. It has not led to a rash of lawsuits: Of the 197 employee complaints since April 1997, 75% have been resolved early in the dispute resolution process—and no employee has gone to court. "We decided forcing people into something would cast doubt on the program," says Kevin Strahan, employment dispute resolution manager.

TRW and others have taken another route. Employees unhappy about the arbitrator's decision can still sue. TRW says of fewer than ten cases arbitrated so far, only one is heading for court. TRW also changed a provision requiring the employee to pay part of the arbitrator's fees, reducing it to a flat $100.

Many companies with mandatory arbitration plans are standing firm. Despite the setbacks, a majority of courts have upheld the policy. But, considering how well the voluntary policies work, it would seem to make sense to replace mandatory arbitration with voluntary plans. As Evan Spelfogel, a New York lawyer, says, "Why ask for trouble and give plaintiff's bar anything to hang their hat on?"

III-8: Reinventing Workplace Regulation

DAVID I. LEVINE

In the United States, more than 100 laws regulate everything from safety to discrimination to overtime rules.[1] Unfortunately, workplace regulations often do not work well for employees, for employers, or for regulators. Nobody is satisfied with the current system of regulation. Employees and

their unions complain of continued discrimination, lack of safety, and other problems. Employers complain of the high cost of regulations, an adversarial relation with regulators, and the rigidity of many "one-size-fits-all" regulations. Even regulators are unhappy. Rules are difficult to modify even decades after the regulators realize they are out of date. For example, one agency used an 18-foot chart with 373 boxes to describe its rulemaking process.[2] Inspections are rare, frustrating many regulators' desire to ensure safe, legal, and nondiscriminatory workplaces. In addition, rules often require regulators to play "gotcha" and count minor infractions. For example, paperwork violations are the most common source of violations written up by OSHA. The resulting system often leads to, as one author put it, *The Death of Common Sense.*[3] Most regulators would prefer to use common sense so they can assist compliance by those companies that want to play by the rules, while focusing enforcement on the worst offenders.

AN ALTERNATIVE

The good news is that an alternative exists, one based on creating incentives for companies and workers to solve their own problems. The proposed system is based on *conditional* deregulation, where companies with good records of compliance can choose to work with their employees to improve compliance and face fewer regulations, inspections, and penalties. To ensure the company does not reduce safety, increase discrimination, or otherwise worsen employees' lives, employees or their representatives must approve each alternative plan.

When the system works, regulations will be more flexible and will achieve their goals more effectively (for example, providing more safety at lower cost). The methods used to meet these goals will be designed to fit the needs of each organization and its workforce, reducing the costs of compliance. In addition, more managers and employees will have the authority and the incentive to ensure the company complies. The new system also will provide incentives for companies to be proactive in working with their workforce to search out and solve problems. Companies that provide good workplaces will be rewarded with regulatory flexibility. These positive incentives will be in addition to existing negative incen-

tives such as fines, the costs of workers' compensation, or the threat of a union drive. The outcome should be safer, fairer, and less discriminatory workplaces that are both better places to work and more productive.

Importantly, regulators will be able to spend less time and energy at the majority of workplaces that intend to comply with the spirit of the law. This change will free up regulatory energy to focus on the "bad apples." (At the same time, some fraction of regulators' resources will need to be redirected to providing training materials and other assistance to workplaces that are moving to the new system.)

The potential disadvantages of the proposed system are equally clear. Companies might merely go through the motions of setting up alternative systems, while reducing safety and ignoring the statutory rights of their employees. In this scenario, a system of conditional deregulation will diminish the already-weak enforcement powers of the regulators. Self-regulation without oversight is not a recipe for compliance.

Fortunately, one group has an interest both in effective regulation and in a flexible and productive workplace—the workforce. A premise of the proposed system is that the employees must collectively approve any plan for achieving a regulation's goal. For example, employees can provide oversight when considering new means to achieve the goals of a safety regulation. They might choose to exchange more flexibility in weekly hours for an end to mandatory overtime: and they can approve an employee involvement group to improve working conditions or safety that might otherwise run afoul of labor law. In all these cases, if the workforce agrees, it is often inefficient for the federal government to mandate one-size-fits-all regulations.

There is no single best way to ensure employee involvement in approving the alternative plans. At the same time, the approval process must meet minimum standards concerning adequate information, adequate training, and a fair selection process for employee representatives.

Each sphere of regulation, from safety to wages and hours, suffers from a common set of problems: rigid, command-and-control regulations, with one set of regulations for all workplaces over a certain size, coupled with an adversarial and legalistic enforcement mechanism. Each sphere of workplace regulation also has similar problems of employer opportunism such as mismeasuring compliance or failing to meet minimum standards. In addition, each sphere has the feature that the workforce and the regulators share most objectives.

Under this proposal, companies and workers could jointly agree to modify the regulations in any one sphere or in several. This proposal provides the economy of scale of having a single representative body in place for all issues that arise. Because of the common issues that arise in each sphere of workplace regulation, proposals for reform of specific arenas will systematically miss the advantages of a unified framework for employee-monitored self-regulation.

The proposal draws on the long tradition among economists of advocating performance-based regulations. It also enables employers (with their workforce) to design alternative means to achieve the goals of any regulation. Furthermore, those who are successful in this endeavor would be treated differently from those with poor records. For environmental regulations, preliminary evidence indicates that performance-based regulations can achieve performance similar to that of command-and-control regulations, but cost about one third less. (Moving to performance-based regulations is already a priority of the Clinton administration's proposals for reinventing regulations.)[4] It is plausible that similar cost savings can be achieved in other spheres of workplace regulation.

Employee involvement is an important complement to performance-based regulations because measuring performance is so often problematic. For example, rewarding low rates of reported injuries gives managers incentives both to reduce injuries, and to penalize employees who report their injuries. Empowering employees to approve the safety plan and to monitor its results reduces the difficulties with managers intentionally distorting the measures used to gauge performance.

SAFETY AND HEALTH

Every year more than 6,000 Americans die of workplace injuries, an estimated 50,000 people die of illnesses caused by workplace chemical exposures, and six million people suffer nonfatal workplace injuries. The good news is that fatality rates have been declining over the last 20 years, particularly in the sectors most heavily inspected by OSHA. The bad news is that injury rates (as best we can measure them) have not declined. Injuries alone cost the economy more than $110 billion a year.[5] These numbers are high in absolute terms, and they are also high compared with other nations such as Sweden and Japan (even acknowledging difficulties in international comparisons.)[6] Moreover, in the previous five years, OSHA had not inspected three fourths of the work sites that suffered serious accidents in 1994 and early 1995.[7]

More regulation does not seem to be the answer: after the IRS, OSHA may be the most hated part of the federal government.[8] The reasons for this hatred are easy to understand. As OSHA itself describes the problem:

> In the public's view, OSHA has been driven too often by numbers and rules, not by smart enforcement and results. Business complains about overzealous enforcement and burdensome rules. . . .

Too often, a "one-size-fits-all" regulatory approach has treated conscientious employers no differently from those who put workers needlessly at risk.[9]

THE ROLE OF EMPLOYEE INVOLVEMENT IN IMPROVING SAFETY

Improving safety and health requires that managers and employees actively participate in identifying and eliminating hazards. A number of enterprises have already established mechanisms for such employee involvement. For example, in one survey about 75 percent of establishments with more than 50 employees reported having safety and health committees, as did 31 percent of smaller ones.[10]

MANDATORY PROGRAMS

About 10 states currently have laws that require employers in some of all sectors to sponsor safety committees.[11] A majority of state workers' compensation systems are beginning to require workplaces to establish a safety and health program, at least in hazardous sectors.[12] Most of these required programs contain minimum standards similar to those listed below.

Although no careful evaluation exists, preliminary evidence on the effectiveness of such committees is favorable. For example, both state and business officials agree that mandated safety and health committees have contributed to the $1.5 billion decrease in injury costs experienced by Oregon employers between 1990 and 1993.[13]

VOLUNTARY PROGRAMS

OSHA's well-respected Voluntary Protection Program recognizes companies with excellent safety programs. VPP employers have injury rates about 40 percent lower than the average of their industries (although it is unclear how much of the decrease is due to the actions measured by the VPP program). More generally, employers that voluntarily adopt safety and health programs have lower injury and illness rates than do other employers, and their managers often attribute the difference largely to the existence of the program.[14]

Unfortunately, current federal law discourages such safety and health programs instead of encouraging them. One reason is that the National Labor Relations Acts' definition of "company unions" is broad enough to forbid many safety committees. Another reason is that OSHA does not systematically provide incentives for proactive safety and health programs. (OSHA does provide a small incentive in that good faith efforts can lower fines slightly.) Even if a safety and health program identifies a better and cheaper way to achieve a safety goal, OSHA does not grant a waiver from its detailed regulations.

Fortunately, the situation is changing, and OSHA is moving to encourage proactive safety and health programs. For example, in a pilot program called Maine 200, OSHA targeted the 203 companies in Maine with the most injuries over the preceding years. Each company in this group was allowed to choose either to undergo an immediate and detailed safety inspection, or to create a safety and health program meeting certain minimum standards. All but two of the companies opted to create a safety program.

Preliminary results of Maine 200 have been impressive. Participating companies have identified and eliminated 55,000 hazards in the program's first year—as many hazards as OSHA identified in the entire state during the previous eight years. In addition, the injury rate declined at 59 percent of these companies, sometimes dramatically.[15] OSHA is currently expanding this program to any state that will help it identify the companies with the worst safety records.

In construction, OSHA has begun rewarding worksites with a written safety program and a trained safety person. OSHA rewards such sites by promising that any OSHA inspections will focus only on the four main deadly hazards, not on minor violations such as paperwork violations or poor communication about possible hazards.[16]

ENSURING MINIMUM STANDARDS

In the writings of safety professionals such as industrial hygienists, ergonomists, union safety representatives, and regulators, a consensus is arising about the elements of adequate safety programs. Such programs must ensure that both managers and employees have the training to understand safety, incentives to improve safety, and the authority to make safety-enhancing changes. To be more specific, the following elements are common to most proposals for an adequate safety and health program:[17]

- Managers and employees receive training and education about identifying and controlling hazards. They (or outside experts they choose) perform periodic workplace inspections to identify hazards.

- Managers and employees have incentives to participate fully in the safety and health program. Employees or their representatives have the authority to develop recommendations to the employer with assurance that the employer will respond to recommendations in a timely manner. Employees are protected against retribution due to their contributions to the safety program.

- When accidents occur, an emergency response plan is implemented and first aid services are available. An investigation to eliminate root causes follows each accident.

- The employer provides appropriate medical surveillance for all health hazards.

- Written records include a description of the safety and health program, records of injuries and illnesses, and plans to abate hazards. These abatement plans have timetables and procedures to track progress.

Good processes matter, but so do results. Under this proposal, employers with very high accident and illness rates (compared with their industry) or with fairly high accident rates and no pattern of improvement would lose the presumptions otherwise due to employers with good safety programs. (Employers requesting exemptions would be required to submit their OSHA safety and health logs and workers' compensation records to OSHA so that OSHA could compare its safety record with its industry.) For employers with poor safety records, or those in particularly dangerous industries, additional certification of the safety program by a third party such as the workers' compensation insurer may be required. (Workers' compensation insurers are good choices to make these certifications because they save money from reducing injury rates. Several states require insurers to certify safety plans as adequate.)

Finally, not all regulations would be automatically waived if workers approve the voluntary plan. In situations with hard-to-detect hazards that may lead to rare or long-to-develop harms, even trained employees will have trouble dealing with the scientific complexities involved. In these situations, OSHA should continue to promulgate regulations.

OSHA has already proposed some incentives for excellent safety programs and records. These include OSHA inspections focused on major hazards rather than every hazard, lower fines, and lower priority for random inspections.[18] Unfortunately, these incentives alone will not be very effective, because fines are almost always trivially small and random inspections are very rare.

OSHA could provide more effective incentives by giving automatic waivers from detailed command-and-control regulations to safety programs that achieve the goals of each rule. In addition, OSHA could agree that for approved safety programs, all complaints except those involving imminent danger would have to satisfy the internal safety procedures before OSHA would inspect the workplace. For example, a worker would first have to submit a suggestion or complaint to the in-house safety committee. Only if this committee then found no need for action (or did not act in a timely fashion) could the worker call in an outside regulator. OSHA does not have time to inspect every complaint and still engage in sufficient random inspections of the most dangerous workplaces; giving deference to excellent in-house systems will permit them to focus their scarce resources on the most dangerous and worst-run workplaces.

Permitting companies to exempt themselves from OSHA regulations if they have a safety program creates a risk that some companies will establish sham programs that reduce safety. Fortunately, employees have an interest in a safe workplace and are ideally placed to oversee the workplace safety plan. In addition, under this proposal, employees can threaten to disestablish the safety program, causing OSHA to revert to detailed regulations coupled with an inspection if the employer does not follow through on agreed safety and health improvements. Preliminary case studies and statistical evidence suggest that the combination of employee involvement in health and safety and the ability to call in safety regulators when disputes arise can lead to better outcomes than either alone.[19]

DISCRIMINATION AND HARASSMENT

The United States is unique among industrialized nations in permitting companies to fire employees without the need to show cause. Ironically, the United States is also unique in having the most expensive and conflict-laden legal system, one that frustrates both employees and managers. Alternative dispute resolution programs such as mediation, arbitration, and ombudsmen have the potential to increase fairness in dismissals, promotions, and other management actions, while also reducing costs.[20] The key is to ensure these alternative dispute resolution programs are not mere shams, but actually provide due process under the law.

Employees have statutory rights to a workplace free of discrimination and sexual harassment. Unfortunately, surveys suggest that several million employees each year perceive they have been sexually harassed or discriminated against. Evidence of continued discrimination is not just from self-reports. When matched pairs of employees (black and white, Anglo and Hispanic, or male and female) are sent for job interviews, employers are more likely to offer white Anglo men employment, especially for better jobs.[21]

Workers have a statutory right to appeal to the EEOC, and eventually to the court system, for redress. Unfortunately, many workers cannot enforce their statutory rights. When employees bring charges before the EEOC, they find themselves at the back of a line almost 100,000 people (18 months) long.[22] When the EEOC does find the employer guilty of malfeasance, most claims do not result in meaningful monetary damages. Lawsuits, although occasionally leading to enormous awards, are largely the preserve of those in high-wage and high-status occupations, and are irrelevant in practice to most of the workforce.[23]

Even without the backlog, many victims of discrimination do not find EEOC enforcement well-suited to their problems. Some find the EEOC process too adversarial. Many do not want to bring formal charges, but want low-cost, low-intensity dispute resolution procedures. Sometimes the employee wants nothing more than a formal apology or for the behavior to stop.[24] Other employees find the EEOC process too costly, particularly if they need a lawyer at some stage. A third group of employees finds the EEOC process too public. For example, the EEOC process does not permit anonymous complaints as would be possible through the in-house ombudsman in many companies.

In short, many employees find themselves with no workable recourse to discrimination. Some quit and suffer unemployment or wage declines: others continue to work after what may have been largely a misunderstanding, with no simple means for clearing up the misunderstanding; and others endure work with bosses who persist in violating their rights.

At the same time, nonunion employees in the private sector are employed at will, meaning the firm is allowed to dismiss the employee "for good cause, for bad cause, or even for cause morally wrong."[25] Many states have carved out several exemptions to pure employment at will, most importantly based on employers' handbooks or other promises that imply an employment contract.[26] Unfortunately, these protections, like those against discrimination, apply in practice primarily to high-wage employers who can afford a lawyer.[27]

While many employees feel their rights are not protected, many employers resent the cost of litigation and regulation and what they perceive as EEOC's combative and anti-employer stance.[28] Two bad effects can result if employers find it expensive to dismiss people from protected groups. First, fear of lawsuits may stop them from dismissing unsatisfactory employees from these protected groups, reducing efficiency and incentives. In addition, employers may resist hiring the disabled, blacks, or females because they fear future lawsuits.[29] When the courts do find a contract was implied, many employers

resent the high costs of lawsuits and the uncertainty and risk relating to the (small) chance of very large damages.[30]

The cost of the EEOC process already provides companies with some incentive for developing good in-house processes for the avoidance and resolution of discrimination cases. But current employment law does nothing to amplify this incentive, and it should.

THE ROLE OF EMPLOYEE OVERSIGHT IN CREATING CREDIBLE ALTERNATIVE DISPUTE RESOLUTION PROCEDURES[31]

While no legal system alone can end all discrimination, this proposal should both reduce discrimination and lower the costs of fighting discrimination. Alternative dispute resolution procedures can reduce costs, increase the speed with which problems are resolved, and increase both employees' and employers' satisfaction. A key element of alternative dispute resolution procedures is that they can be flexible and tailored to the needs of the organization and its members.[32] For example, in-house dispute resolution procedures often provide employees with the choice of either confidential or public means of addressing complaints. In a setting where many employees are not native English speakers, in-house procedures might ensure that any appeals board of workers and managers had at least one speaker of each party's native language. In many complaints, the main need is for better communication; in-house procedures can begin with mediation, not the more legalistic EEOC procedures. . . .

CRITIQUES

The main critique of in-house systems—even those approved by the workforce and meeting high standards—is that some workers will lose compared with the status quo. For example, some safety programs will not be sensitive to complaints that would be valid under OSHA and that an OSHA inspector would have caught, and some in-house dispute resolution procedures will be manipulated by management, endorsed by a discriminatory workforce, or poorly run.

These problems are serious, but ultimately the criticism is unconvincing. Many workers now work in unsafe conditions and are not treated fairly. Given the inadequacies of the current system and the likelihood of continuing funding cuts for regulatory agencies, the current system is unlikely to become more effective at protecting workers without dramatic reforms, and indeed is likely to get worse. This proposal must be judged by whether it improves safety, lessens discrimination, and improves the situation for most workers, not by whether it is perfect.

Some unions have opposed past proposals for various forms of employee representation committees in the United States because they are too close to company unions. At the same time, some managers have resented proposals for works councils as thinly disguised entry points for unions. The evidence supports neither view strongly—for example, no evidence exists that union organizing has increased or decreased in states that begin requiring safety committees.

An additional argument against permitting workers to renegotiate regulations in areas such as safety is that they may agree with management (perhaps under the threat of job loss) to reduce safety or other protections below the socially optimal level. (Recall that because of workers' compensation and social security disability insurance, often neither workers nor employers pay the full cost of injuries.) It is likely that workers and managers at some workplaces will agree to reduce safety below the level that OSHA now requires on paper. Unfor-

tunately, given OSHA's resources for enforcement, under the status quo OSHA has almost no ability to enforce safety rules in workplaces where workers and managers do not want to obey them. Thus, it is unlikely that many workplaces will reduce their level of safety, although it may remain below the socially optimal level.

One obstacle to the new system is the required change in the priorities of regulators. Currently, as noted above, regulators are often required to inspect after every complaint and to write up all violations, no matter how minor. Under the new regime, many regulations would be waived for workplaces with effective internal systems. Regulators would need to redirect resources from nitpicking inspections to providing training materials and other resources for in-house systems. (Inspections at companies without effective in-house systems would remain an important part of regulators' jobs.) Congress would need to provide sufficient resources to regulators so that they could assist compliance, particularly in the early years when participants in in-house systems will need the most training.

A further issue for any proposal for employee representation, ranging from unions to works councils, is the question of the proper scope for representation. This proposal assumes that the workplace (for example, a single store in a large retail chain) is appropriate. In employers with multiple worksites, a company-wide employee council might help make policy, along with establishment-specific councils. Furthermore, special versions of these rules would be needed at workplaces such as construction sites where many employees work only a short while.

Politically, this proposal has many hurdles. The current system has relatively strong workers' *de jure* rights on paper, but often not in practice. After a generation of expansion in *de jure* rights for employees, many advocates for employees look to the law, not to employees and employers, to protect workers' rights. *De jure* rights are only likely to improve workers' lives if these advocates are willing to trade off some unenforceable rights on paper for improved protections in practice.

At the same time, many critics of employment protections feel that complete deregulation is the answer. Everyone agrees the current regulatory system has many shortcomings. Unfortunately, continued discrimination coupled with the many imperfections in labor markets makes it unlikely that complete deregulation will enhance the workforce's well-being. Similarly, although savings are possible, budget cuts which destroy the limited regulatory capacities of the enforcement agencies are also unlikely to improve things. It is in the long-run interests of both managers and employees to improve regulation, even if not along the lines of this proposal.

Finally, many proponents of reinventing regulation focus on the importance of measuring outcomes, not processes. This proposal, in contrast, promotes a focus on both outcomes and a meta-process (that is, an employee-led process for approving the process). The reason to involve employees is simple—because outcomes are always difficult to measure, employers will face incentives to game any outcome measurement system. In many cases, we can achieve better results with a combination of outcome measurement and employee-led monitoring of internal processes.

CONCLUSION

Almost all observers of the American workplace think it desirable to have both more flexible regulations and greater employee participation in the regulation and resolution of workplace issues. The government has substantial control over the first, but must be concerned that any flexibility will be used by employers to defeat the goals of the regulations. In contrast, the government has few mechanisms for encouraging employee participation.[33] Fortunately, the proposed system both promotes flexibility in regulation and, by using employees to monitor management, increases employees' voice in how their workplace is run. Thus the government moves from discouraging to encouraging employee involvement in decisions at the workplace, and at the same time it reduces direct government regulation.

It is important that the proposed new system is voluntary. Each employer has the option of establishing an alternative system with high standards and employee oversight, or the option to remain subject to the current regulatory scheme. The government provides incentives to those employers with good records of success and good programs to work with their employees to ensure continued progress. Often, an important incentive is the prospect of being freed, albeit conditionally, from detailed command-and-control regulations.

In short, the status quo provides poor incentives to workers and managers—it encourages them to concentrate on the letter of the regulation while ignoring the goal of the law. The reinvented system provides incentives for workers and managers to achieve and exceed the standards of today. The status quo also provides poor incentives for regulators; for example, OSHA inspectors, who are forced to play "gotcha" instead of finding flexible and creative ways to improve safety. The reinvented system permits many employees of regulatory agencies to focus on compliance assistance, while others focus on the truly bad apples. Finally, the status quo relies on top-down regulations, while the reinvented process encourages workers and managers to improve compliance, with flexibility to meet local conditions.

Under this proposal, an employer can establish an alternative regulatory system in any single area of workplace regulations such as safety, dispute resolution, or wage and hours rules. However, the new system can be fruitfully applied to all these areas of regulation. Creating a single employee committee to provide oversight for all spheres costs less than creating separate oversight mechanisms. This approach to reinventing regulation, by providing employers incentives to work with their employees, has the potential to improve both the condition of the workplace and its productivity.

Notes

1. GAO [General Accounting Office]. *Report on Workplace Regulation,* Washington, D.C., June 1994.
2. *Regulatory Systems,* Accompanying Report of the National Performance Review, Office of the Vice President, Washington, D.C., September 1993.
3. Philip K. Howard. *The Death of Common Sense* (New York: Random House, 1994).
4. Al Gore, *Common Sense Government* (New York: Random House, 1995).
5. *The New OSHA,* Department of Labor, URL http://www.osha-slc.gov/Reinventing. 1995.
6. Joel Rogers and Richard B. Freeman, "Who Speaks for Us? Employee Representation in a Nonunion Labor Market," in Bruce E. Kaufman and Morris M. Kleiner, eds., *Employee Representation: Alternatives and Future Directions* (Madison, Wis.: IRRA, 1993).

   Some analysts dispute the need for any safety regulation. They assume that workers have good information before taking jobs or that workers quickly find out about hazards and find it easy to move between jobs. In this setting, employers will face market incentives to provide the efficient amount of safety because unsafe employers will need to pay higher wages that compensate workers for hazards.

   Unfortunately, the empirical support for this theory is mixed. In addition, a number of market failures suggest government intervention is called for. For example,

information on safety and (especially) health risks that may take decades to materialize is far from perfect. Moreover, the presence of social insurance implies that injured workers do not pay the full cost of their injuries; thus, the free market will lead to inefficiently little safety. Finally, even if markets work well, we should still favor proposals such as this one that reduce the costs of the politically chosen level of safety regulation.

7. Bob Port and John Solomon, "OSHA Never Saw 75% of Fatal Sites," *San Jose Mercury News,* September 5, 1995, pp. 1E, 5E.
8. Edward E. Potter and Judith A. Youngman, *Keeping America Competitive: Employment Policy for the Twenty-First Century* (Lakewood, Colo.: Glenbridge, 1995).
9. *The New OSHA,* Department of Labor, URL http://www.osha-slc.gov/Reinventing, 1995.
10. Commission on the Future of Worker-Management Relations, *Report and Recommendations,* U.S. Department of Labor, U.S. Department of Commerce, Washington, D.C., 1994.
11. Ibid.
12. OSHA [Occupational Safety and Health Administration]. *Review and Analysis of State-Mandated and Other Worker Protections Programs,* June 1995.
13. "Oregon Safety Committees Touted," *Occupational Safety and Health* (September 1993), pp. 26–27.
14. GAO [General Accounting Office]. "Workplace Safety and Health Programs Show Promise," Testimony before the House Committee on Education and Labor. GAO/T-HRD-92-15, 1992.
15. *The New OSHA*, Department of Labor, URL http://www.osha-slc.gov/Reinventing, 1995, Appendix 1.
16. Ibid., Appendix 2.
17. See, for example, ibid., Appendix 3.
18. Ibid.
19. Paul Adler, Barbara Goldoftas, and David I. Levine, "Ergonomics, Employee Involvement, and the Toyota Production System: A Case Study of NUMMI's 1993 Model Change," *Industrial and Labor Relations Review* 50/3 (April 1997): 416–437; David

Weil, "Enforcing OSHA: The Role of Labor Unions," *Industrial Relations,* 30/1 (Winter 1991): 20–36.

20. May 1991 article explains several market imperfections that may lead employers to have inefficiently or unfairly little protection against unjust dismissal. David I. Levine, "Just Cause Employment Policies in the Presence of Worker Adverse Selection," *Journal of Labor Economics,* 9/3 (July 1991): 294–305.

21. Marc Bendick et al., "Measuring Employment Discrimination Through Controlled Experiments," Fair Employment Council of Greater Washington, Inc., Washington, D.C., May 1993; George Glaster, Wendy Zimmerman, et al., "Sandwich Hiring Audit Pilot Program Report," Urban Institute, Washington D.C., 1994; David Neumark, Roy J. Bank, and Kyle D. Van Nort, "Sex Discrimination in Restaurant Hiring: An Audit Study," National Bureau of Economic Research, Cambridge, MA, 1995; Michael Fix and Raymond J. Struyk, eds., *Clear and Convincing Evidence: Measurement of Discrimination in America* (Washington D.C.: Urban Institute Press, 1993).

22. Shannon P. Duffy, "Casellas: EEOC Suffering Backlash," *The Legal Intelligencer,* June 20, 1995, p. 1.

23. John J. Donahue, III, and Peter Siegelman, "The Changing Nature of Employment Discrimination Litigation," *Stanford Law Review* (May 1991).

24. Mary P. Rowe, "People Who Feel Harassed Need a Complaint System with both Formal and Informal Options," *Negotiations Journal* (January 1990), pp. 1–12.

25. Jack Steiber, "Employment-At-Will: An Issue for the 1980s," 1983 IRRA Proceedings, Industrial Relations Research Association, Madison, WI, 1984, p. 2.

26. Potter and Youngman, op. cit., p. 141.

27. Commission on the Future of Worker-Management Relations, *Report and Recommendations,* U.S. Department of Labor, U.S. Department of Commerce, Washington D.C., 1994, p. 30.

28. Potter and Youngman, op. cit., p. 141.

29. Donahue and Siegelman, op. cit.

30. Joseph Goldstein, "Alternatives to High-Cost Litigation," *Cornell Hotel and Restaurant Administration Quarterly,* 36/1 (February 1995): 28 ff.

31. This section draws on the Commission on the Future of Worker-Management Relations, *Report and Recommendations,* December 1994, pp. 29–30.

32. Commission on the Future of Worker Management Relations, *Report and Recommendations,* Washington D.C., U.S. Department of Labor: U.S. Department of Commerce, 1994, p. 28.

33. Ibid., p. 27.

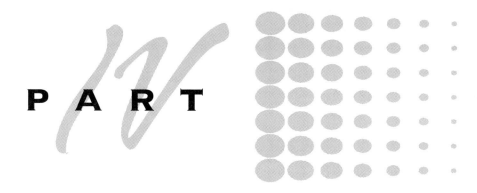

PART IV

IMPLEMENTING COMPENSATION AND BENEFITS

From its earliest roots to the present day, compensation has been central to HRM. Compensation responsibilities grew from the routine clerical tasks of payroll administration to include the design and administration of a host of sophisticated incentive pay and benefit packages. Employers are interested in minimizing costs while attracting, retaining, and motivating an effective labor force. Employees, whatever their level, are interested in their own financial well-being and security. The tensions between these interests are major factors in the dynamics of compensation. The multiple realities of compensation are the subject of the articles in Part IV.

The design of pay plans is the focus for the next section of articles. To be effective, pay must affect employee behavior. "How American Workers See the Rewards of Work" (Peter V. Leblanc and Paul W. Mulvey) documents that employees view compensation much differently than management, particularly when it comes to pay for performance. Stock options are currently a popular form of compensation; but, according to Samuel Greengard's "Stock Options Have Their Ups & Downs," HR is finding there are many associated problems.

Compensation approaches vary substantially across firms. We offer two examples to illustrate. IBM's need to accommodate the new workforce drives "Paying the People in Black at Big Blue" by Andrew S. Richter. Michael Lewis (excerpt from *Liar's Poker*) reveals his ambivalence about the substantial bonus he earned as a first-year bond trader.

Sanford Jacoby's *Modern Manors* (excerpt included in Part I) describes the sometimes feudal nature of the relationship that developed between employer and employee in the early part of the twentieth century. Fulfilling employee needs through employee benefits, some of which became legally required, was an important aspect of the relationship. As we move into the twenty-first century, the roles of employer, government, and employee in meeting employee needs are being reconsidered (see also Part VIII). The debate about changes in legally required economic security programs like Social Security continues. "What, Me Worry?" by Robert W. Thompson considers the Society for Human Resource Management's perspective on the human resource management implications of Social Security reform. Ellen E. Schultz's "Pension Cuts 101" indicates that recent changes to employer pension plans have often been at employee expense. Pressures of rising costs and employee concerns for choice have led many employers to provide vouchers for health care coverage rather than a particular health care plan (Amy Gage, "Employers Pass Buck on Insurance").

IV-1: How American Workers See the Rewards of Work

PETER V. LEBLANC AND PAUL W. MULVEY

Cradle-to-grave employment is no longer the norm, yet Americans remain surprisingly loyal to their employers. But they expect to be rewarded well for this loyalty—and for good performance. The message to employers is, if you can't guarantee me a retirement, fine, but reward me fairly while I'm here.

Clearly, downsizings, mergers and acquisitions, and other organizational changes of the 1990s have been a wake-up call that workers no longer can depend on their employers as the paternalistic, lifelong providers of the past. Despite this trend, employees are still surprisingly loyal to their organizations, but there's a catch. According to new research, that loyalty is being threatened by employees' dissatisfaction with their pay and the methods used to determine pay.

These are findings from a new study on the "Rewards of Work," conducted by Sibson & Company. The study shows that nearly 80 percent of U.S. workers are committed to their employers and 66 percent believe their employers are supportive of their work efforts. Only 16 percent of American workers say they intend to leave their employer voluntarily during the next year, despite the many opportunities available in a tight labor market.

Yet only 60 percent of those workers reported being satisfied with their level of job security. The study reveals that workers' commitment to their organization and intention to leave are significantly related to their satisfaction with their compensation.

Reprinted from *Compensation and Benefits Review* (January–February 1998): 24–28.

The kicker is that the amount of pay and benefits workers receive is only part of it.

The most important factor in determining employee commitment or intention to leave is not pay, but the pay system. That is, employees who are more satisfied with the system and process used to determine their pay are less likely to leave and are more committed to their employer. Among the pay system elements studied were the following:

- The process for setting job grades and bands
- The amount of information provided about the pay system
- The process for determining raises
- The type of pay system used
- Leader discretion on pay decisions

Furthermore, workers today have clear preferences for how they want this pay system to be designed. The "Rewards of Work" study surveyed 2,250 full-time U.S. workers, a nationally representative sample, working in a wide variety of industries across the country. Almost 1,500 workers returned the surveys for a 66 percent response rate. Sibson conducted the research in conjunction with PSI, a Tampa-based international market research and consulting firm.

The "Rewards of Work" survey addressed pay system preferences and five categories of the total rewards strategy including pay, benefits, work content, affiliation, and career. Respondents were identified as a "core worker," "knowledge worker," or "leader." Core workers are nonexempt individual contributors; knowledge workers are exempt individual contributors; and leaders are managers of individual contributors.

PAY SYSTEM PREFERENCES

U.S. workers today want rewards to be focused on the individual—not the team, group, or company—and they want increased pay to be fixed, that is, delivered to their base pay rather than in the form of one-time payments such as bonuses or incentives.

According to the research, employees who report the strongest preference for individualized and fixed rewards such as merit pay are also the highest performing. Sibson's "Rewards of Work" study suggests more than a Dilbertesque frustration with the workplace. Employees are demonstrating a deep, profound dissatisfaction with the way their performance is evaluated and rewarded.

The study revealed a wide gap between the rewards preferred by employees versus employers. For example, workers prefer permanent base pay increases based on merit, while management is fonder of one-time variable pay systems, since these systems cost less and are more short-term focused. Merit pay—fixed raises for good performance—is the pay system of choice for U.S. workers. But employers are trying to keep fixed costs down while continuing to motivate top performance.

The answer, for many companies, has been to deemphasize merit pay in favor of variable, reearnable payments. From the employers' perspective, the good news is that the study showed the most highly committed and performing workers are predominantly rewarded through merit pay and/or individual incentives—both pay-for-performance approaches. Ironically, however, 80 percent of workers on individual incentives report that they would rather be on a different pay system. The challenge is to improve the individual incentive plans that are working for employers so that they also appeal to employees.

Most employers believe that merit pay has outlived its usefulness, but employees obviously don't agree. There is much interest among companies in variable pay for group performance, but overreliance on those systems and ignoring individual pay for performance could be a big mistake.

WORKERS DISLIKE TEAM REWARDS

Employers and employees also disagree when it comes to team rewards. According to an earlier survey Sibson conducted in conjunction with the Association for Manufacturing Excellence, employers reported that group or team incentives and special recognition programs are the most effective pay systems for a team environment. However, in spite of the prevalence of teams in American companies today, the new study indicates that team pay and cash recognition programs currently are not attractive incentives for employees. Workers' lack of interest in team pay implies that employers are simply not rewarding teams as effectively as they could. The research also shows that all workers—whether they work as part of a team or not—prefer to be rewarded for their individual contributions with permanent pay increases. Employees seem to prefer increases to their base pay because they appear in every paycheck. Also, recognition programs are known to be controversial if not managed fairly and generously.

GUARANTEED PAY RAISES ARE POPULAR

While not as popular as merit pay increases, "pay for membership" is a popular choice among employees. Workers report that pay for membership programs, such as raises that come with seniority, cost-of-living increases, or across-the-board adjustments, offer at least two major advantages. First, workers are entitled to the pay increases for as long as they are employed, and second, payments received are permanent changes to their base pay. However, the study also showed that lower performing and committed workers are those who are most commonly on pay for membership plans.

WHAT AMERICAN
WORKERS BELIEVE

Almost half (49 percent) of the employees surveyed are satisfied with their overall level of pay. However, satisfaction with the level of pay is linked to annual income. Only 32 percent of workers earning less than $25,000 a year are satisfied with their overall pay, but 69 percent of those earning at least $60,000 annually are satisfied. Salaried workers tend to be more satisfied with their overall pay than hourly workers.

People are also slightly more satisfied with the raise they received this year than with the pay increases they received in previous years. Almost half (46 percent) reported that they are satisfied with their most recent pay raise, with leaders (54 percent) being more satisfied than knowledge workers (46 percent) and core workers (42 percent). Salaried employees (54 percent) and those with an annual income of at least $60,000 (53 percent) are far more likely to report satisfaction with their most recent raise than hourly employees (39 percent) and those with less than $25,000 in annual pay (36 percent).

The study also found that, while many workers feel that they should be paid more, they do not feel this way about their co-workers and superiors. More than half (56 percent) of the surveyed workers said they don't believe their CEO is worth his or her pay. And almost six in ten (58 percent) said their organization's senior management team is not worth its pay. Surprisingly, only 55 percent believe that entry-level workers are worth the pay they receive.

WORKERS ARE UNHAPPY
WITH PAY SYSTEMS

In addition to dissatisfaction over pay vehicles, many U.S. workers also expressed discontent with the way pay increases are calculated. Only one-third of the employees surveyed (31 percent) said they are satisfied with the way promotions are decided in their organizations. In addition, only one-third (32 percent) are satisfied with how their raises are determined, and less than one-fourth (22 percent) are happy with the system used to assign their jobs to a pay grade.

The research showed that many American employers could be doing better when it comes to the process for rewarding their employees. Workers are frustrated and see numerous opportunities for improvement. Change is necessary not only to improve worker perceptions but also because it has an impact on important organizational outcomes, such as commitment to the employer, performance above-and-beyond expectations, and intentions to leave the employer.

To improve employees' perceptions of their pay system, companies should share more information about the pay system on a timely basis and include employees in some aspects of the pay system design. For employers, the silver lining is that it is far less expensive to fix problems with how employees are rewarded than it is to fix the amount of rewards employees receive.

Many workers are also dissatisfied with the influence their supervisors have in making pay change decisions or with the quality of feedback they receive from their supervisors or co-workers. In the total sample, just 30 percent expressed satisfaction with supervisors' influence on pay. And only about a third (35 percent) are happy with the amount of pay information shared by employers.

Employees are skeptical of pay systems in general. While workers are loyal to their organization, they are also more critical of the techniques, systems, and processes used to determine their pay. As the labor market of talented people continues to shrink, this issue should be a key focus for companies attempting to retain and motivate people.

MOST WORKERS
ARE SATISFIED WITH BENEFITS

Overall, more than two-thirds of employees (68 percent) are satisfied with the value of the benefits they receive from their employer. There are some large differences among various employee groups, however. For example, at companies employing more than 5,000 workers, 82 percent of the employees are satisfied with their benefits, compared with just 48 percent at companies with fewer than 50 employees. Employees earning at least $60,000 a year are far more likely to be satisfied with their benefits than those earning less than $25,000 a year. Also, while 70 percent are satisfied with paid time off from the job, only 39 percent are satisfied with their unpaid time off.

WORK FEEDBACK
FROM MANAGEMENT

A majority of workers are also frustrated with the communication and feedback they receive from management about their performance and what they can do to be rewarded differently. If management is really interested in motivating workers, it should pay close attention to workers' strong preference for effective merit pay programs. Since a good merit pay system requires a credible performance feedback and rating system, employers would also benefit from improving their performance management approaches. The point is, group incentives are no replacement for individual base pay incentives for performance. People want to be rewarded for what they personally have contributed.

On the other hand, workers believe they have jobs that are personally fulfilling. For example, workers responded that they have jobs that require them to use a complex set of skills (67 percent), are challenging (69 percent), and are important or significant (90 percent). Fewer, although a majority, report that they are allowed to have autonomy (59 percent).

TRAINING AND DEVELOPMENT
AND PROMOTIONS

In addition to their satisfaction with job security, a majority of workers are satisfied with the amount of personal growth and development in doing their current job. In contrast, employees are not happy with their opportunities for training and development or the actual amount of training and development they receive. Furthermore, workers do not agree that promotions and promotion procedures are handled well by employers. In line with the changes in today's labor market and the "new" contract, employees expect their employers to keep them employable.

AFFILIATION AND JOB STATUS
ARE OKAY

Workers are generally satisfied with the organization's reputation, their job status, and their work environment. Specifically, slightly more than half (54 percent) are satisfied with the status given to their individual jobs. Even more believe that they have a safe (82 percent), clean (82 percent) work environment and that their equipment and tools are up-to-date (73 percent).

CONCLUSIONS

Many of the findings of "The Rewards of Work" study have important implications for employers. Although employees are concerned about their pay, they are more concerned about how they are paid. This has implications for the "new" contract with their employers. Simply throwing more money at people will not necessarily increase satisfaction with pay. People want to know that the "system" for administering pay is effective, fair, and inclusive. If employers are able to design pay systems that take into account employee preferences, concerns, commitment, and performance, retention will likely increase.

IV-2: Stock Options Have Their Ups & Downs

SAMUEL GREENGARD

Like many chief executives, Howard Schultz was thrilled when his company, Starbucks Corp., went public in June 1992. On the first day of trading, the stock closed at $21.50—up from an opening price of $17. Not only did the CEO's net worth zoom, the coffee retailer had finally reached the big leagues. But instead of hoarding his beans, Schultz decided that he would give some of them back to employees in the form of stock options. At a time when other firms offered options only to key senior executives, Schultz made them available to everyone working 20 hours a week or more, including those standing behind the counter at a local Starbucks store.

Today, Seattle-based Starbucks has a market capitalization somewhere in the neighborhood of $4.2 billion and about 2,100 stores in Asia, Canada, the United Kingdom, and United States. But Schultz hasn't veered away from his original philosophy of giving employees a stake in the company. More than 10,000 of the firm's 26,000 workers participate in the plan, which Starbucks refers to as its "Bean Stock" program. They've made down payments on houses, purchased cars, and paid for their college educations. Meanwhile, the company has managed to cut turnover to approximately one-third the industry norm.

Stock options. These days, the words are everywhere. And it's not difficult to understand why. Pick up a newspaper or click on the television and you're likely to hear about some young entrepreneur who's worth tens of millions—sometimes even billions of dollars—through options. There's Jeff Bezos of Amazon.com, whose paper wealth is somewhere in the neighborhood of $10 billion—despite a 1998 salary of $81,840. There's Michael Dell, who's worth a cool $22 billion as founder and chairman of Dell Computer. And then there's Bill Gates, whose personal fortune resides somewhere in the galaxy of $105 billion—almost all from Microsoft stock.

But behind the glitzy façade and the media hoopla, stock options have quietly become a way for companies to attract, retain, and reward workers. They're also a way for organizations to align the workforce with shareholder value. From Amazon.com to Xerox, companies are turning to stock options in record numbers. And while the great bull market of the 1990s has unquestionably fed into the frenzy, it would be a mistake to tag the phenomenon solely to the popularity of stocks. To be certain, options have become an entrenched compensation strategy—and are profoundly altering the corporate landscape.

TAKE STOCK OF THE PAST

The idea for stock options is actually rooted in the 1930s, though the practice didn't take place in any real way until the 1960s. At that time, major corporations began offering top executives stock options as a way to boost personal income and tie performance to shareholder value. Then, in the 1980s, Congress slashed tax rates and the stock market awakened from a 10-year slumber. CEOs like Disney's Michael Eisner and Toys "R" Us CEO Charles Lazarus began to garner headlines for receiving huge options windfalls, which totaled tens of millions of dollars.

Since then, the popularity of stock options—not to be confused with Employee Stock Ownership Plans (ESOPs), which are geared toward retirement savings—has zoomed along with the stock market. According to Sanford C. Bernstein & Co., the total value of shares set aside for options grants in the United States increased from $59 billion in 1985 to $600 billion by 1996. More than 90 percent of public companies now have employee stock-option programs. And, recently, the practice has begun to spread to Japan and other countries.

"Stock and stock options are becoming the preferred currency for compensation programs in the United States," notes Heidi Toppel, a regional practice leader for Watson Wyatt Worldwide. "More employers are providing stock options beyond the executive management level. In most cases, the goal is to align workers and shareholders, boost retention, and allow employees to share in the company's success."

Companies find stock options so attractive for a basic reason: they don't cost them anything yet they boost pay. Thanks to a glitch in tax law, the options don't have any cash value. What's more, when workers exercise options, the tax code allows the company to deduct the gain as an expense, despite the fact it hasn't spent any money.

Ultimately, the wealth is created by the stock market itself and the company can boost its profit by reducing labor expenses. "In a sense, it's funny money," says Mike Butler, who heads the employee ownership consulting practice for Hewitt Associates.

Employees like stock options because they can buy their company's stock sometime in the future, but at the market price when issued. For example, a person who is granted an option at $50 a share hopes the stock will rise. If the price climbs to, say, $75 a share, the holder can exercise the option and net a taxable profit of $25 per share. However, if the stock drops to $25 and doesn't bounce back, the options expire worthless. Ditto if a person holds onto the stock too long or it never rises.

Yet, despite their enormous popularity—and success—stock options can create problems. In some cases, companies have struggled to keep vested employees on the payroll once they've cashed in options to the tune of millions of dollars. In fact, companies like Oracle and Microsoft have hundreds, even thousands of employees that have joined the "millionaire" club as a result of stock options. Other firms have learned the hard way that if the company's stock crashes or remains stagnant for a prolonged period, it can wreak havoc. "There are lots of issues to grapple with. It's not as simple as starting a program and expecting it to succeed," warns Butler.

XEROX EXPLORES ITS OPTIONS

Paula Flemming knows that fact well. As director of HR effectiveness at Xerox Corp. in Stamford, Connecticut, Flemming has struggled with an array of issues to build a viable program. Although the company has had a profit-sharing program in place since the early 1970s, it opted to change the mix from 100 percent cash to 50/50 cash and stock in 1998. In January 1999, it awarded $8.2 million in stock options to 48,000 of the firm's 52,000 U.S. employees. After one year of employment, an employee is eligible to receive options, which are valid for eight years. An employee is considered vested a year after receiving the first options.

A key in setting up the program, says Flemming, was ensuring that the right underlying metrics were in place. Instead of using return on assets as an indicator, Xerox opted to use growth and earnings per share. "We wanted to tie the program into shareholder value," she explains. Moreover, the company increased the maximum payout for the profit sharing program from 10 percent to 15 percent of total wages.

"The biggest message the company is trying to send to employees centers on ownership. An employee who has a stake in the company's performance is far more likely to help it grow and boost its stock value. The program also lets employees participate in the same wealth accumulation opportunity that has been available to executives for years. Performance-based pay is an effective way to motivate a workforce," she adds.

However, Xerox is a prime example of the challenges and risks of stock options. Last May, the stock peaked at nearly $64 a share. After the company announced lower than expected earnings in October, the stock price plummeted to the low 20s. Today, all employee stock options are underwater, meaning that employees are unable to buy them. And that, says Flemming, presents a barrier—especially if the company's stock performs poorly over the next several years.

However, in the past, Xerox execs who have held options for extended periods have enjoyed the greatest gains; the stock has always recovered from downturns. As a result, she and other human resources executives provide constant education about stock investing in general and the company's options program in particular.

Butler believes that the tremendous growth of stock-option programs is partly an attempt to remain competitive and attractive in the labor marketplace. In an era of reduced stability and job security, "It's a natural way to encourage employee loyalty. It's a way of saying, 'You might not work here forever, but while you're here, we expect 110 percent—and in return we'll share the wealth with you.'" However, he also argues that these programs are partly a result of "executive guilt." Over the last two decades, says Butler, "CEOs and senior executives have reaped millions of dollars from stock options, and now many of them feel that stock options are necessary at the employee level in order to avoid a feeling of inequity among employees."

Of course, not all stock options are created equal—and the way different companies approach the issue varies greatly by industry. High-tech entrepreneurial companies—including many of the Internet high flyers that have popped up over the last few years—depend heavily on stock options to provide compensation. Many pay salaries far below market value. Yet "a certain type of person—often someone in their 20s or 30s, and usually without a home and family—is attracted because of the opportunity to hit the options jackpot while doing work that's interesting," says Butler. In fact, some work at two, three, or even five startups before making any real money in stock options—almost always through an initial public offering (IPO). Others never hit pay dirt.

STOCK OPTIONS CAN PRESENT CHALLENGES

All that glitters isn't necessarily gold. What happens to a company that winds up with dozens, even hundreds of millionaires who no longer *need* to come into work because they have all the financial security they'll ever require? Do they run for the exits in droves—taking valuable intellectual capital with them? Not necessarily, experts say. For one thing, a well-designed program will continue to grant options every year, so that a person can continue to accumulate wealth through the company's stock. For another, many of the workers who are attracted to these high-tech, entrepreneurial companies find the work stimulating. "Pay isn't the only issue, or even the primary issue for some workers. It's the ability to have an impact and do something exciting," Butler explains.

Consider Broadcom Corp., an Irvine, California, company that manufactures microchips and other components used in cable modems, DSL modems, digital cable set top boxes and high-speed networking gear. The company went public in 1998, and since then it has seen its stock rise six-fold. The net result? More than 75 percent of the firm's 800 plus employees are millionaires on paper. Yet the company only lost four employees last year, says Nancy Tullos, vice president of human resources. "It's a stimulating place to work, employees feel a sense of ownership, and senior management has been smart enough to create ongoing stock incentives to keep people at the company," she explains.

Tullos admits that a downturn in the stock could present difficulties, but she believes the reason for lagging stock performance is crucial. "If Broadcom started missing key design wins and experiencing internal problems, then we would have a reason to be concerned. If it's simply a reflection of the market, then we feel there's no reason to worry. The key is that we don't want to lose our edge and we don't want employees to lose their edge," she explains. Yet, as the firm matures and stock options represent less of a potential windfall, she points out that Broadcom will begin paying higher salaries and providing other benefits.

Indeed, there's also the issue of pay equity, which can create headaches for everyone. Because some employees join a company on the ground floor—before an IPO—they might receive a larger number of stock options than someone who starts later. However, the company might find it necessary to pay the latter employee more—in order to make up some of the difference. The net result, particularly at these entrepreneurial companies: a manager might earn $50,000 a year in wages while a subordinate receives $75,000. Likewise, those who join a company later might not see the same kind of appreciation in the company's stock as those who join a start up.

Of course, that's a far different scenario than for mainstream companies such as Citicorp, Kodak, Merck, Starbucks, United Airlines, and Xerox. In the majority of cases, workers at these firms aren't looking to get rich from stock options, they just hope to accumulate money for a down payment on a house or a trip to Europe.

That's the case for Jessica Gleeson, who works in the corporate training department at Starbucks. She started at the company in 1990—serving coffee in a Seattle store—while attending the University of Washington. A year later, CEO Howard Schultz announced Starbucks would offer stock options to employees who work at least 20 hours a week.

Gleeson purchased stock from the options, then sold it in 1995 for a $15,000 profit. That became the down payment on a new home. Now, she's preparing to fly to Paris for a year-2000 celebration—also funded from company stock that she sold recently. "Bean Stock has definitely given me a much stronger feeling of ownership in the company," she says. In fact, a couple of years ago, Gleeson devised a way to save the company $1 million a year by reducing in-store waste. "People wind up treating the organization's money like it's their own money," she adds.

According to Helen Chung, a spokesperson for Starbucks, the stock-option program fits into an overall HR strategy, which includes an array of other benefits. The Bean Stock program provides options based on the annual success of the company, and every year the board of directors decides how many options will be available to workers. In 1998, for example, workers received stock options equal to 14 percent of their annual wages. After a year, an employee is 20 percent vested; after five years a worker is 100 percent vested. The company also operates a separate stock investment program (SIP), which allows employees to buy shares outright through the company every quarter at a 15 percent discount.

HOW MUCH LONGER WILL STOCK OPTIONS SOAR?

Despite the enormous success of stock options, potential storm clouds loom. One of the things that have made options so appealing is the stellar bull market of the 1990s. In an environment of rising stock prices, options succeed.

However, experts agree that a prolonged bear market could it make it nearly impossible for companies to use options effectively. In addition, critics have continually lobbied Congress and the Financial Accounting Standards Board (FASB) to change the tax code to make options an actual expense—something that could cost major corporations hundreds of millions of dollars a year. So far, attempts to change the system have fallen mostly on deaf ears.

If fact, it's a pretty good bet that the situation won't change anytime soon. "Stock options have clearly changed the corporate landscape," says Toppel. "They have become a key form of compensation and an important part of the economy. When a program is successful employers and employees come out ahead."

IV-3: Paying the People in Black at Big Blue
Compensation Management and Cultural Change at IBM

ANDREW S. RICHTER

IBM's odyssey from industry domination to near failure to reemergence as a major competitor has been well chronicled, especially in terms of the financial measures of performance. Many reasons for the turnaround have been advanced. First, IBM was greatly aided by the rise of network computing. After struggling through the PC and client–server revolutions, IBM got the second chance it needed as the networked world came full circle to appreciate the critical role of large-scale enterprise computing, IBM's traditional strength. Second, IBM was able to climb out of its crisis through massive and well-publicized cost reductions, most notably workforce reductions. Third, under Louis V. Gerstner Jr.'s leadership, IBM rejected the pressure to remake itself into a number of smaller, narrower companies and instead came to fully appreciate the power of its size and ability to offer customers global and seamless solutions spanning hardware, software, and services.

Reprinted from *Compensation and Benefits Review* (May–June, 1998): 51–59.

REVERSAL OF FORTUNE: THE ROLE OF CORPORATE CULTURE

But these factors alone cannot tell the whole story. Understanding why a leaner, but still massive IBM could survive in the networked world requires an understanding of why IBM nearly failed in the first place. Sluggishness in exploiting new technologies and losing touch with customers and the marketplace were all critical parts of the recipe for disaster that can be linked to dysfunctional organizational dynamics and individual behavior patterns. And, although its impact is not easily measured, a new emerging culture at IBM has been a major factor in the company's rebirth.

There is no clearer evidence of this than the recent feature story in the new-age business journal, *Fast Company* (October-November 1997). Entitled "IBM's Grassroots Revival," the article aims to give readers "the real story of how Big Blue found the future, got the Net, and learned to love the People in Black," the industry's ubiquitous, downtown, techno-cool hipsters. It also provides "rules for radicals" taken from interviews with some of IBM's most celebrated visionaries, change agents, and rabble-rousers. Their words convey a picture that is very different from the stereotypical IBMer bedecked in a white shirt, blue suit, and more rules (and penalties) than the NFL. (Several remarks taken from the *Fast Company* piece appear later in this article.)

CORPORATE CULTURE: FROM JARGON TO REALITY

Like many companies, IBM seeks to establish and maintain a "high performance culture." However, a high performance culture means little more than any culture that will produce a high level of business perfor-

mance. The attributes of that culture vary tremendously by context. The qualities of a high performance culture for an established retail chain, an upstart service business, and a consumer products company that is losing market share may be very different. Further, in addition to context differences, all cultures evolve over time. Indeed, the company that thinks it has found the ideal culture for all time is, much like a celebrated computer company in the late 1980s, surely headed for a painful fall.

In simple and practical terms, a corporate culture can be defined as the aggregate of values, attitudes, and behavior patterns that are so ingrained in an organization that they are seldom discussed or even noticed. This is exactly why changing culture is so hard. One of the surest indicators of culture change is often nothing more than a sense of discomfort when things are not quite as they are expected to be. Relationships of cause and effect lose some of their predictability. Changes may not seem wrong so much as disquieting or uncomfortable. In the course of this review, "discomfort factors" will be highlighted in relation to many of the changes and initiatives discussed.

A culture is seldom highly visible to those enmeshed in it. However, to those outside of it, even subtle nuances may be quite telling. This is why one principal culture-changing tactic is to bring in people from the outside (including the celebrated People in Black, among others). Joining IBM in late 1995, I got an effective short course in the dynamics of culture in a two-word response to a proposal that was circulating at the time. The author of the response, in what was apparently perfectly sound IBMspeak, stated that he/she "non-concurred."

When I asked if anyone was allowed to simply "disagree," my colleagues laughed, but we all understood that language has some of the most subtle and yet pervasive impacts on culture. At IBM, endless discussion (leading to inaction) was often a substitute for open discussion (leading to decisive action). Two-and-a-half years later, I hear a lot more disagreement and a lot less nonconcurrence.

The culture that is leading to high performance for IBM has three general characteristics, which constitute the core of its performance management plan.

- **Winning** is an obsession. If the essence of the business is competition, this should be obvious. However, for a business that totally dominated its industry and at one time was bigger than its seven biggest rivals combined, winning came to be a presumption. Caution held sway over risk-taking.

- **Execution** is a cornerstone of winning. If speed and decisiveness are hallmarks of a successful information technology (IT) competitor today, it was not always so. It was not that long ago that being "better" was more important than being "first." New models and systems were introduced only after they were demonstrably bullet-proof. As the industry moves to Web years and Java years, the first company to market gets both the profits and the "mind share."

- **Teaming** is something that every business wants to do or thinks it wants to do. But teaming is not something that always comes naturally to an organization as large, diversified, and complex as IBM. The statement has often been made that many of IBM's senior executives preside over businesses that are themselves *Fortune* 100 or 500 companies. The spirit of the new emphasis on teaming (and winning) is captured by John Patrick (author of the "Get Connected" manifesto that ushered IBM into the network computing revolution), who told *Fast Company* "I never put a business-unit name on my card. People ask me, 'What division do you work for?' It doesn't matter what division I work for. If IBM wins, everyone wins."

WHITHER COMPENSATION MANAGEMENT? (OR WITHER, COMPENSATION MANAGEMENT!)

It is hardly unusual at a compensation conference or other professional gathering for a consultant or corporate compensation manager to stand up and boldly proclaim in fairly self-congratulatory tones that compensation professionals are indeed change agents. What is frustrating is that such pronouncements are almost always followed by a disclaimer that goes something like this: "Of course, compensation cannot lead change; it can only support change." It is a principal contention of this article that such disclaimers are a bit of a cop-out. Of course, no one assumes that corporations and their employees are Pavlovian dogs, who, when exposed to the stimuli of changing reward structures, immediately change their behavior. Rewards, like most aspects of culture, often work in subtle ways. Dramatic changes in rewards can signal who will advance and who won't, highlight emerging role models, and generally shake up expectations about the overall terms and conditions of the employment contract.

Compensation, like any strategic HR function aimed at shaping a culture, can travel neither ahead of the business, nor very far behind it. It has to be sufficiently conversant with the vision of the business and its evolving needs to continuously produce solutions and improvements as the business evolves. As a partner with senior executives and line managers, compensation must constantly interact with the leadership, rather than exist as a downstream activity. If the leadership of the business is actively seeking to change the core vision and rules for working, competing, and winning, compensation cannot be sitting on the sidelines waiting for the dust to settle before it produces "supporting" solutions. Among other things, this involves an acceptance of risk that has not always been the hallmark of HR or compensation professionals.

THE CHALLENGE FOR IBM

For IBM, the challenge in compensation management boils down to three inter-related goals:

- As a business partner, produce programs and policies that make sense to senior management in its quest to change the business. The goal here is business effec-tiveness, rather than making popular programs per se.

- Deliver a package that is viewed as rele-vant and appropriate by a broad spec-trum of employees, including the People in Black, Generation Xers, and Baby Boomers as well as employees who have more traditional views. The goal here is to attract and retain—but to be more attrac-tive to some than to others and to be more likely to retain some than others.

- Operate with principles, orientations, and methods that mesh with the values, attitudes, and behaviors that are reshap-ing every other aspect of IBM's busi-ness. This is walking the talk. This is focusing on how we do things, rather than on what we do.

There is no lasting victory in the effort to achieve these goals, although there is always the possibility of defeat. What we can say is that we have made considerable progress in the last few years in changing many of the most basic assumptions and rules surrounding reward management at IBM. However, this effort will perpetually be work in progress.

COMPENSATION AND BUSINESS EFFECTIVENESS

Many companies like to state that their pro-grams accomplish *both* internal equity and external competitiveness. These statements are often facilitated through convenient definitions of what constitutes internal equity and competitiveness. For most com-panies, however, there is a clear emphasis on one factor or the other. Clearly, in the world of compensation, IBM's "old" culture was most apparent in the company's strong emphasis on internal equity over external competitiveness. In any given salary grade, accountants, development engineers, HR professionals, programmers, and manufac-turing managers would be paid comparably off the same salary structure, irrespective of what market data said about trends for each job family. "Competitiveness" was under-stood to mean overall competitiveness or the averaging of some job families being overpaid and others being underpaid.

This approach was built during the years of IBM's near-complete domination of its industry. In many respects, it was entirely logical and functional, given that environment. It is hard to emphasize mar-ket competitiveness in compensation when a company is larger than its seven biggest rivals combined. The focus on internal equity was one solution to managing a huge and hugely successful business. But it also had its costs. Maintaining it required two things: a complex and cumbersome decades-old point factor system that was largely a black box to anyone other a few people in compensation, and a career con-cept that was based on the expectation of serial promotions.

For a new generation of leaders who live under constant pressure to win against relentless competition, this model could not last. Compensation's response to the demands for change was fourfold.

1. *Marketplace Rules.* In 1994–5, the com-pany made a highly visible switch from a single salary structure (for non-sales popu-lations) to different salary structures (and merit budgets) for different job families. This process has created a certain amount of ongoing tension, especially among those in the job families that are paid somewhat less. However, it delivers an extremely clear message: A market-driven company must watch the market closely and act accordingly.

There is discomfort here, but it is unavoidable. Employees, managers, and even sometimes executives have complained that taking different actions for different job families constitutes playing favorites. Actually the reverse can be argued quite persuasively. It has been the process of taking different actions for different job families that has allowed us to achieve a roughly consistent competitive marketplace positioning for those groups. It is a matter of shifting the focus from internal comparisons to external comparisons. As a culture changes, some very basic definitions (e.g., competitiveness) change with it.

2. *Fewer Jobs, Evaluated Differently, in Broad Bands.* The second response was to scrap the job evaluation system and traditional salary grades at the same time. The new approach was dramatically different. To understand the old point-factor plan (derived from the National Metal Trades Association system) required wading through a two-inch binder of paper. The new system, which at heart is a classification approach, has no points at all and is adequately explained by a single chart (see Exhibit 1). This level of simplicity was important for enabling global implementation. The old system contained ten different factors; the new one has just three (skills, leadership requirements, and job scope).

The change in job evaluation methods provided a convenient juncture to review the number of titles and the current state of job documentation. In the United States, the number of separate job titles was reduced from over 5,000 to less than 1,200. Position descriptions were shortened and clarified. Managers, rather than HR professionals, were given the responsibility of assigning their employees to bands.

The shift from 24 salary grades to 10 broad bands was intended to communicate not only a new career model, but also a new organizational model. It wasn't accidental that there were no automatic combinations or mappings of former grades to new salary bands. As with the introduction of job family market pricing, the new approach had a significant discomfort factor. More than a few employees found themselves banded with other employees who had been previously located in different (i.e., lower) grades. No one's pay was changed, but the new approach delivered a message about rewards and the value of contributions.

The band structure was adopted as one tool for creating a flatter organization that could deliver goods and services to market faster. As such, it was one response to a clear distaste for hierarchy, especially unnecessary hierarchy, on the part of People in Black (and the IT industry as a whole). Reducing the number of levels should create more open and rapid discussion and resolution of issues, rather than endless discussion.

The new career model replaced serial promotions with a broader concept of personal growth and development. This in turn created even greater pressure on the compensation management system, since it is one thing to have broad bands, but entirely another thing to appropriately utilize the full span of pay opportunities they contain. This is especially the case in a culture that tended to promote one-size-fits-all solutions with a pay program that tended to drive most employees to their salary-grade mid-point, thus reinforcing mediocrity.

3. *Letting Managers Manage (. . . Pay).* If People in Black have little patience for hierarchy, they have even less for bureaucratic staff functions that deprive them of the ability to make decisions to run their business.

EXHIBIT 1   IBM's New Job Evaluation Approach

Band	Skills required	Leadership/Contribution	Scope/Impact
1			
2			
3			
4			
5			
6			
7			
8			
9			
10			

Factors: Leadership/Contribution
Band 06: Understand the mission of the professional group and vision in own area of competence.
Band 07: Understand departmental mission and vision.
Band 08: Understand department/functional mission and vision.
Band 09: Has vision of functional or unit mission.
Band 10: Has vision of overall strategies.

Both the band and the approach are global. In the U.S., bands 1–5 are nonexempt; bands 6–10 are exempt. Each cell in the table contains descriptive language about key job characteristics. Position descriptions are compared to the chart and assigned to bands on a "best fit" basis. There are no points or scoring mechanisms. Managers assign employees to band by selecting a position description that most closely resembles the work being done by an employee using an online position description library.

That's it!

An abbreviated schematic illustration of the new—and simple—IBM job evaluation approach.

David Gee, who presides over IBM's alpha-Works (which shares IBM products and software while still under development with anyone who's interested) operates out of a physical space in the Silicon Valley dominated by a poster announcing, "I cannot be managed by anybody." One could only imagine his reaction to the traditional IBM "grid" approach to managing base salary increases. This approach created a matrix of performance appraisal scores and compa-ratio ranges to dictate (to the tenth of a percent!) the size of increases to be granted.

The new system is markedly different. Midpoints don't exist. Compa-ratios don't

exist either. Managers get a budget, some coaching, and a tool they can use in many different ways. The essence of the coaching is: either differentiate the pay you give to stars versus acceptable performers or the stars won't be around too long. The tool, which is basically a spreadsheet, lets managers rank employees on a variety of factors (e.g., critical skills and results) before deciding on how to carve up a budget. Which factors the manager uses and how he or she weights them is up to the manager. Alternatively, managers who bristle at the notion of any rating system can simply input salary increases directly with an explanatory comment of one or more sentences that records their rationale.

This new approach, which contrasted sharply with IBM's preexisting culture of emphatic uniformity and controls, gained immediate acceptance, especially among first-line managers. Somewhat to the amazement of the compensation team that designed it, the tool actually elicited fan mail (e-mail, of course) from all parts of the corporation, including, most notably, the technology cognoscenti.

HR has passed the baton to line managers when it comes to making individual pay decisions. The only remaining challenge is to make sure that line managers use their newfound powers wisely. While it is much too early to say for sure, the early indications are that the People in Black (and managers of every other conceivable stripe) do make the right decisions about pay. They also appreciate having the decisions left in their hands.

4. *Big Stakes—and Line of Sight—for Stakeholders.* As IBM began to fail in the late 1980s and early 1990s, every nonexecutive employee's cash compensation (outside of the sales realm) consisted of base salary (plus overtime, shift premiums, and assorted other adjustments). Pay-at-risk was a foreign concept for a company that perceived little risk in its leadership of an industry. IBM's business problems of the early 1990s quickly brought about a serious review of this thinking. Although variable pay for all employees is hardly a radical or original concept, it nevertheless represented a major departure for IBM.

By 1997, most IBMers around the world had 10% or more of their total cash compensation tied to performance. What is significant here is that this "opportunity" was built out of decreased merit budgets in some countries and pay cuts in others. There is no clearer way to present a stakeholder concept than to have people pay for their stakeholdings.

Performance affects the plan in two ways. The plan's funding rides on a combination of the performance of IBM and key business units. The allocation of the funding for any business unit is based upon the performance appraisal rating of each employee. There are only three ratings, and a top-rated employee receives two-and-one-half times the award of an employee with the lowest ranking. (Awards are calibrated as percentages of pensionable earnings.)

Once again, there is a significant discomfort factor. Variable pay at target, globally, has typically required more than twice the funding of merit increase programs. While the funding of the plan is based on a stakeholder concept, the allocation of funds has a tremendous amount of line-of-sight dynamics.

The discomfort factor here is intentional. In an environment where winning has been emphasized, accountability for results—both for executives and employees—is going to rule. Once again, reward management may not immediately change behavior, but it does signal a radical change in the rules of the game.

● ● ● ● ● ● ● ● ● ● ● ● ● ● ● ● ● ● ● ●

CREATING A RELEVANT PACKAGE

The changes in the reward structure that help managers change how business is conducted would probably fail if employees on the receiving end of those changes did not accept and support them. The challenge is heightened by the fact that IBM is demographically so diverse. Even setting aside IBM's non-U.S. operations (which account for roughly half of the employee population), the company represents a huge melting pot. More than a few HR managers have dreamed of the luxury of a less diverse workforce with a far more homogeneous set of needs and values. Consider that the average age of the Microsoft workforce is in the mid-twenties. People in their forties are rare; retirement-eligible people are virtually unheard of. IBM's average age is just over 40 and our population truly runs the gamut from Generation Xers to Baby Boomers to Depression and War Babies. Selling a rewards package to one group is hard enough; selling to all is daunting. The compensation response to selling the new programs to this diverse population has been fourfold here as well.

1. *Embracing Diversity.* In 1996, IBM announced benefits coverage for same-sex partners of employees. While this could be viewed as a response to the needs of a specific segment of the employee population, the message had far broader implications. First, it was another indication that IBM's practices would be market-driven. Our recruiting efforts, like our customer base, encompass all groups in society. Second, it reemphasized many of our core values, including the fact that the employment contract is based on skills and contribution, rather than other considerations.

Not surprising, the announcement of domestic partner benefits was discomforting to some and opposed outright by a few others. All in all, however, the announcement demonstrated to the People in Black and a lot of other groups that IBM's work environment can and will be as open and free as has become the expectation in our industry.

2. *Expanding Options.* No form of compensation is more synonymous with the IT industry than the stock option. Silicon Valley lore and the prospect lists for the nation's top private bankers are filled with young millionaires who made their fortunes with either founders' stock or stock options in startup or fast growth ventures. In contrast, IBM traditionally had reserved most of its stock options for executives.

For IBM's package to have credibility with the People in Black, options had to

become a part of the picture. However, IBM was not and is not prepared to give options to 240,000 employees worldwide.

The answer was to make options a part of the mainstream package, but on a selective basis that aims to retain top talent in key skills areas. Starting from a fairly small group, the number of nonexecutive optionees has been expanding aggressively. It doubled last year and will double again this year. Rather than granting a few options to many, the strategy has been to make significant grants to key contributors who represent a high retention priority.

This tactic has also created some discomfort. Options have not been granted as recognition for past achievements, but rather based on the expectation of future contributions. Beyond the broad issue of "haves" and "have nots," there are instances of employees who have received grants reporting to managers who have not. Still, the overriding principles remain clear. Options will be used to retain key skills. The program will not make everyone happy, but it does provide credibility for the total package.

3. *Expanding Employee Choices—and Responsibilities.* IBM has traditionally had an extensive benefits program. Although the benefits were often quite generous, many of the designs were both somewhat out of the mainstream and, in some cases, quite paternalistic. Nevertheless, for many years the company was something of a fixture on *Money* magazine's annual list of the 10 companies having the best benefits.

At a time when the company is trying to improve the competitiveness of its overall package, any changes to the benefits package can provoke emotional responses and charges of takeaways. The solution has been to follow two overall principles which have guided many of the actions already described. The first is to respect marketplace practices. If our competitors offer a benefit that we do not, employees can and should expect IBM to develop a similar benefit. On the other hand, if IBM offers a benefit or level of benefits not found in the industry, continuation of the practice will be questioned.

The second principle is to remind employees as often as possible that their total rewards are a package. As such, IBM can afford to spend only so much on the total package and, by definition, what gets spent on benefits significantly influences what can be spent on cash compensation. This message has been delivered a number of times and undoubtedly will continue to be a mainstay in the overall communication process.

A variety of benefit offerings have been redesigned or replaced. An archaic "survivor income plan" was replaced with a more contemporary group life insurance program. In the health benefits arena, employee contributions have been increased and new alternatives in provider networks are being added. In both instances, employees will have greater choice in terms of selecting the type of benefit they want or the extent of coverage they need. They will also have greater responsibility for sharing in the costs, especially the costs of high-end benefits. While some have viewed this as a takeaway, a growing percentage of employees (especially those with work experience in other companies) recognizes that all we have done is to adopt some fairly common marketplace practices.

People in Black are not necessarily known for their commitment to a single-employer, college-to-retirement career concept. A critical piece of the culture and the employee–employer contract is the implied career concept. Clearly, IBM will need to more crisply define a career concept for future capital accumulation programs in order to strike a balance between making long service attractive for top contributors and allowing sufficient portability and choice for those not interested in long service.

4. *Straight Talk.* People in Black are often a touch cynical when it comes to corporate communications that are less than forthright. Then again, so are employees who have lived and worked through serial downsizings. While it is probably almost a foregone conclusion, open, candid communication is a key component of the effort to enlist the hearts and minds of employees in new approaches to rewards. The spirit of the new communication efforts is very well captured by a series of pieces IBM has sent out to employees under the general title of "Straight Talk About . . . " (e.g., "Pay," "Base Pay Increases," etc.—see Exhibit 2). These have a near-absence of sugar coating and have stressed overall principles (like marketplace competitiveness). Further, in something of a break with past practices, there has been an effort to address a broader audience rather than communicating simply through line managers. Finally, the communications team *within* compensation and benefits is being expanded to provide a more continuous and consistent stream of communications.

CAN PEOPLE IN COMPENSATION AND BENEFITS WEAR BLACK TOO? (WALKING THE TALK)

The short answer to the above question is that if they do not, they will quickly lose credibility. In the current environment, compensation and benefits (and all of HR) need to do two fundamental things to gain the respect of the People in Black. The first is to do what they do! As the passion for network computing and e-business solutions grows within IBM, it is vital that HR demonstrate its own finesse and passion through using the latest technology to improve programs and services. The second is to think the way they think. Some of the People in Black interviewed by *Fast Company* offered up

EXHIBIT 2 Taking a Page out of *Straight Talk About...*

Straight Talk About
Annual Base Pay Increases

The IBM Base Pay Program is designed to give managers the flexibility to deliver pay increases that support business needs and result in appropriate compensation for you.

This brochure provides a brief, yet important, review of how your manager makes base pay increase decisions under the IBM Base Pay Program.

A Brief Review of Bands and Pay Ranges

Band Pay ranges
All non-executive IBM positions have been placed into one of 10 broad bands. There are five non-exempt bands (1–5) and five exempt bands (6–10).

Each band has a minimum and maximum amount of allowable base pay for the position in that band. In other words, for any job in the band, base pay must be at or between the minimum and maximum base pay range amounts.

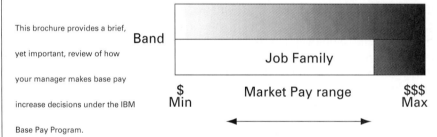

Market Pay ranges
Each position at IBM has been assigned to a market pay range representing competitive base pay practices for positions within that job family. Each market pay range includes a minimum and a maximum base pay amount. The market pay range for your position will always fit into the band pay range.

IBM's objective for base pay and other cash compensation is to attract, retain and motivate high-performing employees. To achieve this objective, IBM develops market pay ranges using competitive pay data from dozens of salary surveys. The pay information is sorted by industry, geographical location, company size and job family. By using multiple surveys, IBM is able to double-check the accuracy and consistency of the data each survey provides.

"rules for radicals" that may be as relevant for HR professionals as they are for Java application developers.

1. _HR Business_ = _@Business._ There is no shortage of network computing solutions coming out of compensation and benefits these days. The new base pay approach described earlier is run entirely off a Lotus Notes tool that managers can access. An interactive training module for this tool is also available online. Another new tool on the Lotus Notes platform is our Total Rewards Report, which can be accessed by employees at any time. This report provides information about every form of compensation they receive as well as every benefit provided.

Internet–extranet solutions have not been ignored either. In cooperation with technologists at Bankers Trust and consultants with Integrion (IBM's financial services technology consortium), access to the 401(k) plan became available over the Internet in 1997. It is not unusual to see 401(k) home pages and even account views. However, getting the system to offer full transaction capabilities in a secured environment for the 200,000 existing accounts (and over $15 billion in assets) truly tested our capabilities in adapting technology to larger user-populations and data sets—a feat also known as developing scaleable solutions.

In another partnership (this time with John Hancock), a state-of-the-art extranet solution (a secure linkage between company intranets) was developed for our Long-Term Care Plan.

In all of these initiatives, we have always asked for user feedback both in the development phase and in the post-rollout phase. While we have gotten lots of positive feedback on simplicity, intuitiveness, and methodology, the height of success was in the specific phraseology used by some of those giving the feedback. High scores on

somewhat antiseptic user satisfaction rates are one thing—but, having an application described as _"cool"_ is quite another.

2. _Rules for Radicals._ In the _Fast Company_ article, a number of IBM's most celebrated e-business change agents offered some of their accumulated wisdom in the form of "rules for radicals." If HR is indeed a business partner to these leaders, then some of their rules ought to be applicable to the design and implementation of compensation and benefit programs. In fact, they are.

For example, take John Patrick's remarks on getting to market quickly versus getting there when you achieve perfection: "Make the calendar your friend. Set a date by which something has to happen and work from there. Don't wait until your project is perfect. Get it out and see how people react." This has been a major modus operandi for compensation and benefits, since so many of our delivery dates are carved in stone. For base salary increases, there is a common review date for all employees, who expect to see their increases on May 1. The tools their managers will use are designed, refined, and rolled out on the basis of that reality. Sometimes this leads to what we call 80/20 solutions (e.g. 80% solved, 20% to-be-solved), but getting to market cannot be sacrificed. In the 1997 version of the Lotus Notes base pay managers' tool, we wanted to enable managers to see each employee's recognition awards and stock options in addition to the cash compensation. This was the only item on our wish list that didn't make it to the tool in time. Instead, it was an enhancement to the 1998 version of the tool.

What about deliverables that don't have a set delivery date? Pat Sueltz, who is vice president for IBM's e-business software, told _Fast Company,_ "I don't walk the talk, I _run_ the talk. We used to think in Web years—one Web year equals three months in a normal year. Now we think in Java years. We jump a

Java year every other month." That sort of urgency has affected almost every project in compensation and benefits. One example is the worldwide design and full implementation of the new job evaluation system and broad bands, which was accomplished in less than a year. Another example is the widespread use of IBM's ACT (i.e., Accelerate Change Together) session process. In this process, teams from a broad variety of functional and business backgrounds are brought together for two or three days to solve a specific business problem. At the end of their session, they meet with a panel of sponsoring executives who hear their recommendations and must accept or reject them on the spot. Once a recommendation is approved, 30-, 60-, and 90-day checkpoints are set up to make sure that full implementation occurs. ACT sessions have successfully tackled problems ranging from recognition for technical professionals to creating greater differentiation in pay.

Perhaps the most important rule for compensation and benefits came from David Gee, the Program Director for alphaWorks, who told *Fast Company,* "Part of our job is to shake up the status quo. We *want* to get in trouble. . . . My management tells me, 'If we're not getting four protest calls a week, you're not doing your job.'" There is a lot of wisdom here. Important changes cannot be made without breaking a little glass. Changing the rules of the game for rewards invariably creates winners and losers. Therefore, we need to acknowledge that, at least in the short run, our goal must be greater business effectiveness and not universal admiration. We could reduce the noise level by reducing the magnitude and pace of change. However, there would still be the sound of doors shutting as People in Black and a variety of other talented people leave to seek opportunities in more hospitable environments.

IV-4: Liar's Poker
An Excerpt
MICHAEL LEWIS

Bonus day, when it arrived, was an enthralling reprieve from my daily routine of chatting with investors and placing bets in the markets. Watching the faces of other people as they emerged from their meetings was worth a thousand lectures on the meaning of money in our small society. People responded in one of three ways when they heard how much richer they were: with relief, with joy, and with anger. Most felt some blend of the three. A few felt all three

distinctly: relief when told, joy when it occurred to them what to buy, and anger when they heard that others of their level had been paid much more. But the look on their faces was always the same no matter what the sizes of their bonuses: They looked sick to their stomachs. It was as if they had eaten too much chocolate pie.

Being paid was sheer misery for many. On January 1, 1987, 1986 would be erased from memory except for a single number: the amount of money you were paid. That number was the final summing-up. Imagine being told you will meet with the divine Creator in a year's time to be told your worth as a human being. You'd be a little edgy about the whole thing, too, wouldn't you? That's roughly what we endured. People felt a wave of pure emotion waft over them immediately on the heels of a year of single-minded pursuit of success, and it made their stomachs churn. Worse, they had to hide it. The game had to be played. It was rude to gloat too soon after being paid and embarrassing to show anger. The people who had it best felt unpunctuated relief. They had been paid pretty much what they had expected. No surprise. No reaction. Good. That made it easier to seem impassive. It was over.

My own compensation meeting was late in the day. I met with my jungle guide, Stu Willicker, and the sales manager of the London office, Bruce Koepgen, in one of the *Gone with the Wind* dining rooms. My jungle guide simply listened and smiled. Koepgen, said to be destined for greatness in Salomon Brothers, spoke for the organization.

I'd like to say I was as cold and calculating as a hit man facing a Mafia don after the job has been done. But that just wouldn't be true. I was more on edge than I had expected. All I—or anyone else—really wanted to know was the size of my bonus. But I had to sit through a much longer speech, for reasons I didn't at first understand.

The managing director shuffled some papers in front of him, then began. "I have seen a lot of people come through here and shoot the lights out in their first year," he said, then named a few young managing directors as examples. "But I have never seen anyone have the kind of year that you have had." He began to list names again. "Not Bill, not Rich, not Joe," he said. And then: "Not even [the Human Piranha]." *Not even the Human Piranha? Not even the Human Piranha!*

"What can I say," he said, "but congratulations?" He spoke for about five minutes and achieved the desired effect. When he finished, I was prepared to pay him for the privilege of working at Salomon Brothers.

And I thought I knew how to sell. The boss put my small abilities to shame. He pushed all the right buttons. Most of the cynicism and bitterness I was developing for the organization melted. I felt deeply reverent about the firm, my numerous bosses, John Gutfreund, the AT&T trader, and everybody who had ever had anything to do with Salomon Brothers except perhaps the opportunist. I didn't care about money. I just wanted this man to approve of my performance. I began to understand why they gave you a talk before they give you the money.

Like priests, paymasters in the Salomon empire followed a time-honored pattern. The money always came as an afterthought and in a knot you had to disentangle. "Last year you made ninety thousand dollars," he said.

Forty-five was salary. So forty-five was bonus.

"Next year your salary will be sixty thousand dollars. Now let me explain those numbers."

While he was explaining that I was paid more than anyone else in my training class (I later learned that three others were paid as much), I was converting ninety thousand dollars into British pounds (fifty-six thousand) and putting that into perspective. It was certainly more than I was worth in the abstract. It was more than I had contributed to society; Christ, if social contribution had been the measure, I should have been billed rather than paid at the end of the year. It was more than my father had made when he was twenty-six, even factoring in inflation, which I did. It was more than anyone else my age I knew made. Ha! I was rich. I loved my employer. My employer loved me. I was happy. Then the meeting ended.

And I thought again. When I had a moment to reflect, I decided I wasn't so pleased. Weird, huh? This was Salomon

Brothers, remember. These were the same people who had me blowing up customers with exploding AT&T bonds. They were perfectly capable of turning the same fire-power on me as they used on my customers. I had done their dirty work for a year and had only a few thousand dollars to show for it. Money out of my pocket was money in the pocket of the man who has sung my praises. He knew that better than I. Words were cheap. He knew that too.

I decided, in the end, I had been taken for a ride, a view I still think is strictly correct. I wasn't sure how many millions of dollars I had made for Salomon Brothers, but by any fair measure I deserved much more than ninety thousand dollars. By the standards of our monopoly money business, ninety grand was like being on welfare. I felt cheated, genuinely indignant. How else could I feel? I looked around me and saw people getting much more when they hadn't generated a penny of the revenues themselves.

"You don't get rich in this business," said Alexander when I complained privately to him. "You only attain new levels of relative poverty. You think Gutfreund feels rich? I'll bet not." Wise man, Alexander. He studied Buddhism, which he liked to use to explain his detachment. On the other hand, he was three full years out of the training program and no longer constrained by the band. The firm had just paid him a fantastic sum of money. He could afford his lofty sentiment.

He had, however, put his finger on the insatiable hunger for more felt by anyone who had succeeded at Salomon Brothers and probably at any Wall Street firm. The hunger or, if you will, the greed took different forms, some of which were healthier for Salomon Brothers than others. The most poisonous was the desire to have more *now:* short-term greed rather than long-term greed. People who are short-term greedy aren't loyal. Salomon Brothers people in 1986 wanted their money *now* because it

looked as if the firm were heading for disaster. Who knew what 1987 would bring?

Shortly after bonus time, London traders and salespeople—along with Ranieri's people in New York—began to stream out the door for more money elsewhere. Big guarantees were still being made by other firms to Salomon traders and salesmen. The older employees, who were playing for real money, had been bitterly disappointed. They had expected, say $800,000 and had received only $450,000. There simply wasn't enough to go around. It had been a terrible year for the firm, yet somehow each person individually felt he had done well.

A year after I arrived I was able to look around me and count on two hands and a foot the number of people who had been with the firm longer than I. All but three of the twenty or so older Europeans who had set the office pace in the age of the two-bottle lunch had left for greener pastures. Each was quickly replaced with half a dozen geeks, so that though people were quitting as fast as they could find other jobs, the firm expanded.

Finding the bodies was simply not a problem. By the end of 1986 traces of the American collegiate madness appeared in Britain. There was the same eerie popular feeling that no job was worth taking outside investment banking. I was called upon at the end of the year to give a talk to the Conservative Students Society at the London School of Economics. If there was a place on earth able to resist both a Conservative Students Society and the temptation of Salomon Brothers, it was the LSE, a traditional hotbed of left-wing sentiment.

The subject of my speech was the bond market. That, I figured, would keep them away in droves. Anything about the bond market promises to be long and dull. Yet in the event more than one hundred students turned up, and when one seedy-looking fellow who was guzzling a beer in the back shouted that I was a parasite, he was booed down. After the talk I was besieged not with abuse, and not with questions about the bond market, but with questions about how to get a job at Salomon Brothers. One young British radical claimed to have memorized the entire starting lineup of the New York Giants because he had heard the personnel director at Salomon was a Giants fan (true). Another wanted to know if it was a fact, as he had read in the *Economist,* that people at Salomon Brothers didn't stab you in the back but came at you head-on with a hatchet. What was the best way to show that he was sufficiently aggressive? Was it possible to go too far, or should he just let it all hang out?

At its peak in mid-1987 Victoria Plaza contained nine hundred people and looked more like a day-care center than the flagship office of a global empire. The ever-apposite Dash Riprock looked up one day and said, "Just the managing directors and the kiddies." By then I knew what he meant almost before he said it; I had an inbuilt Dash Riprock decoding device. The average length of service of my colleagues in London fell rapidly from six years to less than

two years. Their average age, once well into the thirties, was about twenty-five.

Throughout early 1987 a tired old joke circulated that a sign was soon to be posted beside the exit from the trading floor: WILL THE LAST ONE OUT PLEASE TURN OUT THE LIGHTS? Then a fresh new joke (to me, at least) made the rounds. Only it turned out to be true. The head trader of British government bonds (called gilts) had quit. The managing directors of the London office fell to their knees (figuratively speaking) and pleaded with him to stay. He was the backbone of a new and fragile enterprise, they said. Screw backbones, he said, he had been offered much more money by Goldman Sachs, and he was going to get while the getting was still good. He was, after all, merely a trader trading his services. What did they expect? They expected, they said, for him to forget about trading for a moment and consider the importance of loyalty to the firm.

And you know what he said to that? He said, "You want loyalty, hire a cocker spaniel."

IV-5: What, Me Worry?
Social Security Reform Could Impose Paperwork, Education Burdens for HR

ROBERT W. THOMPSON

Many Americans old enough to have begun thinking seriously about retirement are familiar with the goofy character Alfred E. Neuman, the icon of the late, great humor publication, *MAD* magazine. Neuman's

freckled, gap-toothed, big-eared, grinning countenance provided the visual image they'll remember. But it's also hard to forget the pithy saying that Neuman applied to virtually everything in life: "What, me worry?"

When it comes to preparing for their "golden years," some Americans seem to have adopted the same devil-may-care attitude that Neuman did. According to former Treasury Secretary Robert Rubin, in 1998 the national personal savings rate averaged less than 1 percent of after-tax income, ranking the United States with Canada as "the lowest by far of the G-7 countries, and lower than many developing countries."

To a certain extent, Americans' neglectful attitude toward amassing retirement income is understandable. After all, why worry about having enough money stashed away for retirement when you still feel hale and hearty? Wouldn't it be nice to take that thousand bucks that you've saved up to put in your IRA and instead treat yourself to a well-deserved vacation or a 32-inch TV with all the goodies?

Besides, there's always Social Security to rely on. Or is there?

Up until five or so years ago, the bad news seemed to come mostly from economists, talking heads, and government bureaucrats. They warned us that we needed to truly rethink the Social Security system, cautioning that when the baby boomers reached 65 and started retiring in droves in the early twenty-first century, they'd run through the nation's collective retirement savings like a hot knife through butter. Today, with the next millennium right around the corner, the warnings sound less like the cries of alarmists than the sound of common sense. The need to rejuvenate, reform, or even scrap Social Security has become a top priority of congressional leaders, business executives, Clinton administration officials, and—lest we forget—the presidential candidates.

But human resource professionals may be thinking: "What does this have to do with me, at least in my work capacity? Isn't this mostly a nonworkplace issue that will primarily affect employees as taxpaying citizens? Sure, the payroll deductions that we send to the Social Security Administration may go up. But won't the accounting systems take care of that fairly easily?"

It's hard to provide a clear answer at this point, simply because there are so many vastly different Social Security reform plans being circulated, creating so many options to consider. Some proposals, if enacted,

would cause few headaches for HR professionals. But the ones that currently are dominating the debate are definitely worth watching because they involve "privatizing" the system in one way or another. The current Social Security system could be either replaced or supplemented by new "personal retirement accounts" that would give individuals more choices about how to invest their retirement money.

Even if Congress were to enact a reform plan that didn't directly increase the tax burden on employers, whatever comes to pass likely will be so complicated and daunting that employees will have no idea what to do next. Where are those anxious employees likely to turn for answers? The HR department, of course.

PRIVATIZATION: DEFINITIONS AND EXAMPLES

Simply put, privatization means shifting investments to the private sector. In the Social Security arena, it entails taking some or all of the money now going into the Old-Age, Survivors and Disability Insurance (OASDI) fund—or Social Security trust fund, as it is commonly called—and shifting it into individual accounts over which employees would have some control. Currently, employers send all payroll deductions required under the Federal Insurance Contributions Act (FICA) to the Social Security Administration, which by law must invest the collected taxes in government securities. (The current FICA tax rate is 7.65 percent on the first $68,400 of income. Both employers and employees pay the tax. Of that amount, 6.2 percent goes toward Social Security and the remainder toward Medicare.)

Although the various privatization plans differ as to how much control employees would have over their investments, most of the major reform proposals would allow employees to invest in private securities, such as stocks. Supporters of privatization say this would allow employees to accumulate retirement savings at a much faster rate because the rate of return on stocks is generally much higher than on low-risk but low-interest government bonds.

Under another form of privatization, FICA payroll deductions would continue to flow into the Social Security trust fund and to be managed by the federal government. However, the Social Security Administration would no longer be required to buy government bonds with the money; instead, it could invest the money in private-sector stocks and bonds. Wall Street types, of course, would love to see the enactment of either type of privatization, which would result in an infusion of capital for U.S. companies.

One concern accompanying privatization is that, if employees are given wide leeway in investing the money that's in their personal retirement accounts, they could make unwise decisions and buy stocks that ultimately plummet in value. This problem, of course, can affect even the most savvy investor. But it could pose severe problems for people in the lower and middle income brackets, who often have no experience with equities. Therefore, some privatization proposals would require that employees invest a proportion of their funds in fixed-return vehicles, such as government bonds. Other proposals would allow the government to set guidelines channeling investments into certain low-risk equities.

· · · · · · · · · · · · ·
DISTRIBUTING THE PROCEEDS

There has already been a great deal of debate about how the money should be managed once an employee reaches normal retirement age (currently 65 years of age, but potentially going up to 68 or even 70). A major question is whether retirees should be able to receive all of the proceeds of their personal accounts

as soon as they leave the workforce, or whether they should be required to spread their receipts out over a period of years.

There are three basic ways to pay retirement benefits: annuitizations, timed withdrawals, and lump-sum payments. Under the first approach, the retiree contracts with an annuity provider, generally an insurance company, to provide income for an agreed-upon length of time. The contract specifies the premium to be paid to the provider, the monthly amount to be paid to the retiree, and the interest rate that will be calculated over the life of the annuity. Interest rates may be fixed at the onset or they may be tied to the return on investments. The most common of annuities is the life annuity, which pays benefits for the remainder of the individual's life. Social Security is a prime example of a life annuity system.

Timed withdrawals, sometimes called "self-annuitizations," are a cross between annuities and lump-sum payments. Under that approach, a retiree would determine how much he or she wanted to receive each month for a specified period of time, and then would find an investment manager or record-keeper to handle the details.

Advocates for women are particularly concerned about the possibility that Congress, if it approves personal retirement accounts, might allow retirees to receive lump-sum payments as soon as they retire. One cause of concern is the possibility that male retirees, whose earnings continue to outpace those of women, might exhaust the nest egg—leaving their spouses with little to live on after the husbands die, which historically occurs first. Another, less morally grounded reason is that many people simply lack the discipline to manage a large amount of money that falls into their hands at one fell swoop.

Therefore, some proponents of privatization want to stipulate either that lump-sum payments be limited to a certain portion of the retirement accounts' value or that retirees be required to purchase annuities for the full amount of their accounts' value.

Mandating annuities would pose another problem: There currently is little market for private annuities, so they are expensive to buy. The United States' largest provider of annuities is the federal government, in the form of the Social Security Administration. Private insurance companies aren't often called upon to sell policies to individuals who have come into a great deal of money and want to make sure that they receive a small portion of it each month for the rest of their lives.

According to Congress's General Accounting Office (GAO), which in June issued a report, "Social Security Reform: Implementation Issues for Individual Accounts," the administrative cost of buying an individual annuity in the current market is "relatively high, averaging a one-time charge of about 5 percent of the premium." The GAO says that if Congress required retirees to annuitize their personal account balances, the cost of buying an annuity would drop due to economies of scale. Also, mandating annuities would eliminate the high cost of adverse selection. Under a voluntary system, the people most likely to buy annuities would be those who expected to live to a ripe old age. In contrast, those with serious health problems or reckless lifestyles would be more likely to opt for lump-sum payments.

Compared with annuities, the administrative costs of the Social Security system are very low—less than 1 percent of outgo, according to the American Academy of Actuaries. This low overhead in part results because the government can take advantage of economies of scale. But another explanation is that employers do much of the legwork by sending taxes to the IRS and W-2 forms to the Social Security Administration. Even small increases in administrative costs can result in major reductions in the amount of retirement income.

The GAO and others say there are several answers to the problems involving annuities. One idea is to follow the example set by Chile, which in 1981 established a pension system that has become a much-touted model and has helped revive that country's economy. In Chile, workers automatically have 10 percent of their wages sent by their employers to their individual savings accounts; a worker can add an additional, tax-deductible 10 percent of his or her wages to the account. Upon retirement, workers are required to purchase annuities representing 70 percent of the average worker's salary; after buying the annuities, the workers can receive the remainder of their account balances as lump-sum payments.

● ●
SOURCES OF CONCERN FOR EMPLOYERS

Employers and organizations representing them, including the Society for Human Resource Management (SHRM) are closely watching the debate to be sure that what Congress does, if anything, doesn't impose heavy administrative burdens on them or increase their payroll taxes. A major worry of employers is that, should personal retirement accounts be authorized, the new administrative and record-keeping responsibilities might fall heavily on employers' shoulders.

One option is for administration of personal retirement accounts to be centralized at the Social Security Administration. But a drawback, as the GAO notes in its June report, is that "the current centralized Social Security record-keeping system was not designed to maintain records on individual accounts that are owned and managed by individual workers." The Social Security Administration's system is based on annual reporting; in contrast, a personal retirement account system that involved equities, the value of which often fluctuates wildly from day to day, would require a continuous flow of administrative hustle and bustle.

"The current reporting and tax collection system does not include other administrative activities that would need to occur under an individual account system, such as creating systems to collect and record individual investment choices, transmitting contributions to investment managers, recording account value changes, sending periodic account statements, and providing payout entities with necessary account information," the GAO wrote. "While an investment manager could perform some of these activities, under a centralized system, government agencies would likely assume many of these responsibilities."

A second option is one that would involve employers: setting up a decentralized administration and record-keeping structure, possibly based on the current systems for 401(k) plans. However, while the number of employers sponsoring 401(k) plans has risen dramatically in recent years, the proportion is still relatively low. According to the GAO, only 25 million Americans participate in a 401(k) plan. "Under a 401(k) model, employers, especially those that currently do not provide any retirement plan, would bear the additional cost and responsibility of creating an infrastructure to quickly deposit contributions and provide employees with links to and choices among funds," the congressional agency concludes.

If employers were called upon to bear additional costs and responsibilities, some might decide to change or reduce the benefit packages they now offer, "thus possibly undermining the overall goal of pension plans and individual accounts: improved retirement security," the GAO says. Also, according to the report, a decentralized system probably would lead to additional government oversight and regulatory responsibilities.

Then there's the problem of how to ensure seamless administration of personal retirement accounts if an employer went out of business. Approximately 650,000 employers go out of business or start new businesses each year, for a turnover rate of some 10 percent. "Once an employer went out of business, making corrections to individual accounts would be difficult, if not impossible," the GAO says.

SHRM'S POSITION ON REFORM

Because of the likelihood that Congress in the near future would make the first major reforms of the Social Security system since 1983, the SHRM Board of Directors last February debated what type of policy position the Society should take. A position paper, which the board adopted, includes the following key points:

- Social Security, by promoting a work ethic and individual dignity, differs from social welfare programs, and any legislative reforms should continue that approach.

- Any reforms should be implemented over time, with the greatest change reserved for those individuals with the time to accommodate the change.

- The self-supporting design of the system should be changed from the "pay as you go" basis, under which the current generation of workers provides retirement income for preceding generations, to a system that is actuarially balanced.

- SHRM opposes proposals for directly increasing payroll taxes in future years to maintain benefits and ensure solvency.

- There should be some amount of privatization, accompanied by "essential" investor education led by the government. When employers provide investment education, they should be protected against fiduciary liability.

- Account balances should be converted to life annuities upon retirement.

- Investments in equities should be applied to a "broad market," including Standard & Poor's 500 stocks, so that portfolios are diversified. These investments also should shift more of the burden of protecting against inflation to individual retirees.
- The normal retirement age should be indexed to life expectancy.

It should be evident by now that understanding, let alone implementing, Social Security reform is a complicated task. Not everyone agrees with congressional leaders, the Clinton administration, and Wall Street

that the current system needs major restructuring. Some think tanks, such as the left-leaning Economic Policy Institute, and many leaders of organized labor believe the current system needs to be fine-tuned—not scrapped. But as an increasing number of baby boomers start thinking about what they'll do in their retirement years, they'll become increasingly anxious that Social Security, as now structured, is not the safety net they once envisioned. So, HR professionals need to be aware that major reforms are likely early in the new millennium, and that they had best be prepared.

IV-6: Pension Cuts 101
Companies Find Host of Subtle Ways to Pare Retirement Payouts

ELLEN E. SCHULTZ

When International Business Machines Corp. announced the latest changes in its pension plan last year, David Finlay, a senior engineer in Colorado, went to his basement and hauled out boxes of benefits brochures collected since he joined IBM in 1972. It wasn't too hard for him to figure out that through the 1970s and 1980s, various changes had been for the good. It took a lot longer to figure out what happened in the 1990s.

When he was done, months later, what he discovered dismayed him. In the past decade, the company made change after change to its pension plan, reducing Mr. Finlay's future benefits each time, by his reckoning. According to the 55-year-old engineer's calculations, he will retire in 10 years with a $57,700 annual pension, compared with $71,200 it would have been without the revisions of the 1990s.

IBM, which declines to comment on Mr. Finlay's analysis, is a case study in the manifold, complex ways large companies have been whittling away pensions over the past decade, a pension-paring spree that hasn't ended yet. An examination of hundreds of federal filings reveals such cuts at a host of big companies, including Ameritech Corp., Duke Energy Corp., Dow Chemical Co., Kmart Corp., Lucent Technologies Inc., and Southern Co. The upshot of the pension changes, which are often highly complex and poorly explained to employees, is that millions of people will retire with pensions that are sharply lower than they once would have been.

"If your pension has changed in the 1990s, it probably changed for the worse," says Norman Stein, a pension-law professor at the University of Alabama at Tuscaloosa.

● ● ● ● ● ● ● ● ● ● ● ● ●
PROFIT CENTER

Sometimes companies cut pensions when business is bad, but that isn't what's happening here. Employers are imposing the pension cuts at a time when profits are lush and when most pension funds are fully funded or overfunded, thanks to the long-running bull market. Paring future payouts, in such an environment, renders plans even more overfunded.

That isn't just a comforting feeling to companies. For some, it is also a new profit center. That's because accounting rules allow excess pension income to flow to the bottom line, where it can boost operating income and smooth earnings.

Some of the changes are so complex that even government pension experts aren't sure how they work. Created by consulting firms and companies' finance departments, the maneuvers flourish with little oversight. They go well beyond the "cash balance" system that caused an outcry last year after *The Wall Street Journal* reported that the new-style plan could cut older workers' pensions as much as 50%.

Some companies make subtle changes to the benefit-calculation formulas of traditional pension plans. Others take advantage of pension-law loopholes to eliminate early-retirement subsidies, and still others adjust compensation formulas to lower the amounts that count toward a pension. Says Brooks Hamilton, a lawyer who runs a pension consulting firm in Dallas: "Never have so few plundered so much from so many."

"CHANGES," NOT "CUTS"

Federal law bars employers from retroactively cutting benefits an employee has earned. But it is perfectly legal to cut the rate at which benefits are to be earned in the future, or to eliminate future benefits altogether.

A company that is reducing future pension accruals of its employees is supposed to make this clear to them. Few do. In regulatory filings, companies typically cite "changes" or "modifications," not "cuts" or "reductions," and the brochures given to employees are typically vague. In IBM's case, a brochure for some 1995 changes did contain a reference to "lower value" for certain workers. Still, in 1999, even while employees were complaining bitterly to lawmakers about adoption of a cash-balance plan, almost none realized that the 1995 changes had already transformed their plan.

One of the most common ways companies cut pensions is by changing the formula they use to calculate monthly retirement checks. Under traditional plans, payments generally are based on three items: years of service, an average-salary figure. and a multiplier, such as 1.5%. All three can be changed. Southern Co., for instance, reduced its multiplier to 1% from 1.7%. Benefits were reduced 25% to 33%, by a Southern official's calculation, although employees of the Atlanta utility age 35 or older could remain subject to the old formula.

It might seem the years-of-service and average-salary elements would be immutable, but in fact, companies can manipulate these elements, too. They can cap the years of service that count toward a pension. And on salaries, instead of taking the employee's highest three years of pay, they can take an average of 10 years or even an entire career.

WEARAWAY

Kmart and Manpower Inc. froze their pension plans, so that neither future salary increases nor added years of service could increase the benefit. When Kmart froze its pension plan in 1996, it quickly turned it from underfunded into overfunded—and pumped $63 million of pension income into its bottom line for 1998. A spokeswoman for Kmart says employees have the opportunity to participate in 401(k) retirement plans that supplement the pension. Manpower, which froze its plan at the end of February 2000, has no comment.

When a company changes its pension formula, employees can face months or years before their expected future retirement benefit gets back up to where it was before the change. In the meantime, they are essentially earning no benefit. "Wearaway," pension designers call this phenomenon.

Duke Energy made a complex adjustment in the early 1990s to the way it incorporates Social Security into its pension formula, a move that halted the accruals for the oldest workers for months or even years, the company acknowledges. Duke later converted to a cash-balance plan, again reducing accruals for some, although this time the change didn't affect those closest to retirement. Wearaway doesn't violate the law against cutting already-earned pensions so long as the employer provides the original, larger benefit to anybody who departs before working his or her way through the wearaway period.

At IBM, pension cuts began in 1991 when the company lowered the multiplier in its traditional plan to 1.35% from 1.5%. Mr. Finlay calculates that this and other 1991 changes reduced the pension he would draw at 65 to about $69,500 a year from $71,200. IBM also capped the pension, meaning that years worked beyond 30 wouldn't increase it.

Asked about Mr. Finlay's conclusions, IBM said in a written statement: "We are not saying your information is correct. We are saying only that we have decided not to participate" in an article about the changes.

● ●
DROPPING A SUBSIDY

IBM's next significant move came in 1995. The company wanted to drop an early-retirement subsidy, which it had added to the plan in 1991 to encourage older workers to leave. The subsidy, which let 55-year-olds retire with nearly the pension they would have at 65, "encouraged departures," so it

"served us well," Donald Sauvigne, then head of retirement benefits at IBM, told an actuaries' conference in Vancouver, British Columbia, in 1995, according to a transcript. But IBM found it also had the unwelcome effect of encouraging people to stick around until at least age 55. "So we had to design something different," Mr. Sauvigne said.

What they came up with was, indeed, very different: a pension-equity plan. This is a hybrid that consultants Wyatt Co. (now Watson Wyatt Worldwide of Bethesda, Maryland) devised for RJR Nabisco Holdings Corp. in January 1993, when Louis V. Gerstner Jr. headed RJR. In April 1993, Mr. Gerstner arrived at IBM, and soon it, too, began planning a shift to the new structure, though it isn't clear what Mr. Gerstner's role was. Ameritech, Dow Chemical, Motorola Inc., and U S West Inc. (now part of Qwest Communications International Inc.) all have adopted similar plans since then.

Like its better-known cash-balance cousin, a pension-equity plan wipes out any early-retirement subsidy and produces smaller retirement payments for many older workers. Both plans differ from traditional pensions, under which employees earn as much as half their ultimate benefits in their last 5 to 10 years on the job. In contrast, under these newer types of pensions, the value of a worker's benefit grows at a more level rate throughout his or her employment.

A cash-balance plan provides employees with hypothetical accounts that grow each year with a company contribution, usually based on salary plus interest on the hypothetical balance. In contrast, the "accounts" in a pension-equity plan grow each year when the company contributes an amount representing the multiplication of a person's average pay over the prior five years or so by a factor that increases with service. There's also usually interest credited to the account, but it is embedded in the calculation and isn't evident to employees. "The plan took me months to understand," IBM's Mr. Sauvigne told his actuarial colleagues at the conference—and he was a 25-year benefits veteran.

FINLAY DIGS IN

It also challenged Mr. Finlay. When he started studying IBM's pension moves in 1999, the engineer would bicycle home from work to a subdivision on the outskirts of Boulder, Colorado, and stare at his computer till nearly midnight. He spent weekends developing spreadsheets and reverse-engineering the algorithms with the information he hauled from his basement. He even took his laptop computer to a genealogical conference his wife was attending in Colorado Springs so he could fiddle with the material. His wife, MaryAnn, didn't mind. "We want to know where we stand," she says.

One thing Mr. Finlay eventually says he figured out was that the embedded interest rate went down with age. It was 5% for employees under age 45, 4% for those 45 to 55, and 0.5% for years above age 55. Yet it was other aspects of the formula shift that were reducing his pension, not this. By his calculation, the 1995 changes reduced his prospective pension to about $57,700 annually from the previously estimated $69,500.

"I'm a Goldwater conservative, a Vietnam vet, and a Republican, but I'd support a union coming in here if it would force the company to open up its books on what it's doing," he says. "If I were 10 years younger, I would have left. It tells you something about a company when it does something like this to people."

That most IBM employees didn't protest back in 1995 isn't surprising. Like most companies, IBM unveiled the pension-equity plan as a move that involved "changes" and "a new formula," according to its government filings. In its handouts to

employees, IBM said the changes were "the result of a recent study which concluded that the plan should be modified to meet the evolving needs of IBM and its increasingly diverse workforce, and align more with industry practices and trends."

The brochure did note that employees "will see varying effects" and that those retiring early will "see lower value." Mr. Finlay didn't think much about the change at the time, and neither did many of his colleagues. "I did not realize the significance of the impact," says software engineer Ken Buckingham, 44, a 20-year, second-generation IBM employee in Charlotte, North Carolina. "I had not a clue that this wasn't a traditional pension plan. They have a right to make these changes, but I resent the surreptitious nature in which they made them."

LUCENT'S CHANGES

Companies sometimes communicate pension reductions so poorly they're mistaken for enhancements. Consider the changes Lucent made in 1998. It cut the multiplier in its traditional pension plan to 1.4% from 1.6%, reducing future accruals. Yet a company brochure given to employees said: "For most employees, these changes will provide a greater annual pension benefit than the amount currently provided by the plan."

A Lucent spokesman says the brochure wasn't misleading because of other modifications, such as a 401(k) change and an updating of the salary part of the pension formula. But that update was a routine one made periodically to advance the period on which the salary average would be based, and would have been made even if the multiplier hadn't been cut.

Other companies improve their 401(k) savings programs when they cut pensions, obscuring the cuts by emphasizing "total" retirement benefits, including whatever an employee might save in his or her 401(k). On this front, Lucent did something more complicated in 1998. It reduced the amount it matches when employees put money into their 401(k) accounts to 50 cents on the dollar from 66.6 cents, but it added a "variable" match based on earnings-per-share growth. "We took the base down but gave employees more upside potential," the spokesman says, adding that in the past two years, the combination has resulted in a larger corporate contribution.

Employers rarely say that the reason they are changing their retirement plan is to save money. Instead, no matter what kind of change they are making, companies generally tell employees roughly the same things. "The changes keep us competitive with others in our industry," noted Lucent in an employee brochure that is typical. "Lucent's success depends on attracting, retaining, and motivating top performers." A Lucent spokesman says the changes were intended to take away a "sense of entitlement" among employees and to reward performance.

Similarly, when IBM converted to a pension-equity plan in 1995, it sent a memo to managers saying the goal was "to attract and retain the people we need for the future" and to "align more with industry practices and trends." When IBM switched to a cash-balance plan four years later, its brochure for the staff said the change was to help "attract, retain, and motivate" employees.

● ● ● ● ● ● ● ● ● ● ● ● ● ● ● ● ● ● ● ●
GERSTNER'S EXPLANATION

Later, at the annual shareholders' meeting last April, Mr. Gerstner stressed that the company's most recent pension maneuver was accompanied by various compensation enhancements. The combined moves eliminate "a sense of entitlement," he said. IBM also has a 401(k) retirement plan, but the chairman said that its pension plan had been "woefully out of date. It did not address the realities of employee mobility in the new marketplace. Our old pension plan was created at a time when employees joined IBM for life," he said. But "we anticipate that only 10% of our new hires are likely to reach 30 years of service with IBM."

Most of IBM's leading competitors "do not provide a pension plan at all," Mr. Gerstner added. "We must find a balance between the needs of our shareholders and the needs of all our employees."

Certainly, the shareholders have fared well. At the actuaries' conference in 1995, IBM's Mr. Sauvigne said the adoption that year of the pension-equity change had some immediate payoffs. "The new plan is a lot less expensive than the predecessor plan," he said. "We took a lot of dollars out of the liability line on Day One just by flipping the switch."

Indeed, the year before, IBM had reported pension expense of $11 million. In 1995, the year it converted, it reported pension *income* of $252 million, of which about half was attributable to the stock market and the rest to the pension change. Over the next four years, pension income boosted the company's operating income by $1.8 billion, according to federal filings.

Then came the 1999 announcement of a switch to cash-balance, a system that by this time had become controversial. The move caused such an uproar among middle-age staffers that IBM made a partial retreat, increasing the number of older employees it let remain in the old plan. Still, the move paid off for IBM; last year, it saved an added $184 million—6% of pretax income—through reduced pension expense, according to government filings.

Mr. Finlay wasn't affected because he decided to stay in the prior plan. But if he hadn't made that choice, he calculated, IBM's latest switch would have cut his annual pension to about $45,800. He says he recruited volunteers around the office to test-drive his spreadsheets.

FREEZING THE PLAN

For employees, bad news can continue even after a conversion to a cash-balance plan. What has happened at some big companies illustrates the variety of ways managements continue to pare pension benefits.

For instance, six years after Interpublic Group of Cos. converted to a cash-balance pension plan, the ad agency went further and froze the plan. CBS Inc. adopted a cash-balance plan but closed it to new employees. MCI Communications converted to cash-balance but later, following its merger into WorldCom Inc., stopped providing contributions to the hypothetical accounts in the plan. And retailer Casual Corner Group changed the compensation formula in its cash-balance plan to exclude bonuses.

Casual Corner acknowledges it made its move to save money. CBS says that it increased its contribution to 401(k) plans and that many employees will now get stock options that can be used for retirement savings. WorldCom and Interpublic decline to comment.

Companies can cut pensions even as employees walk out the door. If a plan allows departing employees to take a lump sum instead of a lifelong stream of monthly payments, the lump sum can be worth 30% to 50% less than the present value of the monthly pension (called an annuity). That's because federal law allows lump-sum payments to exclude the value of an early-retirement subsidy, provided employers give employees a choice between a lump-sum payment and the monthly annuity.

This helps explain why hundreds of large employers began offering lump sums in the 1990s. The savings got even greater after employers successfully lobbied Congress in 1994 to let them use a bigger discount rate when calculating the lump sums. The change results in lower lump-sum payouts.

PROPOSED LEGISLATION

Last week, the House passed a pension bill with a variety of provisions that would make further pension reductions possible, including one that gives companies greater leeway to cut early-retirement subsidies. The bill would also allow companies with already-overfunded pension plans to put more money in the plans, even as their pension obligations shrink. That makes it more likely that the pension plan will contribute to the company's bottom line.

Increasingly, companies are asking employees to make irrevocable decisions about their pensions, such as whether to remain in an old plan or choose a new one. Motorola, for instance, allowed 70,000 employees to make a one-time choice in April of whether to move into the new pension-equity plan, which started July 1, or stay in the old plan.

If employees can't compare the value of the options, they can't make an informed choice. Mary Fletcher, a marketing-services trainer and 14-year veteran of IBM, was presented with a lump-sum option last year when IBM prepared to sell a unit with 3,000 U.S. employees to AT&T Corp. Only after she hired a financial adviser to help with the calculations did she realize that the lump sum was worth 30% less than the monthly pension. The annuity's present value: $101,000. The lump sum she was offered: $71,500.

Still, Ms. Fletcher, 47, took the lump sum. Almost all employees do, figuring they can invest the money and eventually end up with more.

Ms. Fletcher is simply glad to be off on her own. Even though she is "a numbers person," she says, when it came to IBM's pension plan, "they were always changing things. So we were always confused."

IV-7: Employers Pass Buck on Insurance

AMY GAGE

If you work full time, your employer spends about $4,000 on your medical insurance each year. What if your manager handed you that money and let you pay for your own health care instead?

It could happen. IBM is among the blue chip companies weighing the pros and cons of "defined contribution" plans for employee health care.

Benefits plans in general are giving employees more choices. For example, PTO banks, short for "paid time off," allow people to pool their vacation and sick days, and use their time off as they please.

Twin Cities companies such as Land O'Lakes, Carlson Cos., and U.S. Bancorp give their workers several health plans from which to choose. Employees who pick a less expensive plan may opt to put more money toward dental insurance, for example.

Those who want the Cadillac health plan may have to pay some of the cost themselves. "It's the first step in a defined contribution plan," says Cathy Tripp, health care practice leader at William M. Mercer in Minneapolis, a human resources consulting firm.

It's unlikely that any employer would leap from offering a single health plan to making employees shop for their own insurance. Still, health care costs are rising quickly enough that many employers are tempted to make employees more responsible.

"Employers could distance themselves from the decision," Tripp explains. "They could fix their costs and be able to budget it."

Advocates of defined-contribution plans say employees would be better health care consumers if they knew the true cost of treatment and prescriptions. The $10 copayment at the doctor's office masks the real cost of $70, Tripp says. The $9 prescription costs more than four times that much.

Health care costs likely will rise 9 percent nationally this year and as much as 15 percent in the Twin Cities, according to Tripp. "Our market doesn't have a lot of competition," she explains.

The rising cost of health care is a top concern among executives from large and small companies, according to a poll of 400 business leaders conducted last November by *Twin Cities Business Monthly* magazine.

Although defined-contribution plans may be convenient for employers, they could wreak havoc with employees' lives. People who are healthy could get by with cheaper health plans and pocket the extra cash.

But people with chronic conditions, whether allergies or diabetes, could have a harder time finding affordable insurance because they would be buying as individuals, not as part of a pool.

"That's the biggest disadvantage of all: How do you deal with the equity issue of sick employees having to pay more?" Tripp says.

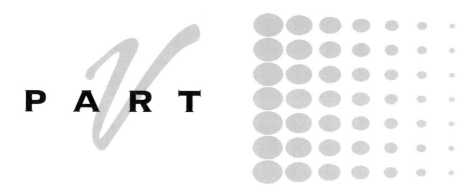

PART V

DEALING WITH DIVERSITY AND DISCRIMINATION

Viewing HRM in context, as we have been trying to do in this book, we see that HRM's history has been a mixture of apparently traditional and dramatically new responses to a continuously unfolding business and social environment.

We see such mixtures in many places. For example, when we compare the world as it seemed when we were younger to how it seems today we see that sometimes the same words continue to be used, but the phenomena they refer to are dramatically different. To illustrate, consider "school discipline." Recently, several times a year now, the news has reported that a schoolchild has shot a teacher or other students. Schools throughout the country are installing sophisticated technologies to prevent children from bringing weapons to class. When we reflect on the disciplinary problems of our own school experiences, our teachers seemed to be preoccupied with students butting in line and chewing gum. Clearly, both eras had discipline issues. However, the issues raised today appear to be so much more dramatic and complex that it is easy to miss any underlying commonality with those of the past.

We see similar changes in HRM when we compare the first HRM (then called personnel administration) courses we taught with what we teach today. Certainly, back then there were issues to address (e.g., "right-to-work" laws, Boulwarism, and job enrichment). However, much like the contrast between chewing gum and shootings in schools, this book reveals that HRM now deals with matters that make earlier concerns seem hardly to be issues at all. Today's issues appear to be so much more important, dramatic, and complex that important commonalities may be obscured. However, when we see things in context, the fundamental commonalities are more apparent. Recall how in Part I Jacoby demonstrated that the workplace has been a locus where people with different interests have struggled with each other over distribution of crucial resources and privileges. The workplace continues to be a crucial location where people battle over resources that play major roles in their life choices.

Today, as before, conflicts over privileges, preferences, and resources stimulate many issues that HRM practitioners must address. As the issues and interests change, so often do the labels, the specific social concerns, and the manner in which they are expressed. But the basic general aim to legitimate various claims continues. However, because the nature of the specific issues changes, HR managers continuously deal with new challenges.

Among the most salient social challenges today are an increased ratio of females to males in the workforce and changes in society's racial composition. In Part V we explore how these and other social changes have altered the dimensions on which struggles at work take place and have thereby altered the challenges for HRM practitioners.

Our objective is to show the scope of matters now in play, rather than to treat any of these issues in depth. Therefore, we present a large number of relatively brief articles. In this particular part, we focus on diversity and discrimination, which have become central HRM concerns as social attitudes, lifestyles, and the distribution of social power have changed.

Recently, issues about diversity and discrimination have attracted a great deal of attention both in the media and in HR practice. The substance of these issues has changed considerably over the last few decades. Early on, these issues were typically addressed in such terms as "affirmative action" and quotas; more recently, emphasis has shifted to how diversity can contribute to organizational performance. In this part, we deal with both phases.

Although many of our selections deal with more recent concerns, the relationship to the past must be considered. For example, Arthur P. Brief, Robert T. Buttram, Robin M. Reizenstein, S. Douglas Pugh, Jodi D. Callahan, Richard L. McCline, and Joel B. Vaslow suggest that, despite progress, subtle racism continues.

Significant changes in the demographics of American society have created changes in the composition of the workforce. In recent years, the number of people with different cultural and linguistic backgrounds in the workforce has grown substantially. In "Babel at Work" Timothy Aeppel reveals the linguistic and other complications these changes can involve. The next selection, a brief piece from the *Wall Street Journal* on the Bamboo Ceiling, deals with demographic groups whom early affirmative action efforts treated, at most, only peripherally.

In contrast to this recent development, both early affirmative action and the more recent treatments of diversity and discrimination have focused heavily on women. Even here, there have been important changes as the roles of women at work have evolved. Insight into some of these changes is provided in the next selection in which Cynthia F. Cohen reviews some legal matters that gender stereotypes have stimulated. However, despite all that has been done, Cohen shows that the effects of traditional gender stereotypes unfortunately still operate.

Of course, women have traditionally played a role in the workplace even when they have not been in it. Outside the work site they have been supporting their husbands' careers through business-related entertaining and so forth. However, even these roles seem to be changing as the women who play them see themselves differently. The case of Lorna Wendt, described by Betsy Morris in "It's Her Job Too," helps us to see a side of the gender issue that is real and becoming more widely discussed, although it is omitted in most human resources

textbooks. The next selection by Gene Koretz, "A Womans' Place Is..."
explores some of the subtle ways women today may be denied opportunities to
succeed.

Subtlety is intriguing. Many current incidents are called harassment and this
word suggests that some of these issues may not be so subtle. However, the next
selection (Daniel Niven's "The Case of the Hidden Harassment") suggests that
even harassment can be invisible sometimes. Similarly in "The Glass Table,"
Charles Michaels describes a situation in which potential harassment would not
have been spotted if a staffing meeting had not taken place around a table with a
glass top.

The number of dimensions which HRM practitioners deal with under the
heading of diversity discrimination has continued to expand as an increasing
number of social groups seek to have their concerns addressed. One fairly recent
addition to HRM concerns pertains to people holding unconventional sexual orientations. This is not a new source of diversity in the workplace, but the openness
about the matter and the power of the voice that openness has engendered are
new. So far the major impact has been in one of HRMs longest standing functions: overseeing employee benefits. The selection "More Companies Offering
Same-Sex-Partner Benefits" captures some of the challenges.

Taken together, the selections on discrimination and diversity in this part
reveal that several changes have resulted in new challenges for HRM. In the next
part, we will explore the ways that HRM practitioners are attempting to grapple
with the impact of these and other challenges that recent social changes have
introduced.

V-1: Beyond Good Intentions
The Next Steps Toward Racial Equality in the American Workplace

**ARTHUR P. BRIEF, ROBERT T. BUTTRAM,
ROBIN M. REIZENSTEIN, S. DOUGLAS PUGH,
JODI D. CALLAHAN, RICHARD L. MCCLINE,
AND JOEL B. VASLOW**

. . . .

EXECUTIVE OVERVIEW

Blatant racism is rarely observed in contemporary corporate America. This is partially attributable to the good intentions of many corporate leaders to establish racial equality. However, these good intentions have not always been enough to eliminate discrimination in employment. Discrimination still exists because a more subtle form of racism has emerged in recent years, one not necessarily alleviated by current popular programs such as diversity training.

. . . .

WHERE WE ARE TODAY

Racial slurs and derogatory remarks are heard rarely in the contemporary American workplace. This is consistent with the findings of survey researchers that indicate a dramatic shift in the racial attitudes expressed by white Americans.[1] Just 50 years ago, public opinion polls showed widespread acceptance of segregation and discrimination based upon race; today, these polls demonstrate that blatant racist attitudes are no longer popular and racist expressions are socially unacceptable. The corporate community undoubtedly deserves some credit for this shift. The efforts of Digital Equipment Corporation, General Electric, Pacific Bell, Xerox, and many other corporations to establish racial equality as a standard for doing business are well documented.[2]

Is it safe to assume that if one hears no evil, there is no evil? We think not. Blatant racism has been replaced by a more subtle form of racism that reflects an adherence to such traditional American values as individualism rather than open bigotry.[3] Managers, in attempting to fulfill seemingly reasonable business objectives, may create conditions conducive to these new racist attitudes. Only by understanding the nature of the new racism, including how it is activated, can managers avoid the unintentional promotion of segregation and discrimination in their organizations. Given the many visible efforts evident in corporate American to achieve racial equality, the intentions of most business leaders are good ones. But, as recently demonstrated by Texaco's agreement to pay $140 million to resolve a lawsuit brought by its black employees who charged the company with racial discrimination, good intentions may not be enough.[4] Such intentions have often proven inadequate because of the subtle force for wrongdoing that the new racism represents.[5]

EVIDENCE OF RACIAL DISCRIMINATION IN THE WORKPLACE

If one does not hear derogatory remarks about blacks or antagonistic statements aimed at them, what proof is there of racism in the workplace? One could take the attention focused by the media and civil rights groups on a relatively few companies as evidence of a problem, but there are better data available.[6] First, one might consider the frequency with which racial minorities report being victims of workplace discrimination. For example, more than 52,000 allegations of racial discrimination were filed with the Equal Employment Opportunity Commission during the 1992–1993 fiscal year against private sector employers.[7] Allegations of discrimination, of course, do not constitute proof of such. Aggregate data concerning the financial and professional positions of blacks relative to whites, however, suggest that many EEOC plaintiffs are not merely crying wolf. According to the U.S. Census Bureau, between 1979 and 1993 the real income of white families increased by 9 percent, while the real income of black families did not change. The Bureau also reported that in 1993, blacks earned less than their white counterparts in all jobs at all levels. Moreover, recent research indicates that these disparities in pay persist even after controlling for differences in job qualifications.[8] Finally, studies indicate that blacks, in fact, do not proportionally occupy certain kinds of positions, particularly those above the very bottom level of organizational hierarchies. Indeed, although blacks represent approximately 12 percent of the U.S. population, they make up less than 5 percent of the management ranks and considerably less than 1 percent of senior executives.[9]

Blacks are segregated not only vertically; some evidence also shows rather striking forms of horizontal segregation in the workplace. A recent study of newly hired clerical employees of a large commercial bank in the Northeast found that blacks were four times more likely than whites to be assigned, after five months on the job, to a black supervisor.[10] Importantly, when the researcher who discovered this pattern of segregation queried management about it, the bank's managers reacted with surprise. Not only did they claim they were unaware of such a pattern, they professed no knowledge of any policy or custom of job assignments that would lead to the segregation of employees by race. It seems the segregation that occurred was not consciously endorsed by the managers; some subtle yet powerful force was operating to match supervisors and subordinates by race.

This force not only results in segregation within an organization, but apparently may also prevent blacks from entering the workplace. The Fair Employment Council of Greater Washington, Inc. sent out teams of black and white job candidates matched in terms of sex, age, personal appearance, articulateness, and manner to apply for the same jobs.[11] The pairs also were equipped with similar fictional job qualifications. While blacks were favored over whites in 5 percent of the encounters with prospective employers, whites were favored over blacks in 29 percent of them. In fact, the black applicants were often told the job was already filled while their white counterparts were granted interviews for the position. This behavior is a prime example of what one scholar has termed "passive racism."[12]

The findings of social science research on race in the workplace are highly mixed. Numerous studies show that blacks often are treated more poorly than whites (for example, they are recruited less readily and their performance is rated lower).[13] Other research, however, shows that blacks are treated the same as or better than whites.[14] Closer review of this literature indicates that white subjects who suspected their racial attitudes were being investigated did not tend to treat blacks unfavorably; however, when the purpose of the studies was well hidden, at least some whites felt free to act on their negative racial attitudes.[15] If our interpretation of these mixed findings is correct, then it seems reasonable to conclude that some subtle form of racism was operating in these studies. That is, those whites harboring negative racial attitudes restrained themselves from expressing anti-black feelings unless they felt they would not be identified as racist. Blatant racism is dead or dying and has been replaced by a new form of racism.

. . . .
THE NEW RACISM

What is the nature of this new form of racism to which we have been referring? Until recently, the constellation of beliefs and values underlying this new form has been examined primarily by psychologists and political scientists who have used labels such as symbolic racism and modern racism to describe the new form of racism.[16] According to these scholars, old-fashioned racism was characterized by open bigotry and belief in the pre–Civil War stereotypes of blacks. It resulted in public policies supporting segregation and other forms of racial discrimination. Today, the majority of whites endorse the principles of integration and equal access or opportunity for persons of all races. But some whites, while endorsing these doctrines, vociferously oppose such policies as affirmative action, forced busing, and government payments to welfare recipients (who are mistakenly perceived as mostly black). This opposition is based on feelings that blacks are not sufficiently self-reliant, self-disciplined, or otherwise do not adhere to the values embodied in the Protestant Ethic.[17]

New racists believe that discrimination is a thing of the past; blacks are pushing too hard and moving too fast; public officials and other elites, through such policies as

affirmative action, have ensured that the gains blacks have made are excessive and, therefore, unfair; racism is bad.[18] This last belief sharply separates the new racism from the old. New racists define racism in terms of its blatant, old-fashioned version and see open bigotry as socially unacceptable. This rejection of open bigotry is likely tied to awareness of historical events such as the slave trade, the Holocaust, and other inhumanities. People who have adopted these new racial attitudes view their beliefs not as racist, but simply as facts. The successes of the civil rights movement may have reduced white guilt, allowing some whites to feel indignation about the perceived pushiness of blacks.

People subscribing to these new racial attitudes will refrain from engaging in discriminatory actions unless those actions can be somehow justified. Since such people recognize the social undesirability of being seen as bigots, those harboring anti-black feelings will not act against blacks unless their actions can be interpreted as nonracist. This phenomenon has important implications for understanding the conditions under which those who have adopted the new, negative racial attitudes will act upon their views, and when they will not. The new racist will not reject a black candidate for a sales position based explicitly upon his or her distaste for working with blacks; rather, he or she would rationalize that a customer population that is predominantly white would be more responsive to a white salesperson. Such business justifications are likely to provide new racists with the excuses they need in order to act out their negative feelings towards blacks.

Consider a sign posted in the headquarters of the Lincoln Yellow Cab Company in Springfield, Illinois, during the fall of 1995. The sign read: "Effective immediately. Do not pick up any black males unless you feel it is safe. If you do not feel safe with the way they look do not pick them up! There has

[sic] been too many robberies lately, and they have all been by BLACK MALES."[19]

Certainly, driver safety and security are legitimate business considerations for any cab company. Armed with this justification, the author of the sign at Lincoln Yellow Cab may have felt little compunction about setting racially discriminatory policies based on negative experiences with only a few representatives of the black male population.

As another example, consider the comments of the human resource director for a Chicago factory about hiring black job applicants: "You are going to have more problems than when you hire either a white or hispanic employee. . . . Absenteeism is going to be more of an issue, drugs will tend to be more of an issue . . . and the kind of work ethic . . . the eagerness to put out as much as possible [will not be as great with a black employee]."[20] This individual would probably be reluctant to publicly describe all blacks as lazy drug addicts. Yet by casting his opinions in terms of subordinate job performance, he betrays a grossly stereotypical manner of viewing others. As one scholar said of the human resource director's remarks, "This is a new way of couching some of the same kind of stereotypical thinking."[21]

Finally, consider the case against Shoney's restaurants. In late 1992, Shoney's agreed to a $132.5 million settlement in response to charges the company discriminated against its black employees. White managers were allegedly ordered to "lighten up" their restaurants—a company euphemism for reducing the number of black employees—and to hire "attractive white girls" instead.[22] Only 1.8 percent of Shoney's restaurant managers were black, and 75 percent of its black employees held jobs in such low-paying, non-customer-contact positions as dishwasher.

A former Shoney's vice president said these statistics were the result of the chief executive officer's unwritten policy that "blacks should not be employed in any posi-tion where they would be seen by customers."[23] The chief executive officer himself admitted, "In looking for anything to identify why this unit is under-performing, in some cases, I would probably have said this is a neighborhood of predominantly white neighbors, and we have a considerable amount of black employees and this might be a problem."[24] Thus, the practice of making hiring and promotion decisions on the basis of race was justified on the basis that the company's clientele might be "put off" by black employees.

As disturbing as these examples are, it is all the more troubling to realize that the new racist ideology may manifest itself in exceedingly more subtle ways. It is all too easy to translate stereotypical differences between blacks and whites into the modern language of person–organization fit. When it comes to fit, contemporary executives speak in terms of "attitudes," "belief systems," "values," "style," and "personality" in fuzzy terms that might easily be used by the new racist as a stand-in for skin color. Thus, the stereotype of blacks as lazy becomes translated as a black job candidate who is "not really enough of a 'self-starter' to fit in." If this obfuscatory language is not enough protection for those subscribing to the new, negative racial attitudes, they may avail themselves of a legacy of managerial teachings that explicitly support the notion that factors such as race are legitimate and useful criteria on which to base hiring and promotion decisions. Take, for example, the lesson taught by Chester I. Barnard in his 1938 book, *The Functions of the Executive*. He described the informal executive organization as one whose purpose is to communicate "intangible facts, opinions, suggestions, suspicions, that cannot pass through formal channels."[25] For this informal organization to function appropriately, Barnard prescribed that it select and promote to executive positions people who are compatible with those already in place. He stated, "Perhaps often and certainly occasionally men cannot be promoted or selected, or even must be relieved, because they cannot function, because they 'do not fit,' where there is no question of formal competence. This question of 'fitness' involves such matters as education, experience, age, sex, personal distinctions, prestige, [and] race. . . . "[26]

One would not expect to see such directives moving through formal channels today. Rather, concerns over race and fit would likely be treated as other intangible facts, opinions, suggestions, and suspicions. An emphasis on racial fit, while betraying the application of racial stereotypes, is quite consistent with the long-standing (and often challenged) assumption that similarity among top-management team members will promote organizational functioning.[27] Unfortunately, given the degree of vertical segregation that persists in contemporary organizations, blacks undoubtedly are placed at a disadvantage as companies pursue what Loden and Roesner call the "homogeneous ideal."[28] Perhaps this is why, more than three decades after the publication of Barnard's advice to executives, a black manager wrote "I believe that many of the problems I encountered were problems of fit. . . . I was out of the 'place' normally filled by black people in the company. . . . "[29]

. . . .
TRICKLE DOWN RACIAL ATTITUDES

The existence of business justifications likely will free those who have adopted the new, negative racial attitudes to act in a discriminatory fashion. Regrettably, when these attitudes exist at or near the top of an organization, their damaging effects can be compounded. When questioned by a reporter about the sign instructing drivers not to pick up black passengers, the owner of the Lincoln Yellow Cab Company described earlier said it had been posted by

a secretary at the request of her supervisor.[30] It is unclear whether the secretary agreed with the policy contained on the sign. However, the implication was that she was "just following orders."

When business justifications for discrimination issue from the upper levels of an organization, subordinates may enforce racist policies simply as a matter of compliance with authoritative directives. When executives air concerns over blacks fitting in, their managers may interpret these concerns as directives to treat blacks differently, and subordinates are likely to heed these instructions. In fact, both history and research suggest that subordinates will follow such directives, even if they harbor no anti-black feelings.[31]

Observers of all sorts of organizations have long recognized the dark underside of obedience to authority.[32] Philosopher Hannah Arendt, commenting on Adolph Eichmann's role in Hitler's Final Solution, concluded, "It is the nature of every bureaucracy . . . to make functionaries and mere cogs in the administrative machinery out of men."[33] An employee, she wrote "for the sake of his pension, his life insurance, the security of his wife and children [is] prepared to do literally anything."[34] Nobel Prize–winning economist Herbert A. Simon observed that "the employee sign[s] a blank check, so to speak in entering upon his employment," because it is "the price of retaining [a] position, securing a higher salary or other advantages."[35] In the words of a former senior executive: "What is right in the corporation is not what is right in a man's home or in his church. What is right in the corporation is what the guy above you wants from you."[36]

These disturbing quotations imply that organizational members will tend to comply with what they hear as orders from above, even when doing so conflicts with their personal values, causes discomfort, and involves actions that they otherwise would consider as immoral, illegal, or unthinkable.[37] But what about the subordinate who shares the new, negative racial attitudes of his or her superiors? Since the manager or executive subscribing to the new, negative racial attitudes is likely to initiate discrimination by providing some sort of business justification, subordinates who subscribe to the same negative attitudes are relieved of the task of concocting an excuse for expressing their anti-black sentiments. Moreover, because the subordinates are in a position to claim that they were just following orders, they are more likely to feel free to behave in a discriminatory fashion without fear that they ultimately will be judged as a racist. In this circumstance, the new racist ideology can have a most devastating impact on promoting racial equality in organizations.

OBSERVING THE NEW RACISM IN ACTION

Ideally, one would want to test the truth of our assertions about the new racism in a corporate setting. But, measuring business justifications to discriminate, racial attitudes, and levels of discrimination in the workplace presents a host of problems regarding access to organizations, legal concerns, and ethical issues. Thus, we conducted three studies that simulated business settings. Every attempt was made to maximize the realism of our simulations. Two of the studies, for example, relied upon an elaborate "in-basket exercise." An in-basket exercise is a simulation of the paperwork that arrives in the mailbox of the typical manager. These exercises often have been used for training and selecting managers; and, in fact, have been shown to be predictive of managerial success.[38]

While the subjects participating in the experiments all were non-black university students, they did vary in terms of academic major and employment status. Neither of

these factors, however, affected the findings obtained, indicating some degree of generalizability. (For more on the subjects and other features of the studies, see the Appendix.)

Subjects in all studies were randomly assigned either to receive or not to receive a business justification to discriminate from their "boss." In one study, for instance, subjects received a memorandum in their in-baskets requesting them to rate the qualifications of candidates for the soon to be vacated position of vice president of human resources. Those given a justification to discriminate from their "boss" were told:

> Given that the vast majority of our workforce is white, it is essential we put a white person in the VP position. I don't want to jeopardize the fine relationship we have with our people in the units. Betty [the outgoing vice president] worked long and hard to get these folks to trust us; and I do not want her replacement to have to overcome any personal barriers.

As shown in Figure 1, subjects who received the business justification rated black candidates significantly lower on a five-point scale than those who did not receive the justification. This finding was consistent across all three studies, with different types of subjects, suggesting business justifications to discriminate can lead to discrimination.

In two of the studies, the degree to which subjects subscribed to the new, negative racial attitudes was assessed directly several weeks before the simulations. Their attitudes were measured with the Modern Racism Scale, a measure frequently used in social psychological research.[39] (See Table 1 for the measure.) In one study, subjects were told they were assisting a faculty member with a consulting project and were asked to review the credentials of ten candidates, selecting three of them to be interviewed for a marketing position. Three of the candidates were black and qualified for the position, two were white and also

FIGURE 1   Mean Ratings for Qualified Black Candidates in Each Instruction Condition

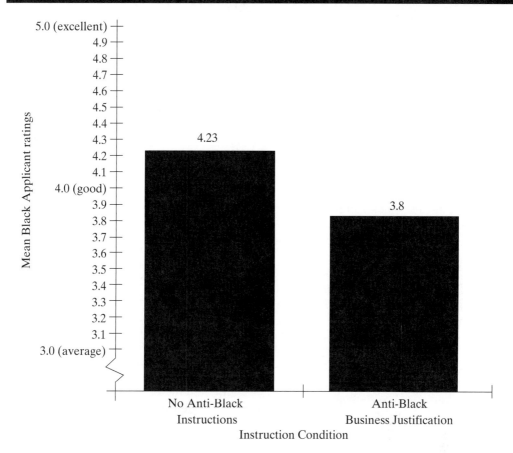

qualified, and the remaining candidates were white and unqualified. Subjects randomly assigned to receive a business justification to discriminate were told the following in a memorandum from the "president" of the "client firm":

In the past, we have kept our [marketing] teams as homogeneous as possible. We feel that similar people will have similar goals and ideas. Importantly, the particular team to which this person will be assigned currently includes no minority group members. Our organization attempts to match the characteristics of our representatives with the characteristics of the population to which they will be assigned. The particular

territory to which your selected representative will be assigned contains relatively few minority group members. Therefore, in this particular situation, I feel that it is important that you do not hire anyone that is a member of a minority group.

As shown in Figure 2, subjects receiving the justification to discriminate selected significantly fewer qualified black candidates to be interviewed. Indeed, 37.5 percent of the subjects receiving the justification selected no black candidates, thus choosing unqualified whites over qualified blacks. Second, for those subjects harboring new racist attitudes, the business justification to discriminate served as a releaser, freeing

TABLE 1 Items from the Modern Racism Scale

- Blacks have more influence upon school desegregation plans than they ought to have.
- It is easy to understand the anger of Black people in America. (reverse scored)
- Over the past few years the government and news media have shown more respect to Blacks than they deserve.
- Discrimination against Blacks is no longer a problem in the United States.
- Over the past few years Blacks have gotten more economically than they deserve.
- Blacks should not push themselves where they are not wanted.
- Blacks are getting too demanding in their push for equal rights.

(McConahay, Hardee, and Batts, 1981)

them to act against black candidates. With the justification, subjects scoring high on the measure of new racism selected an average of only .53 blacks to be interviewed, while subjects scoring low on the racism measure selected an average of 1.10 black candidates. In contrast, when no justification to discriminate was given, high and low prejudiced subjects behaved similarly, selecting 1.88 and 1.80 black candidates, respectively. In a third study, prejudiced subjects were also found to treat blacks particularly unfairly when supplied with a business justification to discriminate.

Because they were simulations, these studies may not mirror perfectly what is happening in corporate America. But they suggest that if a manager justifies discriminatory behavior on the grounds of seeking to realize a seemingly reasonable business objective, his or her subordinates may accept the justification, and, in fact, treat blacks unfairly. Moreover, the justification probably will prompt subordinates subscribing to the new, negative racial attitudes to act in a particularly discriminatory fashion.

● ●
BEYOND GOOD INTENTIONS

The well-intentioned executive concerned about racial equality in an organization should consider these suggestions:

LOOK AT THE NUMBERS

For a given position, what proportion of black applicants are hired compared with the proportion of whites? For a given position, what proportion of black occupants are promoted compared with the proportion of whites? For a given position, what is the turnover rate among blacks compared with the rate for whites? Are blacks clustered in certain occupations or at particular organizational levels? Do blacks feel they are treated the same as their white counterparts? Based on employee attitude survey results, do black and white employees, occupying similar kinds of jobs, report comparable levels of satisfaction with supervision, co-workers, promotional opportunities, and pay?

If the numbers look right and black employees feel equally treated, managers can stick to the policies, procedures, and practices they have in place. If there are signs of racial discrimination, managers must make a firm commitment to fix the problem. Responsibilities for organizational effectiveness, as well as legal and moral obligations, give no option but to act. Because most managers already are looking at their numbers, it may be the failure to act, or to act effectively, that is the source of the problem. Texaco, for instance, apparently collected and analyzed much of the data being called for; but it also is apparent that

FIGURE 2   Mean Number of Blacks Selected for High and Low Prejudice Subjects

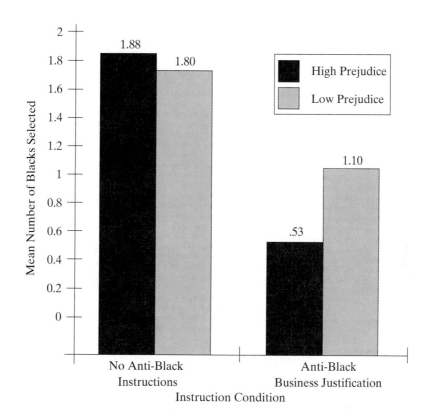

the company's response to its analyses was not effective.[40]

DO NOT STOP AT STAMPING OUT BLATANT RACISM

Diversity training will probably not destroy old-fashioned racial stereotypes. Despite recent evidence to the contrary,[42] old-fashioned racism and its tenets—white supremacy, black inferiority, and racial segregation—are dead or dying in America. To attack these beliefs through diversity training, therefore, is likely to have little effect. Indeed, new racists, when participating in such training, may be the very ones to lead the charge against old-fashioned racial stereotyping, for they recognize the social

undesirability of such blatant racism. New racism is more subtle and complex, emphasizing that discrimination is passé and stressing that black gains are too fast, excessive, and unfair. An alternative to diversity training is to expose people to the sorts of behaviors that are to be expected and to provide an incentive for engaging in them. At Harvard Pilgrim Health Care, a Boston-area managed care company with 8,500 employees and $2 billion in annual revenues, executives are expected to promote more minorities and women into the ranks of senior management and to make their employees feel the company supports diversity. Importantly, the annual appraisals of Harvard Pilgrim's executives capture how well they are meeting these expectations and their bonuses reflect their appraised performance.[43]

ELIMINATE VAGUE SELECTION AND PROMOTION CRITERIA

New racists will not act on their anti-black feelings unless given a nonracist justification for doing so. Executives must eliminate even seemingly reasonable business rationales that can be used as justifications to exclude blacks. Vague talk of matching people to jobs in terms of such things as social background, lifestyle, or even attitudes, beliefs, and values in order to achieve harmony, comfort, or ease of adjustment is to be avoided. If one is sincere about matching on the basis of values, those values need to be clearly articulated and carefully assessed. Techniques are available for accomplishing this.[44]

ENFORCE TOUGH RULES

Language control is not enough. Discourse about doing business is too diffuse to regulate completely. Tough rules need to be specified and enforced regarding the treatment of blacks. Obviously, many such rules are mandated by federal, state, and local governments; but organizational leaders must move beyond attempts merely to comply with legal regulations. In regard to hiring, for instance, the following sort of affirmative action rule may be required: When choosing between black and white candidates with comparable credentials, the black is to be selected. Although such treatment might be demanded to overcome the subtle but powerful forces of the new racism, we see a backlash in some quarters against these kinds of rules. For example, California recently voted affirmatively on an initiative to ban racial preferences in all aspects of state government operations, including employment. Senator Philip Gramm of Texas has spoken in favor of a presidential executive order abolishing federal affirmative action programs.

The employment playing field in America often is balanced against blacks and an official color-blind stance alone will not level that field. But affirmative actionlike rules will work only if the words and deeds of an organization's management indicate the rules are to be followed. After settling its employees' lawsuit against the company for racial discrimination, Shoney's has become a model for articulating rough rules and enforcing them. Blacks have been hired, promoted, and equitably paid, and racially abusive managers have been fired.[45] A legal crisis is not necessary to prompt a company into action. Inland Steel represents one of many companies that put tough, effective rules in place before a crisis erupted. Management at the company listened to the concerns of its black employees and put into place an award-winning affirmative action program.[46]

ENCOURAGE PRINCIPLED DISOBEDIENCE

Any experienced executive knows that significant organizational change is hard to achieve. Eliminating racial discrimination is a case in point. Attempts at language control and rule enforcement may not be enough to rid an organization of a pattern of decision making that over the years has become a part of the social fabric of the organization and of the larger society in which it is embedded. Subordinates, no matter what steps top management takes, may interpret instructions from above, correctly or incorrectly, as requiring that blacks be treated disadvantageously. In response to such perceived instructions, subordinate managers should be encouraged to disobey, to question what they believe their superiors' wishes to be.

Knowledge about how to encourage such principled organizational disobedience is scarce, but some orders clearly demand disobedience. Kelman and Hamilton in their powerful book, *Crimes of Obedience,* provide a number of ideas for facilitating such principled disobedience. First, disperse authority. By holding managers accountable to both their line superiors and to a human resource staff executive for hiring, promoting, and other personnel decisions, the window is left open to question directives from either party. Second, redefine the role of the loyal subordinate. By condemning loyalty construed in terms of unquestioning servitude and by praising the people who have the courage to question troublesome orders, blind obedience may become stigmatized. In addition, endorse peer discourse. By helping to create a norm of openness among subordinate managers, the critical discussion of instructions from above, the articulation of misgivings, the reinforcement of doubts, and analyses of how to respond may be facilitated.[47]

In some organizations, acting on these ideas would constitute nothing less than a revolutionary change in management style. But a revolution may be precisely what is required to eliminate racial discrimination and other forms of organizational wrongdoing. Many organizations now have in place policies and procedures for swiftly investigating allegations of discrimination and, if wrongdoing is detected, appropriately punishing guilty parties. It is feasible to expand such practices to include the investigation of individuals who might have known about incidents of discrimination but remained silent. Persons found guilty of such silences should also be punished appropriately, if organizational leaders have made it clear that it is the duty of every employee to bring to the attention of management alleged incidents of discrimination and that failure to do so will have negative consequences.

As Roosevelt Thomas and other leading thinkers on diversity have stressed, the forces driving discrimination in the work-place are many, and any legitimate attempt to combat discrimination must be multi-faceted.[48] If there is a history of discrimination in an organization, nothing short of a wholesale attempt to change the racial culture within that organization is likely to succeed. To accomplish such massive change, some organizations, sometimes under pressure, have chosen to establish a partnership with a civil rights group such as Jesse Jackson's Rainbow Push Coalition or the National Association for the Advancement of Colored People.[49]

The dynamics we have described in this article may not be limited to issues of race. Recent research indicates that the new racist ideology may have a counterpart where gender is concerned.[50] Although they have not been the focus of this article, the savvy manager will keep an eye out for new forms of sexism, ageism, and other potentially hidden forces driving discriminatory practices. Moreover, the problem we have addressed is by no means exclusively an American one. Ample evidence documents subtle forms of racism in many advanced economies.[51]

Racial discrimination in corporate America is a real problem in need of executive action. Efforts to resolve the problem have not been wholly successful and strategies are called for. The nation's business leaders can contribute more to achieving equality among the races by recognizing that their organizations are essential vehicles for social change. The burden of change, however, is not the sole responsibility of business. Educators (perhaps especially, professors of management), government officials, and, most importantly, individual citizens of all races share the burden of ensuring that skin color does not denote differences in knowledge, skills, abilities, expectations, motivational levels, or any other human characteristic that helps determine economic outcomes. When our collective responsibilities are fulfilled, we all will gain.

Appendix

In all three experiments we reported, subjects were undergraduates enrolled in a private university in the southeastern United States. None was black. Approximately 34 percent of the university's undergraduate population is drawn from the southeastern United States, 27 percent from the northeast, and the remainder from elsewhere in the United States and internationally. In the first study, 76 business students participated: 42 percent were female and 30 percent were employed. Subjects played the role of a chief financial officer of a restaurant chain in a business simulation. The simulation has been used successfully in prior research concerned with a different topic, producing no substantial differences in results across samples of students, corporate controllers, and top managers.[52] For details regarding the first study, including a description of how the credentials of the "job applicants" were verified, see A.P. Brief, R.T. Buttram, J.D. Elliott, R.M. Reizenstein, and R.L. McCline, "Releasing the beast: A study of compliance with orders to use race as a selection criterion," *Journal of Social Issues,* 1995, 51, pp. 177–193.

Eighty-four psychology students participated in the second study reported. Approximately 46 percent were female. Subjects in this study were led to believe they were assisting a

faculty member with a consulting project. Details of the study are found in R.M. Reizenstein and A.P. Brief, "Just doing business: Compliance and racism as explanations for unfair employment discrimination," a paper presented at the 1995 annual conference of the American Psychology Society in New York.

The third study reported, using the same business simulation as in the first study, relied upon 137 business students as subjects: 42 percent were female and 35 percent were employed. See S.D. Pugh, A.P. Brief, and J.B. Vaslow, "Prejudicial hiring practices: The roles of authority, legitimacy, and modern racism," a paper presented at the 1996 Academy of Management Meetings in Cincinnati, for the details of the third study.

For more on the ideas presented in this article, see A.P. Brief and E.L. Hayes, "The continuing 'American dilemma': Studying racism in organizations," in C.L. Cooper and D. Rousseau (Eds.), *Trends in organizational behavior—Volume 4* (Chichester: John Wiley and Sons, 1997), and A.P. Brief, R.T. Buttram, and J.M. Dukerich, "Collective corruption in the corporate world: Towards a process model," in M.E. Turner (Ed.), *Groups at work: Advances in theory and research* (Hillsdale, N. J.: Lawrence Erlbaum and Associates, 1997).

Notes

1. For example, see Schuman, H., Steeb, C., & Bobo, L. 1985. *Racial attitudes in America.* Cambridge, MA: Harvard University Press.
2. Jackson, S.E., & Associates. 1992. *Diversity in the workplace: Human resources initiatives.* New York: The Guilford Press. Graham, L.O. 1993. *The best companies for minorities.* New York: Plume.
3. For example, see Kinder, D.R. 1986. The continuing American dilemma: White resistance to racial change 40 years after Mydral. *Journal of Social Issues.* 42:151–171; McConahay, J.B. 1986. Modern racism, ambivalence, and the Modern Racism Scale in J. Dovidio and S. Gaertner (Eds.). *Prejudice, discrimination, and racism: Theory and research:* 91–124.

New York: Academic Press, and Sears, D.O. 1988. Symbolic racism. In P.A. Katz and D.A. Taylor (Eds.), *Eliminating racism:* 53–84. New York: Plenum Press.
4. Eichenwald, K. 1996. Texaco to make reward payout in bias lawsuit. *The New York Times.* November 16:1 and 23.
5. For example, see Herbert, B. 1996. Workday racism. *The New York Times.* November 11:A15.
6. For example, see Kerwin K. 1997. The smudgy legacy AT&T's new prez left behind. *Business Week.* February 3:36–37; Smith, E.L., & Kelly, J. 1996. Jackson puts the push on Mitsubishi. *Black Enterprise.* August: 16.

7. The Commission is the federal agency charged with interpreting, administering, and enforcing laws to ensure all applicants and employees are treated similarly without regard to protected characteristics such as race.

8. See Cancio, A.S., Evans, T.D., & Maume, D.J. Jr. 1996. Reconsidering the declining significance of race: Racial differences in early career wages. *American Sociological Review.* 61:541–556.

9. Morrison, A.M. 1992. *The new leaders.* San Francisco: Jossey-Bass. Also see, for example, Powell, G.N. and Butterfield, D.A. 1997. Effects of race on promotions to top management in a federal department. *Academy of Management Journal.* 40:112–128.

10. Lefkowitz, J. 1994. Race as a factor in job placement: Serendipitous findings of "ethnic drift." *Personnel Psychology.* 47:497–513.

11. Bendick, Jr., M. Jackson, C.W., & Reinoso, V.A. 1994. Measuring employment discrimination through controlled experiments. *Review of Black Political Economy.* 23:25–48.

12. Essed, P. 1991. *Understanding everyday racism.* Newbury Park, CA: Sage Publications.

13. Stone, E.F., Stone, D.L., & Dipboye, R.L. 1992. Stigmas in organizations: Race, handicaps, and physical unattractiveness. In K. Kelly (Ed.), *Issues, theory, and research in industrial/organizational psychology.* Amsterdam, Holland: Elsevier Science Publishers.

14. Stone et al. 1992.

15. Stone et al. 1992.

16. See Kinder 1986, McConahay 1986, and Sears 1988.

17. For example, see Kinder, D.R. & Sears, D.O. 1981. Prejudice and politics: Symbolic racism versus racial threats to the good life. *Journal of Personality and Social Psychology.* 40:414–431.

18. McConahay 1986.

19. Long, R. 1995. Cabbies told to pass up Black men. *The Times-Picayune.* November 2:A3.

20. Hayner, D., & Johnson, M.A. 1993. In the workplace, two perceptions. *The Great Divide: Racial attitudes in Chicago, Chicago Sun-Times special reprint.* 14–15. Chicago: The Chicago Community Trust.

21. Hayner & Johnson. 1993:14.

22. Watkins, S. 1993. Racism du jour at Shoney's. *The Nation.* October 18:424–428.

23. Watkins 1993:424.

24. Watkins 1993:427.

25. Barnard, C. 1938. *The functions of the executive.* Cambridge, MA: Harvard University Press. 225.

26. Barnard 1938:224.

27. For example, see Essed 1991; and Thomas, Jr. R.R. 1991. *Beyond race and gender.* New York: American Management Association.

28. Loden, M., & Rosener, J.B. 1991. *Workforce America: Managing employee diversity as a vital resource.* Homewood, IL: Business One Irwin.

29. Quoted in Jones, E.W. 1973. What it's like to be a Black manager. *Harvard Business Review.* 51:114.

30. Long 1995.

31. Such a compliance argument is developed in A.P. Brief, R.T. Buttram, and J.M. Dukerich. 1997. Collective corruption in the corporate world: Towards a process model in M.E. Turner (Ed.), *Groups at work: Advances in theory and research.* Hillsdale, N.J.: Lawrence Erlbaum and Associates.

32. Katz, R.L., & Kuhn, D. 1978. *The social psychology of organizations.* New York: Wiley.

33. Arendt, H. 1963. *Eichmann in Jerusalem: A report on the banality of evil.* New York: Viking Press: 289.

34. Arendt, H. 1978. *The Jew as pariah.* New York: Grove Press: 232.

35. Simon, H.A. 1945. *Administrative behavior.* New York: The Free Press: 133.

36. Quoted in Jackall, R. 1988. *Moral mazes: The world of corporate managers.* New York: Oxford University Press: 6.

37. Kelman, K.C., & Hamilton, V.L. 1989. *Crimes of obedience: Toward a social psychology of authority and responsibility.* New Haven, Conn.: Yale University Press.

38. For example, see Frederiksen, N., Saunders, D.R., & Wand, B. 1957. The in-basket test. *Psychological Monographs.* 71. No. 428. Lopez, F.M. 1966. Evaluating executive decision making: The in-basket technique. *AMA Research Study.* No. 75. New York: American Management Association, and Thornton, G.C.

1992. *Assessment centers in human resource management.* Reading, MA: Addison-Wesley.

39. McConahay, J.B., Bardee, B.B., & Batts, V. 1981. Has racism declined? It depends upon who's asking and what is asked. *Journal of Conflict Resolution.* 25:563–579.

40. Eichenwald, K. 1996. Records signal lawyer's role in Texaco suit. *The New York Times.* November 15: C1 and C2.

41. Also see Wynter, L.E. 1996. Business and race. *The Wall Street Journal.* December 4: B1.

42. For example, see Hernstein, R.J. & Murray, C. 1994. *The bell curve: Intelligence and class structure in American life.* New York: The Free Press.

43. Deutsch, C.H. 1996. Corporate diversity in practice. *The New York Times.* November 20: C1 and C15.

44. For example, see Chatman, J.A. 1989. Improving interactional organizational research: A model of person–organization fit. *Academy of Management Review.* 14:333–349.

45. Gaiter, D.J. 1996. How Shoney's belted by a lawsuit, found the path to diversity. *The Wall Street Journal.* April 16: A1 and A6.

46. Bollier, D. 1996. *Aiming higher.* New York: AMACOM.

47. Kelman and Hamilton, 1989.

48. For example, see Thomas. 1991; Thomas, Jr. R.R. 1992. Managing diversity: A conceptual framework. In S.E. Jackson et al. (Eds.), *Diversity in the Workplace.* New York: The Guilford Press and Loden & Rosener. 1991.

49. For example, see Holmes, S.A. 1996. Size of Texaco discrimination settlement could encourage more lawsuits. *The New York Times.* November 17:20; and, Holmes, S.A. 1996. Boycotts rarely have impact on bottom line. *The New York Times.* November 15:A4.

50. See Swim, J.K., Aiken, K.J., Hall, W.S., & Hunter, B.A. 1995. Sexism and racism: Old-fashioned and modern prejudices. *Journal of Personality and Social Psychology.* 68:199–214.

51. Pettigrew, T.F., & Meertens, R.W. 1995. Subtle and blatant prejudice in Western Europe. *European Journal of Social Psychology.* 25:57–75.

52. Brief, A.P., Dukerich, J.M., Brown, P., & Brett, J. 1996. What's wrong with the Treadway Commission Report? Experimental analyses of the effects of personal values and codes of conduct on fraudulent financial reporting. *Journal of Business Ethics.* 15:183–198.

V-2: Babel at Work

A 3Com Factory Hires a Lot of Immigrants, Gets Mix of Languages

TIMOTHY AEPPEL

Morton Grove, Illinois—Draped from the ceiling in 3Com Corp.'s sprawling modem factory in this Chicago suburb is a sign of the times: 65 different national flags, each representing the origin of at least one person who has worked here since it opened 2½ years ago.

The plant employs 1,200 people, the vast majority immigrants. They speak more than 20 languages, including Tagalog, Gujarati, and Chinese. English, of varying degrees, ties them together.

"If there's a problem, I call over somebody who speaks the person's language to help," says Thai Chung, a 33-year-old refugee from Vietnam who manages Line 12, one of a dozen assembly lines.

That doesn't always work. A few days ago, Mr. Chung, a wiry man who spends much of his day striding up and down his line, wanted a janitor to clean up some grease. He spoke to him in English but obviously wasn't understood even after repeating himself slowly. He thought the man might be Polish; so he enlisted Vesna Stevanovic, one of the assemblers on his line. But she's from Serbia and couldn't speak to him, either. "I'm not even sure he's Polish," says Ms. Stevanovic, gazing over the frames of pink eyeglasses. "I don't know what he is."

The janitor eventually got the message. Nobody knows how. Stella Foy, a gruff 57-year-old Chicago native who also works on the line, says simply: "Around here, you point a lot."

Many factories, as they hire more immigrants, are being plunged into an industrial Tower of Babel. Earlier waves of immigrants tended to have more in common, such as the East Europeans who flocked to the steel mills a century ago. Now factories, running faster and using increasingly complex equipment, might seem to need such commonality among their workers more than ever.

A HIGHLY DIVERSE GROUP

Churning out modems around the clock, 3Com's workers could hardly be more diverse. Urbane Asians with multiple college degrees work alongside people only recently arrived from Central American villages. Serbs work with Bosnian Muslims, as well as Iraqis, Peruvians, and South Africans. Managers think at least a third of their workers wouldn't mind if asked to work Christmas—as they were two years ago—because they don't celebrate it.

Overcoming language barriers is just one of the challenges. Some immigrants come from countries where you seldom say "please," and certainly not to someone you

consider your social inferior. That aloofness can cause hurt feelings. The factory also has its own hierarchy, based largely on language ability and background. Those who speak the best English and are the best educated are the most upwardly mobile.

Saji Korah is one of them. "I have a bachelor's degree in economics from India and an associate's degree in computer programming," the 34-year-old says in crisp English. Yet his job today, riveting brackets onto circuit boards, could be done by someone far less educated.

MORE SCHOOLING

It's monotonous, and he makes it clear he has no intention of doing such work for long. He is going to school part time for yet-another degree, in computer-information systems. He dreams of becoming one of the plant's roving technicians.

Asked whether he has problems communicating with less-well-spoken colleagues, he says, "Sometimes, I have trouble following their pronunciations." Standing nearby, Suresh Patel says he has trouble, too, but mainly in understanding American-born workers. "Sometimes, they talk too fast," he explains.

In dealing with such difficulties, 3Com's approach is simple. Its managers don't even try to accommodate cultural quirks—probably an impossibility anyway. They just make it clear that they expect newcomers to adapt to the factory's methods. "They're here because they want to be here, so we start with that assumption," says Tom Werner, vice president of manufacturing for the company's two big Chicago-area plants.

In addition, the company continually designs and redesigns the work to fit the varied workforce. When Richelle Ho, a 23-year-old from the Philippines, steps up to her post on Line 12 as her shift starts, a laminated sheet explaining her task hangs above her workstation. A few sentences direct her to put strips of yellow tape over the "gold fingers," the part of the printed circuit boards that will eventually plug into a computer. But the page is dominated by a big color-coded drawing, showing the outlines of the product and arrows pointing to the gold fingers.

Language isn't a big deal to Ms. Ho, who speaks fluent English. At lunchtime, however, she usually joins a clique of Filipinos, and they talk in Tagalog, the main language in the Philippines. But she comes from a region where another language, Cebuano, is spoken, and, she says, "I don't speak Tagalog very well."

If any job on the line becomes too complex, it is broken up into narrower slices to make it easier to learn. Mary Ellen Smith, director of manufacturing, says: "We keep as much simplicity in the process that we can. The key is that anyone can come in and do that job."

The factory doesn't have much choice but to hire a lot of immigrants. Many native-born Americans wouldn't consider taking the often-tedious entry-level jobs. But for John Phan, a 35-year-old who came from Vietnam a decade ago speaking little English, operating a machine on Line 12 is a step up. He makes $10.05 an hour, compared with $7.50 an hour he previously earned at a plastics factory.

Mr. Phan's English is heavily accented, and he admits he sometimes can't understand co-workers. But that hardly matters; he seldom has to talk. He knows when a machine is running low on components, for instance, because a white light flashes on a pole jutting up from the top of it. One machine even talks to him: "Be careful, the feeder section may move," coos a soothing female voice, just before a big metal rack known as a feeder automatically shifts out into the corridor. "These machines are very smart," he says.

HOW HE MANAGES

When he must communicate, Mr. Phan has options. He often works alongside another Vietnamese, Peter Mac. "Sometimes we speak Chinese, sometimes Vietnamese; I know both," Mr. Phan says. Moreover, the English-fluent supervisor, Mr. Chung, can speak those languages. Indeed, of the 25 workers on Line 12 in this shift, only 3 are native-born Americans. The largest group is 10 workers from India, and the line includes an Iraqi, an Ecuadorian, a Guatemalan, and a Serb, as well as a handful of Filipinos.

But when offering a full breakdown of his team, Mr. Chung—himself still haunted by a harrowing escape by boat from Vietnam to Thailand in 1981—carefully separates the three Vietnamese from the three who consider themselves "Chinese people from Vietnam." Such distinctions are important, deeply intertwined with personal identities, though most Americans encountering all this for the first time might be baffled.

Mr. Chung says he doesn't intentionally group people according to nationality, yet some of that happens anyway. The lines have considerable autonomy to arrange workers any way that helps them meet production goals; if putting together fellow nationals is beneficial, so be it. That's why the "functional testing" section of line 12 is staffed today by two Indian men—one of them Mr. Patel—who always work together. "It makes it easier," explains Mr. Patel, adding that when nobody else is around, he and his colleague talk to each other in their native Gujarati.

They observe a kind of linguistic etiquette: Workers know that when with someone from their own "group," they can slip into their own language. But if an outsider is involved, it's English.

However, this sort of consideration goes only so far. Eleanor Punay, from the Philippines, tries to explain why she often was offended when she first started here. "Where I'm from, you say 'please' and 'thank you' a lot, maybe even too much."

GETTING REASSURANCE

As she speaks, she glances nervously toward a man operating a machine a few feet away; she doesn't want him to hear her. Lowering her voice, she says: "Let's just say there's some countries where they don't say it as often as you'd want." Early on, she adds, she spoke about the matter to her sister, who works in a hospital with many foreign doctors, and the sister assured her it wasn't personal.

Ms. Punay's co-worker doesn't look up, and it's unclear whether he heard any of this. But a few minutes later, he tucks his last finished modem onto a black plastic rack and pushes it over onto Ms. Punay's worktable without a word.

"Thank you," she says. He pops back into his chair and turns back to his work.

Immigrants work on every part of the assembly line, but especially on the second half of it, doing jobs like inserting final components by hand, testing products, and packaging them. The front end of the line is heavily automated, with machines such as "chip shooters," which put tiny electronic components such as silicon chips onto the circuit boards as they move down a conveyor belt. Each circuit board, though only about the size of a slice of toast, ultimately carries about 200 parts.

Yet most people on the line don't need to know the technical details. Even those running the machines are mainly expected to refill parts and do minor adjustments. If a machine breaks down, teams of technicians and programmers swoop in.

Language ability is a litmus test for advancement. You can't run a line or become a roving technician if you have serious trouble with English. Yet even those on their way up sometimes worry about their accents or verbal ticks.

"I get really frustrated," says Mr. Chung, the supervisor, despite his excellent English. Talking about technical issues is no problem, he says, "but sometimes I'm talking to someone, and I want to explore something deeper, something important; but I can't get into it." He figures his English conveys, at most, 70% of what he is thinking on personal matters. What bothers him more, he adds, is that he sees other immigrants who have been in the United States far less time than he has and, he thinks, speak better.

A BIT OF ENVY

Like many of the plant's upwardly mobile immigrants, Mr. Chung is proud of what he has accomplished. He owns a three-apartment house with his brother and likes to travel; he has visited Paris. Yet he feels thwarted in his ambitions. He dropped out of college after his junior year and took a factory job to make money to help bring his other relatives over from Vietnam. Now, he looks with some envy at his older brother, who finished college and works for the Federal Aviation Administration. "He's doing real well, better than me," he says wistfully.

Those at the plant with good English and ambitious to advance can choose from an array of training courses beyond the basics needed for their immediate jobs. The courses cover everything from leadership skills to how to run a chip shooter. Workers can even take a course on drawing up an instructional sheet similar to those hanging over their workstations; they practice by writing one for making a peanut-butter-and-jelly sandwich. Training also relies heavily on lots of illustrations and on-the-job practice.

Hattie Curry is one of the few Americans on Line 12. A native of North Carolina, she started working for the company seven years ago, before this plant opened; the company, acquired by 3Com last year, was then known as U.S. Robotics.

Ms. Curry notes the increase in immigrants at 3Com and says working with them hasn't always been easy for her. "Before I worked here," she says, "I hadn't been around a lot of foreign people; I didn't understand their ways." As a newcomer, she thought some with more skills were reluctant to train her and tried to block her advancement. "Now, I know that's just their way," she says. "They don't mean to be mean." But she has changed her own style: "I handle them more firmly now; I've become stronger."

Yet despite all the blending of people on the factory floor, it stops in the lunchroom. From a corner table, three Indian women look over the rest of the big dining area. A table near the checkout is occupied almost entirely by African-American women. The table next to them, by Indian men. And so it goes around the room. "We share our food," says Jashwanti Bodhanwala, a mother of two who has been in the United States for 23 years, as if that entirely explains the apartheid-style dining.

One thing the lunch groups do is to facilitate gossip. The room is one of the few places, besides the outdoor smoking areas, where people relax and swap rumors.

Ms. Bodhanwala tugs off a piece of moist, spicy Indian flatbread, and spoons onto it a lump of homemade mango chutney from a plastic container. Asmabahen Patel, sitting opposite her, offers some mustard pickles. "Of course, if you weren't here," says Ms. Patel, gazing at a reporter, "we'd be speaking Gujarati."

V-3: Helping Asians Climb through Bamboo Ceiling

The familiar term "glass ceiling" connotes difficulties that women managers have breaking into senior executive ranks. An emerging term, "bamboo ceiling," applies to Asian and Asian-American employees and their troubles moving into U.S. management posts.

Though U.S. companies pursue Asians for technical jobs, they often shun them for managerial spots. Many corporate executives say Asians often are passive and self-effacing, lacking management skills and possessing cultural values that hurt their ability to succeed as bosses.

The University of Illinois at Chicago has begun a one-year program to give foreign-born engineering Ph.D.s a strong dose of American culture, especially in the ways of American managers. "Too often, Asians come to believe that if you know jokes or understand American slang or get pronunciations down pat, you can communicate," says assistant vice chancellor Judy Curry, who helps lead a seminar on intercultural communication. "But there's a need to identify the differences in values between Asian and Western cultures."

Among other things, students learn how to make small talk, ask for a raise, turn someone down gracefully—and shake hands: "up and down four times, dry, firm, eye contact and a smile," Dr. Curry says.

They also follow the Chicago Bears and the stock market, giving classmates weekly stock tips.

Next semester, professors in English, history, management, and political science will weave together other aspects of Asian and U.S. business cultures.

V-4: Glass Ceilings and Glass Slippers: Still Stereotyping after All These Years?

CYNTHIA F. COHEN

In *My Fair Lady,* Henry Higgins inquires "Why can't a woman be more like a man?" Similarly, research indicates that women who work in male-dominated professions must attempt to fit in the male culture to avoid being treated as outcasts.[1] Many women in business have attempted to do exactly this. They have dressed in acceptable versions of power suits and have behaved as their male counterparts do, carefully avoiding being overtly feminine. They do this, in part, because the defining behavioral characteristics of the majority typically affect the evaluations of behaviors of minority members of the organization.[2] Unfortunately, in organizations that are not diverse, members of minority populations tend to be stereotyped with negative characteristics and are typically viewed as less qualified than their majority group counterparts, solely as a function of class membership. Individual differences tend to be ignored in favor of preconceived notions that are rooted in beliefs about group characteristics. Simply stated, stereotypes can be a very powerful influence on one's career and certainly are one of the factors that have contributed to the glass ceiling that women have such difficulty shattering.[3]

Obtaining information about specific situations that demonstrate the deleterious effects of stereotypes on job advancement is difficult because organizations are not usually open about behaviors that are discriminatory. However, a landmark legal case provides insight into one situation where stereotypes played a significant role in a partnership decision.[4] Ann Hopkins was being considered for a partnership with Price Waterhouse when she received feedback from her review that suggested she was too "macho," she "overcompensated for being a woman," and that she should "take a course in charm school."[5] When the Policy Board explained the decision to place her candidacy on hold, Hopkins was advised to "walk more femininely, talk more femininely, wear make-up, have her hair styled, and wear jewelry."

This assessment of Ms. Hopkins was based on input from the partner review procedure. The process of selecting new partners occurs annually and the procedures are very elaborate. A senior manager is considered for partnership when the partners of his or her local office propose he or she be considered. Written proposals recommending the candidates are distributed to all the partners of the firm (when Hopkins was considered there were 622 partners). Each partner is asked to provide input on any candidate about whom they

Written especially for this volume by Cynthia F. Cohen.

have knowledge. All the candidates are then ranked on explicit criteria. There is an Admissions Committee that reviews each candidate. This committee prepares a summary of the evaluations and makes a recommendation to the Policy Board who then decides whether to place the candidate on hold or to place the candidate on the partnership ballot.

Although Hopkins was rated very highly in a number of categories, her interpersonal skills were considered to be a problem. The decision to place Hopkins's partnership decision on hold was based primarily on concerns about her interpersonal skills. Some of the input suggested that she was difficult to work with and did not get along well with her staff. However, some appraisals appeared to be gender-based and potentially stereotypical. In addition to the remarks noted earlier, some partners were concerned about Hopkins's use of profanity, although another partner believed that this issue arose only "because she is a lady using foul language." Hopkins was also described as having "a lot of talent" but lacking in "social grace." The District Court found that sexual stereotypes were "part of the regular fodder of partnership evaluations."

The reliance by Price Waterhouse, at least in part, on these stereotypes was found to be discriminatory under Title VII of the Civil Rights Act and Ms. Hopkins was awarded partnership status as a part of the remedy. Thus, the landmark Supreme Court decision, *Price Waterhouse v. Hopkins,* extended the definition of discrimination to include sexual stereotyping.[6] However, the presence of sexual stereotyping in the workplace is not, in and of itself, illegal. The Supreme Court explicitly stated that the stereotypes must be firmly linked to organizational decision making in order for them to be found discriminatory.

A later case with similar themes, *Ezold v. Wolf, Block, Schorr, and Solis-Cohen,* also involved a partnership decision and allega-

tions of gender bias based on stereotypes. The District Court found, among other things, that Ezold was "criticized for being 'very demanding' and was expected by some members of the Firm to be nonassertive and acquiescent to the predominantly male partnership. Her failure to accept this role was a factor that resulted in her not being promoted to partner. However, several male associates who had been evaluated negatively for *lacking* sufficient assertiveness in their demeanor *were* made partners" [emphasis from the original court decision].[7] The decision of the District Court was eventually overturned by the Court of Appeals based on the determination that the District Court analyzed the evidence improperly with respect to the determination of pretext and substituted its judgment for the judgment of the firm.[8] The decision of the Court of Appeals has been subject to criticism that it permits stereotyping and discrimination to exist under the pretext of subjective decision making.[9] More recent cases continue to explore the legal consequences of stereotypical expectations. For example, in *Greenbaum v. Svenska Handelsbanken NY* (SNY), the District Court found that "the word 'aggressive' was used by SNY officials to describe a form of excellence when describing male traders but was viewed as a ground for disqualification when considering a woman like Greenbaum. . . . SNY applied standards for promotion that were inappropriately stereotypical and gender-biased."[10]

Price Waterhouse v. Hopkins, Ezold v. Wolf, Block, Schorr, and Solis-Cohen, and *Greenbaum v. Svenska Handelsbanken NY* (SNY) illustrate the dilemma that women face: they often work in a male-oriented environment to which they are expected to adapt, but they are also held to different standards of behavior based on stereotypes about sex. Women are then left wondering whether charm school would have been more valuable than business school.

On the other hand, women who demonstrate more "feminine" characteristics at work may also find that they receive poor evaluations because they do not fit the male profile. A case in point is *Milligan-Jensen v. Michigan Technological University* in which a female public safety officer was subject to criticism because the male-oriented uniform she was required to wear was ill fitting and was told by her supervisors that she "had the lady's job" and wore "the woman's badge."[11] Wearing the glass slipper is no guarantee that one can shatter the glass ceiling. Obviously, this presents a no-win scenario for women who wish to advance. This paper examines the problem with and persistence of stereotypes in the workplace, reasons why the issue is not often raised by women, reasons why organizations should address this issue, and strategies for organizations that want to do so.

Preventing sex stereotypes from affecting the workplace is a very difficult task because sex stereotypes are so firmly entrenched in business and society. Many sex stereotypes are institutionalized to the point that many people, women included, fail to notice them. Interestingly, research indicates that even when women have experienced sex discrimination in their careers, they do not tend to see this as a sustained pattern for themselves or other women.[12] Acceptance of stereotypes appears to be common among women in leadership roles who are typified by the comment "As a woman, I found out I always had to work harder and longer. I've always had to confront situations in order to get what I need."[13] Breaking the glass ceiling becomes significantly more difficult if the women who do break it do not recognize the impact of patterns of gender stereotypes that might have delayed their own progress.

There are two basic forms of sex stereotypes: one which attributes certain characteristics to men and women; and one which dictates what behaviors and characteristics are appropriate for men and women. The first category includes the belief that women or men are unsuitable for certain jobs or job duties because of their sex. Patterns of job segregation by sex (such as thinking that only women can be nurses and only men can be police officers) reflect this stereotype. Although there continues to be debate about the origins of gender segregation at work, there is no doubt that it is a persistent characteristic of the workplace in the United States, Great Britain, and a great many other industrialized countries. Despite the fact that Title VII generally prohibits hiring on the basis of sex, gender segregation has continued to exist in the United States.

Another example of this category of stereotyping is the creation of "female ghetto" jobs in organizations. When women tend to occupy certain jobs, they often become devalued or imbued with "feminine" characteristics. One job that has recently come under stereotyping scrutiny, unusually enough, is that of managing partner in law firms. One legal recruiter was quoted as saying "I wonder how much the job of managing partner might become a girl ghetto in the worst-case scenario. It's like, you're the mother. Take care of that."[14] Although others dispute this point of view, a female managing partner indicated that she carefully considered this possibility when accepting the position by having "a very clear understanding that my major role would be in strategic and financial planning. . . . One does want to make sure firms are not stereotyping women into personnel issues and HR issues."[15]

In the same vein, women are often the focus of stereotypical expectations concerning their roles as primary child care providers. In *Fisher v. Vassar College* the District Court ruled that "there is also direct evidence that the Biology Department, perhaps still deeply rooted in the tradition of the hard sciences, was unable to overcome the stereotypical view of women as either scientist or wife— but not both." [16] In fact, the court noted that in the past 30 years, no married woman had been tenured in the hard sciences (which was defined as mathematics, physics, chemistry, geology, biology, and computer science). Despite a research record that exceeded those of men who applied for tenure, Fisher's scholarly accomplishments were discounted because she took time to raise a family. Despite her many scholarly accomplishments, the fact that she was married and had a family caused her male colleagues to "wonder about her commitment." The refusal to evaluate individual performance but, instead, to rely on a group's generalizations is the very definition of this type of stereotyping. This creates serious barriers to the success of women in male-dominated jobs and professions. This, in turn, keeps the percentage of women low and permits the second form of stereotyping to occur.

The second form of stereotyping segregates appropriate behavior by gender. For example, in the Price Waterhouse case, remarks from the partner review process described Hopkins as too "macho" and suggested that she be "more feminine." The partners' comments reflect the attitude that, because she is a woman, these behaviors are unacceptable. Similarly, in *Ezold* and *Greenbaum,* aggressive behavior is considered a negative quality for women, but a positive quality for men. Research indicates that women in nontraditional jobs tend to display traits and behaviors that are more similar to their male counterparts than they are to women in traditional occupations.[17] It is obvious that this becomes a lose/lose proposition for many women: they must somehow learn to operate in the framework of a male-dominated work place, but they may be punished for exhibiting the same characteristics for which men are rewarded.

Stereotypes can affect careers in even more subtle ways than the documented comments made in the cases previously cited. These may include who is invited to certain business lunches, who is assigned to certain high-visibility and high-reward tasks, and who is perceived as a fast tracker. A recent complaint to the EEOC by a woman principal at Morgan Stanley Dean Witter alleges that "the firm excluded women from golf outings, excursions to Las Vegas, and entertainment at strip clubs in New York and other cities."[18] When organizations sponsor trips to strip clubs, a particularly devastating gender stereotype is perpetuated. This objectification of women works in an insidious manner because the organization legitimates the use of and belief in stereotypes in the workplace. A sexualized atmosphere can be a contributing factor to the development of stereotypes, so it is not surprising that allegations of stereotyping frequently contain allegations of sexual harassment as well.[19]

Although the use of stereotypes in making employment decisions is illegal, making use of the provisions of Title VII is a daunting task for the person who has been discriminated against. It has often been suggested that some women do not exercise their rights under Title VII even in the face of persistent discrimination. There are several reasons why this occurs.

First, as previously mentioned, many women often believe that they must tolerate stereotypes to fit in. In these situations there is no real recognition, even by the victim, that the stereotypes represent a valid concern. Therefore, any inability to cope with stereotypes is viewed as the woman's problem rather than the organization's problem. Clark, Caffarella, and Ingram found that although all the women in leadership positions they interviewed indicated they had experienced discrimination and/or stereotyping during their careers, they "wrote off these experiences as something to be expected, 'the cost of doing business.'"[20]

Second, in situations where the use of stereotypes is recognized as problematic, a woman may fail to take action because she does not want to be labeled as a troublemaker. She may decide that taking action to correct the situation will be more harmful to her career than the continued presence of the stereotype itself. Ironically, taking up a cause of action that relates to sexual stereotyping often reinforces the dominant group's belief that women do not fit in to the exclusive upper levels of the organization. When women "buy in" to this concept, they also help to maintain the status quo and do little to make cracks in the glass ceiling for others to come through.

Finally, some women may be discouraged by the lack of sufficient remedies available from Title VII. For many years, Title VII provided only "make whole" remedies for individual victims of discrimination. These include job reinstatement, back pay, promotions, and so forth. However, there were no punitive damages or damages for emotional distress. Thus, victims of discrimination had no choice but to return to the discriminatory environment if they sought Title VII remedies. The Civil Rights Act of 1991 did make some changes in available remedies. Punitive and compensatory damages were added for intentional discrimination, but were limited based on the number of employees in the organization. For the largest organizations, the limitation on these added damages is $300,000. Because of the limitation of these remedies, causes of action concerning sex discrimination are also filed as torts or even under state worker's compensation laws where there are no such limitations.

In addition to make whole and other monetary outcomes, court orders may also result from Title VII claims. An example would be an order requiring the employer to cease a discriminatory practice. Unfortunately, when these practices involve the attitudes and actions of a number of people in the workplace, it is doubtful that this remedy alone will prove effective. Even a well-intentioned employer may have difficulty enforcing rules and procedures adopted to comply with the court order. Given the nature of these remedies, a victim of sexual stereotyping may feel there is very little to be gained through filing a complaint.

Even though Title VII remedies do not prove adequate for many potential complainants, this does not mean that employers should ignore problems of sexual stereotypes in the workplace, hoping that a complaint will never be filed. There are a number of reasons why employers should address this problem before a formal complaint is filed with the EEOC or local state human rights agency.

If for no other reason, the prospect of litigation should be a deterrent. The employer's attorney's fees usually eclipse the cost of the legal remedy. In addition, if the employee prevails, the employer is usually required to pay the employee's attorney's fees, too. There is also the company image to be considered. An organization that is a defendant in a well-publicized discrimination case runs the risk that public reaction will be adverse, possibly affecting sales and the ability to attract good employees in the future. Even if the case is eventually settled out of court, there can still be attendant adverse publicity.

Moreover, organizations that fail to mitigate the effects of discriminatory stereotypes find themselves in a very weak position when personnel decisions are eventually challenged. In the Price Waterhouse case, the District Court Judge determined that "Price Waterhouse intentionally maintained a partnership evaluation system that permitted negative, sexually stereotyped comments to influence partnership selection."[21] It is obvious that employers who fail to deal with this problem perpetuate the use of sex stereotypes at work and place the organization in the position of intentionally permitting the personnel systems to operate in a discriminatory manner.

Of even greater concern is the effect on employees who must work in an environment that operates on the basis of stereotypes. These employees will not be used to their fullest advantage because stereotypes often limit the opportunity to perform certain tasks or certain jobs. Both the individual and the organization will suffer as a result of this underutilization. As the characteristics of the workforce continue to reflect a greater percentage of women and minorities, this underutilization will grow and problems of morale will occur as more and more employees are alienated from the mainstream culture of the organization.

What strategies can employers use to address the problems of workplace stereotypes? There are several immediate areas that managers can address relatively easily: (1) educate employees about sex stereotypes, (2) reinforce the educational effort through leading by example, (3) use objective performance evaluation criteria, (4) take appropriate action when stereotypes persist, and (5) continue to work to diversify the organization.

The Supreme Court noted that Price Waterhouse failed to "make partners sensitive to the dangers [of stereotyping] to discourage comments tainted by sexism."[22] This implies that educational efforts on the part of Price Waterhouse would have been looked upon favorably by the Court and reinforces the importance of having a systematic effort to educate employees about stereotypes. Education can provide employees with a greater awareness of the existence of and problems with using stereotypes. Although this is an important element in changing stereotypes, it is not always successful.[23] It is, therefore, unrealistic to believe, especially where there are no broader based efforts to change the organi-

zation culture, that stereotypes can be eliminated easily in this manner.

In addition to educational efforts, it will also be necessary for managers to lead by example. The overriding factor in the Price Waterhouse case appeared to be the failure of senior managers to recognize and deal with the existence of stereotypes in the review process. Similarly, in other legal cases, the actions of managers hold particular weight in establishing proof of illegal use of stereotypes. Therefore, managers need to have even more extensive training in identifying and preventing the use of stereotypes than do other employees.

Another problem that can be addressed involves performance evaluation criteria. The more subjective the criteria, the more likely stereotypes will influence the evaluation. Therefore, organizations should work to make performance standards as objective as possible. Ridding the organization of the effect of stereotypes requires evaluating individual efforts without regard to group characteristics. Care should be taken, particularly when promotion or evaluation processes seek input from a large number of organization members, that those individuals are provided with specific, objective criteria on which to base the evaluation. Open-end comments about perceptions of performance invite the types of stereotypical remarks found in the evaluation processes at Price Waterhouse and Svenska Handelsbanken. When these stereotypes enter any formal personnel process, managers should make it clear that they are inappropriate and that they should not influence the employment decision. This will not only help to preserve the legal status of the decision-making process, it will also reinforce the educational effort. If managers continue to reject the use of stereotypes, awareness should further increase and the commitment of management to removing this from personnel decisions is evidenced.

Managers also need to deal effectively with recalcitrant managers or employees. In the original Price Waterhouse trial, Judge Gessel found that over the years "[o]ne partner repeatedly commented that he could not consider any woman seriously as a partnership candidate and believed that women were not even capable of functioning as senior managers—yet the firm took no action to discourage his comments and recorded his vote in the overall summary of the evaluations."[24] Individuals who repeatedly offer inappropriate evaluations or continue to make stereotypical comments to co-workers should be singled out for special educational efforts. If no change occurs, the organization should not solicit their comments for formal review processes. It may even be necessary to initiate disciplinary action in egregious situations.

These strategies provide only a narrow solution to symptoms of a much broader problem rooted in the organization's culture and societal expectations. Addressing the larger problem of changing the organization culture is necessary for at least two reasons. First, the narrower approach primarily emphasizes removing stereotypes from formal personnel processes. In the absence of a broader emphasis, stereotypes may continue to exist informally beneath the surface of the evaluation process. They may be unarticulated, but they will continue to contaminate the work environment. Second, if stereotypical comments are or have been made during formal personnel procedures, there is a very strong likelihood that problems of discriminatory attitudes such as stereotypes exist in other day-to-day activities.

There are several actions that can be taken. One is the introduction of cultural diversity classes into the training and education programs offered by the organization. This goes beyond the stereotype awareness training suggested earlier. This broader effort can have many forms including inten-

sive three-day diversity seminars, video training series, and even a full-time position devoted to the diversity issue. Indeed, "corporate pluralism" is an important goal of several organizations including Digital Equipment, Inc., Ortho Pharmaceutical, and Pillsbury.[25]

Perhaps more important is diversifying organizational membership. Stereotypes exist, in part, because there are few women or minorities in organizations, particularly in leadership roles. The very scarcity of individuals from these groups permits the existence of a dominant group culture and perpetuates the expectation that "normally" these jobs are not occupied by women or other minorities. As organizations change racial and sexual composition, the ability to evaluate individuals on their performance, rather than the presumed characteristics of their group, increases.

In addition to this broad-based approach to changing the organization, managers may also want to consider informal means by which employees could express their concerns about problems they have encountered with stereotyping in the organization. For example, employees might be asked to participate in an informal group discussion about barriers they have experienced in the organization. An informal meeting to encourage this type of discussion can be an eye-opening experience for a manager. Typically, an informal meeting is less intimidating than a formal complaint system and can expose problems about which the manager was previously unaware. Also, as opposed to hearing a single formal complaint, an informal group setting can include many voices that have had some of the same experiences. This lends weight and more credibility to the problems raised. Obviously, if the meeting reveals a problem with stereotyping in the organization, the organization must take appropriate action. This would include many of the actions previously discussed.

If significant problems with stereotyping appear to exist (or even other discriminatory actions based on sex) the organization can set up more formal complaint mechanisms. There are a variety of ways to do this including ombudspersons, investigators, and official complaint systems. Each of these methods has its strengths and weaknesses that the manager will want to evaluate.

For example, in organizations that have little history or experience with complaint mechanisms, the ombudsperson approach may be preferable. Employees who are otherwise reluctant to bring up these issues may find that an ombudsperson system is easier to use than procedures that require them to speak to their manager first or to fill out a written complaint as the first step. Because no specific action can be taken without her permission, the employee can discuss the problem with the ombudsperson before deciding whether to pursue the complaint. Even if the employee decides not to pursue the matter, it gives the organization information about the existence of problems. At the very least, more effort can be put into dealing with the general problem company wide. If the employee decides to pursue her complaint, the organization is given an opportunity to resolve the problem before it enters the legal system.

Although workplace stereotypes are very difficult to address, organizations that attempt to address this problem from both approaches will benefit in many ways. As employee awareness increases, stereotyping will be less likely to enter personnel decision making. When stereotyping does occur, correct action by managers will reinforce the employer's commitment to removing bias from these decisions. Obviously, the personnel procedures will be greatly improved because they will focus on relevant job behaviors instead of illegal and irrelevant stereotypes. This will not only reduce legal exposure but will also provide greater procedural and substantive justice for employees. Personnel procedures will do what they are supposed to do: provide for the fullest utilization of the skills and abilities of employees.

Most importantly, encouraging pluralism in the organization will provide a work environment that is not only more productive but offers greater respect for individual differences. This will be especially critical in the future because the workforce will have a greater percentage of women and minorities than ever before. At the same time, it does not appear that stereotypes are likely to fade anytime soon. One has only to examine the contents of popular culture, including music videos and video games to see that stereotypes continue to exist and gain reinforcement. Women continue to be portrayed as either sexual objects[26] or as those in need of rescue.[27] It seems likely, therefore, that organizations that are able to overcome problems with stereotyping will be more successful than those that do not. In the best of all possible worlds, a rich cultural diversity in organizations will mean an end to stereotyping and a beginning for pluralism so that glass ceilings and glass slippers no longer need apply.

Endnotes

1. Bradley, H. (1989). *Men's Work, Women's Work,* Minneapolis: University of Minnesota Press, p. 70.
2. Reskin, B.F., McBrier, D.B., Kmec, J.A. (1999). "The Determinants and Consequences of Workplace Sex and Race Composition," *Annual Review of Sociology,* 25:335–61.
3. Meyerson, D.E. and Fletcher, J.K. (2000). "A Modest Manifesto for Shattering the Glass Ceiling," *Harvard Business Review,* January/February: 127–137. (Included in this book.)
4. *Price Waterhouse v. Hopkins,* 109 S.Ct. 1775, 49 FEP Cases 954 (US SupCt-1989).
5. *Hopkins v. Price Waterhouse,* 578 F. Supp 1109, 38 FEP Cases 1630, (DC DC-1985).

6. Cohen, C.F. (1989). "*Price Waterhouse v. Hopkins:* Mixed Motive Discrimination Cases, the Shifting Burden of Proof, and Sexual Stereotyping," *Labor Law Journal,* 40:723–728.

7. *Ezold v. Wolf, Block, Schorr and Solis-Cohen,* 751 F. Supp 1175, 54 FEP Cases 808, 1990.

8. *Ezold v. Wolf, Block, Schorr and Solis-Cohen,* 983 F.2d 509, 60 FEP Cases 849, 1992.

9. Kuhles, B. (1993). "Ezold Reversed: Glass Ceiling Reinforced?" *New Jersey Lawyer,* January: 1.

10. *Greenbaum v. Svenska Handelsbanken NY (SNY),* 67 F. Supp 2d 228, 1999.

11. *Milligan-Jensen v. Michigan Technological University,* 767 F. Supp 1403, 59 FEP Cases 1014, 1991.

12. Clark, C.M., Caffarella, R.S., and Ingram, P.B. (1999). "Women in Leadership: Living with the Constraints of the Glass Ceiling," *Initiatives,* 59:65–76.

13. Ibid.

14. Flaherty, K. and Ward, J. (1998). "The Other Side of the Glass Ceiling," *The Connecticut Law Tribune,* June 1, 1998.

15. Ibid.

16. *Fisher v. Vassar College,* 852 F. Supp 1193, 64 FEP Cases 1346, 1994.

17. Terborg, J.R. (1977). "Women in Management: A Research Review," *Journal of Applied Psychology,* 62:647–64.

18. Wise, D. (2000). "EEOC Finds Gender Bias at Morgan Stanley," *The Legal Intelligencer,* June: 4.

19. *Jenson v. Eveleth Taconite Company,* 824 F. Supp 847, 61 FEP Cases 1252, 1993.

20. Clark, Caffarella, and Ingram at [11].

21. *Hopkins v. Price Waterhouse,* 578 F. Supp 1109, 38 FEP Cases 1630, (DC DC-1985).

22. *Price Waterhouse v. Hopkins,* 109 S.Ct. 1775, 49 FEP Cases 954 (US SupCt-1989).

23. Dunnette, M.D. and Motowidlo, S.J. (1982). "Estimating the Benefits and Costs of Anti-sexist Training Programs in Organizations," in *Women in the Work Force,* ed. H.J. Benardin, New York: Praeger, 156–82.

24. *Hopkins v. Price Waterhouse,* 578 F. Supp 1109, 38 FEP Cases 1630, (DC DC-1985).

25. *Newsweek,* "Past Tokenism," May 14, 1990:37–43.

26. Seidman, S. A. (1999) "Revisiting Sex-role Stereotyping in MTV Videos," *International Journal of Instructional Media,* 26:11–22.

27. Sherman, S.R. (1997). "Perils of the Princess: Gender and Genre in Video Games," *Western Folklore,* 56:243–58.

V-5: It's Her Job Too
Shot Heard 'Round the Water Cooler

BETSY MORRIS

Once upon a time, a good corporate wife was to be seen and not heard. She was to make sure nothing, but nothing, came between her man and his work. She was to shield him from the tedious and distracting details of domestic life. She was to raise beautiful, well-mannered children and maintain a beautiful, well-appointed home, making it look effortless. She was to work the charity circuit—to be the belle of the

charity ball and also its unpaid CEO. She was to smile through scores of business dinners. And she was never, ever, to make a stink. Even in the worst of times, even when things unraveled, she was expected to know her place and, if need be, to slip quietly off-stage. Lorna Wendt did all of these things except the last. When her 32-year marriage to GE Capital CEO Gary Wendt came apart two years ago, she raised a big ruckus. She wanted half of the $100 million she estimated he was worth. She wanted to tap

Reprinted from *Fortune* (February 2, 1998): 65–78.

what she considered her rightful share of the treasure-trove of unvested GE stock options and pension benefits accumulated during the marriage but not due until later in his career. She wanted respect. She wanted acknowledgment, just once and writ large, that society valued all those things she'd done on the home front. As with executive pay, the amount one needs to live on wasn't the issue. The money was merely a way of keeping score.

And Lorna Wendt did score when Connecticut Superior Court Judge Kevin Tierney handed down part of his ruling last month. She came away with $20 million—far less than the $50 million she'd sought, but far more than the $8 million plus alimony that Wendt had originally offered. She got half the hard assets—breaking the glass ceiling that often exists in upper-crust divorces, where wives are more likely to get what the judge thinks they need according to a practice known in the divorce bar as "enough is enough." And while Judge Tierney didn't give her any of her husband's stock options outright, he did rule that those granted during the marriage were marital property and that she should be compensated for some of their value.

The Wendt case has launched a thousand cocktail-party conversations and struck fear in the hearts of primary breadwinners everywhere. A lot of men are still incredulous of her demands. In a big-bucks case like hers, "the question becomes, Is the person who is making the money—is that person's contribution greater than the person who stays at home and runs the house?" says Robert Stephan Cohen, a New York divorce lawyer. "I'll tell you, having represented a number of high-net-worth individuals—they don't think so. They think the contribution of the at-home spouse is important, but not equal." Yet Lorna Wendt has elicited cheers from lots of career women and stay-at-home women alike. No matter that immense portions and impor-

tant nuances of the judge's ruling still aren't known. (We still don't know, for instance, how close she came to the 50% mark or where Judge Tierney came out exactly on the value of a corporate wife.) He released just a 28-page summary of what is expected to be a 450-plus page decision. No matter the unlikelihood of this very proper, soft-spoken, 54-year-old woman straight out of another era becoming a feminist symbol. Her case has struck a chord.

It isn't hard to see why. Sure, Lorna Wendt is rich, privileged, hardly Everywoman. (She told the court that she needed a $10,000-a-month clothing budget.) But as the woman behind the success story, she has come to stand for the many things that wives still mostly end up doing and that society seems mostly to take for granted: child rearing, tending a family's emotional and spiritual needs, and the unglamorous stuff like car pools, doctor's appointments, sympathy notes. Lorna Wendt has become a lightning rod for the tensions that swirl around what has traditionally been called women's work. In a poll conducted by Yankelovich Partners for *Fortune*, far more women (57%) than men (41%) say this kind of support is extremely important to a man's career. Far more women (51%) than men (28%) feel that the duties of a corporate wife—travel, entertaining, and charity work in addition to child rearing and housework—are extremely important to a husband's success.

The Wendt case also highlights the struggle this country's courts have had over the past three decades in determining how to divide fairly the goods in this age of divorce and women's rights. Just 14 years ago, the *Guide to American Law,* a legal encyclopedia, defined the legal concept of marriage this way: "A husband has the obligation to support a wife and a wife has the duty to serve." The notion that in divorce the husband would wind up with most of the property and the wife with alimony support influenced divorce settlements for a long time. The advent of no-fault divorce laws around 1970 and the large-scale entry of women into the labor force caused courts in many states to divide assets more equitably.

But what's equitable? In community property states—there are nine of them—courts consider all income and property that accumulate during a marriage to be owned equally. In only a handful of those (notably California) does that mean a mandatory fifty-fifty split. The rest of the states are equitable distribution states, in which courts attempt to divide property fairly, taking into consideration such factors as length of marriage, the contributions of both spouses, ages and health, and, of course, prenups.

Increasingly, women have been asserting that it isn't just the spouse who brings home a paycheck who provides economic value. "We can't put a price tag on things like children. We don't say they're worth $7 billion, nor should we," says Martha Fineman, a Columbia University law professor who testified on behalf of Lorna Wendt. "The problem with domestic labor is that it is consumed. You don't have anything left over except the children. You don't have it left to divide."

Increasingly, divorce lawyers say, courts have been responding to the notion of marriage as a partnership. In lower-asset divorces, judges already are often steering cases toward more of a fifty-fifty split. It is in the high-asset cases—where the primary breadwinner often argues that his success has resulted from a special gift or talent—that big gaps still exist. But even here, the stay-at-home spouses are getting a lot more assertive. "They're beginning to say. 'Hey, I'm a full partner.' I think as housewives, they didn't ever look at it that way before," says Eleanor Alter, a New York divorce lawyer.

What impact Lorna Wendt's case will have on all this is difficult to say until the judge renders his full opinion. Attorneys for both sides have received copies of the judge's rough draft but won't share it because it is exactly that: rough. Pages are missing and out of order; some are hand-written. Still, Lorna Wendt's lawyers are willing to discuss several of the draft's highlights. While she has scored big in some areas, she seems to have suffered setbacks on some of her major arguments. "Judge Tierney didn't put a dollar value on her contributions but seems to have found that Lorna Wendt's contributions, while substantial, weren't as great as Gary Wendt's," says Sarah Oldham, one of Lorna Wendt's attorneys. "He found that her contributions don't justify what she's asking for." Judge Tierney's draft, she says, also finds that marriage is not a commercial partnership and that it would be up to the Connecticut legislature to create a presumption of a fifty-fifty asset split in a divorce. Even so, Oldham says, "she's gotten the door open" in winning half of Wendt's hard assets and in persuading the judge that perks like stock options are marital property.

Divorce laws vary by state, and the Wendt case won't set binding legal precedents. But the judge's full ruling is being breathlessly awaited by lawyers all over the country, and it is bound to have some influence on the tactics of divorce lawyers and the thinking of judges. Already, Lorna Wendt has removed some of the stigma associated with putting up a big public fight.

At first glance this might seem like a commotion over an anachronism. After all, in 84% of the marriages in this country both spouses now have jobs. Yet the topmost rungs of corporate and professional America still are heavily populated by "traditional" couples. And while it has become very un-PC for a company to have any overt expectations of its employees' spouses, the truth is that at many places it's still very difficult for a man to get into the executive suite without a corporate wife.

That's why Lorna Wendt has been so adamant. "I complemented him by keeping the home fires burning and by raising a family and by being the CEO of the Wendt corporation and by running the household and grounds and social and emotional ties so he could go out and work very hard at what he was good at," she says. "If marriage isn't a partnership between equals, then why get married? If you knew that some husband or judge down the road was going to say, 'You're a 30% part of this marriage, and he's a 70% part,' would you get married?"

With such arguments, she has stirred the pot in a lot of other divorce cases. Just since her case went to trial a year ago, two of her star witnesses, Columbia's Fineman and Stanford University economist Myra Strober, have served as consultants in divorce cases across the country. So far, one or the other or both have taken part in the cases of cellular-telephone pioneer Craig McCaw and his ex-wife, Wendy, in Washington; Charles Morgan Jr., CEO of information services provider Acxiom Corp., and his ex-wife, Jane, in Arkansas; Jamie Coulter, CEO of the Lone Star Steakhouse chain, and his ex-wife, Gayla, in Kansas; and more.

For divorce lawyers it's merely a gold mine, but for a growing number of women it's a full-fledged movement—a nonfiction version of the *First Wives Club*. Lorna Wendt has encouraged others to speak up. "The divorce system is really discriminatory against women in big-money cases, still very patriarchal," says Melita Easters Hayes, who went through a high-profile divorce from Atlanta computer executive Dennis Hayes but has kept mostly silent about it until now, at least in public. She spends a lot of time counseling other similarly situated women through their divorces. Lorna Wendt has begun the Foundation for Equality in Marriage, which she hopes will carry on her cause through a speaker's bureau and other educational programs. By the time its board held its first meeting last

month, she had already received nearly 1,000 E-mails.

Nobody is more stunned by all this than Gary Wendt. "I was really unprepared," he says. "I had no idea of the venom that was going to be spewed at me. I mean, we really thought this thing was going to be settled on the courthouse steps." His side of the story is very different from hers. He has always maintained that he was worth a lot less than she claimed—approximately $21 million at the end of 1995, when the case began, and roughly double that now. (The big difference in their valuations: taxes—he has deducted them—plus unvested stock options, restricted stock, and other deferred benefits that he says have no current value because he needs to continue working to get them.) He says he did offer her half. "Factually the story was 'Man Has $20 Million, Offers Wife $10 Million,'" he says. But he believes his wife and her lawyers turned the case into a feminist political football. "By manufacturing phony numbers, they created the issue," he says.

For Lorna Wendt, it has been a rather breathtaking metamorphosis from 1960s housewife to star of the TV newsmagazines. She is a gracious woman, warm and ever so polite. Whatever she might be feeling, she expresses no rage or bitterness. Some anger, yes, and tears. But when she talks about Wendt, she is diplomatic, protective even still.

She and Wendt grew up in small towns in Wisconsin (they met in high school in Rio, Wisconsin) in much humbler circumstances and simpler times. Her father was a Lutheran minister, but the person in the family she really looked up to was her mother, a cheerful, giving person who did all her own baking and canning and raised six children. Her mother set an example, she says: "Don't think of yourself first. Husband, family first." And Lorna tried to live up to the example. "I wanted to be the best wife. I drove myself to live up to these things that I had seen my mother and other women do. I would support Gary and follow him. In those days women just did not say, 'I don't want to move, Dear.'"

She went with him to Cambridge, Massachusetts, where he attended Harvard Business School. She worked to help support them and typed his papers at night. Then they moved to Spring, Texas, outside Houston, where he worked for a developer; then to Atlanta; then to Coral Gables, Florida; and finally to Stamford, Connecticut, where they settled in 1975 when he joined GE Capital. She took her duties seriously, smoothing the way for each move, building new community and church ties each time, caring for their two young daughters. And it is important to her that even though she became wealthy and privileged, she never forgot her roots. She still does the ironing and shovels snow. She has always sung in the church choir. Until 12 years ago, she taught piano to schoolchildren.

Her introduction to the role of corporate wife came in Texas, where Wendt's boss and his wife were luminaries on the Houston social scene and included the Wendts in some of their big black-tie parties. "We began to get a glimpse of what maybe could be," Lorna Wendt says.

Her education continued in earnest after the move to Stamford and GE Capital. "When we came in to meet the CEO's wife, I mean, wow. She was somebody up there on that pedestal." The woman in question—Valerie Stanger, wife of GE Capital's John Stanger—was studied and emulated by the other wives. They would watch how she dressed, how she acted, how she entertained. "You'd watch to see how she treated others and how she always had a kind word and was very interested in people," Lorna Wendt recalls.

Lorna Wendt was a quick study. "I have books at home telling me exactly what you should do as a corporate wife," she laughs. "First of all, you were a good wife. You're not going to make demands on your hus-

band that will take his time away from his business. You're going to be a good mother, and by that I mean keep your children in control. We don't want any scandal going on with the children."

She considered herself the CEO of the Wendt family. She never dreamed of asking her husband to call a plumber or of calling him home to tend a sick child, even though one of their daughters was hospitalized frequently as a baby. That was her job—running everything smoothly "so he wouldn't have any worries when he came home at night."

In her more public role, she learned she had to look and dress the part: tasteful, never too flamboyant, but not too conservative either. And it mattered, she says. If you didn't fit the bill, you stood out, and other wives—and husbands—would notice. She would overhear conversations on the private jet: "'Gee, did you see her dress?' Or, 'She didn't talk very well.'" Lorna Wendt recalls. It could be the kiss of death.

She was expected to entertain—sometimes extravagantly, sometimes informally, at the drop of a hat. (Just how much entertaining she did is a bone of contention.) She had Wendt's colleagues over for a New Year's Day lobster dinner little more than a week after the birth of their first child in 1968. In the early years she'd often throw together a dinner party on scant hours' notice. "I would do it and I wouldn't rebel. Because I was supporting Gary, and I don't think that's wrong." She carried through with her last big black-tie Christmas party at their house on Erskine Road in December 1995, despite having learned about a week before that Wendt wanted a divorce. Much of her life was a command performance. "You were always to have a smile on. You always acted as if you wanted to be there, liked everyone you came in contact with. . . . Acting as if, I spent my whole life acting as if."

As GE Capital spread across the globe in the past 10 years, the couple spent more time on business trips. By the end, Lorna Wendt says, she was traveling five or six months out of the year. In the summer of 1995 they visited Italy, France, and London on a business trip, then flew to Bermuda in July, then headed to Eastern Europe for "a three-week summer vacation"—a van ride through eastern Germany, Austria, Poland, and Hungary with another GE couple. She says, "Gary wanted to get a feel for the countryside and culture" because GE was going to be expanding into those markets.

Each year, GE Capital would reward its top producers by sending them on lavish trips to places like Bali, Singapore, China, Egypt, Greece. She would accompany Wendt for two or three weeks at a time. They were dream trips, and for the most part she greatly enjoyed them. But it wasn't all a piece of cake. Each week the GE Capital award winners would change, but the activities would not. Each week, for the most part, she would attend the same tours, see the same sights, hand out awards to the wives during the culminating black-tie dinner—each time acting as if it were as special as her first. "I would pride myself. Even if Gary didn't want to go on that bus trip again—you know, Napoleon's tomb for the seventh time—I did. I took my job seriously because I remembered when I looked up to the CEO's wife."

She had come to understand along the way the importance of the game. GE demanded a lot from its employees. So it "was very good at dangling carrots in front of wives' noses," she says. "I remember when we first got to GE, it was: Wow, I may get a chance to go to Europe in the fall. Okay, all right, you can work hard. You can stay at the office longer."

Throughout business history, of course, wives have been an important part of the equation, and companies have known it. "Wives are significant and very important—however they are disposed," says one consultant who has advised many CEOs on personal matters over the years. They can hurt an executive by being "uppity," by doing too much shopping and social climbing, he says. "Or they can put a different spin, a more humane spin, on their husbands so the business associate or client says to himself, 'If this gal is so great, there must be more to this guy than meets the eye.'" Adds Gerard R. Roche, chairman of the executive search firm Heidrick & Struggles: "Just to be able to come home like a warship back into the harbor and find solace, encouragement, and support, and have no big guns shooting at you—it can be an enormous advantage." The best executives are those who lead fully integrated lives, he says, "where you can't tell the difference between their working life, their social life, their relaxing life. There is a thread that goes through it all: their affairs of state are constantly in mind."

That, obviously, requires a supportive wife, and Linda Schlenker has been one twice over. Her first husband was the chief financial officer of a Florida HMO, and during that three-year marriage, 15 to 20 evenings a month were business functions—ball games, symphony concerts, dinners on the road with prospective joint venture partners. "He would have me go along for the light conversation and to take some of the business off the evening," she says. Afterward he would often consult her about whether the attendees would make good business partners. "Everything I did revolved around the success of my husband's business," she says.

Now, in her second marriage, she plays the same role for her current husband, Ron Schlenker, who owns a manufacturer's rep firm in Minneapolis. They've been married 2½ years and "We hardly ever eat a meal in our home," she says. "I consider myself a key element in this corporation. I am very much an equal partner. He says since we've been entertaining as a team, his business has grown appreciably."

Not everybody is still so keen on the role. Another twice-married corporate wife says she, too, was very supportive of her first husband, a high-profile New York attorney. It was she who gave him the encouragement to move to the big time when he was being wooed by a large New York law firm earlier in their marriage. "He kept suggesting Denver and other places that would be better lifestyle choices," she recalls. But she would tell him: "You're too good to waste yourself in a smaller city."

He did accept the job and became a big success. She raised the children and picked up the pieces during his frequent and unpredictable business trips. "When he was the Cub Scout master, I did most of the projects. He volunteered to collect for the American Heart Association—I was the one out in the snow collecting," she says. After 30 years of marriage, her husband left her for a younger woman. She eventually remarried a successful businessman, but now she has her own life. "I pick and choose what I do."

Looking back, she doesn't feel that she had much choice in the arrangement. "I was a product of the 1950s. I graduated in 1955, and in those days, you were practically a failure if you weren't married a week after graduating from college," she says. "Had I lived in the 1990s, I would certainly be out working. I would have a nanny and a career. I love to juggle. I would have liked to have been in this generation. I know exactly what I would have done. I would've gone into television, anchored the six o'clock news."

Surely, with so many women in the workforce, the corporate wife's job description must be changing? To some extent it is. Modern-day corporate wives aren't so ceremonial. They aren't expected to drop everything and hop to. A few have their own careers. They most certainly are freer to gripe about their husbands' work loads. But if anything, the job has gotten even tougher. It often requires more travel. It often

requires that wives be more knowledgeable about current events and the business. There has been a boom in so-called work vacations given as awards to top producers. And corporate wives are still expected to pick up all the pieces at home.

Indeed, it seems the more things change, the more they stay the same. Numerous studies indicate that men in traditional marriages tend to earn more and get promoted more than those in dual-career marriages. "Consistently, again and again, those who do best in corporate organizations still very much come from the traditional family," says Linda K. Stroh, associate professor of organizational behavior at Chicago's Loyola University. "The higher up you go, the likelier it is that you will have a traditional marriage." There is, of course, the chicken-and-egg question: How many wives of successful executives stop working simply because they can afford to? Some researchers are finding that that doesn't happen as often as you might think. Myra Strober, one of the professors who testified in the Wendt case, recently completed a study of Stanford University's graduating class of 1981. She found that as husbands climbed the corporate ladder, wives' careers often fell by the wayside. After relocations, children, "you know the rest of the story. What's the chance she can come back to her career track in a way that's satisfying?" She calls these wives—two-thirds of the stay-at-homes in her study—Reluctant Homemakers. "People say, 'Isn't the Lorna Wendt problem a problem of the past? Women in their 30s and 40s aren't going to play that role.' Perhaps fewer of them will, but it goes with the way jobs are designed. In many corporations today, it takes such single-minded devotion to get to the top."

That's certainly true in the case of Ron Howard and his wife, Nicki, who might be considered a 1990s version of the corporate wife. She has the usual roster of awards dinners and business functions to attend for

Ron, a technology entrepreneur who founded a software company in 1977 and then saw it through a merger, a spinoff, and a combination last month with Atlanta-based Hayes Microcomputer. (He is now the CEO of the new company, Hayes Corp.) Nicki entertains business associates in their home, but only about twice a quarter. "It would be unfair to make her take an ongoing role in the maintenance of business relationships," he says. "She has tremendous burdens already."

He tries hard to spend as much time as possible with his two children, ages 6 and 8, curtailing his trips as much as possible. He even managed to coach Little League last spring. But often he's at his computer until midnight or 1 A.M. He worked Christmas day. "It is not even so much the time work takes," he says, "as the monopoly of brainpower, even when I'm home." Nicki takes care of the home, the finances, the children, the personal relationships. "I could never do what I do without her," he says. "If it were not for her, I would have a very, very emotionally deficient life."

It's not just the business world that is still depending on corporate wives. "The people who are running large charities are the corporate wives," says Carol Lee Daniel, who is in the midst of a divorce from her husband, Richard Daniel, the retired vice chairman of Mellon Bank in Pittsburgh. Most high-level Mellon wives of her generation did a lot of charity work, she says. Their organizations could "pretty much count on getting some underwriting from the bank," she says. And conversely, "It reflects well on the bank, and the bank is very proud of it." She served as president of the Twentieth Century Club, a prestigious women's club in Pittsburgh. She helped create and then co-chaired the Donald C. Winson Award dinner, a black-tie fundraiser for the American Cancer Society. She has also chaired the society's Snowflake Luncheon. "I've worked on the ballet ball, the sym-

phony ball, the Family House Polo Match," she says. "Can you believe it, I have actually taken classes in napkin folding?"

After years of fulfilling the unsung duties of a corporate wife, a woman develops a sense of partnership—a sense of entitlement, a sense of ownership. When Melita Easters began dating Dennis Hayes, Hayes Microcomputer Products was still just a small modern company; he had just moved it out of his house. She was a journalist and wrote press releases and speeches for him. After they were married, and as the company grew, she continued her involvement. She still wrote speeches, and organized bigger events like dinners at Atlanta's High Museum of Art.

"Dennis would call me and say, 'I'm bringing some guys over, can you do supper?'" she recalls. She took cooking lessons, bought a big double freezer, and stocked it with steaks. "I always knew it was his company, but I felt very involved in the blood, sweat, and tears equity of it. In our case, it was a decision that I would not work but be increasingly supportive of his career. It is often an economic decision of the couple that the wife do all those things women do."

That's not the way her ex-husband, Dennis, sees it at all. The things she did for the business, he says, could have been done by others. "It would have been a lot cheaper to hire somebody," he muses. He's not shedding any tears for his ex-wife. She had help in maintaining the house and help in caring for the children, which freed her to do a lot of other things. And he says, though they had no prenuptial agreement, the terms of their marriage were always clear to him. "In our marriage, our household was what we had in common," he says. Other than that, "your business interests are yours, and mine are mine."

Easy as it is for wives to come to believe that what's mine is yours and vice versa, it just isn't so legally, says Robert Epstein, one of the attorneys who represented Gary Wendt. "When people get married, it is romantic to say they become one," he says. "But there is no such thing as a partnership created by marriage." Legally, he says, you can kiss that notion goodbye. Kiss goodbye, too, the notion that Lorna Wendt is entitled to 50%, Epstein adds. "While we don't deny she made significant contributions, Mr. Wendt also made a contribution as a father and as a husband and providing her with a wonderful home and a lifestyle that is certainly very special," he says. "We do deny that she was significantly responsible for Mr. Wendt's success. Sure, Mrs. Wendt did what every wife does: She did some dinner parties and traveled with her husband."

It is that kind of logic and language that seems to be inspiring any number of women to fight back. After seven years of marriage and two children, Melita Hayes fought a scrappy enough battle during her 1988 divorce. At that time, she ended up with, among other things, a hefty temporary alimony and 10% of the Hayes company. But she became an even bigger force two years ago as Hayes was emerging from Chapter XI bankruptcy protection. She joined a competing group that was trying to acquire Hayes at the time. That effort failed, but in the meantime the company bought her stake for $11 million, way more than its initial offer, she says. "I don't think Dennis had any idea I would end up playing that kind of role in the bankruptcy," she says. She has now made it "something of a mission" to counsel other women through divorces. "You see women settle for far less than they should" because the process is so gruesome, she says. Ladies to the end, many of the wives aren't ready for the bare-knuckle brawl that occurs in divorce. "You see women living in million-dollar houses but who are stuck buying groceries on chump change," she says.

Carol Lee Daniel, the Mellon Bank wife, can say very little about her divorce case, which is scheduled for trial next month. But it has been very painful. Her husband, who is 70 years old and retired, is claiming that she was not a good corporate wife, she says. But when she asked some of the other wives to testify on her behalf, she says, one wife told her: "Hell, yes. At every one of those dinners you were sitting across the table, smiling just as hard as I was."

Even Linda Schlenker, who remains an enthusiastic corporate wife in a happy second marriage, has her guard up this time. Her first husband didn't give her much credit for the role she had played. Nor did he give her much in a divorce settlement. She ended up in debt and with a job that paid only $28,000 a year. She is now armed with a prenup.

But the most visible and influential member of this group is, of course, Lorna Wendt. She believes her marriage began to unravel when she began to stand up for herself—when she began to do Outward Bound trips about six years ago. (Wendt was on the board, and their first trip was together.) Outward Bound tests your inner strength. It teaches you about yourself. It also teaches teamwork. And Lorna Wendt got hooked. "I found out that other people valued me for what I thought, that I have a mind, that I can have a difference of opinion," she says.

She began to assert herself more. She had always loved music and continued to sing in the church choir and in the Greenwich choral society, and she began to beg off on some of the business trips if she had a concert. "I never did neglect my duties as a corporate wife," she says. "I would always check with him first. But if I could sure squeeze in another Outward Bound trip, I would."

She believes the breaking point came on the van trip through Eastern Europe three summers ago. It was vacation, but also business, she says—breakfast, lunch, and dinner. "You'd be out most of that time with men, and you'd always have to have that smile on your face and be interested," she says. In Warsaw she asked if she could be excused from one of the business dinners so she could go out on her own for Italian. "Gary threw a fit. I didn't go. It was part of my independence. I think as I got stronger, he couldn't quite field it." A spokesman for Gary Wendt says he was angry but that it wasn't the first time she had refused to attend a dinner.

For his part, Gary Wendt won't comment on what led to the divorce. He and Lorna Wendt agreed as part of their case that they wouldn't make allegations about who is at fault. But he definitely gives the impression that he feels in the latter stages of their marriage she wasn't living up to her end of the bargain. She hardly entertained during those years, he says. "We built a very nice home in North Stamford, and one of the things I expected out of that was the very nice home could be used for entertaining and business situations. I could never persuade her and I finally gave up." There was a lot of travel, he adds. "For the last seven or eight years, I have viewed it as one of the important parts of my job to lead the expansion internationally, and so I did a lot of travel and I would frequently ask her to go along. I wanted a companion. She had the choice, and sometimes she would go and sometimes she wouldn't." Over time, though, "I was lonely. I was working very hard, and it didn't seem like there was anyone to share it with."

Shortly before the divorce proceedings began, he took up with another woman who was 10 years his senior. "I found somebody one day who was happy, and that's why I was attracted to her. She was a happy person."

The fireworks began when he refused to cut Lorna in on the tremendous wealth he stands to reap at the end of the career she feels she helped make possible. He says he'd never thought about marriage as an economic partnership. "I didn't before. I haven't since. I don't understand that," he says.

So she got tough. She decided she would play the game his way. She said to him: "If Jack Welch said, 'Gary, there's somebody else I really want to bring onboard; thank you for all your hard work all those years,' you would be out working your hardest to get the best damned deal you could. And I'm just doing the same."

And that, perhaps, is the most shocking aspect of the Wendt case—that a wife of her stature and credibility and good grooming could make such a public fuss. If Lorna Wendt can stand up for herself, then anybody can stand up. Perhaps the real message conveyed by the uproar over the case is this: Get it straight on the wife thing. If it's really important to have somebody home raising the kids, then put your money where your mouth is. And if you don't, then don't any longer expect her to keep smiling and act like a lady. Those days are gone.

V-6: A Woman's Place Is . . .
Men Frown on Female Execs Abroad

GENE KORETZ

American women seeking to climb the corporate ladder via overseas positions face steep odds. While females account for some

Reprinted from *Business Week* (September 13, 1999): 28. ©1999 The McGraw–Hill Companies, Inc.

30% of students in MBA programs, they're only 14% of those chosen by Corporate America for foreign postings. And a big reason, suggest two studies presented at the Academy of Management's annual meeting in Chicago last month, is that their male bosses overestimate the problems awaiting them overseas.

In the first study, researchers from Loyola University in Chicago surveyed 261 women who worked abroad and 78 of their mostly male supervisors in multinational corporations. They found that the women saw both their ability to adapt to foreign cultures and the attitudes of foreigners toward female ex-pats more favorably than bosses did.

In the second study, researchers at Loyola Marymount College in Los Angeles surveyed 323 managers in Germany, Mexico, and the United States about their views of the performance of American women working overseas. U.S. male managers were significantly more doubtful about American women's effectiveness than were their U.S. female counterparts or German and Mexican managers of either sex.

In sum, U.S. male managers exhibit "unfounded bias" against American women in overseas positions—a bias that researchers believe hampers females' selection for such assignments.

V-7: The Case of the Hidden Harassment
What Happens When a Manager's Responsibilities Clash with an Employee's Right to Privacy?

DANIEL NIVEN

Jerry Tarkwell, a real estate lending manager at Filmore Trust, marched out of his office toward the associate's wing of the bank's eighteenth-floor offices. "I need the Thompson Properties file right away," Tarkwell said to the associates' secretary. "Do you know where I can find it?"

"It's probably on Jill's computer table. I was helping her enter the new figures this morning."

"Thanks." Tarkwell headed down the hallway and knocked on the door marked "Jill McNair, Associate." McNair didn't answer, so he opened the door and walked over to the computer table piled high with folders. As he shuffled through the files, Tarkwell glanced at what was written on the computer screen. It was an electronic mail message McNair had sent earlier.

Can you walk me out again tonight? He's in today and I'm sure he'll be waiting for me. He leaned up against me when I was at the coffee machine this morning and whispered some disgusting stuff about how great he is in bed. I don't want another episode like the one in the hallway Monday night. I should have left when you did, but I thought he'd already gone.

I'm sorry you have to put up with this. Get back to me. I'll be ready to go whenever you are.

"Oh, that's awful." Tarkwell felt sickened as he got up to leave. "God, I wonder who's doing this?" He grabbed the Thompson Properties file, returned to his own office, and called the company's equal employment officer.

"Tarkwell was in your office a little while ago looking for the Thompson file," shouted the secretary as Jill McNair walked briskly down the hall.

Reprinted from *Harvard Business Review* (March–April, 1992): 12–23.

"Damn, I was supposed to hand that over to him an hour ago," McNair thought as she opened her door. The computer screen immediately caught her eye. "Oh no," she gasped, "I can't believe I left that on." The ring of her phone made her jump.

"Hi, Jill, it's Jerry. I'd like to talk to you right away. Can you come down to my office?"

"Sure," she said weakly and then hung up the phone. "I'll bet he read it," she thought. "What am I going to do now?"

McNair knocked on Tarkwell's door and went in. "Sit down, Jill. I have something rather disturbing to discuss with you," Tarkwell began. "I went into your office to pick up the Thompson file. I'm afraid I read what was on your computer screen."

Jill looked at him angrily. She clenched her fists in her lap.

"Let me tell you first how sorry I am that you've been . . . put in that kind of situation." Tarkwell shifted uncomfortably. He was having trouble finding words that wouldn't embarrass them both. "I need to know who's been doing this to you so we can put a stop to it. I called the equal employment officer, and she explained the steps to resolving a case of this sort. First you. . . . "

McNair cut him off. "You had no right to read my personal e-mail, and you had no right to call EEO before talking to me. This is my problem not yours, and I don't want this getting around. Do you have any idea what can happen to me and to my career if people find out about this?"

"I didn't tell them who'd be bringing the complaint," Tarkwell said. "You just have to write a letter, and they do an investigation."

"Don't you understand?" she asked, seething. "It would be his word against mine, and he's senior to me." She wished she hadn't let that slip. "I'm the one who's going to get hurt. If this gets investigated by EEO, everyone in this building could be questioned. I'll

probably get transferred, and then I won't have a chance at promotion. And who'd want to work with me? Every man in the company would be afraid I'd report him if he so much as opened a door for me."

"Look," Tarkwell reasoned, "nobody here has to find out. I'm sure the EEO will do whatever you feel is best. You know you can't go on working under these conditions."

"I won't have my privacy invaded," McNair said flatly. "There's nothing you can do."

"But it's a federal law," Tarkwell demanded. "This company has to maintain a workplace free of sexual coercion, and as your manager, I have to report this. It's company policy."

"I've got too much at stake here," McNair answered, reaching for the door. "So just stay out of it, Jerry. I can take care of it myself."

● ●

HOW CAN TARKWELL BEST RESOLVE THIS ISSUE?

Five experts on sexual harassment in the workplace examine his options.

Jill wonders who will want to work with her if she brings a complaint. The answer often is no one.

CHERYL WANG, A FORMER
INVESTMENT BANKER, NOW A
PUBLIC TELEVISION PRODUCER

Jerry, although I know you will be talking to lawyers, people from human resources, and equal employment officers about Jill McNair's case, perhaps I can offer you another perspective—the perspective of someone who understands what Jill is going through. I too was a victim of sexual harassment.

In my case, however, the managers were not as enlightened as you are. They heard my harasser make comments like "let's go see a porno film" or "let me pet your sweater." They knew that intelligent women like me weren't getting assigned to exciting, high-visibility projects. They saw that women were leaving the department, one by one. And they did nothing. You, on the other hand, have recognized that what Jill is experiencing is sexual harassment. And, most important, you are treating this as a serious problem.

Unlike the managers I encountered, you want to help. But you won't be helping Jill by forcing her to bring a complaint against the harasser. She is already a victim of someone else's unwanted actions. Don't compound her sense of victimization by pushing her into another situation she doesn't want to be in.

Perhaps the best way to help Jill is to show her how to take control. Show her that there *are* options. But first make damn sure that those options really do exist.

Find out what the sexual harassment policy in your office is. Does the message that sexual harassment is illegal and will not be tolerated come through loud and clear? Does that message come from top management? Are seminars held so that all employees understand what sexual harassment is and what to do if they encounter it? Is there a complaint system in place? If so, does it work? Do the employees trust it?

I suspect that the answer to these questions is no. If Filmore Trust did have an effective way of dealing with sexual harassment, Jill wouldn't feel as if she had to accept harassment as a necessary evil of her job. And managers like you would know specific steps to take that wouldn't jeopardize the victim or the company.

If you really want to help Jill and Filmore Trust, you must convince the company to educate its employees and to establish a good system for handling sexual harassment complaints. Ultimately, you will be helping not only Jill but other potential victims as well. The chances are good that Jill is not the only person at Filmore Trust experiencing sexual harassment.

These are long-term solutions that will take time to implement; however, you and Jill also need immediate help. Two options for the short-term are:

- Call a meeting of your department and discuss sexual harassment. Tell your employees that Filmore Trust and you will not tolerate any behavior that is sexual in nature, unwelcome, or unreasonably disruptive.

- Find an expert on sexual harassment who doesn't have any ties to Filmore Trust and give his or her name to Jill. Obviously, Jill doesn't trust the way your company would handle a sexual harassment complaint. Perhaps she might have greater confidence in advice coming from someone on the outside.

In the meantime, let Jill know your concerns but don't dismiss hers. The unfortunate truth is that a sexual harassment victim who makes a formal complaint to management without the protection of an established, trusted complaint procedure risks losing his or her reputation, job, or even career.

I know. When I brought my complaint to senior management, one of my greatest fears was retaliation. I wrote a letter, just like the one you are suggesting Jill write. In response, management thanked me for bringing sexual harassment to its attention and told me not to worry. I was promised it would be "business as usual" around the department.

But it wasn't. Instead of starting an investigation of my harasser, management started an investigation of me. It stole positive performance reviews out of my employee file and then told me my work was unsatisfactory because there weren't any good reviews on record. Colleagues who had once been sympathetic now didn't want to get involved. Others just stopped talking to me. Conversation would halt when I entered a room. So I sympathize with Jill when she wonders who will want to work with her if she brings a complaint. The answer often is no one.

And don't think that "nobody here has to find out." Long after I left my company, I heard that people were gossiping about the financial settlement I had received—and this in spite of a gag order.

Like other victims of sexual harassment, Jill hopes that the problem will eventually go away. Unfortunately, sexual harassment doesn't stop on its own. It simply goes somewhere else, finds someone else—unless people like you step in.

A mandatory investigation policy discourages reporting; Filmore Trust should offer some options.

> MARY P. ROWE,
> SPECIAL ASSISTANT TO THE
> PRESIDENT, OMBUDSMAN, AND
> ADJUNCT PROFESSOR AT THE SLOAN
> SCHOOL OF MANAGEMENT AT
> MASSACHUSETTS INSTITUTE OF
> TECHNOLOGY

People who feel harassed need options and choices—especially if they lack conclusive proof of the harassment. This case appears to present two unacceptable choices for manager Jerry Tarkwell and no desirable options for Jill McNair. Moreover, Filmore Trust's policy will not work in the company's interests either. No party's interests are served well here.

Let's start with the company. Filmore Trust needs an environment where sexual harassment is absent or at least rare. This will occur where employees can and do speak up and get incipient harassment stopped on the spot, where managers offer options so people who feel harassed have some control over what happens, and where reporting harassment and asking for help will not damage someone's career.

My research and experience indicate that while a mandatory investigation policy may appear to be helpful to harassed people, it actually discourages reports of harassment. Mandatory investigation especially threatens careers when the only evidence is "he said/she said" (though more evidence might be found in the Filmore Trust case). This is because responsible managers hate to take action in such a case, so no one gets punished, and the alleged offender does not feel truly acquitted.

What about McNair's interests? They are the same interests I listed for Filmore Trust. In addition, McNair values her privacy and fears reprisal. Tarkwell's interests are probably similar.

How can Filmore Trust meet the interests of all parties? The company should offer four sets of options for dealing with harassment:

1. *Counseling for Direct Negotiation.* Filmore Trust should offer off-the-record counseling so that employees can learn to negotiate the problem effectively. With the help of an employee assistance program or an ombudsman, for example, McNair might choose to learn how to confront the harasser directly or write that person a private letter. Drafting a clear, factual letter will help McNair think through her evidence, compose her mind and feelings, and help her select and pursue an option for action. Sending or hand delivering (and keeping a copy of) a letter is statistically likely to end the harassment, at no cost to privacy. It also provides more evidence, if harassment continues or the offender retaliates, that the alleged sexual approach actually happened and was unwelcome.

2. *Informal, Third-Party Intervention.* McNair should be able to seek informal assistance from a human resources manager or other appropriate person. The third party would intervene as a shuttle diplomat or mediator. Informal intervention usually

does not include adverse administrative action. The third party could deliver a warning and write a memo to his or her own file.

3. *Formal Investigation and Action.* McNair should be able to request fact-finding and judgment. If she knows she has choices, she will be more likely to make a formal complaint, but this option should not be pursued against her wishes.

4. *Generic Approach.* McNair should be able to ask Tarkwell or another appropriate manager—off the record and without providing the name of the alleged offender—for a harassment prevention effort. This choice could trigger an apparently routine training program in the relevant department. Or McNair could ask that the department head send a departmental letter that includes examples of sexual harassment and a strong statement of company policy. If McNair has the option to ask for such action without anyone's name being used, then the harassment can be stopped at no cost to anyone's privacy or rights. In my experience, the generic approach will stop the alleged harassment about four-fifths of the time, and it helps to affirm company policy. It also fosters an atmosphere where people can feel comfortable taking a direct approach if they are harassed and where they will feel less afraid to ask for an investigation.

There should be no adverse administrative action against an alleged offender without a fair—probably formal—process. If any of the informal options are chosen by McNair, then Tarkwell must follow up immediately, several months, and one year later to be sure that the alleged harassment has ceased and that there has been no retaliation.

For women, Japanese companies are hotbeds of harassment.

MIKIKO TAGA,
FREELANCE JOURNALIST AND
AUTHOR OF *CORNERED CHILDREN*
AND *SINGLE MIND*

Jerry Tarkwell does not have to choose between respecting Jill McNair's privacy and putting a stop to sexual harassment. His accidental knowledge of McNair's harassment has given him, whether he likes it or not, the responsibility to do both.

It would be irresponsible to follow blindly "company policy" if to do so would undermine its original intent (presumably to help employees deal with harassment). Doing nothing, however, is also not an option. Sexual harassment involves the entire company, not just two people. Tarkwell therefore cannot let the issue go now that he knows something is going on.

As long as McNair refuses to report her case, Tarkwell will, by definition, be threatening her privacy in any attempts to talk to her about it. But McNair has already crossed the line between private and company life by using company equipment (e-mail) to tell her colleague about her sexual harassment. While Tarkwell must urge McNair to report her case, he must refrain from reporting it to the company's EEO until she assents.

Regardless of whether McNair ultimately reports her case, Tarkwell must make this his opportunity to attack the problem of sexual harassment and to raise company consciousness about it. Anything less would be shirking his responsibility of creating a safe working environment for his staff.

In Japan, on the other hand, a Jerry Tarkwell would have no cause to even mention his knowledge of Jill McNair's case to her, and the ethical problem presented by this situation would not have surfaced. Few Japanese companies have any sexual harassment policy in place.

Indeed, consciousness of sexual harassment here is so undeveloped that the very issue of the protection of privacy has yet to surface. For women, Japanese companies are still hotbeds of harassment.

The first sexual harassment suit filed in Japan was in 1989. The woman, who was

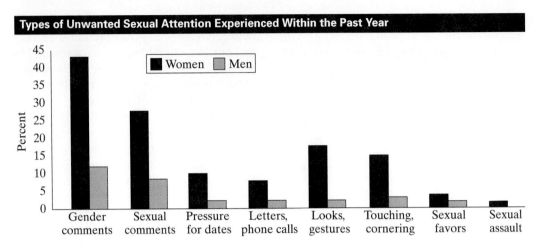

Types of Unwanted Sexual Attention Experienced Within the Past Year

In national surveys, when employees are asked if they have been sexually harassed, the average annual response rates are 15 percent for women and 5 percent for men. But when asked in the Klein Associates survey if they have been subjected to the legally defined forms of unwanted sexual attention listed in this chart, employees report dramatically higher numbers.

being harassed by her immediate supervisor, complained to his boss, only to find that his boss condoned his actions and blamed her for inviting them. In other words, the men stuck together.

Within such a context, a woman must go beyond those immediately involved in order to be heard. But once she does, the rest of the company eventually finds out, she is further harassed, and, generally, she ends up quitting.

If she does file suit, she will most likely do so more out of a desire for revenge than of a feeling that her rights have been violated. Japan has such a long history of male dominance that there is no collective belief

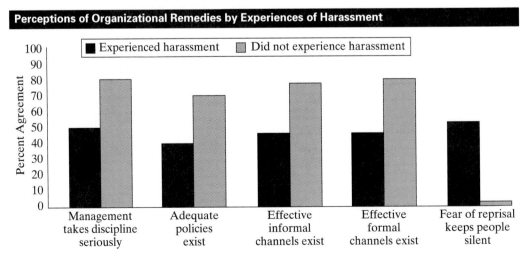

Perceptions of Organizational Remedies by Experiences of Harassment

Employees who have experienced sexual harassment find most organizational complaint systems don't offer enough confidentiality or protection from retaliation.

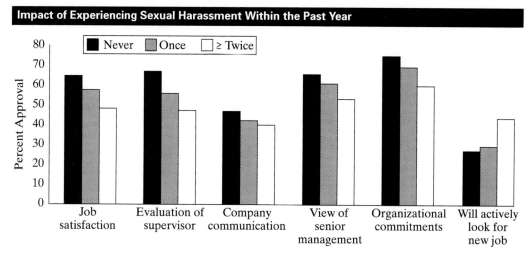

Impact of Experiencing Sexual Harassment Within the Past Year

As employees experience multiple or extreme incidents of sexual harassment, their opinion of their companies' managers, and jobs declines.

that a woman should be the equal working partner of a man.

I endured two years of sexual harassment—though at the time I did not know the term—while I was employed at a large manufacturing company. The older female employees taught the younger women that it was a mark of "female maturity" to respond to harassment by smiling and ignoring it.

During my stay in the United States (1983 to 1988), I was shocked to learn that there was a name for such hateful behavior. In 1989, when I published my book *Single Mind,* I was able to introduce the term sexual harassment to Japan.

In the three years since, the term *seku hara* has gained currency as the media has legitimized its usage. (In fact, seku hara is a trivialization of the term sexual harassment, further proof of the widespread insensitivity to this issue.) There have been three sexual harassment suits filed in Japan that I have followed; two have been won, and the other is still pending. Though this sounds promising, and though anti-seku hara campaigns would seem to indicate substantial change, the situation is, in fact, far from progressive. In effect, the message is "Watch out, guys.

We know women are emotional, so we will have to step lightly for our own protection."

Ultimately, sexual harassment is less an issue of company policy than one of personal responsibility in a management position. Tarkwell has shown that he takes the company's policy seriously; now he should follow through on his commitment by ensuring that McNair's situation is justly resolved and by raising office consciousness about harassment.

Jill McNair should not be pressured into becoming an unwilling martyr.

JUDITH P. VLADECK,
SENIOR PARTNER AT VLADECK,
WALDMAN, ELIAS & ENGELHARD,
COUNSELLORS AT LAW

Jerry Tarkwell should respect Jill McNair's request for privacy. She is not obliged by law to press charges of harassment and should not be required to do so against her own better judgment. McNair is probably realistic about the potential damage to her career. She has no doubt seen the lack of sympathy and support available to a woman who complains about harassment. She should not be pressured into becoming an unwilling martyr.

If Tarkwell is concerned about McNair's complaining later that she was not protected by the company, he could ask her to provide a memo stating that she had considered her options and rejected the company's offer of assistance. If she declines to provide such a memo, Tarkwell should write his own memo to that effect and place it in McNair's personnel file. It would likely protect the company in the future.

Tarkwell, having alerted the EEO of his knowledge that a company employee was imposing on other workers, is in the difficult position of any good citizen who learns of a malfeasant in his community. If the victim refuses to press charges, the bystander cannot do so. Having encouraged the victim to do what he thinks is correct, he must accept her decision.

Obviously, a conscientious person such as Tarkwell could suggest that the company's harassment policy, with assurances of confidentiality, be circulated and posted again.

Whether McNair can be disciplined for refusing to cooperate in an investigation is a more difficult question. While reporting harassment is protected by law and retaliation against a person who does so violates federal law, failing to report is *not* protected by any clear statutory language. It might be argued that discipline for failing to report is a form of discrimination in itself. A woman who is required to report sexual harassment is being deprived of equal terms and conditions of employment, in that, unlike the men who are not subjected to the harassment, she is burdened with an obligation to come forward and place herself at risk.

Unfortunately, in many jurisdictions, a woman in McNair's position is at risk of discipline or termination for failing to disclose information requested by the company. In New York, for example, an employer who fired McNair for remaining silent could do so with impunity.

A subsidiary question arises concerning Tarkwell's conduct. If Tarkwell had not looked at McNair's computer screen, he would not have known about the problem. While it may be understandable that Tarkwell went into her office while she was not there to look for documents that he needed at once, his reading of her electronic mail message was inappropriate and an invasion of her privacy. McNair, unfortunately, has no right to the privacy of her personal e-mail, unless the company has some rules protecting the privacy rights of its employees.

Jill McNair is in the unenviable position of a woman trying to make a career for herself, who is likely to get battered for not publicly fighting back against the sexual harassment she is suffering and who risks ostracism and abuse from her colleagues if she does complain.

Only the EEO can determine if the potential harm to employees outweighs the complainant's concern for privacy.

LEE CHESTER GARRON,
EQUAL EMPLOYMENT
OFFICE–AFFIRMATIVE ACTION
TRAINING MANAGER FOR DIGITAL EQUIPMENT CORPORATION

Like many companies, Digital doesn't deny that sexual harassment exists in the workplace. Digital encourages managers and employees to take advantage of sexual harassment training, which examines the issue and develops solutions to harassment in any given work situation.

At Digital, 90% of all sexual harassment claims involve individuals who are not aware that their behaviors are offensive or unwelcome. And 90% of these claims are settled by an apology and a promise by the harasser to correct permanently his or her behavior. The remaining 10% might be settled with some disciplinary action.

A great deal of consideration should be given to validating any claim of sexual harassment, even before a full-fledged investigation takes place. This allows for the possibility that an employee might be filing a claim to offset poor performance or getting revenge for a personal relationship "gone sour." Evidence must be secured to avoid a "his word against mine" situation.

In the case of Jerry Tarkwell and Jill McNair, Tarkwell did exactly what I would recommend by first contacting Filmore Trust's EEO for instructions. Even though McNair demands that no further steps be taken, Tarkwell should continue to consult with the company EEO so a decision can be made about how to react to McNair's requests for anonymity. Only there can it be determined if the potential harm to the victim or other employees outweighs the complainant's concern for privacy. Tarkwell is responsible for acting on any issues that affect his employees, so McNair's situation cannot be ignored. At Digital, Tarkwell would be held accountable for his employees' behavior.

Tarkwell must pursue the issue, first to find out if the complaint is merited and then to ensure that no other incidents of harassment occur. Tarkwell can suggest that McNair seek the advice of another manager if she feels uncomfortable talking about it with him, and he must convince her that a company policy exists that will protect her. Every company's sexual harassment policy must contain a "no retaliation" stipulation promising that the complainant will not incur any kind of reprisal as a result of a claim.

Programs and policies assuring employees of their right to bring forth, without reprisal, issues that they feel are affecting them negatively are paramount to any positive or reasonable resolution in issues of sexual harassment. Many cases are resolved with simple, positive intervention—when the offended employee is convinced that the company will stand behind its policies, standards, and values. Helping employees understand not only their right to utilize the internal open-door process but also federal EEOC guidelines on sexual harassment and their right to use these avenues to find a resolution is very important. The prevention of sexual harassment in the workplace is the employer's responsibility.

To implement this policy successfully, Digital managers and supervisors are encouraged to know their environment and subordinates—as well as raise their level of awareness through sexual harassment training courses. The training involves role playing of actual sexual harassment situations and lively follow-up discussion in which attendees share their thoughts and ideas about the implications of sexual harassment. Digital's EEO also offers "Train the Trainer" seminars for human resource professionals to learn more about the issue and prepare them to train others. Digital's goal is to bring resolution to a sexual harassment claim and ensure the investigative process satisfies both the employee and management.

V-8: The Glass Table

CHARLES E. MICHAELS

Alice Graham was the Vice President for Human Resources at a medium-sized grocery chain. She scheduled a meeting with

Margaret Samson, a management-level employee who had worked for the company for six years. Margaret had never been among the top performers in the company, but her performance had been acceptable until lately. In the past six months, Mar-

Written especially for this volume by Charles E. Michaels.

garet's performance had slipped to unacceptable levels. Margaret worked for Ed Morton, one of the fastest-rising Group Managers in the entire corporation.

The current trouble with Margaret started last week and has caused a furor in the company. A routine management meeting was held in a new location with a glass-topped conference table. Margaret and Ed, as usual, sat together at the meeting as did many participants and their bosses. During this particular meeting, several managers noticed that throughout much of the meeting, Ed had his hand up Margaret's skirt. Word of Ed and Margaret's behavior reached John Riggs, the company's CEO. Mr. Riggs asked Alice Graham to look into the situation. Alice spoke with all of the participants of the meeting and determined that the behavior was clearly inappropriate. Ed Morton was interviewed and then fired for his part in the situation even though he was seen as one of the company's best young managers.

Alice's problem now concerned what to do with Margaret. Her performance had been slipping and the company had considered terminating her even before the incident at the meeting. If she willingly participated in the behavior at the meeting, she would be fired just as Ed had for the same offense. Determining willingness was the problem. Margaret could have been a victim of sexual harassment. Since she worked directly for Ed, she might have been hiding the harassment for fear of Ed firing her or taking it out on her at work. She may have been suffering in silence and that might also explain her recent drop in performance.

In addition to the people at the meeting, Alice had set up meetings with other female employees who worked for Ed, now or in the past, since managers that engage in sexual harassment usually harass more than one woman. Alice also set up the meeting with Margaret.

Alice sat at her desk ten minutes before the meeting with Margaret. John Riggs, the CEO, asked Alice for a recommendation of what action to take with Margaret. What should Alice ask Margaret and how should she make her decision?

V-9: More Companies Offering Same-Sex-Partner Benefits
Study Finds Tight Labor Market Is a Factor

Washington, Sept. 25—More companies are offering health insurance benefits to partners of gay and lesbian employees than ever before, including more than 100 of the *Fortune* 500 companies, a new study has found.

As of August, 3,572 companies, colleges, universities, states, and local governments were offering or had announced that they would offer health insurance coverage to domestic partners of their employees—

Reprinted from *The New York Times* (September 26, 2000): C2.

an increase of 25 percent from last year, the study found. In August 1999, 2,856 of these companies, educational institutions, and governments offered such benefits.

Sixty-five percent of those in the survey provide domestic partner benefits to same-sex and opposite-sex couples; 35 percent offer benefits only to same-sex couples, the study found.

The study was conducted by the Human Rights Campaign, a Washington-based group that represents gay, lesbian, and transgender Americans.

"Employers have discovered that these benefits help attract and keep the best workers, a critical consideration in the current tight job market," said Kim I. Mills, education director for the Human Rights Campaign and an editor of the report.

Among *Fortune* 500 companies, the number of employers offering benefits to domestic partners increased 46 percent, the study found, to 102 this year from 70 in 1999.

The Big Three automakers—Daimler Chrysler, General Motors, and Ford Motor—announced in June that they would offer health benefits to the same-sex partners of their 466,000 hourly and salaried employees in the United States. This was a "landmark move" in the effort by corporate America to provide such benefits for gay and lesbian couples, the report concluded.

Coca-Cola also announced in June that it would extend health coverage to domestic partners, joining General Mills and Pillsbury, two other leading food producers that offer these benefits.

Boeing decided last October that it would offer health coverage to nonunion members and their partners. Honeywell, another leading aerospace company, provides benefits to domestic partners.

Until this year, the two largest American companies offering same-sex benefits had been I.B.M. and Citigroup, Ms. Mills said. Both companies are based in the New York area, where gays and lesbians are more politically and economically influential than in the Midwest.

"There is a cultural shift taking place," Ms. Mills said. "People want to be open about their lives in the workplace. The public attitude is that this kind of discrimination is wrong."

In May 1998, President Clinton issued an executive order prohibiting discrimination based on sexual orientation in the federal civilian workforce. To date, all cabinet-level departments and 24 independent agencies have adopted nondiscrimination policies with regard to sexual orientation. But the federal government does not provide same-sex benefits for its employees.

Ninety state and local governments or government agencies, however, provide domestic-partner health benefits, the report showed. Since August 1999, Connecticut and Washington have added benefits for state workers, joining California, New York, Vermont, and Oregon. In addition, 12 cities and counties have added or announced that they would begin to offer these benefits, including Atlanta; Phoenix; Montgomery County, Maryland; and Albuquerque.

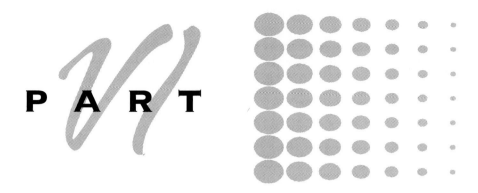

PART VI

GRAPPLING WITH ISSUES

In the previous part, we saw how social changes have created challenges for HRM to deal with diversity and discrimination. Although these may represent the most widely publicized recent challenges, they are not the only ones that social changes have put before today's HRM professionals. In this part we consider some of the others.

Throughout the book we have stressed the need to appreciate the impact of social and economic environment forces on what organizations must do to manage human resources effectively. Among these forces, one that seems always crucial is the tightness of the labor market. In the first selection, "The Wild New Workforce" Michelle Conlin and Peter Coy (with Ann Therese Palmer and Gabrielle Saveri) explore how the recent tight labor market for talented people is driving organizations to institute more individualized and flexible approaches to compensation.

Also, throughout the history of HRM, changes in technology have had profound impacts on all aspects of organizations including HRM. The next two selections, by Stephanie Overman and Sharon C. Zehe, explore some of the implications of newer technologies for employee privacy.

We then turn our attention to the topic of work-related stress. This is not a new concern. For example, the noted historian Daniel Rodgers (1974) in writing of industrial work in America tells us that back in 1860 the term "neurasthenic" or nervousness was viewed almost as a national disease. Thus, workplace-related stress is not as recent a development as the popular press might lead one to believe. However, while not a new issue, the realities of modern work seem to be associated with a number of demands that are believed to threaten both physical and mental health. The next selection, "Business Travel" illustrates some of these threats.

Another set of HRM issues that has recently captured considerable attention is sexual behavior at work. While throughout the history of our culture, sexual conduct has posed concerns, it seems that it is only recently that these concerns have become major workplace issues. Two simultaneous trends seem to have produced this situation: Social norms about sex have changed greatly. The opportunities for sexual contact between men and women in the workplace have increased due to several factors including the growing number of women employed in organizations, altered work roles that seem to entail more emotional contact between male and female employees (e.g., increased travel), and less structured work. Such changes may have eliminated the barriers that previously constrained sexual activity.

However, we must be cautious about asserting or even implying that sexual activity among employees has *actually* increased. Caution is needed because much of the evidence suggesting an increase has appeared in the media and popular press (such as the cover story in *Fortune* "Addicted to Sex" that we reprint in this part). Such increased coverage could be due to several things other than a rise in the incidence of workplace sex. For one, sales is a prime goal of publishers, and, as it is often said, "Sex sells." Second, changes in norms have made it easier to talk about sex in "polite conversation" than was the case only a few years ago. In short, it would be risky to conclude from the greater frequency of discussions in the popular press that there have been actual changes in the amount of workplace sex. Nevertheless, it cannot be denied that organizations are spending more effort trying to define appropriate relationships between men and women in the workplace. This section contains several articles from major business publications that reveal key dimensions of this issue. We have already mentioned Morris's "Addicted to Sex" which provides both an overview and some specifics about what appears to be taking place. Then, Carol Hymowitz and Ellen Joan Pollock consider how previous policies on romantic relationships at work have unraveled.

As we noted earlier, the provision of benefits is a long-standing matter for HRM practitioners. As we have observed in the previous part with the treatment of same-sex benefits, benefits involve people with different interests promoting their specific preferences. Given the political agendas involved and the fact that providing benefits is not what most work organizations were created to do, it is not surprising that someone might suggest getting rid of employee benefits entirely. Craig J. Cantoni's article raises this provocative position.

When you have completed the readings in this part, you should be very comfortable with a key premise of this entire book: the substance of the issues that HRM practitioners confront may be, in large measure, a product of dynamic social and political economic processes in the larger society. Of course, which is cause and which is effect is an open question. We do not treat the opposite direction of causality (that HR issues in the workplace can have an impact on social and political economic progresses in society) very much in this book, except to conclude this introductory essay to Part VI by suggesting that it probably operates and we invite you to consider it too.

VI-1: The Wild New Workforce

MICHELLE CONLIN, PETER COY, ANN THERESE PALMER,
AND GABRIELLE SAVERI

Guys like Reed Kingston scare the pants off CEOs. Two months ago, Kingston, a partner in Ernst & Young's Cupertino (California) office, waved goodbye to his huge, ergonomically correct office, razor-sharp secretary, and consulting work with some of Silicon Valley's most glamorous companies. Today, he does scut work like bookkeeping off a second-hand laminate desk for a voice recognition startup called Voci Corp. The offices are in the back of a grimy machine shop. As the company's vice-president of sales and service, he has no assistant, no benefits, and no salary.

What makes Kingston so worrisome? He's anything but the stereotypical, tattooed twentysomething with a bungee-jumper attitude about corporate loyalty. Kingston is, in fact, a 42-year-old company man—the type of hard-working, sober citizen who has been the backbone of corporate America for generations. Spending his entire 18-year career at the Big Five firm, he finally made partner three years ago. He has a wife, twin four-year-old daughters, a huge home, and an even bigger mortgage. "I'm risk-averse," Kingston says.

The really scary part is how many Reed Kingstons there are. Their worker wanderlust, fueled by stock options, signing bonuses, and the chance to take on a bigger challenge, is not restricted to Silicon Valley anymore. With the tightest labor markets in 30 years and unprecedented opportunities beckoning, it's a wonder that more members of the wild new workforce haven't cleared out their cubicles and leveraged themselves into better gigs. After all, when

budget hotels offer managers free BMWs, pancake houses in Texas dole out $4,000 signing bonuses, and Deloitte & Touche gives away new Jeep Wranglers and $15,000 checks to employees simply for referring new bodies, then every worker should feel emboldened. If this boss won't provide a raise, stock options, extra time off, or whatever, then another one will.

So how is it that the growth in real hourly compensation has actually slowed—from a 4.3% annual rate in the third quarter of 1998 to 2.3% this year? Necessity begets invention, and businesses that have little or no pricing power with their customers have been getting pretty crafty about cooking up ways to cope with a labor market that would have devastated them a decade ago. They know that big across-the-board raises would wreck profits, so they simply refuse to hand them out. In fact, annual raises have fallen from 5.2% in 1990 to 4.2% in 1998 and 1999. Meanwhile, variable pay—stock options and bonuses often tied to performance goals—is increasing. This is a way to compensate superstars in the expansion without locking in higher fixed costs that will be burdensome in a downturn.

● ● ● ● ● ● ● ● ● ● ● ● ● ● ● ● ● ● ●
SHREDDED CONTRACTS

The new compensation isn't free, although it is cheaper. Still, companies have little choice when the job market looks like a city gripped by a speculative real-estate boom. "When the valuable properties are surging, some average lots on the extreme perimeter go for irrational prices," says Bruce Dennis, president of startup Sevant Inc. in San Jose, California.

Reprinted from *Business Week* (December 6, 1999): 39–46. ©1999 The McGraw–Hill Companies, Inc.

Something else is going on here, though—something that will likely outlast the current hiring crunch: Just as the New Economy is dismantling the old rules of commerce, the new workforce is shredding the contracts between employers and employees. Employers are giving up rigid wage scales in favor of flexible compensation. They are learning to live with high turnover and abolishing seniority-based pay. "We're in a dramatic transformation," says Hewitt Associates LLC compensation consultant Paul Shafer. "We're moving toward person-based pay."

And the trend away from corporate loyalty that began in the 1980s when companies eliminated layers of mid-career employees has now flipped in favor of the worker. In this environment, an employee who remains loyal to an organization is penalized. After all, if the woman in the next cubicle can jump to another company for a 20% raise, a signing bonus, and stock options, why should you wait around for that 4% merit hike?

That's where Reed Kingston was. Week after week, underlings would come and tell him that they were being wooed by dot.com startups promising rewards and challenges that Ernst & Young could never match. "I found it harder and harder to tell them why they should stay," he says. So, he joined them—trading his security and six-figure salary for the chance to make a fortune and a big difference in the life of a new company.

● ● ● ● ● ● ● ● ● ●
PRECIPICE

How long business can continue to plug the holes in the dikes is unclear. Much depends on whether the Reed Kingston syndrome spreads further down into the workforce. Already, warns John Challenger of Challenger, Gray & Christmas, Corporate America "is dangerously close to the precipice" as it tries to keep up.

Before business goes over the edge, it's more likely that economic growth in the United States will moderate, and the job market will loosen up. It's a safe bet that nobody will be doling out "smart-dress" allowances, free flying lessons, or new cars as they are today. What will remain is an altered employment relationship in which increasingly independent workers negotiate their own way through their careers. "These seem to be tendencies that aren't driven by the business cycle," says Daniel J.B. Mitchell, a professor of management and public policy at the University of California at Los Angeles.

One side effect that could create tension: the stark contrasts in the workplace as companies lavish bonuses and fat salaries on new hires, while existing workers bump along with compensation low enough to keep the overall average down. "[Companies] can't afford to be concerned with internal equity," says Eric Larre, a consultant with Aon Corp.

And the differences across industries are stunning. In computer manufacturing, pay for nonsupervisory workers rose 12% in the third quarter, according to the BLS. For telephone communication workers, in contrast, the BLS says pay actually fell 0.7%. Dan H. Marks, president of auto dealer Libertyville Classic Group Inc. in Waukegan, Illinois, says his technicians are getting 10% fewer hours of warranty work this year, and average wages are off about $80 a week.

● ● ● ● ● ● ● ● ● ● ● ● ● ● ● ● ● ●
JUGGLING JOB OFFERS

These tensions between the haves and the have-nots are fueling a lot of new resentments. At workplaces everywhere, new hires with no experience are swaggering into the office with pay packages far bigger than those of veteran staffers. Elite employees are making so much money so quickly and are juggling so many job offers that they live in constant fear of making the wrong decision and blowing their chance of getting their "two commas" and retiring at age 40.

Many companies recognize the need to keep the troops happy—with special bonuses and soft perks. California-based Cheesecake Factory Inc. pays salaries 20% above market rates, according to *People Report,* a human resource journal. But it also gives stock options to all its general managers. They also get to drive shiny new BMW 323's. Sounds expensive. But the company says it has actually saved money, losing only two general managers in the last two years in an industry where 38% turnover is average.

TIS, a Manhattan-based e-business consulting firm, keeps its turnover to a minuscule 3% by hiring for the long term. It avoids one-dimensional, work-over-the-weekend geeks. Instead it looks for people who have compelling outside interests and encourages them to bring their passions to work. In his spare time, Senior Software Engineer Andrew Peterson is a tightrope-walking juggler. On any given day at TIS's hip downtown Manhattan offices, he can be seen practicing in his circus gear.

For all the enlightened approaches that the new workplace is inspiring, there are plenty of companies getting more out of their workers the old-fashioned way—by simply loading on the work without upping the pay. That's exactly what Sivivian Merrick says happened to her at MCI Communications Corp. Merrick joined the company—now part of MCI WorldCom Inc.—in 1997 in a job taking orders for phone service. MCI gave her a $37,000 salary and a fancy title: "provisioner engineer."

In a class action pending in federal court in Houston, Merrick and others allege the engineer title was a disingenuous way for MCI to get around paying workers overtime. Merrick says she worked 70-hour weeks, subsisting on fast food and minding her 4-year-old son Mister while she worked into the night. MCI says it won't comment on pending litigation.

Throughout the economy, the speedup is well under way. The 40-hour week has all but disappeared: Americans now log 260 more hours a year than they did a decade ago. Pharmacists and government workers have already won suits awarding them extra pay for overtime work. Flight attendants at Continental Airlines are mulling a class action over a requirement that they show up at the airport 45 minutes prior to the flight's departure. Their gripe: They don't start getting paid until the door to the aircraft has slammed shut.

Whether it's longer hours or clever tricks to boost productivity, companies are finding ways to get the job done without paying more. Fargo (North Dakota)-based Tharaldson Enterprises, the country's largest private hotel operator, puts the laundry right behind the front desk so check-in clerks can wash linen in their free time. Maids are paid by the room, not by the hour.

Another option is to tap new pools of labor, including immigrants, offshore workers, the disabled, prison inmates, welfare recipients, and senior citizens. Mark Gregory, a fast-food operator with shops in the Midwest, is looking into getting special permits to allow him to hire 14- and 15-year-olds to pick up the slack. Gregory already tried sending recruiters to the parking lots of competitors and offered workers leaving their jobs an extra $2 an hour if they'd come work for him at a new Arby's.

Gregory is one of many business owners who say that without immigrants, they might have to switch off the lights. He's down to one English-speaker, and the cost of training the others, plus the extra compensation, will crimp his operating margins by 4%. Immigrants are filling jobs across the economy and doing everything from washing dishes to doing the heavy thinking in some of the nation's top research laboratories. Glovia International, an El Segundo (California)-based software company, says 90% of the software developers in its Pro4 division are on H-1B visas, which allow "specialty occupation" workers to enter the United States for employment. They come from Japan, South Korea, India, Russia, Mexico, Ireland, and Britain.

The other way to tap foreign labor is to follow General Electric Co.'s lead, pushing work offshore—directly or by demanding that suppliers do so. Microsoft Corp. and RealNetworks Inc. use a Bangalore, India, company, Aditi Corp., to handle customer e-mails.

How much longer can companies keep pulling these rabbits out of their hats? The H-1B visa program is under constant assault by labor groups who say it is just a way to undercut the American worker. And Southfield (Michigan)-based Quality Information Systems Inc. in October pleaded guilty to federal felony charges of visa fraud for running what Peter Tangalos, an attorney for 25 former QIS consultants, says was "a sweatshop for computer consultants."

In the end, no amount of juggling and clever tactics will completely reverse the power of workers to get higher wages at some point. Even now, the low rise in nominal wages may be artificially depressed by the fears of economic downturn that were in the air when budgets were set in late 1998. For now, the outlook for 2000 seems tame: Hewitt Associates says raises will stay at 4.2%. But if salaried employees who have been putting in extra-long hours to keep up with the sizzling economy demand more when budget season gives way to salary review season, then the figure could jump.

The good news for employers is that by making compensation more flexible, they are better prepared for the inevitable downturn. If things go bad, it's easy enough to stop giving signing bonuses, tell the temp workers to go home, and cancel the BMWs. That's both good and bad for the economy: Lower compensation erases consumer buying power at a vulnerable moment, but it preserves employer profits.

However the economic cycle plays out, the workers will never willingly go back to the old ways. In the New Workforce, even gray-templed loyalists like Reed Kingston are taking the kind of chances once reserved for a circus. And employers, like it or not, are learning to keep a lot of balls in the air.

VI-2: HR Managers Are Urged to Guard Employee Data Privacy

STEPHENIE OVERMAN

U.S. human resource managers must address the European Union's concerns about employee privacy or risk having a

HR News by Stephanie Overman. Copyright 1999 by Society for Human Resource Management. Reprinted with the permission of HR News published by the Society for Human Resource Management, Alexandria, VA, in the format Textbook via Copyright Clearance Center.

solution imposed upon them, a representative of the Society for Human Resource Management (SHRM) told participants at a meeting on the thorny topic.

"If we fail, the [European Union] legislature will step in," said Gerry Crispin, SPHR, vice president at large on SHRM's Board of Directors.

"We can't tolerate a situation in which the data we need to conduct business cannot be transferred," said Crispin, vice president of Shaker Advertising Agency of Oak Park, Illinois, and director of client staffing strategies in the firm's East Brunswick, New Jersey, office. "If a company can't access data, it is not conducting business."

U.S. officials, as well as companies and their HR managers, have been searching for a response to the European Union (E.U.) directive issued last year that prohibits companies from transmitting personal information to countries that do not offer "adequate" privacy protection (*HR News,* March, p. 1).

But the E.U. has not begun enforcing the directive, and several European countries have not passed the national laws necessary to carry it out.

U.S. Commerce Department officials have been trying to persuade European officials to accept a system under which U.S. companies would adopt a code of behavior and be allowed to regulate themselves.

U.S. and E.U. officials planned to meet in late June to further discuss the "safe harbor" concept in which businesses, by committing themselves to privacy principles, would seek approval from European commissioners to transmit personal data to and from the United States.

Under these principles, companies collecting personal information would provide three types of notification to individuals about whom information is being collected:

- What statistics are being collected?
- Why is the information being gathered?
- Which organizations will receive the data?

Individuals would be given an "opt out" mechanism that would permit them to decide whether and how personal information was used. The safe harbor approach would not automatically make all U.S. data transfers legal; companies would have to sign on to the principles.

In April a delegation of U.S. companies met with German data protection officials to discuss the acceptability of *Privacy & American Business's* customized model contract.

The Hackensack, New Jersey–based Center for Social and Legal Research, publisher of *Privacy & American Business,* reported that "German data protection officials thought the *P&AB* model was the best they have seen."

The model contract is conceived as a contract between affiliates of a U.S. company operating in an E.U. nation and the corporate unit in the United States that would be receiving and processing personal information about individuals in E.U. member states. It offers a comprehensive framework designed to ensure data protection and provides means of enforcement against errant U.S. data controllers or processors.

The nonprofit Center for Social and Legal Research said there is clearly a trend toward stricter regulations on the transfer and processing of personal data around the world. The new data protection systems set standards for the processing and transfer of all identifiable personal data—both consumer and human resource data.

Surveys show that consumers are concerned about how businesses use their personal information. But employees have registered strong confidence that employers handle their information properly, perhaps because the U.S. workplace is so regulated, with laws, government regulations, and voluntary standards specifying what employers can and cannot do in relation to their employees.

However, with the new directive, this standard of privacy protection in the HR context will not be enough to secure unhindered transfers of personally identifiable data to the United States from E.U. member states and from other nations with comprehensive, government-controlled data protection regulations.

PRIVACY ASSUMPTIONS

"The biggest issue, from my perspective, is that in this country we have certain assumptions about privacy that are just not standardized across all industries and companies," Crispin said in an interview following the meeting.

"We don't always disclose every transaction involving employee or candidate data. We don't disclose how long information is going to be retained," he said. "There are no standards, nothing that says, 'By such a time, data will disappear.'"

In the United States, privacy is not treated with the same kind of reverence as it is in many other countries. Crispin said, "We are a more public kind of society, but because of the incredible richness of emerging technology, the ability to find everything there is to know about everyone has increased.

"Privacy will become a much more important issue over the next several years. We should be working on it now. If we don't tackle it today, it will be much more difficult to deal with effectively down the road."

Crispin urged HR professionals to "come to the table in their own corporations. Find out what their company is doing about maintaining and disclosing all information. As employees become more educated they are asking more questions," not just in European companies but in U.S. organizations as well.

At the May meeting, Donald Harris of HR Privacy Solutions, a consulting practice in New York, discussed developing an HR information code of practice that could head off domestic pressure for legislation.

Harris said such a code also would strengthen sound management practices, build employee trust, and lay a solid foundation for planning and developing new uses of HR technology.

He said the most important elements of an HR code of practice would include data subject support and redress for data subjects, verification of compliance, and penalties for noncompliance.

Alan F. Westin, editor of *Privacy & American Business* and co-chairman with Harris of the meeting, noted that Australia and Canada are about to pass omnibus national public-private sector legislation to bring them in compliance with the E.U.

Japan also is looking at an industry-led model that is less regulatory, Westin reported.

VI-3: Beware Abridging E-Speech
Blanket Bans on Personal E-Mail and Internet Use at Work Can Lead to Trouble—for Employers

SHARON C. ZEHE

By now, most employers know they need to set policies concerning the personal use of the Internet and e-mail in the workplace to prohibit harassing e-mail or forbid access to pornographic Web sites.

As a result, some employers simply have banished all personal use of the Internet and e-mail so they don't have to act as a watchdog.

But what if an employee violates this "no personal use" policy by accessing his favorite union Web site to see what the union has to offer? What if an employee

---

Used with permission of Sharon C. Zehe.

sends a message to another employee, or to her manager, criticizing a management policy?

Can the employer fire these employees for violating the "no personal use" policy or for insubordination?

Recent federal agency decisions suggest they cannot be fired. And that means it's time to rethink outright bans.

How big an issue is this for employers? A March survey of Minnesota's largest publicly held companies by the *Star Tribune* shows that nearly 20 percent do not permit employees to use e-mail or Internet access for personal reasons. Most respondents (79.5 percent) permit personal use, but with some restrictions.

TOLERABLE DISSENT

The National Labor Relations Board (NLRB), a government agency that sets and enforces rules that protect an employee's right to organize, recently ruled that when a company terminated a computer programmer for sending a less-than-flattering e-mail about his company's proposed vacation policy, it had violated the National Labor Relations Act (NLRA). The company claimed it had fired the programmer for failing to treat others with courtesy and respect, not for the content of his message. But the NLRB ruled that even though the message contained flippant and grating language, it was not so intolerable as to lose the protection of the law.

Some background: The company had offered a new vacation program to employees that suggested employees actually would get more days off. The programmer didn't think the statement was correct, and sent an e-mail to all employees, explaining that the policy was not what the company claimed.

The chief operating officer offered the programmer a choice: Either apologize for the message or lose his job. The programmer chose termination, and filed a complaint with the NLRB. The board found that the employer had retaliated against the employee for engaging in "concerted activity" protected by the NLRA, and ordered the company to reinstate the employee with back pay.

The interesting part about this case is that the programmer was not in a union. He wasn't even trying to start a union. He simply wanted to ensure that employees understood that the vacation policy was not as great as the company had stated it would be.

The lesson for employers from this case? When deciding to terminate an employee for misuse of e-mail or the Internet, ask yourself whether what the employee was doing was protected activity. If the activity relates to conditions of employment or a complaint, and it furthers a group interest, it is protected under the NLRA.

That means employees who are campaigning for a safe workplace probably are protected from termination or retaliation under the act, but an employee who conducts an e-mail campaign for her own promotion probably is not.

ESSENTIAL COMMUNICATION

What about complete bans on personal use of computers and e-mail? The NLRB has issued a memorandum that suggests these policies are unlawful because of the importance of e-mail for communications for employees. Many companies provide laptop computers to employees and e-mail is the major source of communication between employees; also, it is hard to distinguish between working time and non-working time for professional employees. The heavy reliance on electronic communication demonstrates the importance of computers and of e-mail in the workplace. Therefore, employers should not prohibit employees from personal communications via e-mail.

What's an employer to do? First of all, establish a policy that addresses a specific issue. If the goal is to prohibit harassing or discriminatory messages, create a policy that states just that.

If the goal is to prohibit release of trade-secret information or prevent downloads because of potential virus problems, limit the policy accordingly.

The act allows an employer to establish rules that balance its rights with an employee's. But don't issue a blanket policy prohibiting all non-business communications.

Second, if your company has an e-mail or Internet usage policy, make sure it is enforced consistently. If the policy states that occasional personal use is acceptable, yet you are aware that some employees abuse this policy, don't choose to enforce it when you learn an employee has accessed a union Web site or is attempting to organize the workforce.

There is nothing more suspect, and potentially unlawful, than an employer suddenly enforcing an e-mail policy once it learns of union activity.

Finally, watch for further developments in this area. It appears the NLRB is not done with this developing area of law and intends to ensure that it is on top of the issues. The board instructed all regional offices to submit all cases involving employee use of computers for protected activities to headquarters. This means the board is aware of the potential issues and plans to address them head-on.

In an age in which employees are becoming more savvy in protecting their rights and increasingly are challenging an employer's right to fire them, more professionals are turning to the act for protection.

Employers need to familiarize themselves with the NRLA and ask themselves whether the employee has engaged in activity that's protected under the act before taking any job action.

VI-4: Business Travel

The World Bank Gauges the Toll Travel Takes on Employees and Looks for Ways to Soften the Effect

JOE SHARKEY

"My husband missed our son's high school graduation due to business travel. None of us has ever forgotten."

A lot of words were spoken at the World Bank's two-day symposium late last month "Stress, the Business Traveler, and Corporate Health" in Washington. But those two declarative sentences, among the many responses elicited by World Bank

Reprinted from *The New York Times* (May 10, 2000): C8.

managers who surveyed traveling staff members and their spouses, packed real wallop. *"None of us has ever forgotten."*

Corporate America, which often prides itself on the supposed invincibility of the legions of men and women it dispatches around the world, could learn a few things about employee health and welfare from the World Bank. The last two years, the bank has sponsored seminars intended to make employers think more responsibly about the effect ever-increasing travel has on employees and on the people closest to them.

The World Bank, an international organization based in Washington, sends nearly 5,000 employees on international business trips each year, for a total of more than 250,000 days away from home. In 1997, the World Bank sponsored a detailed clinical study that discovered that significantly higher rates of health insurance claims were filed by employees who traveled compared with those who did not. Even more remarkable, frequent travelers, who typically regard themselves as tough and resilient, also account for three times the claims for treatment of stress, anxiety, depression, and other psychological-adjustment disorders attributable directly to the demands of being on the road.

This year, prompted by that 1997 study, the bank convened health professionals and managers from 50 corporate and government organizations to discuss follow-up research that was commissioned to examine more closely the psychological impact of frequent business travel.

"We asked our colleagues what's going on?" said Bernhard H. Liese, a senior health adviser and the former medical director of the bank.

The answer that came back, Dr. Liese said, was that adverse effects from travel were "mirrored in the family" as well as in the workplace.

The 1997 clinical study compared health insurance claims filed by 4,700 World Bank managers and professional workers who had taken international business trips with claims filed by 6,000 World Bank employees who did not travel. Across the board, the survey showed a strong correlation between frequency of travel and higher reports of respiratory infections, gastrointestinal distress, skin disorders, and back pain—all understandable, if somewhat surprising, consequences of heavy travel to a wide variety of places.

But the survey's findings of far higher rates of treatment for psychological disorders were especially startling, Dr. Liese said. That is because only about a third of the World Bank's employees in Washington are from North America. The rest come from countries where there is far greater reluctance "to seek treatment from a psychologist," he said.

The follow-up survey on the risks of that psychological stress was by the same team of clinical researchers, which reported: "As international business travel grows, increasing numbers of travelers will be exposed to health risks, including widely varying physical and psychological stressors." In the their report, published in the scientific journal *Occupational and Environmental Medicine*, they added that "business travel is a unique challenge to the health of employees, which to date has not been studied extensively."

High on the list of emotional stresses for heavy business travelers is worry about personal and family lives, including adjustment problems suffered by spouses and children of an employee who is often away from home. Anxiety about the workload piling up back at the office also ranked high on the stress list.

Typically, the researchers said, traveling employees are disinclined to take time off to rest from a tiring business trip. "Although most respondents think it is necessary, very few of them reported that they actually take rest days after business travel," the study said.

Of course, some corporations and bosses pride themselves on instilling a gung-ho workplace culture that presses worn-out corporate travelers to hit the road on demand and show up at the office bright and early on return, no matter where they flew in from the night before.

"Two-thirds of all respondents reported that their managers rarely or never formally grant" a day off after a long trip, reflecting a perceived lack of sanction for taking rest.

Participants at the symposium heard a lot of practical advice on making life easier on traveling employees: train managers to be aware that changing travel dates at the last minute can adversely affect people's lives; be more flexible in allowing travelers to make their own arrangements and to exercise more control over their lives when they are on the road; compensate traveling employees for their weekends; let them call home daily on the company's nickel.

But the most resonant message came from Dr. Liese, who said more attention must be paid to "corporate responsibilities" in employee travel, an area that lies beyond the reach of any governmental workplace or health-and-safety regulator.

Corporations should be accountable, Dr. Liese said, "to their most valuable resource—their staff."

VI-5: Addicted to Sex
A Primal Problem Emerges from the Shadows in a New—and Dangerous—Corporate Environment

BETSY MORRIS

"Most of my patients are CEOs or doctors or attorneys or priests," says Patrick J. Carnes. "They are people with a great deal of power. We have corporate America's leadership marching through here, and they're paying cash because they don't want anybody to know."

Carnes works at a treatment center called the Meadows, an unassuming little oasis of forbearance tucked among the saguaro cactus and sage in Wickenburg, Arizona. His title is clinical director of sexual disorder services, and he is widely considered the nation's leading expert on what has come to be called, for lack of a better term, sex addiction. He says he treated four *Fortune* 500 chief executives last year.

Not far from the Meadows, in the southern part of the state, is another addiction treatment facility called Sierra Tucson. Six months ago it formalized the work it had been doing with sex addicts into an intensive recovery program. Demand has been strong enough to warrant a waiting list, even at an average cost of $850 a day for inpatient treatment that typically lasts 26 days.

If that price seems a little steep, there are suddenly lots of alternatives for a person seeking "The Cure." No fewer than five 12-step programs for sex addicts are now operating free of charge in cities and towns across the country. The National Council on Sexual Addiction and Compulsivity says it gets about 50 e-mails and 30 to 40 phone calls each week from people seeking help for themselves or for a loved one. It has a list of roughly 100 therapists who have experience with sex addiction and says it is adding new names to that list at a rate of about six a week. The Employee Assistance Professionals Association, whose members are often on a company's frontline when an employee has an addiction problem, is offering a workshop on cybersex addiction at its annual conference in October. "It is definitely on our radar screen," a spokeswoman for the association says. "Our folks

Reprinted from *Fortune* (May 10, 1999): 68–80.

are becoming more aware of the fact that sex addiction is prevalent. They are anticipating they could really help people if they were able to bring this up and do a better job of recognizing the symptoms."

As the Bill and Monica drama has shown, sex addiction is not necessarily what you thought it was. It is often not about the pervert, the exhibitionist, or the pornographer, although it can be. It is about your neighbor down the street who turns out to be, as everybody learns during the divorce, a hopeless womanizer. It's about that sales associate with the slinky dresses and flirty smile who can't seem to behave herself when she's on the road. It's about the CEO and his "woman problem." It's about a guy I'll call Mac Henry, who spent most of his career in the chemical industry and is now chief executive of his own small technology company in Phoenix. "I had sex with hundreds and hundreds of women I met in travels and business. Some numerous times, some one time, some whenever I was in town," he says. "I believe you will find a lot of people out there like me. Executives are usually driven, power hungry, and egomaniacs. Hard drinking and women are often part of our story."

So, you ask, what's new? After all, we're well aware of the sexual exploits of athletes and entertainers. The dalliances of public servants were well chronicled way back in the 1970s by Sam Janus, Barbara Bess, and Carol Saltus, who embarked on a study of prostitutes and ended up writing a book instead about their best clients: politicians. It was called *A Sexual Profile of Men in Power.* Surely this kind of stuff also goes on in the executive suite. And anyway, there's fierce controversy over whether hypersexuality can even be called an addiction. The American Psychiatric Association says no, an addiction must be a physiological dependence on chemical substances like drugs or alcohol. What looks like sex addiction is more likely behavior symptomatic of some-

thing else, such as an anxiety disorder, obsessive-compulsive disorder, or manic depression, says Chester Schmidt, a psychiatry professor at the Johns Hopkins University School of Medicine and head of the APA work group on sexual disorders for the latest edition of the *Diagnostic & Statistical Manual of Mental Disorders,* the APA's bible of mental problems. Calling it sex addiction, he says, amounts to pop psychology—although he bets the association will "take another look at this area" in its next revision of the DSM.

But of course there is something new: a seismic shift in social context. Just consider the old clinical labels for this kind of behavior. In women it was nymphomania; in men, Don Juanism. "Ten or 20 years ago you might have had a doctor whose hand wandered, but he was a good doctor, a fine upstanding citizen, a churchgoer, so nobody called him on it," says Al Cooper, clinical director of the San Jose Marital and Sexuality Centre and head trainer at Stanford University's counseling center. These days harassment lawsuits make it very dangerous for companies to allow a sex addict to be a boss.

In the new legal (and, let's face it, political) climate, sex addiction has come out of the closet, much as alcoholism has in recent decades. For much of this century, everybody thought the alcoholic was the bum on the park bench; in the 1970s and 1980s it dawned on people that he was also the guy having three-martini lunches at the private club. Now lunchtime martinis are frowned upon, but circumstances are just right for sex addiction to flourish. Take a group of baby-boomer men and women (yes, women) who came of age during the sexual revolution. Put them into the anxiety-producing pressure cooker of today's work environment. Ratchet up the pressure to produce. Take away time to nurture real family relationships. Give easy access to cybersex, phone sex, prostitutes. Abracadabra: If a person is so inclined, he can fill his addictive need and 15 minutes later be back for a meeting. No hangover. "What other addiction is like it?" asks James Cassidy, who runs an addiction treatment center in Palm Beach, Florida.

Carnes estimates that 6% of the population has this problem. Cooper believes the percentage of men in our society who are sexually compulsive is between 4% and 6%. It is tough to know whether that percentage is increasing, but Carnes and Cooper suspect it is. At the San Jose clinic, Cooper says, "the fastest-growing group is successful professionals. Society is becoming increasingly sexualized. Hard to imagine, but it is. You see things in the paper, more sexual programs in prime time, more advertising. It gives people the impression that sex is the answer." Adds Nancy Friday, author of numerous books, including *My Secret Garden* and *Women on Top*, both about women's sexual fantasies: "All the songs . . . the media . . . are telling you to try it again. Everybody's doing it. Everybody's got it but you." This has fueled great confusion about sex, she says. "For a lot of people, sex has become a substitute for love, for caring, for being truly wanted."

Then, of course, there is the Internet, which brings porn right into your study or office. It's free. It's convenient. You probably won't get caught (which is important, since fear is a powerful impulse control for a lot of people). You definitely won't get AIDS. Want to see? Just close your office door and, for starters, type in Persian Kitty. . . .

Now a lot of people can handle that. But others can't. They tend to be people with a genetic or psychological predisposition to addictive or compulsive behavior. Trauma, which can include sexual or emotional abuse, and the work environment may also play a role. These people can end up compulsive gamblers, heavy drinkers, compulsive exercisers, type-A workaholics. Often they are more than one of the above.

When they address one problem, another pops up. "It's a little like a jack-in-the box," says Carole deLucia, a New York psychotherapist and employee-assistance consultant.

In extreme cases these behaviors look a lot like addictions. In some people, enthusiastic sex becomes excessive sex becomes compulsive sex—and a sex addict can't stop despite truly grave consequences. A 42-year-old television producer in the Dallas area says he nearly sabotaged his career three years ago when he begun using the Internet. Until then he'd mostly buy girlie magazines, throw them away, and see how long he could go (usually two weeks) before buying more. But when he began to surf porn sites on the Web, it consumed him. Before long he found that instead of working on his documentaries, he was locking the door of his home office (so his wife wouldn't catch him) and spending 7 hours of his 10-hour workday downloading porn and compulsively masturbating. "My work was getting very, very stacked up. I lost prestigious jobs because of it," he says. "It was to the point of paralyzing my business." He is now in recovery with Sex Addicts Anonymous.

When Dr. Carnes surveyed 1,000 sex addicts a decade ago (180 of them women), 80% said they'd become less productive at their jobs, often because they were pursuing sex, fantasizing about it on the job, or exhausted from staying up too late doing those things. One of the respondents said he planned his workweek around his affairs.

Where there is sex addiction in the workplace, there is also coverup—which affects lots of people who have to pick up the slack. Louis D. Cox, a New York psychologist, has turned his years of expertise in addiction therapy into a consulting career, advising companies like Sony, AT&T, and American Airlines on how to cope with big egos and compulsive types and have more smoothly running teams.

Not infrequently, he says, there is an addict in the midst. "That person will impact the whole system," he says, as others joke about him, cover for him, lie for him, do his work, or get furious at him.

Sex not only can muck up a corporate culture, it can cause a hailstorm of legal problems, too. Just look at what happened at Astra USA, now a unit of the London pharmaceutical giant AstraZeneca. Astra officials and managers engaged in a continuous pattern of sexual harassment of female sales representatives, according to allegations in an EEOC lawsuit filed last year. This included allowing the highest managers in the company to make sexually offensive comments, engage in unwanted touching, and require female sales reps to socialize with them as a condition of employment, according to the allegations. The socializing included propositioning, grabbing, and kissing, according to the EEOC suit.

Astra USA agreed last year to settle that lawsuit for $9.9 million, without admitting any violations of the law. In 1996, Astra USA had fired its CEO, Lars Bildman, after the harassment allegations surfaced. Last year it sued him, charging him with fraud, breach of fiduciary duty, and waste of corporate assets and claiming that he both engaged in sexual harassment and tolerated or excused the similar inappropriate conduct of others. Now Bildman and his former employer are locked in a ferocious legal battle. Bildman has denied allegations that he defrauded Astra USA or engaged in misconduct against the company. He has also denied all allegations that he engaged in or condoned a pattern of sexual harassment at Astra. In court papers, he is claiming that Astra breached its employment contract with him. He also alleges, among other things, that Astra tried to discredit him by portraying him as a harasser and hired media consultants to try to destroy his reputation and to bias potential jurors and judges. An Astra spokesman says: "The company views this as an effort by Mr. Bildman to distract attention from his wrongdoing." On yet another legal front, Bildman pleaded guilty to criminal charges of filing false tax returns and is in prison.

The company has been picking up the pieces. Lynn Tetrault, Astra's human resources vice president, says the company has installed new leadership and overhauled its corporate culture. "When it became clear that there was a serious problem, we reacted swiftly," Tetrault says. "If you have a person not behaving the way they should, you have people who will do the same. Or you have people who are inclined to turn their heads. Or you have people who don't like what's going on and who leave."

It's not an easy problem to fix. It's not as easy as transferring a Casanova to a different department—although transferring him to a different continent might solve the problem for a while. That's how the *Fortune* 500 have frequently handled these kinds of problems in the past. It's not as easy as sitting the offender down and telling him to clean up his act. In some cases you're dealing with somebody who wants to stop but can't; in other cases you're dealing with somebody who doesn't see that he has a problem.

Consider the story of the Phoenix executive Mac Henry. He grew up in an upper-middle-class family, the charming and hard-partying son of a *Fortune* 500 food-company executive. You know the type—athletic, popular, seductive, oh-so-much fun at a party. He bounced around several colleges without getting a degree and landed a job at a small chemical company. The business was great sport, a great place for his boundless energy, and he had a knack for it. By the age of 26 he had a job at Occidental Petroleum that put him in charge of operations in Ramsey, New Jersey, and also in Santa Ana, California. He would fly first class and ride in limos, all on an unlimited expense account—pretty intoxicating stuff for a young man prone to extremes. "The business world just facilitated my bad habits," he says. Later, as his jobs entailed more globe-trotting, it was nothing to him to work a 14- or 16-hour day, fly to Singapore, fly to Europe, sleep several hours, do it over again, and end the day by drinking and picking up women. He'd been married at 18 and had two young children back in California at the time, but family was something you did on Sunday mornings. On the road, as he was about half the time, he had an endless stream of pretty women—attorneys' wives he'd meet on airplanes, a Merrill Lynch investment banker he met at a cocktail party, a sales manager for Union Carbide who sat next to him on the rental-car shuttle in a snowstorm in Cleveland. After he found out they were staying in the same hotel, he tipped the hotel clerk to get adjoining rooms. "I took her to dinner and spent the night with her. Can you imagine?" he asks. "She'd been married just two years."

Sometimes he had prostitutes. "Any hotel in the world, the bellman or the limo driver will tell you how and when and what. A limo driver picks you up at J.F.K., and all you need to say is, 'I'm in town for a week. I'm looking for beautiful women.' And you slip him a fifty," he says, and he'll either slip you back a list of numbers or have somebody call. But most of the time Henry preferred to court women on his own. The chase gave him a high he likens to a runner's endorphin rush. "It was like clinching the big order, cutting the big deal," he says.

But lest you think this is just a Y-chromosome thing, consider the story of one Tucson small-business owner who started sleeping around in high school after she was forced into sex on a date at age 14. "I was a young lady with low self-esteem and all the things guys wanted at that age. Cute, charming, big breasts, whatever," she

says. For her, too, sex became a power trip. She loved foreign men, and she would fly to exotic places to meet them. She also loved blue-collar workers. And she was so into objectifying men that she once rear-ended another car while ogling some construction workers. "I kind of felt like I had a male ego. I saw myself as the aggressor. It's a big power-lust game," she says.

This didn't help her business. Sometimes she would ruin professional relationships with businessmen by sleeping with them. For a time, she says, "one of my employees was robbing me blind. I should have known. But he was cute; he had charmed me." Even worse, she found herself seeking out lovers "who were not safe to be with." The more dangerous the sexual experience, the bigger the thrill. She finally ended up in a long-term relationship with a man she believes was a sociopath; she is convinced she'd be dead by now had she not eventually joined Sex Addicts Anonymous.

For Mac Henry the sex was all just part of his professional persona. "I was aggressive and successful. I never dreamed I had a problem," he says. And it was all part of the culture. Early on, on the lower rungs of the corporate ladder, "we did a lot of entertaining at strip joints. You'd use your American Express card—all those places took them, even the escort services. They all had legitimate-sounding names." An executive at one of his early jobs remarks that Henry was the "hardest-drinking womanizer" he'd ever met. It was a compliment. "There are a lot of people who can walk that fine line," Henry says.

But those who go over the line usually end up in trouble or in treatment, often both. It's not a pretty journey. Two men sought help at Al Cooper's San Jose clinic recently because of harassment lawsuits. One was being sued for the second time; the other had lost his job. The head of a West Coast hospital also called. He told Cooper he was worried that three of the hospital's doctors were sexually compulsive. He wanted advice on how to intervene.

Yes, there are such things as corporate interventions for sex addicts. Usually the offender is summoned under some pretext to a conference room. There he finds the CEO or another top executive, the general counsel, a human resources executive, and one of the new breed of therapists specializing in this kind of thing. Frequently nothing is said about the employee's sex life, which often is all tangled up with drugs or alcohol. The people in the room may not even know exactly what the underlying problem is. But they know about prolonged absences from work, unfinished tasks, embarrassing behavior. All this has been documented, and the evidence is presented to the employee. He is encouraged, if he wants to keep his job, to meet privately for a psychological evaluation with a guy like Vincent Casolaro, who used to be co-director of employee assistance for Pan Am and now does corporate interventions for a number of *Fortune* 500 companies. Typically, says Casolaro, by the time a case reaches him, "the person is at the end."

Which is how an executive might end up at the Meadows or Sierra Tucson, where treatment often includes therapy to change thought processes and behaviors, role playing, 12-step meetings, and sometimes medication. Both centers say that about one-third of their patients are receiving treatment for sex addiction. Some are gay; most are not. Sierra Tucson estimates that about 80% of those patients are corporate or professional. The Meadows puts that figure at more like 70%.

The Meadows, run by retired Air Force Lt. Col. Pat Mellody, is strictly no-nonsense—an austere little retrofitted dude ranch with a tiny, unheated swimming pool. It has 70 beds, of which about 55 were filled on average last quarter. The typical stay is four to five weeks, at $900 to $1,000 a day—which more than half the time isn't covered by insurance. Here, pleasure reading is usually prohibited; phone calls are limited to 5 or 10 minutes. The only vice allowed is smoking (in "his" and "her" smoking pits to discourage fraternization).

At the Meadows, after extensive medical and psychiatric evaluations, you are grouped with other sex addicts and subjected to a regime that can be both grueling and gruesome. You spend a week in a therapy boot camp called Survivors, picking through your early life for trauma, abuse, neglect, and anything else that might have contributed to your problems. You write an autobiography, detailing all your transgressions and their repercussions, to "get in touch with all the havoc you've caused in other peoples' lives," says Mellody. You get lectures (several hours a day), 12-step meetings (almost nightly), and group therapy (three hours a day) with the likes of Maureen Canning, who had three CEOs in one of her groups in December. "A very high-functioning group," she says. And just how does one conduct therapy with a CEO? "It's like doing a dance. You're looking for a way in, the point that hurts the most," she says. "Then you go for the jugular."

Sierra Tucson is much more resortlike. Everything here has a pretty name. The two dormitories are called Morning Star and Crescent Moon. The medical assessment and detox unit is referred to as Desert Flower, so as not to seem threatening. This place, too, has lots of lectures and lots of therapy, but it takes a holistic approach to treatment that may include horseback riding, massage, or "body nourishment activities" at the recreation center (although this is often locked so that compulsive exercisers can't sneak in to pump iron). It has a much better lap pool. Sierra Tucson has 63 beds and a waiting list.

An important part of the treatment at both places is family week, during which some assortment of spouses, ex-spouses, kids, in-laws, mistresses, and girlfriends gathers to help the addict get even clearer about his problems. That's actually how Mac Henry ended up at Sierra Tucson: not on his own account but because he'd been summoned to attend family week for a family member in treatment for depression and addiction to prescription drugs. Now, family week, as you can imagine, is a solemn affair, and the visiting relatives are asked to take it seriously, forgoing television and newspapers to really focus on the matter at hand. Henry arrived at his relative's family week on a Tuesday with his girlfriend in tow and his golf clubs in the car. He'd gotten a suite at the El Conquistador, a resort and country club in Tucson. "I thought I was on vacation," he says. By Friday, it dawned on him that he, too, might have a problem.

He had not, in fact, been able to walk that fine line. He had gone into business on his own, and his technology company had done well, growing to about $3 million in revenues in 1995, but his drinking and carousing had continued, and he'd gotten more reckless. His wife had filed for divorce; his daughter had made it clear that he was no longer welcome to visit his grandchildren. His son had joined the family business and was put in charge during Henry's increasingly long absences overseas. But with Henry's neglect, the business started to falter. By the time he arrived at Sierra Tucson, his son had gotten fed up and quit, and his credit cards were tapped out. "I was in my own business, not in the corporate world where you have people who can cover for your mistakes," he says. "I didn't have anybody left to cover for me."

During his relative's family week he owned up to an alcohol problem. But he was grouped with some sex addicts, including a doctor, an entertainer, and a McDonald's franchisee who had taxied his girlfriends around in his private jet. As Henry was grilled and prodded by Sierra Tucson's counselors, he came to see how intertwined his drinking was with his sex. "For me, they went hand in hand," he says. "I couldn't have one without the other."

This phenomenon is known as cross-addiction, and it has become better understood in recent years. "I see a lot of overlap," says Stephen Pesce, a New York City psychotherapist and interventionist. His experience was mostly in substance abuse and other compulsive behaviors, but he was finding that those problems were so frequently intertwined with sex addiction—more than 50% of the time—that two years ago he recruited a sex therapist to join his practice. His clients include a handful of athletes and trust fund babies but mostly people in advertising and banking and on Wall Street.

Wall Street, Pesce says, is the worst. "The sex down on Wall Street is unbelievable, with the prostitution and the porn. It is huge," he says. People who choose that kind of work tend to be thrill seekers to begin with. They're under excruciating stress for a big part of the day. At the market's close, "when they come out of there, they are so jacked up they don't know what to do with themselves," Pesce says. Since it's Wall Street, there is no shortage of temptations. "I've got guys who are just dying down there. We've been trying to go out and talk to more companies, and educate them about prevention. But Wall Street doesn't want to hear about it," says Pesce. It is still in the dark ages on this issue.

Just check out the corporate culture at Lev Lieberbaum, a small brokerage firm that got into big trouble last year with the EEOC. The firm employed roughly 300 people at offices in Manhattan and on Long Island. It was the Wild West, and we're not just talking about catcalls, lewd comments, or the hiring of "wow girls" on the basis of their looks, according to allegations in a harassment suit filed two years ago by three employees. We're talking about guys who would ask for oral sex, according to that suit, expose themselves, proposition the women, and make remarks like "Wear a bra—your nipples are getting hard," according to allegations by the EEOC.

The EEOC case was settled last year for $1.8 million, without any admission of guilt. The firm closed last August. The private suit is still pending. Mark Lev, the firm's co-founder, is now doing private investment banking for a firm he won't name. He says the allegations against his firm were "misrepresentative and trumped. The allegations against me were categorically false." But he also says "there is some scintilla of truth in some of the allegations. We had 300 employees; 250 were under 30. When that happens, you're going to have intracompany relationships. It's unavoidable." He blames some of the industry's questionable behavior on a young workforce and a stressful environment. "Part of the business is volatile," he says. "It causes emotional swings. I've sat at Quotron machines all day and seen the market move, and I've watched the faces of young brokers. They don't know how to react to a bad market. They're frustrated; they're emotional. They don't know how to deal with these volatile things, and they react the way they know how, which is not always appropriate."

Sex addiction and sexual harassment are not the same thing, of course. But it's easy to see how a climate of sexual excess can create a spawning ground for the addict. Take the case of a trader who walked away from Wall Street two years ago. He'd grown up in a New York suburb, the youngest of five children, and had decided after graduating that he wanted to be a paratrooper. "I wanted to jump out of helicopters," he says. But a relative convinced him that he could get the same adrenaline rush and make lots more money by coming to work for him on Wall Street. "The needle went into my arm the minute I walked onto that floor," he says.

He started as a runner at 17 and eventually got his own license. He also got married and had two kids along the way. But most days after the market's close, instead of going home he'd go to massage parlors to find prostitutes. "I did that through my first nine years of marriage. My wife didn't have a clue," he says.

He was never a drinker, but he was definitely a gambler. Over the years he found himself taking bigger and bigger trading risks. "When something went down I'd buy more, because I just couldn't take a loss. I got to the point where I was having really big winning days and really big losing days," he says. But he managed overall to win more than he lost. He was able, despite a prostitute habit that was costing as much as $750 a week, to save enough money to finance his recovery.

It took a lot to get him there, though. For a long time he just didn't think he had a problem. "Many of the guys would see prostitutes," he says. "A lot of them talked about it. Certain guys owned massage parlors. There was a lot of bragging about it." It was only when he began to have a serious affair with an acquaintance that he began feeling guilt about being unfaithful to his wife. The prostitutes hadn't really bothered him; they didn't count. "Now that's denial. That's Clinton," he says. "All sex is not sex." He decided that his new affair was true love, gave up prostitutes, left his wife, and moved in with his paramour. But then he began seeing prostitutes again. "It scared me. I couldn't stop."

The torment finally drove him to check himself into Del Amo Hospital in Torrance, California. "I had to convince myself I was going to a resort," he says. "I actually packed my bathing suits." He lasted three weeks at Del Amo before getting kicked out for fraternizing with his girlfriend during family week, then spent four months at KeyStone Center, an extended-care facility in Chester, Pennsylvania. That was four years ago. He reconciled with his wife, and they moved back in together. He returned to his job on

Wall Street for a while. "It was like standing at a roulette table. I knew eventually they'd carry me away on a stretcher," he says. Two years ago he quit, which was tough for a guy with a family to support and no college degree. Since then he has been doing consulting and lots of therapy.

Is Wall Street all that different from other industries? Probably. It is one of those industries, like music or movies, where you're supposed to be outrageous and excessive. When it comes to sexual misbehavior, "it's not just across companies but across industries where you see patterns," says Jill Kanin-Lovers, human resources senior vice president at Avon Products. She has a basis of comparison, having had top-level human resources jobs at IBM, American Express, and Towers Perrin before joining Avon. "It tends to be more in male-dominated fields, where you're dealing with the dealmakers and pretty strong egos and people who feel they are above it all. Sometimes that translates into naughty behaviors."

Female sex addicts are different. But for all sorts of complicated cultural reasons, their problems are even less talked about and more poorly understood than men's. "Women can cover it up a lot better than men," says the Tucson small-business owner. "There really still are those archetypes of women: the goddess, the mother, the whore. We are supposed to be so virtuous, we don't do those sorts of things," she says.

Women may manifest their addiction differently, too. They may choose to become barmaids or exotic dancers. They may have serial extramarital affairs. Many may be less addicted to the sex itself than to the fantasy that goes along with it, says Carol Ross, a counselor at Sierra Tucson. In some research she did with women sex addicts, she says, a conversation with an attractive man could lead to compulsive thinking: "'Wow, maybe we'll go out. What would it be like living together? What would it be like having my first name, his last name? What would our

children look like?' She's created this whole fantasy relationship in an hour."

Different companies have very different standards for what's considered inappropriate. "We had a very senior salesperson who was a very bad actor" at IBM, recalls Kanin-Lovers. "He was one of our best producers, but we fired him. There was no way we could allow him to go unpunished." Still, she says, "I grant you, you can go to other companies that will turn a blind eye if the guy is delivering results. You have companies that will say, 'We care No. 1 about results, so we'll ignore these problems.'"

That might have been the case with Robert Hammer, the former Minneapolis-based manager for headhunting firm Management Recruiters International, according to two lawyers involved in litigation against the firm. "Hammer was a phenomenally successful sales manager, one of their most profitable. Great at bringing in recruiters, very personable," says Lloyd Zimmerman, senior trial attorney on the case for the EEOC. "He fancied himself a ladies' man. It was well known he was a lech. New employees would be warned about him. If he did something wrong, people would say, 'That's Bob.'" In a private suit against Hammer and MRI, one of his account executives accused him of grabbing her posterior, trying to kiss her, and saying all kinds of nasty things. "I think there was an economic benefit in not getting rid of him. He was a producer," says Donald Brown, attorney for the Minneapolis firm Winthrop & Weinstine, which handled that lawsuit. The company won't comment on what went on at the time. Hammer was fired, and two years ago MRI settled the EEOC suit for $1.3 million, denied any wrongdoing, agreed never to rehire Hammer, and sent a letter of apology to the 17 women who had worked for him.

George Antrim III, Hammer's attorney, says Hammer denied the allegations during arbitration in the private lawsuit. "From my perspective, I believed him," Antrim says. He disagrees with characterizations of Hammer as a lecher. "You could talk to a lot of women who worked for Bob who'd also disagree with that. He's a strong personality. People have strong feelings about him. If you talked to 100 people, half would love him, half would hate him."

Some guys never get into trouble at work. Mac Henry was one of those. He had a couple of affairs with colleagues, but those were consensual. He broke them off without much trouble. Now he sits in the sunny corner office of the business that he nearly ran into the ground, with pictures of his children and grandchildren on his bookshelf. He left Sierra Tucson 4 1/2 years ago and hasn't had a drink since. He's had one girlfriend for most of that time and says he hasn't cheated on her. He has a new set of golfing buddies, five other Phoenix movers and shakers who are also recovering from various addictions (two others had problems with sex addiction). "We don't do booze, and we don't do women," he says. He spent last Christmas with his entire family. He has taken his crazy, compulsive, type-A behavior and he has thrown himself into work. He has built his business back up to

$6 million in sales. It got a clean rating from Dun & Bradstreet last fall. "Am I a workaholic now? Damned straight," he says. "I just took a lot of my energy, and I moved it over here. It's a lot safer."

Recently, Mac Henry sent out a memo to his staff, informing them that their computers were company property and that their Internet downloads would be subject to inspection by management without notice. Why did he do it? Because he'd noticed that some of his employees had been downloading the porn sites. One of them had been traveling with him on a plane, and when he turned on his laptop a picture of a nude woman popped up. "If they want to look at porno stuff, that's their business," he said. But not in his shop and not on his time. "I'm not going to enable them," he says.

Increasingly the more enlightened companies are taking this approach, too. It is no longer okay to have wandering hands, no matter how good you are at your job. Hard drinking and womanizing no longer equate to "tough boss, good at taking risks." Sex addiction is no longer an executive-suite perk; it's bad for business. That may not be one of the 12 steps, but it's a step in the right direction.

VI-6: The One Clear Line in Interoffice Romance Has Become Blurred
Companies Change Policies to Deal with Bosses Who Date Subordinates

CAROL HYMOWITZ AND ELLEN JOAN POLLOCK

International Business Machines Corp. used to warn managers that they risked losing their jobs if they had a romance with a

subordinate. In its Managers Manual four years ago, IBM said, "A manager may not date or have a romantic relationship with an employee who reports through his or her management chain, even when the relationship is voluntary and welcome."

Today, IBM managers get more latitude. They can become romantically involved with subordinates as long as they stop supervising them. In management-training sessions and written guidelines, the company stresses that it won't tolerate a mixing of passion and performance reviews; it is up to managers to make a choice.

"If they want to pursue a relationship with a subordinate, we ask them to step forward and transfer to another job within or outside the company," a spokesman says. "The onus is on them to transfer, not the subordinate who may have less flexibility."

This policy change is evident at a growing number of companies, including AT&T Corp., Corning Inc., Xerox Corp., and Fleet Financial Group. And it signals an emerging view in corporate America that romances between bosses and underlings are simply another issue to be managed, not something that can be banned by corporate fiat.

"KNEE-JERK REACTION"

"Fifteen, even ten years ago, there would be a knee-jerk reaction to fire the people involved," says Jay Waks, a labor lawyer at Kaye Scholer, a New York law firm. But today, the attitude is "you just can't control human nature, and you're not going to fire well-trained people simply because they're having a relationship. There's more of a practical view—to manage the relationship rather than ban it."

A decade ago, most companies adhered to a double standard. Typically, while relationships between bosses and underlings were officially barred, they occurred anyway, with employers usually looking the other way. The more powerful and well-liked a boss, the more license he had to romance whomever he pleased. He and his boss often reasoned that "guys will be guys," and counted on women not to make waves.

The power gap in such relationships was generally vast. The women were usually secretaries and often served as second wives

to their bosses, doing all sorts of personal chores at work, from fetching coffee to picking up shirts at the dry cleaners. If the relationship became romantic, she may have felt conflicted about dating the guy who also set her salary, but she often didn't have anyone to turn to for advice.

THE FALL GIRLS

As recently as 1983, a Harvard Business Review article urged companies to make her the fall girl. The article advised executives to intervene in office liaisons and persuade "the person least essential to the company"—the subordinate who is "in almost all cases a woman"—to leave. "If a company sees rats in the basement, they've got to get them out," the article's author, Eliza Collins, said in an interview at the time. She wrote: "Love between managers is dangerous because it challenges—and can break down—the organizational structure."

Asked now about her views on handling office romances, Ms. Collins says, "The organizational climate has changed significantly, so the structure is much more flexible," says Ms. Collins, now a consultant in Rhode Island. "Today people can work out these issues on an individual, case-by-case basis, instead of involving the company, because they are much more sophisticated and there are many more women at high levels." As for her prior comment about "rats," she says: "Eek to that."

Anita Hill's sexual-harassment charges against Clarence Thomas during his Supreme Court confirmation hearings in 1991 triggered a sea change in how men and women eye, compete with, antagonize, and befriend one another in the workplace. In the wake of Ms. Hill's testimony, men and women began a noisy debate over what constituted sexual harassment and what distinguished coercive, abusive relationships from congenial, loving ones.

"We're in a transition with this issue because of changes in the workplace, but at least we've progressed beyond the point where the first thing that happens is the woman gets fired," says Gail Snowden, group executive of BankBoston Corp.'s community-banking group. "We recognize that there is a power dynamic in these relationships—and that two people are involved."

Many companies are so concerned about sexual-harassment problems that they can't bring themselves to come up with a coherent policy covering consensual relationships. Nonetheless, a growing number say they must acknowledge the romances in their midst and encourage disclosure so that one love-struck partner can be transferred or assigned to an objective supervisor. Managers say the efforts can be laborious. Getting employers to disclose their private affairs is often difficult, especially early on when it isn't clear whether the relationship will last.

But these companies realize that romances between bosses and subordinates invariably trigger morale and productivity problems among other employees who believe the subordinate is being favored. Yet "trying to outlaw romance is like trying to outlaw the weather," says one IBM manager who asked not to be identified.

Men and women not only work alongside each other in equal numbers; they also spend the overwhelming amount of their time at work. As executive recruiter Dale Winston puts it: "How many people are leaving work at 5 P.M. to go to a volunteer activity where they might meet someone?" Offices have replaced bars, churches, parties, or gyms as the dominant meeting ground.

"THE TRUTH WILL OUT"

AT&T has 8,000 employees who are married to each other and countless others who have dated at some time in their careers. "Nowadays, the only pause we have is when one reports to another—and we tell people in that situation to come forward so they can change their work relationship," says Burke Stinson, AT&T's senior public-relations manager. "It's not a lot different than asking people who want to work at home because of a sick child to be straightforward. Eventually the truth will out anyway."

About 30% of managers who responded to an American Management Association survey four years ago said they had had one or more office romances during their careers. Among these, 33% of the men and 15% of the women said the romance had been with a subordinate. Overall, 21% thought it was OK to date a subordinate, compared with 74% who approved of dating a co-worker.

With percentages like these, employers worry about losing valued staff over romances that go bust or cause staff turmoil. So on a couple-by-couple basis, they are bending old rules and making up new ones. "We're in a labor-shortage mode, so companies are less precipitous about letting people go for any reason, especially if they're good," says Ms. Winston.

Consider what happened at one high-tech company where a female manager was spending so much time traveling with her boss that she was rarely available to her own staff. Irked and worried that important decisions weren't getting made, one staffer told senior executives that she suspected that her boss and boss's boss were involved—and that their romance was damaging work output, according to Freada Klein, a Cambridge, Massachusetts, organizational-development consultant who advised the company about the situation. "She informed top executives partly to protect her own job and partly out of company loyalty," Ms. Klein says.

Executives confronted the couple, who acknowledged their liaison. Both were star performers. So instead of moving either of them, the company arranged for the woman manager's work to be evaluated by senior executives, as well as a few peers, rather than by the man she was dating. It's a cumbersome review process, but "the company concluded it was a lot better than losing either person," Ms. Klein says.

Staples Inc. learned last October that its president, Martin Hanaka, had had an extramarital affair with a support staffer named Cheryl Gordon. Mr. Hanaka resigned shortly after Ms. Gordon alleged that he assaulted her during an argument at her apartment and he was arrested. According to the arrest report, Ms. Gordon told police that Mr. Hanaka had grabbed her arm and spun her around. The report didn't mention injuries. Mr. Hanaka's attorney said that the executive "never touched" Ms. Gordon and was "not in a romantic relationship" with her. She subsequently dropped the assault charges.

But following Mr. Hanaka's arrest, Staples, a Boston-based discount-office-supplies retailer, said it conducted an internal investigation and concluded that Mr. Hanaka had violated the company's "fraternization policy," which prohibits managers from having a romantic relationship with a subordinate. The company said Mr. Hanaka left voluntarily. Ms. Gordon is also no longer with Staples.

THE EXTRAMARITAL AFFAIR

No company wants to condone an extramarital office romance or one where the power and age gap between partners is quite wide. "It's hard to call those relationships consensual," says Ms. Klein. But Staples' strict policy—found at just 3% of companies surveyed by the American Management Association—may have limited its ability to manage the situation, she believes.

Had Staples had a more flexible approach, "it might have been embarrass-

ing," but Mr. Hanaka could have been approached by another executive and encouraged to end the relationship, while Ms. Gordon "could have gotten fair treatment, too," Ms. Klein says. A Staples spokeswoman says the company "has a clear policy and we honored that policy."

"RUMORS GOING AROUND"

Relationships that pose a conflict of interest can extend beyond direct employees to outside clients, customers, and suppliers. Martha Clark Goss waited about two months to tell her boss that she was dating an outside attorney who did legal work for the Prudential Life department she supervised as a senior vice president. "I didn't work with him directly but I was head of the unit so I felt disclosing [our romance] was the right thing to do," she says. Still, she waited "until I realized it was pretty serious." She went to Prudential's general counsel, whom she says "was straight-laced" but happened to be going through a divorce at the time. If not for that, "he might not have approved" of her romance, but "as it was he told me to go for it," she says.

David Goss also told his boss about the relationship. But they didn't tell staffers for some time. "I feel pretty strongly that you should separate your personal and professional life," Ms. Goss says. At one point, a staffer protectively told her "there are rumors going around that you're dating David Goss." She laughed and said, "That's accurate." The couple married in 1994, three years after they began dating, and Ms. Goss, who is now vice president and chief financial officer at Booz Allen & Hamilton Inc., says she is glad she told her boss when she did.

Another couple she knows who kept their romance secret have paid a price, she believes. Everyone in the company they work at "knew about their relationship anyway," Ms. Goss says. Now that they have split but are still on the same management team, staffers sometimes feel awkward at monthly meetings. "Every once in a while emotions between them flare and that makes everyone else uncomfortable," Ms. Goss says.

Ms. Goss believes that office romances still may "reflect worse on a woman and be more detrimental to her career" than to a man's. She and other executive women who entered the job market in the 1970s haven't forgotten what happened to Mary Cunningham.

Ms. Cunningham, a young M.B.A. straight out of Harvard Business School, arrived at Bendix in 1979 and in little more than a year simultaneously became the company's top corporate strategist as well as a constant companion to then–Chief Executive William Agee. They both denied that they were romantically involved, but after gossip about the couple swelled among staffers, Ms. Cunningham resigned, saying that "false innuendoes" had made it impossible for her to do her job. She and Mr. Agee later married, but continued to deny that they had been involved while Ms. Cunningham worked at Bendix.

A younger generation of women and men may be less concerned about overlap between their personal and professional lives. Younger managers, for example, are much more likely than older ones to have had an office romance. About 38% of those under 35 report at least one romance with either a peer or subordinate, compared with 22% who are 35 and older, according to the American Management Association.

Jim Drury, a 47-year-old district manager at Shaw's Supermarkets Inc., a New England retailer, has seen this generational shift. Mr. Drury says he now employs many married couples who met at Shaw's. He and his wife Lorraine were considered more of an oddity when they became a couple 12 years ago. At the time, he was a manager of Shaw's Quincy, Massachusetts, store, over-

seeing 220 staffers; she worked for him as a front-end manager, supervising 75 to 100 store employees in cash-accounting functions.

NOT REALLY A DATE

They had already worked together for more than two years when Jim asked Lorraine out for dinner. "It wasn't really a date," says Mr. Drury, but by the end of the evening, they knew they wanted to see each other again.

Mr. Drury decided to tell his boss immediately because he worried that if other employees found out, they would question Lorraine's "professionalism and credibility." As she recalls, "Jim told me, 'people like to gossip,' and he wanted to save both of us from that." Still, they both worried that Mr. Drury's boss would be angry.

He wasn't—and came up with the solution of transferring Mr. Drury. "I think the company liked our performance, so they just moved him for our sakes, not their sakes," says Lorraine.

Both have been promoted since they got together and Mr. Drury says he is grateful that Shaw was "way ahead of the curve" about office romances. "What companies have to deal with is whether they want to give up really good people because they happen to date and get married," says Mr. Drury. "Or do they want to put people in a position where they have to be dishonest and deceptive?"

Companies moving toward more open disclosure policies walk a tightrope between sexual-harassment and privacy-rights concerns. IBM four years ago lost a suit filed by a manager who said he was forced out of the company after dating a subordinate. Daniel Manicelli, a 23-year-veteran, won a $375,000 jury verdict, which was upheld on appeal for breach of employment contract, and contributed to IBM's policy change.

● ● ● ● ● ● ● ● ● ● ● ● ● ● ●
THE LONG HOURS

Don Fernando Azevedo, a psychologist in Carey, North Carolina, who has treated a number of people embroiled in messy office romances, believes companies must acknowledge that they are "co-dependents" in these relationships. "They are facilitating them by asking people to work 50, 60, sometimes 70 hours a week. Employees never get home to see their families or out to meet people they don't work with," he says.

"Then they go on business trips together to places like Vail, Colorado, and stay in five-star hotels. They have dinner and a little wine. They're lonely and here's this other person who understands exactly what they're working on, which is a dangerous combination." He advises companies that don't relish managing numerous office romances to "make sure their employees get home every night for dinner."

VI-7: The Case against Employee Benefits

CRAIG J. CANTONI

United Parcel Service's battle with the Teamsters over pensions and part-time workers points to a broader problem: The American system of employer-provided health and retirement benefits has become an anachronism. Employers and employees would be better off if medical coverage and retirement programs were independent of the employment relationship.

To understand why, consider some history. In 1940 only 10% of the U.S. workforce, or 12 million people, were covered by health insurance, primarily through such plans as Blue Cross and Kaiser Permanente, which grew in response to the hardships of the Depression. In 1942 Congress passed the Stabilization Act, which limited wage increases in order to keep prices in check during wartime. The act permitted the adoption of employer-paid insurance plans in lieu of wage increases. In 1945 the War Labor Board ruled that it was illegal to modify or terminate group insurance plans

during the life of a labor contract. Later, the National Labor Relations Board ruled that insurance and pension benefits fell under the legal definition of "wages." Employer-paid benefits had been institutionalized.

The Liberty Mutual Insurance Co. led the way in 1949 by introducing major-medical coverage, a new insurance product that coupled comprehensive coverage with the new features of deductibles and coinsurance. By 1951, 100,000 people were covered by major-medical insurance; by 1960, 32 million; and by 1986, 156 million.

In 1979, 97% of full-time employees in medium-to-large companies had employer-sponsored health insurance. But by 1991, that percentage had declined to 83%. What happened? Employment declined in durable goods manufacturing, in which 93% of workers are covered, and rose in retail, in which only 62% are. And people started changing jobs more often. Even with mandated coverage for departing employees at their own expense (known as Cobra benefits), waiting periods and exclusions for preexisting illnesses often leave job switchers without coverage at least for a time. Less than half of all workers, meanwhile, are covered by private retirement plans.

The most significant cause of the decline in health and retirement coverage has been the growth in the contingent workforce. Often companies are using part-time and contract workers for the express purpose of avoiding the costs—both direct and administrative of providing benefits. Who can blame them?

From 1971 to 1991, the cost of medical care rose almost 70% faster than inflation. Although medical costs have leveled off, the cost of all fringe benefits has soared to 40% of total compensation, compared with 17% in 1955. Corporations spend almost 12% of total revenues on employee benefits, vs. 4.4% in the 1960s. The average employee's benefits package (including payroll taxes) costs just under $15,000.

Add to this the costs of administering benefits and complying with ever-more-complex regulations. The 1974 Employee Retirement Income Security Act alone has spawned regulations that are two feet thick; complying with these rules takes an army of attorneys and benefits consultants, in addition to in-house benefits administrators (about one for every 1,000 employees). Such costs hit small businesses especially hard: The annual cost to a midsize or smaller business of administering a "simple" 401(k) retirement plan is $475 per participant.

What do companies get for this trouble and money? Black eyes—not only from the usual adversaries in the media and government, as UPS is finding out, but also from the recipients of their generosity. Except for the largest and richest companies, which can afford gold-plated programs, benefits are often a source of employee dissatisfaction and distrust, and rarely a source of motivation or productivity. This is particularly true of medical insurance.

Company-sponsored medical insurance creates a paternalistic relationship. The employer plays the role of the munificent parent, who protects the employee-child from the vagaries of life—a role at odds with the economic decisions of running a business. It also gives employers reasons to intrude on the most personal aspects of their employees' lives, from a family's medical history to a worker's sexual orientation (in the case of domestic partner coverage). Once involved with such personal matters, it seems perfectly natural for employers to devote precious time and energy to matters of health and lifestyle, by offering smoking cessation programs, stress reduction classes, cholesterol screenings, health awareness lectures, and newsletters about diet and nutrition. But whatever goodwill such nannyism might generate, it evaporates as soon as the employer increases premiums, switches managed care networks, or denies a claim.

Noncash benefits corrupt the employer–employee relationship in other important ways. When 10% of total compensation is in the form of benefits, it is difficult for employees to put a true market value on their compensation package or to walk away from a job they don't like. From management's point of view, it is difficult to have true pay-for-performance when employees see 40% of their compensation as an entitlement.

What is the answer? Certainly not another Rube Goldberg– or Hillary Clinton–style national health scheme—though that's what Congress is creating, one law at a time. One better idea would be legislation mandating that private employer group health plans be replaced with non-profit, private-sector buying cooperatives, which would be open to everyone, regardless of work or family status. The cooperatives would perform the same role as large employers: getting reduced group rates from insurance companies and managed care networks, acting as consumer advocates, interpreting and explaining coverage, reconciling claim disputes, and educating members about healthy living.

Getting companies out of the retirement business would require changes in tax and pension law to allow people to save as much money in individual retirement accounts as can now be saved in corporate defined-contribution retirement plans.

After 55 years, the time has come for business to correct an accident of history and get out of the benefits business. And if business leaders don't take the lead, government will do it for them—as it has done since World War II.

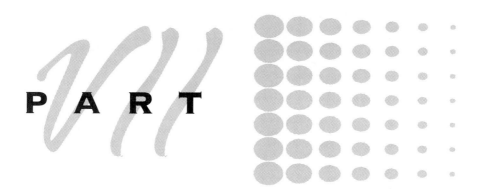

PART VII

INTERFACES OF WORK AND LIFE

Frequently, when we teach management seminars we ask participants at the start of the seminar: *"If you could add one new quality to your life when you wake up tomorrow, what would that quality be?"* Almost invariably, the answer that comes back boils down to "I would like to have more balance in my life." The emphasis tends to be on balancing demands and pressures at work with the desire to spend more time enjoying activities off the job . . . with one's family, partner, or having quality time to oneself.

There was a time, in the 1970s, when the futuristic prediction was that technological advances emerging and anticipated would create a world of increased leisure. People, free from drudgery and leveraging the growing power of the computer, would be more productive, getting work done more quickly and thus having more time to play—or so the argument went. We know this has not panned out that way for most workers. The speed and power of computer technology has reduced and in some cases even eliminated time (to rest) and space (to breathe). The Internet has allowed us to be "on-line" all the time. A project being worked on during a North American day can be picked up and continued by others halfway round the globe and sent back to team members in North America as they sign on the next morning.

Companies facing global competition have placed new and often relentless demands on their employees, so that leisure time and some sense of balance between work and nonwork continues to be tilted towards work. Of course, the nature of work itself is changing and the seductiveness of high technology work and competition can draw people off balance and toward workaholism. Perhaps those who can find balance between their work and other aspects of their lives may be more creative and productive in the long run. Possibly, organizations that create conditions for a healthy interface between work and nonwork in the lives of their employees may be able to hire, retain, and motivate more effective contributions to the bottom-line from these employees. While the evidence on such propositions is not yet clear-cut, there is ample evidence that the tensions at the interface of work and life are real. They are preoccupying people who work in organizations (our seminar participants for example), as well as those who manage and those who think seriously about the tensions and the dilemmas of balance in an increasingly knowledge-based world. The readings in this section capture some of the aspects of these tensions and dilemmas.

The quote from Annie Dillard "There is no shortage of good days . . . " speaks to the need for us to stop at times, to step back from a headlong rush of activity, to take stock of who we are and what our purpose in life might be. We may need less sensation, activity, pursuit of things than we think. We are, in her terms, human "beings" not human "doers."

The excerpt from Leslie A. Perlow's *Finding Time* ("Home Life: Tradeoffs Between Work and Family") is a graphic and sad tale of the tensions in families when one member, in this case the father, gives most of his time to work, even when his wife and child are in distress. The story raises issues about individual and corporate responsibilities for the mental health of employees and their families.

Wayne Muller's article "Time, Priceless Time" echoes Annie Dillard's theme. He writes: "In Commerce we trade time for money. . . . But in the tender country of illness and divorce, we are suddenly desperate to trade money for time." He draws us back to think about the importance of attending to the work-life interface for the quality of our experience.

Aaron Berstein's "Why the Law Should Adopt More Family Leave" argues the case for widening the reach of legislation that permits employees to take leave to care for newborns or illness in the family. The next reading, "Hazardous to Your Career" by Gene Koretz, warns of the costs that may be incurred to people's careers when they take such leaves.

Despite the prolonged health of the American economy, people have lost jobs, sometimes permanently, and many others live with the insecurity of their prospects. *The Economist*'s "Why Willy Loman Lives" tries to identify this discomfort and the need to find ways to protect those who are no longer employable.

Sometimes the interweaving of work and life becomes astonishingly, even tragically, evident. Daniel Sieberg reports the death of a Starbucks' manager, killed while trying to protect an employee ("Starbucks CEO to Attend Memorial for Slain Manager"). The manager's heroism, the way he had lived his life and given it to save another, affected friends and workers alike.

Returning to the issue of "what to do" about work-life imbalances, Pamela Kruger describes in "Jobs for Life" a concerted and considered change effort within the consulting organization Ernst & Young to help its employees achieve more balance between work and other activities. The challenge is great and the attempts to meet it are significant. Finally, Richard Leider and David A. Shapiro describe an incident (in their book *Repacking Your Bags*) that prompted Leider to ask himself a life-changing question: "Does all this (that I do) make me happy?" It is a question worth asking as a way to begin to explore the degree to which the work we do and the life we live meet our personal vision of what is meaningful and satisfying in this complex, overloaded, and richly beckoning life at work.

VII-1: Interfaces of Work and Life

There is no shortage of good days. It is good lives that are hard to come by. A life of good days lived

Reprinted from *The Writing Life*, Annie Dillard (New York: Harper and Row, 1989): 32–33.

in the senses is not enough. The life of sensation is the life of greed; it requires more and more. The life of the spirit requires less and less; time is ample and its passage sweet.

ANNIE DILLARD

VII-2: Home Life: Tradeoffs Between Work and Family
Excerpt from *Finding Time*

LESLIE A. PERLOW

"It was in the thirties. Ice and snow were everywhere. Trees and power lines were down. We had no electricity; we had no heat; we had nothing but a wood-burning stove. I was home alone with our nine-year-old daughter. For six days and six nights we hovered over the stove, desperately trying to keep warm." Allan's wife, Kim, was describing to me the ice storm of 1991. The city had been declared a national disaster area. Allan was scheduled to leave on a business trip to Japan, but the airport was closed, and the trip was postponed for a day. When the airport reopened, Allan left his wife and daughter to fend for themselves. On previous trips to Japan he had been chastised for billing calls home more than once a week. This time he didn't call home for six days. When he finally did call, his family still had no power. His wife and child were freezing, scared, and exhausted. Moreover, they were bitter that they had been deserted. Kim told me:

Reprinted from Leslie A. Perlow, Finding Time: How Corporations, Individuals, and Families Can Benefit from New Work Practices. Copyright © 1997 by Cornell University. Used by permission of the publisher, Cornell University Press.

Our neighbors were horrified. They couldn't believe that Allan would leave me. I was the most hurt and angry of anyone, but I was busy defending him. Allan was in a lose-lose situation. He was afraid of shirking on his work responsibilities, but totally abandoning his wife in a city that had been declared a national disaster was shirking on his family responsibilities. . . . Once he called and found out the situation he did come home the next day.

Allan described his decision to come home:

I felt I had done enough in Japan. I had been to all the meetings, and I had done the best job I could do. I felt my team could handle the rest without me. My wife needed me more, and so I left. . . . I left without having the opportunity to ask my boss. I just decided I needed to go, and I left. . . . I was trying to meet my commitments to everyone, but in the process I managed to piss everyone off. My manager is still mad at me. My wife is still mad at me.

Allan loved his wife and daughter. Yet, he was caught up in the demands of his work, and he often failed to notice how his preoccupation with the job burdened his family. At this point, his wife rarely put up a fight, but she harbored great resentment toward Allan and toward Ditto. "Families are locked out from the start," Kim noted. "The security system doesn't let anyone in the door, and you are locked out from there on. You are locked out of trips, recreational activities, dinners, and celebrations. . . . Families are not a part of the place!"

Kim, herself a social worker, worked three days a week at the university hospital. She explained: "Allan used to be responsible to empty the dishwasher in the morning before he went to work. Now even that is more than he can handle. I used to try to force him to help around the house, but it would always result in an argument. Now, I don't even try. I fear that he is so stressed by work that he will not be able to handle anything else." And then she added only half jokingly, "I would rather have a husband than a dead husband." She said, "I have decided it is just easier to do things myself rather than getting angry. I am too scared about his health to have a fight." According to Kim, "Allan is experiencing all sorts of physical stress from work that is manifesting in side effects. I want to call the doctor, but he refuses. . . . I am so angry at the company that I would not want them at the funeral. I feel so strongly that I actually think these thoughts, and that scares me. I just think that after his death, then they would all act so sympathetic, and yet, no one is doing anything about it now."

While Kim said she had stopped putting pressure on Allan to help around the house because she feared she "could be the one to put him over the edge," she could go on for hours telling stories about events Allan had missed, responsibilities he had shirked, and things she would have liked but could never have asked him to do. One Saturday, for example, she was feeling sick and was depressed about a close relative who had recently died. She said:

It was a rough morning. I wasn't feeling well and then Rachel [their daughter] broke a lamp. I tried several times during the day

to call Allan and tell him to come home. I needed help. I expected him home for lunch. I kept calling, but there was no answer. . . . I was so angry that around four o'clock I took my daughter and marched off to the jeweler and bought a very expensive diamond and pearl ring, in an attempt to console myself. . . . When I got home there was no sign of Allan, but I was feeling better, and I figured he would be home soon. I cooked dinner. . . . But, he never did come home for dinner. . . . He never called, and he didn't get home until nine-thirty that night. I was angry and I let him know that. . . . I threatened him that if he didn't come home it would cost him thousands of dollars because I would buy other things as well. . . . He had gotten wrapped up in working on something in the lab and just lost track of time. . . . He has never done anything quite like it again. . . . He still loses track of time, but he tries to be better about calling.

The only responsibility Allan still had was taking their daughter to piano lessons. Kim believed Allan liked to take her, to stay with her, and to sit with her while she practiced. Still, Kim said, "As much as he wants to do this with Rachel, he is never on time. He will come running into the house at 5:55 to get her for her six o'clock piano lesson, if he comes home at all." Recently, for example,

He picked her up at six o'clock and took her. But then he left a note on the kitchen counter saying that he had to return to work, and could I please pick her up. . . . I happened to stay late at work that night, thinking that Rachel was with her father and so there was no reason for me to hurry home. . . . When I walked in the door at seven-thirty the phone was ringing. It was Rachel. I rushed out to get her. . . . I was very angry that Allan would just abandon her and not make any attempt to get hold of me. He certainly should have made more effort than just to leave a message where I might never get it. . . . It is the only responsibility he has left, and I cannot even count on him for that.

I was still at Allan and Kim's house at 5:15 P.M. when the phone rang. It was

Rachel. She wanted to be picked up. I heard Kim say into the receiver, "Dad will pick you up at five-thirty." But Rachel yelled back, so loud that I could hear her through the phone, "Mom please don't leave me here. You know Dad will never come. Mom please don't leave me here. I am the last one here. Please don't leave me here another time. Please Mom. Please." Kim finally agreed to pick her up. She put down the receiver and turned to me and said, "You see what I mean. We just don't trust him. He has let us down too many times."

Allan was late for everything, Kim said. "He shows up in the third period of school open houses and at the end of basketball games, if he makes it at all. He missed both my MSW graduation and when Rachel won the fourth grade role model contest." She offered, "It is always something: a vendor is visiting, a presentation to the vice-president, or losing track of time. . . . There always seems to be something important, some reason why he cannot be home."

Kim believed the recent layoffs had only added another component to Allan's stress. "After all," she noted, "his income does support the family." She explained: "My theory is that Ditto is trying to keep up with the Japanese and the Japanese work very long hours. Allan tells me stories about his trips to Japan. I know they work until midnight. I also read the booklets on Japan. I know they have no time for their families. They have a wife who takes care of everything and they have very traditional views about women." She added, "I recently read about a Japanese wonder drug 'Regain.' It is filled with caffeine and nicotine and enables you to work harder and longer."

Kim held out little hope for change. She seemed desperate for any suggestions about how to improve her life and Allan's. She admitted, "Divorce may be my only answer. For Allan, I just don't know. I wish Ditto cared more about the mental health of its people. . . . The facade that they are all so fortunate to have a job is absurd."

VII-3: Time, Priceless Time

WAYNE MULLER

In commerce, we trade time for money. Our time is converted into labor, productivity, output, and profit. Whenever we can, we find new, innovative methods for leveraging time into cash.

But in the tender country of illness and divorce, we are suddenly desperate to trade money for time. We pay lawyers colossal fees to guarantee an extra day or two of custodial time with our children. We eagerly employ teams of physicians to increase the possibility of six additional months of life.

Reprinted from *Forbes* (July 5, 1999): 250.

"Time is money," we learned early in our professions. But the equation is flawed. I see it in my counseling sessions, and we all see it with our family and friends. I would like to share two stories (with names and some minor details altered).

John and Mary are getting divorced. Successful in their respective careers, their love for one another has withered for reasons only they can know. They are now trying to divide custody of the children.

Sasha, who was diagnosed with leukemia, took a sabbatical from her job in advertising. She and her husband, a filmmaker, moved to a cottage to walk, to rest, to listen to the quieter voices that teach them what is most necessary.

Time is not money. Time and money are two enzymes that serve very specific functions in our life, and confusing the two can bring us great suffering.

Money traded in the marketplace purchases basic goods and services we cannot provide for ourselves. But how much time should we trade for this money? How do we know when we do not have enough money, and when we do not have enough time? The question is rarely asked, and when it is, it is often too late.

People who have a lot of money and no time we call "rich." People who have a great deal of time but no money we call "poor." Yet the most precious gifts of a human life—love, friendship, time with children and loved ones—grow only in the sweet soil of "unproductive" time.

Adolescents who spend leisure time with their families become less prone to heavy drinking. The less time parents hang out with their kids, the more likely teenagers will develop alcohol problems.

The problem is not simply that we work too much, but that we are paid in the wrong currency. We must be wise enough to render unto Caesar what is Caesar's and unto God what is God's. What if genuine wealth is a fruitful marriage of both time and money, combining material security with those priceless things that grow only in time—time to walk in the park, to read a book, to dance, to put our hands in the garden, to cook meals with friends, to paint, to sing, to meditate, to keep a journal?

Elaine is a professional woman in private practice. She works hard and well, is diligent and honorable in her work. But Elaine lost two husbands—the first in Vietnam, the second to cancer. Now, alone and courageous, she treasures the gifts that only time can bestow. Several days a week she turns off the phone, lights a candle on a small altar and sits quietly. She prays, she gathers pictures. She may go for a walk, and when she walks, she says, she often sings.

VII-4: Why the Law Should Adopt More Family Leave

AARON BERNSTEIN

Since Congress passed the Family & Medical Leave Act of 1993, some 20 million workers of both sexes have taken time off for the birth of a baby or to care for an ill family member. The massive disruptions critics predicted never came to pass. In fact, the economy has boomed, and most employers report few problems accommodating these leaves.

Still, business lobbyists were revving up opposition to expanding the law even

Reprinted from *Business Week* (February 1, 1999): 42. ©1999 The McGraw–Hill Companies, Inc.

before President Clinton proposed it in his Jan. 19 State of the Union Address. Admittedly, the new measure, which would require companies with as few as 25 employees to grant family leave, might cause more difficulties for smaller companies. But given the experience of those already under the Act—the cutoff is now 50 workers—it's time to follow the lead of several states and broaden the law.

In Oregon, for example, state law has covered companies with 25 or more workers since the mid-1980s. "Most small companies here haven't had a problem," says

Betsy Earls, a lobbyist for state employer group Associated Oregon Industries. A dozen other states have narrower leave laws that apply to small employers, most for maternity disability.

NO COMPLAINTS

Even on the federal level, the law already applies to 58,000 worksites with fewer than 50 employees that are part of larger companies based nearby. Some 75% of these places had little or no increase in administrative costs to comply with the federal law, according to a 1996 survey by the bipartisan Commission on Family & Medical Leave. Of course, some might have more flexibility, like the ability to transfer workers among worksites, than independent small companies. Even so, the percentage with no complaints cannot be ignored.

Small employers are already inclined to give some leave benefits—because it's good business. Take Flora Green, who opened her own florist shop in Kendall, Florida, in 1975. From the start, she offered family leave. "We're a real good team, and everyone pitches in when someone takes off," says Green. Last year, she sold her 40-employee firm to a national chain. While some things changed at Foliage by Flora, family leave policy was not one of them.

Green is not alone. Plenty of other small companies offer some family leave, if not the full 12 weeks the Feds want. In fact, 95% of private-sector companies with 25 to 49 employees offer some maternity leave, according to a 1997 study by the Families & Work Institute in New York.

So, why expand the law? First, making leaves mandatory deals with the employers who refuse to be flexible. More important, someday unemployment is bound to rise. The voluntary extension of family leave has come amidst the tightest labor markets in decades. When they loosen, many companies—particularly small ones—may not feel so generous.

VII-5: Hazardous to Your Career
The Risks of Taking Unpaid Leaves

GENE KORETZ

Millions of Americans have availed themselves of the Family & Medical Leave Act of 1993, which permits employees to take unpaid leaves of up to 12 weeks for family or medical reasons. According to a study in the current issue of the *Academy of Management Journal,* however, such leaves may entail significant risks for managers.

In the study, Michael K. Judiesch and Karen S. Lyness of the City University of New York's Baruch College compared the

progress of 523 full-time managers of a big financial-services company who took leaves in the early 1990s with that of their peers from 1993 to mid-1995. Adjusting for age, gender, education, and job factors, they found that leave-takers were 18% less likely to be promoted than non-leave-takers and received 8% less in salary hikes.

The median length of leave was less than two months, and though some lasted much longer, the study found that the length of absences did not affect penalties. (Multiple leave-takers, however, were more heavily penalized.)

Reprinted from *Business Week* (January 17, 2000): 26. ©2000 The McGraw–Hill Companies, Inc.

Not only did leave-takers tend to receive lower job performance ratings for the year in which they took time off, but they also received fewer promotions and smaller salary increases than their peers with similar low ratings. Still, a third of leave-takers did subsequently receive promotions.

Whether they will eventually catch up with their peers, however, is uncertain. The researchers note that those managers receiving early promotions tend to enter an especially fast track, rising more rapidly to higher levels.

VII-6: Why Willy Loman Lives

Two men stand on a stage. One is the hulking figure of Willy Loman, gradually becoming smaller in front of the audience's eyes; the other is his younger and weedier boss, Howard, gradually downsizing his old employee. "You can't eat an orange and throw the peel away," roars the broken salesman. "A man is not a piece of fruit." Meanwhile, Howard patronizes the old man (who decades before had helped christen him) by calling him "kid."

Most of the muffled sobs from the audience during the current, heavily Tony-ed version of *Death of a Salesman* on Broadway occur during the final reconciliation between Willy and his useless son, Biff. But the moment when Howard sacks Willy still stands out in its viciousness. When Arthur Miller's play opened in 1949, one conservative critic called it "a time bomb expertly placed under the edifice of Americanism." Willy Loman, the relentless competitor, became a symbol of the dark side of the American dream that he so firmly believed in. As his wife, Linda, says to Biff: "He's not the finest character that ever lived. But he's a human being and a terrible thing is happening to him. So attention must be paid."

But who is paying attention now? At first sight it seems odd that New Yorkers

are flocking to see such a depressing play. Figures for consumer confidence are sky-high, unemployment at a 29-year low. When people lose their jobs they find new ones pretty quickly. During the interval, young investment bankers sip champagne and express their astonishment that America could ever have been "like that." The most modern figure in the play seems to be the ghost of Willy's brother Ben—an early version of an Internet entrepreneur who keeps on telling his brother how he "walked into the jungle" at 17, walked out at 21, and "by God, I was rich."

Somehow America's chattering classes seem to have forgotten the much-ballyhooed age of uncertainty. Those days in the early 1990s, when the *New York Times* seemed to have a permanent section on insecurity in the workplace and George Bush senior was wandering around New Hampshire mumbling "Message: I care" to laid-off workers, seem almost as distant as the days when salesmen still wore hats. "The current election will be about health care, education, values," one senator says, echoing the views of pollsters. Asked whether her boyfriend, who makes his living selling T-shirt logos round the country, feels insecure, Carol, a fitness instructor who works just round the corner from the Eugene O'Neill theatre, says flatly: "How should I know? He's playing golf in Myrtle Beach."

Reprinted from *The Economist* (June 19, 1999): 28.

Yet the notion that Willy Loman has left the American political scene for the 19th hole in the Carolinas is wrong. To make the obvious point first, as Alan Greenspan, the chairman of the Fed, made it to Congress this week, "The rate of growth cannot increase indefinitely." A nasty stockmarket correction and slightly higher interest rates, and many families across America could be looking at their Visa and MasterCard bills in the same anxious way that the Lomans fret about the payments on the fridge.

A cyclical downturn would certainly push Willy back to center-stage. But the salesman's tragedy was set at the start of America's postwar boom. As Mr. Greenspan has pointed out repeatedly, one reason why wage inflation remains relatively low is the simple fact that many Americans are terrified of losing their jobs. And with good reason. Some 55,231 jobs were shed in May, according to consultants at Challenger, Gray & Christmas. The total for job cuts in the first five months of 1999 was nearly 50% higher than the equivalent figure in 1998. The typical worker changes jobs nine times before the age of 32. "Any Monday morning you can be told you are no longer needed," Mr. Miller recently told the *Los Angeles Times.* "The company is moving to Guatemala." If you pick up any book about the Internet, you will be told that "salesmen" are the next class of people to be "disintermediated." Instead of sending out Willy and his suitcase, Howard would only need to set up a Web site.

Unsurprisingly, the long-term structural trends about insecurity are all up. One poll earlier this year of 500,000 workers showed anxiety about jobs to be three times higher than it was during the 1980–81 recession. And men of Willy's age seem particularly vulnerable. John Schmitt at the Economic Policy Institute points out that if you exclude women (whose careers have become slightly more secure), many of the standard insecurity measures are still worsening. Even if jobs are easy to find, it is hard to take your pension and health care with you. And the older you get, the less likely you are to want to move in search of work.

Nor is it just a matter of losing your job; the problem lies in the whole stress-producing environment of modern corporate America. Mr. Miller once thought of calling his play "The Inside of His Head." It is easy to imagine a modern Willy Loman bemoaning the passing of seniority, being tormented by group evaluation sessions, and spending half his day arguing with his HMO. Even Carol, the Manhattan fitness instructor, complains that her job is now judged on the basis of salesmanship as well as muscle tone. Everybody in America, it often seems these days, is on commission and on trial.

And so, in many ways, they should be. Every country in Europe would kill to have a capitalism that spits out inefficient people like Willy as ruthlessly as America does. Willy's frantic desire to compete, his merry recital of the management clichés of the day ("It's not what you sell; it's how you sell"), his determination to imitate the legendary Bill: all these things are what keeps America ahead of its peers.

Yet the problem of what to do with Willy Loman, and America's other losers, remains. The issues cited by the senator—health care, education, even values—all lead directly or indirectly to the Lomans' door. Last week, Andy Grove, the famously tough boss of Intel (motto: "Only the paranoid survive"), gave a speech on Capitol Hill giving warning to politicians that the social and economic dislocation caused by new technology had only just begun, and that they needed to "grease the skids" to protect the weak. For all its period detail, *Salesman* seems eerily timeless. Willy Loman is far from dead.

VII-7: Starbucks CEO to Attend Memorial for Slain Manager
Mayor Owen Proposes That Anthony McNaughton Be Given City's Highest Honor

DANIEL SIEBERG

The president and CEO of Starbucks will join hundreds of family, friends, and employees Monday at a memorial service for a local manager who sacrificed his life protecting an employee from a knife-wielding assailant.

Howard Schultz, who heads the Seattle-based company with thousands of outlets catering to latte and espresso fanatics, wants to personally honor Tony McNaughton, said a Starbucks source who did not want to be identified.

"They want Starbucks employees, friends, and family," he said. "They want to keep it as private as possible."

McNaughton should be posthumously awarded the highest honor the city can give a citizen who saves a life, Vancouver Mayor Philip Owen said Wednesday.

Owen said he will recommend to the police board, which bestows such honors, that McNaughton be awarded a Certificate of Merit.

Owen, who is chairman of the police board, said there are also plans to pursue a Governor-General's Decoration for Bravery for McNaughton, who was fatally stabbed Saturday while saving an employee from an attacker at the Robson Street coffee shop.

Queen Elizabeth created the Decorations for Bravery in 1972. Since then,

more than 2,000 people have received the awards.

"I'm certainly going to talk to the [police] chief and recommend ... a certificate," said Owen. "A lot of citizens don't step into a situation with conflict, and he instinctively went forward to protect an employee. The sad thing is that he lost his life doing it."

The police board gives Certificates of Merit to citizens who, "on their own initiative and in the face of actual or anticipated danger ... have assisted the police in preventing a crime, apprehending or attempting to apprehend an offender, or made a life-saving attempt."

In the absence of any danger, citizens can be sent a Letter of Commendation signed by the chief constable.

Owen said the procedure to recommend McNaughton will be delayed for a while in order to allow his family and friends to grieve.

Bruce Anderson described his long-time friend, a devout Buddhist, as a "kind, loving, caring man who lived a very peaceful life."

McNaughton's friends have asked to be left in peace while they organize a private service.

"There is no panic to do it today or tomorrow," Owen said. "I'm sure he will receive many recognitions in the future."

Owen added that a park bench could also be dedicated in memory of McNaughton's actions.

Reprinted from the *Vancouver Sun* (February 4, 2000): A3.

VII-8: Jobs for Life

PAMELA KRUGER

What good is a high-powered career if it makes you miserable? What good is owning a beautiful house if you're never home? What good is being passionate about a hobby if you never have the free time to pursue it? Ernst & Young is a cautious firm that has embarked on a bold experiment to address such deeply personal questions about work. The goal, say the people behind these programs, is to create jobs for life.

● ● ● ● ● ● ● ● ● ● ● ● ● ● ●
"SO WHAT ARE *YOU* DOING FOR THE NEXT FIVE YEARS?"

Deborah Holmes laughed off Philip Laskawy's question. The chairman and CEO of Ernst & Young LLP couldn't be offering her a job. It was the fall of 1996. And Holmes, 36, research director of Catalyst, a New York City–based organization that studies women in business, had just presented her analysis of turnover among female employees at E&Y. And the news wasn't good. For years, half of the $5 billion accounting-and-consulting firm's new hires had been women, but the percentage of female partners and managers—not quite 20%—had barely budged.

More disturbing was that E&Y's turnover problem did not involve only women. Holmes's research revealed that corporate culture was producing equal-opportunity angst. A culture that equated face time with commitment and that consis-

tently demanded that its employees sacrifice family for work was clearly out of whack. About 60% of the women and 57% of the men in senior management at E&Y told Catalyst that they were dissatisfied with working long hours. Each year, about 23% of the women and 18% of the men were leaving.

Imagine the cost. E&Y was losing not only talent but also continuity with its clients. And it was spending hundreds of thousands of dollars to fill each vacant position. Holmes told E&Y's leaders that if they wanted to buck that trend, they would have to make sweeping changes in the way they conducted business, and that such an effort would require the full-time attention of at least one person—and probably more than one person.

That was when Laskawy, 59, threw down the gauntlet: "So what are *you* doing for the next five years?" But it wasn't until Laskawy called Holmes at her office later that she finally realized how serious he was. She knew she was staring at what could be an opportunity of a lifetime—a chance to see whether the ideas that she had been developing for the past seven years as a work-life consultant would work in the real world.

"You realize that I'm not guaranteeing anything. My ideas may not work," Holmes hedged. Laskawy agreed: This was no layup. But "whoever cracks this code will be a winner with this workforce," Holmes remembers him saying. "So let's give it a try."

Today, more than three years later, Ernst & Young still hasn't cracked the code, but it certainly has made progress. Laskawy and Holmes are reshaping the work lives of 34,000 professionals in an industry where customer focus is crucial to survival. How do you bring balance to a profession that, by definition, demands brutally long hours? How can work be flexible when a client sets a tight deadline and expects to see you working around the clock to meet it? How do you make it acceptable to talk about personal needs with partners as well as with clients?

In late 1996, soon after Holmes was hired to direct E&Y's newly created Office for Retention, she launched four pilot programs to address those questions. Three of those programs—involving internal networking, mentoring, and external networking—were aimed exclusively at women, and all have proved reasonably successful.

The fourth, and by far the most ambitious, targeted all 34,000 E&Y employees. Its focus: balancing the work-life equation. That program had partners and staffers across the firm fundamentally reevaluating how E&Y does business. And the program wasn't about establishing flextime or job sharing; it was also about incorporating the reality of peoples' lives into the firm's business strategy.

By the end of 1999, 11 of the firm's 50 largest consulting teams and all of its 12 tax-and-audit practices had rolled out retention initiatives. From San Jose, California to Detroit, E&Y consultants, auditors, and accountants began experimenting with a variety of self-generated measures—among them, telecommuting, restricting consultants' travel, even curbing the temptation to check E-mail and voice mail on weekends. (As this article went to press, France's Cap Gemini SA announced that it was acquiring E&Y's consulting practice. That deal will not affect the firm's work-life strategies.)

"What's impressive is the extent of E&Y's initiative and determination to create a wave—a set of changes—that will make the company look like a new organization in five years," says Stew Friedman, on leave as director of the Work/Life Inte-

gration Project (based at the Wharton School of the University of Pennsylvania), which recently did a case study on E&Y's efforts. "There is not just one measure here but a whole campaign that is being mobilized to engage everyone in changing the values and beliefs that drive the company."

Change hasn't come easily or quickly. E&Y remains, by nature, a deeply cautious place: Requests for even the most mundane information take weeks to process, while staffers ruminate over the implications of those requests. And many E&Y professionals still work an obscene number of hours, missing more anniversaries, birthdays, and vacations than they want to admit. Although some offices have seen retention improve dramatically—firmwide turnover among women had dropped by 5% between 1995 and 1998—overall, turnover stands at 20%. Of course, treading water in this hot economy may be an achievement of sorts: A survey of 1,192 major U.S. employers, conducted by the American Management Association, found that between mid-1998 and mid-1999, turnover decreased in only 16% of those companies, whereas it rose in 28% of them. Yet Holmes acknowledges that E&Y has a long way to go. "Some of the work that we started in 1997 is only now beginning to bear fruit," she says.

Perhaps E&Y hasn't won the war, but it has turned life balance into a grassroots crusade with a momentum all its own. Many companies announce work-life programs with much fanfare, only to forget them within months. E&Y avoided that pitfall by implementing three critical strategies: First, Laskawy has made himself a visible and persistent advocate of life balance, ensuring that everyone understands that Holmes's office has his personal backing.

Second, Holmes doesn't dictate policy. Instead, she urges local offices to examine long-held assumptions and to invent their own solutions. In the past two years, hundreds of partners and staffers across the firm have formed "solution teams" to determine the scope and nature of life-balance programs. Says Holmes: "People who live with a problem can solve it better than anyone who rides in from headquarters on a white horse."

Finally, and most important, partners have tried to reflect change in their own work lives. Employees won't back off work until they see their bosses doing the same. So some of the most driven, hardworking partners now make a point of not checking or leaving voice mail on weekends or during vacations. "You simply have to lead by example," says Roger Dunbar, 54, managing partner for the northern California and Pacific Northwest area.

The work-life initiatives have energized E&Y, infusing its people with invention and purpose. Once-sacred truths—"serve the client at any cost," for instance—are questioned openly. In many offices, partners dare to raise their staffers' life-balance issues with clients. In fact, some actually work with clients to reinvent processes, making them family friendlier for employees on both ends. "For me, being part of the process and getting people to talk about these issues has been invigorating," says Jayne McNicol, 34, a senior audit manager in Palo Alto, California, who helped create one of the firm's first life-balance prototypes. Dunbar agrees: "That process has given me my passion back."

THE ACCOUNTANTS: BALANCING THE BOOKS

On the surface, Phil Laskawy is a conventional man who has taken a conventional path. Throughout his 39 years at E&Y, he's toiled and traveled for clients while his wife, Patricia, raised their two sons and worked

part-time from home. Still, Laskawy places high value on balance, even leaving work at mid-afternoon to coach his sons' soccer teams. "My family has always been most important to me," he says. "That doesn't mean I don't work hard. The key is to balance that hard work with the rest of your life."

As he rose through E&Y's accounting ranks, Laskawy began noticing that the firm's female employees, most of whom were married to men with demanding careers of their own, were having a tough time striking that balance—and, as a result, were leaving the company. When he became chairman in 1994, he announced that improving the firm's retention of women would be one of his top priorities. Over the years, he had seen many internal efforts to boost women's retention fail, but he was determined to create a program that would work.

When he heard Holmes's report, Laskawy says, everything fell into place: "This wasn't just a women's issue; it was everybody's issue. We needed to make big, big changes."

From the start, Laskawy made sure that everyone knew how critical he believed Holmes's mission to be. He gave her a staff of three (now up to eight) and named her director of the Office for Retention (OFR)—a newly created function and perhaps the only one of its kind at a major U.S. company.

That wasn't all. Soon after Holmes signed on, Laskawy asked her to present Catalyst's findings to the firm's 2,172 partners at one of its triannual meetings. Then he took her on a six-week "road trip," during which he introduced her to senior leaders at the firm's top 19 offices. Laskawy made a point of telling the partners that Holmes's office was on the 26th floor, just down the hall from his, and that she reported directly to him. "I wanted people to know that this wasn't just a new flavor of the month," he says.

And his support has not flagged: He meets privately with Holmes once a month to plot strategy, and he often talks up the OFR in his companywide voice-mail messages to employees. "Seven times over the past two decades, we've focused on women's issues. But this time, we're seeing real change," one male managing partner told the Wharton researchers. Why? "We now believe that those issues are a real business imperative. And Phil has made them a priority."

Holmes understood how to leverage that support to effect change in a staunchly traditional organization. She had seen companies like E&Y before. A Harvard-educated lawyer, Holmes began her career representing the Alyeska Pipeline Co. in the Exxon *Valdez* oil-spill case. But two years of litigation dampened her interest in a corporate career. So she quit the law, married a musician, and spent the next seven years advising *Fortune* 500 clients on work-life issues, first as a consultant at the Families and Work Institute, in New York, and then at Catalyst.

As a consultant, Holmes had watched many of her clients' best-intentioned diversity efforts fail. At E&Y, she realized early on that her office had to create highly visible prototypes that would involve as many employees as possible. To do that, she began canvassing senior leaders, looking for allies. She wanted to establish the first programs in offices run by partners who were recognized as both innovative leaders and big moneymakers. "I was looking for people who could bring a lot of credibility," Holmes says.

Within two months, she had zeroed in on two offices under Dunbar's aegis—the San Jose and Palo Alto tax-and-audit practices. Despite its stature as one of the firm's most lucrative offices, the San Jose office

was bleeding staff. Set in the heart of Silicon Valley, the roughly 600-person practice—today, it has nearly 1,000 people—was losing so many people to technology companies that by 1997, half of its professional staff had been at the firm for less than two years.

A self-described maverick who sports a beard and peppers his conversation with New Agey contemplations on leadership, Dunbar threw himself into the program. He quickly put together a steering committee of 16 top partners and senior managers. In January 1997, that committee spent a full day with Holmes and her colleague Susan Sweet, 38, thrashing out the causes underlying the retention problem.

At first, some partners pushed for opening a day-care center or starting concierge services. "That's a Band-Aid," Holmes told them, "not an answer to your problem." By the end of that first meeting, the committee had identified the substantive issues that could drive retention—among them allowing telecommuting, making leaders role models, and instituting an evaluation-and-feedback process. The steering committee then created eight teams—made up of 100 mostly rank-and-file managers—to study each issue and to come up with some viable solutions.

Four months later, the teams had generated about a dozen proposals. Some were modest—for example, making every day a casual-clothing day and encouraging people not to check E-mail and voice mail on weekends or during vacations. Other suggestions cut to the core of how people worked, communicated, and related to clients. "Some of those things may sound obvious," Sweet says, "but they have been revolutionary in terms of their impact on the culture."

Walking through the quiet halls of the Palo Alto practice, past a sea of cubicles and cookie-cutter offices, it's hard to envision their clean-cut inhabitants as revolutionaries. But partners and managers bear witness to the change. Take McNicol, a senior audit manager in Palo Alto. Before McNicol started telecommuting, she would spend as many as three hours a day driving between work and her home in San Francisco on the eternally jammed Highway 101. Now she works at home in the mornings and evenings and drives to the office for a few hours at midday, when traffic is lighter. Her daily commute takes 90 minutes. "That's made my life so much less stressful," she says.

Some staffers in those two offices had telecommuted before, but only on an as-needed basis. The pilot represented E&Y's first attempt at creating a program that would work on a large scale. The firm provided qualified employees—those who had, for one thing, a discrete home office—with an ISDN phone line and high-security

---

Principles for Change

How do you make changes in an organization that's mired in tradition? Ernst & Young put these five principles to work.

START AT THE TOP

Chairman and CEO Phil Laskawy has made it clear that Deborah Holmes's Office for Retention is not just window dressing. In a company where office size and location still mean a lot, Holmes's office space is just down the hall from Laskawy's. He also personally introduced her to the firm's top people and promoted her programs in companywide voice mails.

LEAD BY EXAMPLE

When executives work like maniacs, their staffers are likely to do the same. At E&Y, partners try to become models of balance. When the 3-4-5 travel schedule for consultants was implemented, many partners adopted it as well. They also began talking openly about how they meet their own needs, so that others would feel comfortable doing the same.

ONE SIZE DOESN'T FIT ALL

That's especially true in massive organizations like E&Y. So the firm encourages each office and consulting project to set up its own solution teams. An added benefit: Because large numbers of leaders and staffers are involved in the process, the measures had widespread support when they were put in place. "Most people are much more enthusiastic about new ideas that are homegrown," says Holmes, "and the ideas tend to be a lot better."

KEEP IT SIMPLE

In 1997, consultants on E&Y's Detroit project had an idea: Why not offer extra compensation to staffers who log extra hours on the road? But they dropped the idea when it began raising too many questions. "If you want change to be sustainable, you have to keep it simple," says Bob Forbes, the partner in charge of that project.

DON'T FORGET THE BIG PICTURE

No matter what initiatives E&Y's solution teams consider, team members must always consider the corporate mission: to provide top-quality service to the firm's clients. Some teams resist measures that they feel might impede client service, even as other teams embrace those innovations. "Every change that's made has to be in the context of serving the client," says Forbes, "because that's what we're all about."

access to E&Y's computer network. It also threw in a computer, a printer-scanner-fax machine, and office furniture. E&Y legitimized telecommuting by making sure that people could get their work done at home as well as they could at the office.

The biggest change, however, had more to do with how people managed their work than with where they got it done. Like staffers at most professional-services firms, E&Y staffers get assignments from a number of different partners, and little attempt is made to coordinate those assignments. Employees usually accept most projects because billable hours are equated to a person's value to the firm. The result: unlimited work and collective insanity.

As part of the prototype, two committees—one for partners and senior managers, the other for junior staffers—took responsibility for reviewing time sheets to make sure that no one was overburdened. "There are a lot of type-A personalities here who will work themselves to frustration and then quit. We wanted to get to them before that happened," says Jeffrey Calvello, 33, a senior audit manager on one of the utilization committees in San Jose.

The junior-staff committees handed out booklets that describe the number of regular (2,080) and overtime (300) hours that employees should bill annually. And both committees in both offices made it clear that managers and staffers can appeal to their respective committees when the workload seems excessive. In practice, the committees sometimes intervene even when no one complains.

In 1999 alone, according to Sweet, the utilization committees reduced the workloads of 48 people. At one point, for example, Tyler Purvis, 26, a San Jose audit senior, was working nights and weekends trying to keep up with his 12 work projects—and plan his wedding. Before he could protest,

the junior-staff committee discovered the problem. After consulting with Purvis's adviser, the committee found replacements for 5 of his projects. "These days, nobody wants to be responsible for putting someone over the edge," says Katie Jaeb, 34, a partner on the committee.

That sort of thinking, though, hasn't resounded universally in the San Jose and Palo Alto offices. "I know some of the partners think I'm nuts," says Dunbar. "They want to know, 'How can you run a several-hundred-million-dollar practice that way?'" When Dunbar issued the memo absolving staffers from checking E-mail and voice mail while on vacation, nervous partners immediately fired back questions: Were they forbidden to check in? Did the policy include weekends? "I can't stop you from checking in on vacations and weekends if you want to," Dunbar told them, "but you have permission *not* to check in."

For Dunbar, who already had begun to reassess his own relationship to work, the policy took on huge symbolic value. Divorced in 1989 after 20 years of marriage, he came to believe that his marriage failed at least in part because of his 24-7 devotion to work. "I sacrificed everything for work," he says. "I worked all the time—the day before and the day after Thanksgiving. On vacation, I would check in with the office three or four times a day. I couldn't let the phone ring at home without answering it."

Determined now to model the right behavior, Dunbar rarely leaves his staffers voice mail on weekends. "Even if it's more convenient for me to leave a voice mail at 10 P.M. on Friday, I will just record it and save it for Monday delivery," he says. And when he traveled to Greece on vacation with his second wife, he didn't call the office even once. He put another partner in charge, made a copy of his itinerary, and then left instructions on his voice-mail greeting for callers to contact the partner who was filling in for him or, in an emergency, his secretary.

More to the point, employee retention has improved dramatically. Dunbar estimates that turnover in the San Jose and Palo Alto offices has dropped about 15 percentage points since the life-balance initiatives were implemented.

But the offices are still losing valuable people. In this era of startups and stock options, the career path at a professional-services firm looks increasingly tortuous. Why work like a maniac for 12 years to become a partner, when you can make more money faster at a new high-tech joint down the road? Within 18 months, half of the members of the original life-balance steering committee had left the firm. Even some who benefited directly from the measures that were adopted in the two practices have quit to join Internet startups.

Scott Gawel, 29, assistant controller and director of finance in San Jose, was one of the pilot telecommuters. He left E&Y in November to become director of finance at Petopia.com, a San Francisco–based startup. "I had another seven years to go before I'd become a partner at E&Y. During that time, I could be at three different startups." Besides, he adds, as much as the pilot program improved his work life, it didn't change the fact that in a client-driven business, you have to "jump when a partner says jump. Looking down the road, I couldn't imagine both having a family and becoming a partner." Gawel is engaged to be married in September.

Stories like Gawel's only deepen Dunbar's enthusiasm for the life-balance measures. After all, he says, Gawel probably stayed at E&Y a year longer than he would have if the firm hadn't allowed him to work from his San Francisco home. And Dunbar believes that ultimately a more flexible

workplace helps compensate employees for any financial sacrifice. Sanity has to be worth something, after all.

While he weighs expanding the telecommuting program—about 40 employees are on a waiting list—Dunbar is mulling over the possibility of creating satellite offices that would bring work closer to people's homes. He's also requiring partners to undergo annual 360-degree evaluations from staff, peers, and supervisors. Eventually, the results of those evaluations, including how well partners promote work-life balance, will be tied to their compensation. The message: Balance and retention matter.

- - - - - - - - - - - - - - -

THE CONSULTANTS: ARE WE HOME YET?

And then there were the consultants. Holmes soon discovered that E&Y's huge consulting organization—about 37% of its business—posed very different life-balance challenges. Accountants typically work close to home, but consultants often spend months on the road, traveling to visit clients who are located in different states. At one time, E&Y consultants had reveled in the road-warrior role, brandishing their frequent-flier miles and hotel receipts like badges of honor. But now, those demands on their personal lives were breeding resentment.

Increasingly, consultants were complaining openly—and talking with their feet. Turnover remained high, averaging about 20% a year, according to one internal study. And 80% of those who left cited work-life tensions as a primary motivation.

In focus groups with consultants who were working on a Detroit project, stories of missed anniversaries and children's birthdays came pouring out. Even those who lived in the Detroit area were complaining that their schedules were so inflexible that they couldn't even take time to run a simple errand.

More than that, "there was a feeling that top-down communication was virtually nonexistent," says Bob Forbes, 38, the partner responsible for the Detroit project, who helped develop its life-balance prototype. "Nobody felt comfortable saying to a supervisor or a client, 'Hey, I need to go home.'"

Sanity Toolbox

When Ernst & Young launched its life-balance initiatives, the firm didn't just roll out one or two measures. It offered a wide variety of items—some quick fixes, some long-term solutions. Here is a sampling.

THE 3-4-5 TRAVEL SCHEDULE

Consultants can spend months at a time on the road. To ease the grind, the 3-4-5 schedule requires that consultants spend just three nights away from home, four days at a client's site, and day five working either at home or in their home office. Many consultants spend that fifth day at home, catching up on errands.

LIFE-BALANCE SURVEY AND AGREEMENT

Because consultants work on different assignments with different colleagues, each project begins with a comprehensive survey of individual needs and concerns. Consultants and their supervisors then complete a life-balance operating agreement—a contract that spells out staffing requirements, an individual's specific needs, and the way that a supervisor plans to meet those needs.

MAIL-DUTY REPRIEVE

E&Y's tax-and-audit offices in San Jose and Palo Alto came up with a simple innovation: Employees aren't obliged to check E-mail or voice mail either on weekends or while they're on vacation. No one is prevented from doing so, but the message is clear: Checking in when you're off work is unnecessary.

TELECOMMUTING

This is far from a novel solution, but it has gained broad acceptance at E&Y. The company's Silicon Valley offices screen suitable candidates for telecommuting, based on logistics and temperament. Commuting distance, workload, and seniority are also criteria. Then E&Y provides qualified employees with an ISDN phone line, secure access to its network, a computer and other equipment, and office furniture. As a result, employees' commutes are shortened, and their morale is heightened.

WORKLOAD PATROLS

Several factors contribute to unmanageable workloads: First, E&Y accountants get their assignments from a number of partners. Second, little effort is made to coordinate those assignments. And third, employees are loath to turn down billable hours. To address those problems, E&Y's San Jose and Palo Alto practices have each appointed two committees to review employees' time sheets and to make sure that no one is overwhelmed with work. Those committees can remove staffers from assignments, even when no replacements are available. The result? Less burnout.

BEST-PRACTICES DATABASE

Called the Life Balance Matrix, this online database contains descriptions of the best life-balance measures that are used across the firm as well as a list of contacts. The database lets offices share information and resources, so that they can build on one another's success.

In response to that concern, Holmes rolled out the Detroit prototype in the summer of 1997. What evolved from that program and others that were launched at the same time—including a 170-person pilot in Indianapolis—was a radical reinterpretation of how consultants work. Teams confronted the demands of heavy travel and long workweeks. They worked with clients to minimize job stress. And they found ways to bring personal issues into discussions of work assignments and schedules.

Most teams began the process with a 27-question life-balance survey that probed team members' feelings about everything from living arrangements to the expected duration of a project. Then, working together, consultants and their supervisors completed a "life-balance operating agreement" that anticipated personal and professional needs and spelled out ways to meet them.

Life balance was uncharted territory for E&Y consultants, and supervisors were often surprised by what they discovered in the agreement sessions. Take Christopher Mikucki, a manager on a consulting project in Indianapolis. Mikucki, 29, says he had no idea that one of his team members, Marcy Benson, had a commute of more than an hour each way, a drive made more stressful by her client's proclivity for 7 A.M. meetings. He also didn't know that Benson, 23, was in the midst of planning her wedding. "I consider myself a fairly open, personable guy," he says, "but I wouldn't have known about all of that if we hadn't discussed her agreement. That gave her a forum."

Discussions like that also gave Mikucki a chance to air his own concerns. Though driven to succeed at E&Y, Mikucki has interests outside of work that he's determined to pursue. He's married, for one thing. And he's a company commander in the National Guard, overseeing a unit of 140 infantry soldiers—a duty that requires

him to leave work at 4 P.M. a few days a month.

His superiors understood how important the National Guard commitment was to Mikucki. But he also needed the support of his team members. So he and Benson struck a bargain: He would cover for her when she needed to take time off to make wedding arrangements, and she would take on some of his work when he had National Guard obligations.

They also agreed that instead of coming in an hour earlier to prepare for their 7 A.M. client meeting, they would do as much prep work as possible the night before. Mikucki contacted their colleagues in Europe, who typically provided data for those meetings, and urged them to send as much material as possible the night before. A few weeks later, Mikucki and Benson persuaded the client to move the meetings to 10 A.M. That provided the client with more current information from Europe and relieved the client's team members, all of whom had children, of some stress.

Mikucki also took responsibility for checking in on the 40 team members who were working in Paris and Madrid. He discovered that several consultants were quietly working themselves to exhaustion. One young woman had been alone in Paris for five months. She had made just two quick trips home to Indianapolis during that time. Mikucki immediately sent her home for a break; gave her a new, less-stressful assignment abroad; and restructured her old job so that her replacement wouldn't have to work alone for months at a time.

E&Y also hired a full-time human-resources officer for the team in Indianapolis—the first time it had done so for any client site. "When you're in the heat of working long hours, you don't feel comfortable saying to your supervisor, who is working as hard as you are, 'Hey, I don't want to do this,'" says Robert Sydow, 43, a lead partner on the project. "It helps to have a dedicated resource." The firm has since deployed HR officers to 16 other consulting projects.

The most widely used and applauded innovation within the consulting organization, however, is the "3-4-5" travel schedule. Under that schedule, first tested in Detroit, consultants spend three nights away from home, four days at a client's site, and a fifth day "adding value" by working either at home or at their home office.

In practice, that often means flying out early Monday morning, working four long days at a client's site, and then returning home bleary-eyed late on Thursday night. Most teams stagger schedules—some members work Monday through Thursday, and others work Tuesday through Friday—so that consultants are on-site every day.

Still, by mortal standards, that's an enormous amount of travel. But that schedule is a vast improvement on the norm. "The new schedule absolutely made my time away tolerable," says Martin Schyns, 42, a manager at E&Y and a father of two who lives in Lake Forest, Illinois. He worked a 3-4-5 schedule on the Indianapolis project for about a year. Instead of spending Fridays commuting and Saturdays recovering, he got to spend his entire weekends with his wife and young children. "My kids get to see me more often," he says, "and they recognize me when I come home now. If I had to be away five days a week, I don't know whether I'd stay in consulting."

The 3-4-5 schedule is so popular that consulting partners now promote the schedule to clients as part of the up-front negotiations. And clients, typically struggling with the life-balance conundrum themselves, are increasingly receptive. Rich Johnson, 40, CIO of Norton HealthCare, a hospital chain based in Louisville, Kentucky, immediately agreed to try the 3-4-5 schedule when an E&Y partner proposed it. Johnson himself had been a consultant but had changed careers a few years ago because he hated being separated from his wife and children. Now he feels that clients have to change their mind-set. "E&Y's turnover is our problem too," he says. "A shift has to occur on the consumer side of this relationship."

Other clients, impressed by E&Y's pitch for balance, have drawn similar conclusions. Worried about the long hours that their employees were working, senior E&Y partners and the Indianapolis client decided jointly last year to give most of those involved with the project the week of Thanksgiving off. They also offered consultants living in Madrid and their client's staffers health-club memberships and concert tickets. Some clients have even asked E&Y to consult on life-balance issues—an idea that Holmes's office is considering.

Leaders of the Detroit and Indianapolis projects say that their life-balance initiatives have improved employee retention by 10 or more percentage points without hurting client service. But a number of consultants report that their 3-4-5 schedule caused some resentment among counterparts at their clients' firms. "You'd hear a few jokes before you were leaving to go home," one consultant says.

Ironically, some E&Y consultants who live near a client's site also have objected. Working five days a week and commuting from the suburbs, they have less time to spend with their family than do out-of-state commuters who are working on the 3-4-5 schedule. Schyns now works five days a week in E&Y's Chicago office, about an hour's drive from his home. He's looking forward, though, to hitting the road again. "I don't see my kids enough," he says. "I really miss my Fridays."

E&Y may not have worked through all of its life-balance problems, but it is committed to keep trying. Last summer, less than three years after joining the firm, Holmes was made partner, a sure vote of confidence from the firm's leaders. This year, she vows to expand the initiatives by promoting OFR's Life Balance Matrix, an online database that describes the best life-balance practices across the firm.

Meanwhile, Laskawy, who is planning to retire next year, says that he wants to be sure that the firm chooses a successor who will keep pushing the life-balance initiatives. "It's the right thing to do, and it makes business sense," he explains. "Few choices in life are that clear."

VII-9: The Question that Started It All . . .
Excerpt from *Repacking Your Bags*

RICHARD J. LEIDER AND DAVID A. SHAPIRO

Life cannot be hurried.
       —MAASAI SAYING

● ● ● ● ● ● ● ● ● ● ● ● ● ● ● ● ● ●
THE QUESTION THAT STARTED IT ALL . . .

Dick explains how it all began.

Late one afternoon, on a trek through the highlands along the edge of the Serengeti Plains in East Africa, I experience a breakthrough.

It is a year in which East Africa is suffering one of the worst droughts in history. The vast plains are parched, stripped to dust. River beds run bone dry. Fields of lush grass have been reduced to crabbed patches of stiff straw, and the myriad flowers, normally painted in deep shades of green, blue, and mauve, are bleached of all color. Only the dust devils, whirling high overhead and then touching down on the hard, fractured ground seem to prosper.

In the distance, over the scorched Serengeti, move incredible herds of animals—more than 3 million strong—coming together in search of water and food, tracing the hoof-worn trails that are the highways of

their migratory route. They pour steadily across the plains in a broad stream several miles long. It is an extraordinary spectacle, unlike anything else on earth.

The sun is setting, creating water mirages that appear and disappear before our eyes. But the intense heat lingers like a bad dream. It has drained us of all energy. We ride along in our Land Rover, like so many rag dolls strapped in our seats. Small cracks in the vehicle's frame vacuum in clouds of dust that blanket us. The fine silt seeps into our pores until our own bodies feel as dry as the surrounding terrain.

As the leader of this group of twelve midlife adventurers who have traveled 7,000 miles on this "Inventure Expedition" to come face to face with Africa and themselves, I feel especially exhausted. The responsibility of assuring their safety and continued involvement in our process is, at times, almost as oppressive as the heat.

We pull into Magaduru, a small Maasai village in the highlands above the Serengeti. We will be camping here for the night before the start of our backpacking trek in the morning.

A tall, lean Maasai man of aristocratic bearing springs upon our vehicles. He plunges the shaft of his spear into the ground and stands in the pose of the heron, balancing on one foot, bracing the other on the inner thigh of the supporting leg. He

Reprinted from *Repacking Your Bags*, Richard J. Leider and David A. Shapiro (San Francisco, Berrett-Koehler Inc., 1996): 1–7.

adjusts the small sword that hangs on his waist, then throws a worn blanket around his body, with a confidence that imparts style and grace to this simple gesture. His dark, penetrating eyes survey us as if scouting the windswept plain that lies behind. No emotion is revealed on his proud, serious face.

Then suddenly, he breaks into a broad smile and greets us in a combination of English and Kiswahili.

"*Jambo!* Welcome to my *boma!*"

He talks rapidly with our guide, David Peterson, fixing his gaze first on us, then nodding in the direction of his nearby cattle. Loud laughter erupts from the bushes where women and children are hiding.

"What is he saying?" we ask.

David smiles. "He hopes the smell of cattle dung is not too strong for you!"

This breaks the ice. Our laughter fills the air, joining that of our greeter. He introduces himself as Thaddeus Ole Koyie, the village chief. Gripping my hands firmly, he invites our group to be his guests.

In the lively conversation that follows, Koyie, who will be our Maasai guide for the upcoming trek, tells us that he has been educated at missionary school, where he learned to speak English. He does not explain, though, why he has turned his back on "modern" ways. Clearly, he is an influential chief, particularly for a man who is only forty. But there is something more and it implies a powerful sense of place and deep contentment with village life.

The Maasai are intensely communicative in the company of people they know. For reasons of their own, however, they are aloof and suspicious toward strangers. Happily, we don't remain strangers for long.

All of us are quite taken with Koyie. A gregarious and witty man, he has the uncanny ability to move easily between the two worlds of our group and his village, transcending the barriers of language and custom. That night, around the small campfire, when he speaks of the drought, tears glisten in his eyes. Through his passionate eloquence, we come to understand that drought, to the Maasai, is very nearly a death sentence.

Early next morning, as we leave Koyie's *boma* on our trek, I proudly sport a brand-new backpack. It is one of those high-tech ultralight models designed for maximum cargo-carrying efficiency. You know the kind—covered with snaps, clasps, and zippers, full of pockets and pouches, compartments inside compartments, a veritable Velcro heaven—and I have the thing stuffed. I'm a walking advertisement for a Patagonia or L.L. Bean catalogue. But of course, I have to be. As expedition leader, I'm responsible for the entire group. So, in addition to the required group-size first aid kit, I've also been sure to bring along items that will make our trek not just safe, but enjoyable. I'm no Boy Scout, but I certainly subscribe to their motto, "Be prepared." And I have made it a point to be prepared for just about anything.

As we walk along, Koyie keeps glancing at my pack. Time and again, I see him mentally comparing the heavy load I carry with his own, which consists of nothing more than a spear and a stick used for cattle tending. Eventually we get to talking about my backpack, and he expresses his fascination with seeing its contents. Pleased at how impressed he appears to be, I offer to show him my stuff. I look forward to letting him see how carefully I've prepared for our journey and how ready I am for anything.

The opportunity presents itself late that afternoon as we are setting up camp near another *boma.* Proudly, I commence to lay out for him everything in my pack. I unsnap snaps, unzip zippers, and un-Velcro Velcro. From pouches, pockets, and compartments I produce all sorts of strange and wonderful items. Eating utensils, cutting devices, digging tools. Direction finders, star gazers, map readers. Things to write with and on. Various garments in various sizes for various functions. Medical supplies, remedies, and cures. Little bottles inside little bottles inside little bottles. Waterproof bags for everything. Amazing stuff!

At length, I have all the gear spread out. It looks like that photo they always have in the centerfold of the great explorer article that shows everything necessary for a successful trip to the farthest reaches of the planet. Needless to say, I'm pretty satisfied with my collection.

I look over at Koyie to gauge his reaction. He seems amused, but silent. I understand. Surveying the items arrayed about us, I don't know quite what to say, either.

Finally, after several minutes of just gazing at everything, Koyie turns to me and asks very simply, but with great intensity:

"Does all this make you happy?"

There was something very powerful about Koyie's question. His words seemed to hit right at the heart of my deepest values. I honestly couldn't answer him that evening, and even weeks afterwards, I couldn't completely say for sure.

In a split second, his question had gotten me to think about all that I was carrying and why—not just on our trek, but through my entire life.

Compelled by a need to explain it to Koyie—and myself—I immediately began going through all that I had, trying to decide if it *did* make me happy. He and I sat around the fire and talked long into the night. As he listened to me, I listened also, for I found that I was clarifying the core values of my life.

In response to the question, I began to realize the truth. Some of the things did make me happy, but many of them didn't—at least not in any way that made sense to be dragging them along. So as I repacked, I set those things aside, and eventually, gave them to the local villages. I went on the rest of the trek without them. I'm not sure that I'll never want or need them again, but I certainly didn't suffer for not having them at the time.

My load was much lighter after I'd reexamined my needs. And on the rest of the trip, I was quite a bit happier for having repacked my bags. As a result of this experience, I began to assemble my thoughts and feelings about how to *lighten my load.* The insight I've gained has contributed to and been informed by my work as a life and career planning counselor. In discussions with clients, colleagues, and family members, I've developed a new understanding of how important it is to periodically *unpack* and *repack* our bags at various points in our lives.

As my co-author, David, and I have worked with these thoughts, we've made a number of discoveries:

- We've discovered that many people are laboring through their lives, weighed down by attachments that no longer serve them. Patterns of behavior that have helped them get where they are, aren't helping them get where they want to be. As a result, many people feel desperate. They are grieving over the loss of a life—their own. In order to overcome this despair—which we all feel at certain points in our lives—we must confront it, and quite literally, laugh in its face.

- We've discovered that it is possible to simplify one's life without sacrificing the conveniences and comforts we've come to expect. We can *give up* without *giving in.* By having less *in* our lives, we can get more *out of* life. To get to this place, we have to figure out what really matters. We have to examine what's in our bags and decide for ourselves if it's really what we want—and ought—to be carrying.

- We've developed a new appreciation for what the "good life" entails and how important it is that, in creating a vision of the good life for ourselves, we take into account four critical factors: *work, love, place,* and *purpose.*

- We've learned that what we carry "in our bags" defines how we spend our time. And how we spend our time determines how we live and who we are. Sadly, many of us are laboring in ways that are unrelated to the things we really want to do with our lives. It is entirely possible, though, to redesign our lives—to repack our bags—in order to have, do, and be the person we've always wanted to be.

- We've found that happiness has more to do with experiencing than with having. Having is great, but it's not *it*. For most of us, what we're really looking for is a feeling—a feeling of *aliveness*.

Over the past few years, Dick's relationship with Koyie has grown—and the learning has continued. The countless conversations they've had sitting around late night fires and trekking across wind-swept plains have given us great insight into ourselves and our culture. Koyie gently reminds us that the freedom to choose is not something we *have* and therefore can lose, but something we *are*. It is of our deepest essence, just waiting to be called upon.

At every moment, in every situation, we are free to choose a simpler expression of our being. We always have the potential to unpack, lighten our loads, and repack.

For many of us it takes a crisis, mid-life or other, to get us even thinking about what we're carrying. And then, unfortunately, we tend to make decisions from within the crisis. Instead of pausing to reconsider, in a purposeful manner, what we've brought along and why, we're apt to cast everything off and just run. Instead of making rational decisions that prepare us for what's ahead, we tend to come from a position of panic or fear—and the choices we make reflect that.

We can use a process for repacking our bags to stimulate thought on this issue outside of a crisis. We can reflect on our lives in a manner that helps us sort out what's really important—what makes us happy—from what's just weighing us down. We can then map out a new road ahead, one that will get us where we really want to go, with the things we really want to bring along the way.

The process is not something that we experience once and are done with. It's an experience, like Koyie's question, that stays with you, that stimulates thinking and inspires ongoing reflection. We hope you'll find it useful and meaningful no matter where you currently are in life.

There are many ways to engage the process, and you'll discover your own as you proceed. But perhaps the best way to get going is to begin with the question that started it all:

"Does all this make you happy?"

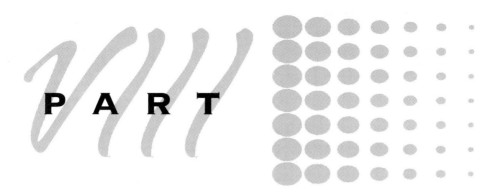

PART VIII

HRM REALITY: ANTICIPATING THE FUTURE

In the conclusion to our first edition of this book we wrote:

"These are times of challenge and turbulence for the HRM profession. Of course, we believe there is a future for the field! However, it is not obvious either what that future will be or how much of its form and content will be created by members of the HRM profession themselves. In part, it will be shaped by economic, technological, and political forces that are influencing the whole of management practice. However, if HRM is to be a healthy, constructive, and innovative force in the organizational world of the twenty-first century, then as professionals, both the academics and the practitioners must rise to the occasion, seize the moment, and play their parts separately and in concert."

These statements remain true today, in the early part of the twenty-first century. As many of the readings in this edition show, HRM as a profession is responding to the challenge of being engaged in the issues of the moment. It is an exciting and challenging arena. New models of HR practice have emerged (we have featured several in this book) and the domain of relevance for HR research and application has changed and expanded, often in unexpected ways. The exponential growth of influence of the Internet and the Web caught by surprise most people writing about the future of management and organization in 1992, when our first edition was published. What lies ahead at the beginning of the twenty-first century? No one knows for sure, of course. We have included a range of readings by authors whose ideas might give us some shape, some anticipation of the next few years. Whatever the future, we remain convinced that HR issues and challenges will need attention from all managers, not just those in the HR profession, a point we made at the beginning of the book.

The reading "Future Trends in Human Resources" discusses existing trends toward outsourcing, continuous learning, and technology-based learning. Expect "quality of life" to endure as a priority Jill Vardy reports on the view that there are no experts in the new Web-based economy. "The future belongs to organizations that emphasize opportunity, learning, and exploration," says expert Kevin Kelly, editor-at-large of *Wired Magazine* in "Jettison Old Notions Of Success, Says Internet Guru."

An article on the future of work in *The Economist* ("The Future of Work and Career Evolution") examines patterns of worklife and predicts more frequent job changing and freelancing. While the old social contract between employers and workers is being shredded, the authors say, it is not clear what will replace it.

Warren Bennis, an acknowledged expert on leadership is interested in the future of leadership. In celebration of his 75th birthday, Kimberly Hopkins Perttula interviewed Bennis. In the interview, Bennis talks eagerly about the need for new understanding and models of leadership for the world of e-commerce and about the increased incidence of transitory work teams. He validates the *Economist* authors' prediction of increased career and job mobility and speaks of the need for people to keep reinventing themselves to face the continuously evolving workplace.

At least some of the workplace of the future will be virtual; a "place" in which employees operate remotely from each other and from managers. Wayne F. Cascio's article ("Managing a Virtual Workplace") provides a thoughtful analysis of this challenge.

A number of readings in Part V focused on discrimination in the workplace. Will the future generate new forms of discrimination? One possibility lies in the realm of genetics. If we can identify causes of dysfunctional behavior through gene testing, will this translate into new means of selecting out "undesirable" attitudes and behaviors in new hires by companies seeking a competitive edge? The reading "Congress Urged to Move on Genetics Legislation" by Theresa Minton-Eversole helps get this issue on the table.

Another sinister aspect of our present and near future is the exploitation of labor in underdeveloped parts of the world, as well as in the United States. What should HR philosophy and practice do about this? "Illegal Child Labor Comes Back" by Brian Dumaine discusses this troubling issue and offers some suggestions.

We conclude this section with three related articles: In a brief excerpt from the book *The Monster Under the Bed*, Stan Davis and Jim Botkin list seven predictions for the shape of business and education. They are succinct and sobering. The next article bears on some of Davis and Botkin's predictions. In "The Quest for Lifetime Employability," Jeanne C. Meister discusses ways that companies can contribute to helping employees find lifetime employability, which is a different aim than lifetime employment, which was once a desirable and sometimes attainable goal. The final reading ("Reconstructing Management Education as Lifelong Learning" by Richard E. Boyatzis and Kathy E. Kram) takes up the present and future challenge of lifetime learning and the role of management education in keeping this process effective.

We hope these readings and the others published in this book inspire the reader with a sense of the richness, range, challenge, and opportunity that face HRM professionals in their daily lives and in their careers. We hope also that they are a positive contribution to those seeking to keep their own learning alive and ongoing.

VIII-1: Future Trends in Human Resources

JOHN McMORROW

THE RISE OF OUTSOURCING: OPPORTUNITIES AND CHALLENGES

The growing importance of career development also stems from other significant changes underway in many corporations. One is an increasing level of outsourcing, as more companies transfer internal operations to outside service providers who can do the job better and more efficiently. In response to this demand, outsourcing companies of all sizes have sprung up. At the same time, downsized or otherwise at-risk employees are increasingly finding employment with the outsourcing firms that replaced them, or are joining the growing contingent workforce selling its services back to larger businesses.

Seth Grimes, principal at Internet consulting firm Alta Plana, sees the move toward a contractual and ad-hoc workforce, and away from traditional, long-term employer-employee relationships, as a positive development. "Employers will increasingly become customers for contractual employees," said Grimes.

Will this trend increase in the future, or will the more traditional employment relationship return? Our panel suggested that both forms of work are here to stay, with the flexible, contingent workforce becoming increasingly important.

"Perhaps one of the benefits of outsourcing is that it focuses the business on its true core competencies," noted Harold Burlingame, executive vice president of AT&T. He believes that it's critical for HR

professionals to understand not only what they're good at, but also which functions they should retain close control of, and which can be outsourced. "We no longer can do everything," said Burlingame. "In determining what should be outsourced and what should be retained, our value is in helping the business make the right choices."

CONTINUOUS LEARNING: THE KEY TO CAREER SUCCESS

As people change jobs more frequently, as they work across geographic and cultural boundaries, and as many become associated more with a single profession than a single company, continuous learning will take center stage. Talent Alliance member companies have increasingly pointed out the need to obtain employees with new skill sets. But in today's economy there simply are not enough educated new hires to go around. Some members of the panel said that the problem lies with the source of young, new workers—the schools. "There's a growing gap between the skill needs of industry and what the public education system can provide," says Brian Lynch of Armstrong World Industries.

If there simply isn't enough high-quality workers to meet the needs of global businesses, then more emphasis must be placed on continuous learning and retraining of existing workers. "The issue is not only how to hire people with fundamentally different skill sets," argued Gary Lewis, project manager at DuPont, "but how to retrain the existing workforce."

Today, educational institutions—from community colleges to prestigious universities—are retooling to meet the needs of

Reprinted from *HR Focus* (September, 1999): 7–9.

business. Education is also booming in the private sector, as organizations make alliances with commercial-education service providers. Moreover, providers of education are delivering more of their programs in corporate customers' classrooms, conference rooms, and cafeterias—wherever there is need.

Jim Smither, professor of management development at LaSalle University, said there is a shift away from traditional classroom-based education. He pointed to new hybrid universities, such as the University of Phoenix, which is a for-profit, non-campus institution, as harbingers of things to come. Smither likened the change in education to what has occurred in healthcare. "Just as managed care has transformed the way medical practice is delivered," said Smither, "so will for-profit, distance learning transform the way education is delivered."

The panel saw several implications stemming from the changing nature of education. First, education will no longer be separated from daily life, and more and more people will try to fit it into their daily schedules, at work and at home. Education delivery will quickly become a 24-hour, seven-day-a-week service. But an important issue is whether employers will allow time for learning, either "on the clock" or through time away from work. Another concern is whether companies will continue to pay for education. The Talent panel suggested that companies will support education, knowing they will receive a return on their investment.

Does this mean that traditional education will become a memory? "I don't think so," noted Allison Rossett, professor of educational technology at San Diego State University. The problem, she said, is that not all employees are suited for the independent learning delivered by innovative programs. She suggested that people become successful learners by developing skills related to "learning how to learn." Both independent

learning and traditional classroom education will be important to employers and employees, and will complement each other.

Whatever the form of education delivery, the Talent panel stressed that continuous learning is key to a successful career. As mergers and acquisitions, downsizing and other events radically change the corporate landscape over the next few years, employees will have to keep their skills and knowledge razor sharp to remain competitive in their careers. As corporations compete for high-quality people, education will emerge as both a necessity and an employee benefit. "New hires will begin seeking opportunities to advance their capabilities," noted Marc Rosenberg, senior consultant with OmniTech Consulting Group, Inc. Rosenberg believes that employees understand the value of knowledge. "They will expect their employers to help them stay on the cutting edge," he said. "Otherwise, they'll go someplace else." DataMain's Jeff Hunter agreed, noting that in the future, the law of supply and demand for highly educated employees will dominate recruiting efforts.

THE EXPLOSIVE GROWTH OF TECHNOLOGY-BASED LEARNING

Because more demands are being put on employees, investment in education is increasing. Corporate spending on training is up 26% over the last five years, according to the latest survey done by *Training Magazine* (October 1998). And technology, along with nontraditional institutions, will radically change the way education is delivered. Programs like Duke University's executive MBA program and Penn State University's World Campus, conducted largely over the Internet, will become even more attractive. In the private sector, hundreds of companies are now selling online. From IT to sales training, the Internet—and intranet—is becoming a dominant force in corporate learning.

Walter Tornow, senior fellow at the Center for Creative Leadership, believes that technology will continue to be used for both performance improvement and communications. Many on the Talent panel noted that the Internet is more than a learning or HR tool; it is the lifeblood of business and "the primary vehicle for commerce and data exchange." In addition, the Internet has dramatically changed the economic model of education delivery, since it makes education available to anyone with a computer, at any time and at any location. And the Internet is cost-effective since it uses a fraction of the business's infrastructure. For these reasons, the panel noted, the World Wide Web will not wither away like so many previous technological innovations.

ARE WE READY FOR "INSTANT KNOWLEDGE"?

What happens when technology enables greater access to greater amounts of information, and when workers increasingly need that information, and need it quicker, to do their jobs? Will they be capable of handling the information glut? Do we fully understand the implications of a much faster, more informed work environment, and will businesses suffer when too much information becomes contradictory or clogs the system? David Jones, professor of management development at LaSalle University, thinks these issues could create huge problems in the future. "The ability to sort through large amounts of immediate information may become one of the new managerial skills," he said. HR professionals certainly will need this new skill. According to Stacy Napper, vice president of HR operations at GTE, "We will probably be most affected by the need for immediate, just-in-time information, data, trends, and services."

The panel saw great challenges ahead if the potential of technology is to be realized. "Simply managing these emerging and evolving technologies will be a big task," noted Manuel London, professor of management and director of the Center for Human Resource Management at the State University of New York at Stony Brook. "The changes in technology, combined with the rapidly changing economic scene, make continuous learning, employee involvement, and commitment all the more challenging," he said.

Several panel members also saw differences in employee demographics as a key challenge to using the new technology. "People need training on how to reach this medium," says Mark Mehler, co-author of *CareerXRoads,* the 1999 directory of the 500 best job, resume, and career management sites on the Web. "Older employees must know how to use a computer; that training is critical," he noted.

Don Kuhn, executive director of UNICON (The International University Consortium for Executive Education), pointed to "the division between those who are computer literate and those who are not" as a major problem area where more must be done.

Organizations also fall into the two categories: the technology-capable and the technology-weak. Creating opportunities that allow organizations to develop technological skills may become a public-policy issue in the future. Quinn Mills, professor of business administration at Harvard University, advocates business-government partnerships at the local and regional level to promote infrastructure. "If you don't have the infrastructure, everything else must wait until you do," pointed out Marc Rosenberg of OmniTech Consulting.

The benefits that come from partnerships are not limited to technology. "In most of the companies I know, HR executives are looking to form partnerships," said AT&T's Harold Burlingame. He noted that companies can come together, despite the competitive nature of business, to create valuable joint services that benefit everyone. "The smart use of technology can make partnerships work even better—this was the basis for the formation of Talent Alliance itself," he said.

QUALITY OF LIFE: AN ENDURING TREND

The Talent panel concluded its discussion by focusing on an issue that has always been at the heart of human resources, and probably will always be: quality of life. "There's an increasing interest in people finding meaning in their lives and in their work," noted Don Kuhn of UNICON. "People are no longer content with income and acquisition alone, but are looking for personal satisfaction." Virtual offices, flex time, increased mobility, and other innovative work arrangements are indicative of a renewed sense of balance that people seek between work and family, and

productive time vs. leisure time. In addition, the changing nature of business and the end of the so-called "psychological relationship" between employer and employee has created a vacuum in the lives of many people. According to Kerry Bunker, of the Center for Creative Leadership, this has created "an enormous threat to our view of meaningful work." He observed that: "While the capacity to communicate has reached new heights, the potential to connect at a human level is being dramatically undermined. Finding a way to balance these two trends will be key to leading people through change and transition."

Perhaps it was fitting that the panel discussion ended on the most "human" aspects of human resources: communications, connections, and balance. The experts agreed that despite the transformations in business, the emergence of a highly technological and global workplace, and new views of the very nature of employment, the dominant HR concerns for the future are much the same as they were in the past: to help people cope with change, successfully find their place in the world of work, and build lifelong careers that are productive and satisfying.

VIII-2: Jettison Old Notions of Success, Says Internet Guru
"There Are No Experts"

JILL VARDY

Ottawa—Every Internet success story creates opportunities for others to succeed, but companies must be willing to abandon their old notions of success, says Kevin Kelly, editor-at-large of *Wired* magazine.

Reprinted from the *National Post* online (May 4, 2000). www.nationalpost.com

"Competitive advantage has gone from the efficient to the nimble. . . . That means you have to be willing to let go of things that are working and head towards the unknown," Mr. Kelly said during a two-hour speech at the commerce 2000 trade show, a conference and exhibition that attracted about 8,000 of Ottawa's technology types.

Mr. Kelly, who at age 48 is the grand old man of *Wired*, advised business people to find younger "mentors" who understand the new economy and don't hold the old notions of risk-averse success. "If you're over 40, surround yourself with 20-year-olds," he said. "That's what I've done."

He warned companies that things are changing so fast that the business virtues of efficiency, productivity, and optimization must be replaced with opportunity, learning, and exploration. And companies must not be afraid to make mistakes. "We tend to think that there are a lot of experts in the new economy, but there are no experts. . . .

The Web is less than 2,000 days old," he said.

He noted that Microsoft Corp., by sending out beta test versions of its Windows 98 software to key customers, got those customers to do the final testing and product evaluation that Microsoft would have had difficulty conducting itself. As a result, he said, customers of Microsoft ended up spending more money evaluating Windows 98 than Microsoft did developing it. "Microsoft harnessed the power of its customers," he said. "Customers completing the product—that's a sign of a new economy."

VIII-3: The Future of Work and Career Evolution

Many still question claims that the patterns of working life are changing. But in the United States the anecdotal signs are increasing: more frequent job changes, more freelancing, more working at home, more opportunity but also more uncertainty. The old social contract between employers and workers is being shredded. It is still unclear what will replace it.

In a slightly shabby classroom in Manhattan, a young man in a neat blue suit introduces himself to the group as Walter—and then sets about describing the lessons from his job search. "Be prepared, know your story, and network, network, network." That was the way that Walter jumped from a job in the construction industry in Canada to one in human resources in New York; and, if the current job does not work out, that will be the way that he will jump to his next job. The network will be ready, his "brand" established. The teacher repeats the mes-

sage: start preparing now for the job after the one that you are looking for at the moment, because "you are going to be doing this again."

What on earth would "Organisation Man," that stolid icon of the 1950s, make of the Five O'Clock Club? An "employee advocacy organization" with 20 branches around America, most of the club's members are 35–55 years old and a third of them earn more than $100,000 a year. The club offers plenty of regular career advice but it is based on two things that Organisation Man avoided like the plague: disloyalty and feelings.

Rather than allowing jobs to define their lives, as Organisation Man did, the club's members are encouraged to decide on their own goals—to imagine what sort of person they want to be in 40 years' time, for example—and then to design their careers around that goal. The club also caters to people whose needs are more psychological than financial, such as the Internet manager who has made $3 million in the past 18 months "but still feels left behind."

Reprinted from *The Economist* (January 29, 2000): 89–92.

Naturally, the club owes at least some of its success to America's booming economy, but its founder, Kate Wendleton, insists that it has also thrived because it is catering to fundamental changes in working life. And she is not alone. McKinsey, a consultancy, has warned its clients that the most important challenge for companies is "the war for talent." Business magazines are full of details about "why it pays to quit," how you should be "hot desking" with colleagues, "telecommuting" from home, and generally reconsidering your whole future.

Yet there is also a more pessimistic school of thought. Many on the left, particularly in Europe, believe that the same forces—technology, globalization, the shift towards services—are leaving workers to the mercy of a new and ruthless variety of capitalism. In a new book, *Sharing the Wealth* (Norton, $24.95), Ethan Kapstein of the University of Minnesota argues that governments are now playing a game of "beggar-thy-labor" which will stir up a social backlash against globalization.

In continental Europe unemployment stands at 10% and more people are being forced to accept part-time work. In Japan, according to the *Asahi* daily newspaper, the number of businessmen diagnosed as clinically depressed has risen rapidly. *Sararimen* check into their shrinks on Saturdays and Sundays because the more frightening meetings happen on Mondays. In the United States, critics point out that, despite eight years of economic growth, lay-offs over the past two years have been more widespread than ever.

Meanwhile, median wages for male workers are still lower in real terms than they were in the 1970s.

What on earth is happening? The broad answer is that it depends on where you live and what you do. The "insecurity" that is suddenly so frightening to a *sariman* in Tokyo has long been normal for a construction worker in Dallas (and not that odd for

a construction worker in Tokyo either). There are also different costs: an unemployed worker in Germany receives benefits many American workers can only dream about. On the other hand, most arguments about "the end of the career" usually end up focusing on the world's biggest, most flexible and fastest-changing labor market—the United States.

Some pour cold water on the whole idea that the traditional American career is disappearing. David Neumark, an economist at Michigan State University, points to plenty of professions—teachers, doctors, even labor economists—in which job-hopping remains rare, and to plenty of others, such as the building trade, in which job-hopping has been the norm for generations. The basic measure of job stability is how long people have been in their current job. In 1998 the median figure was 3.6 years, a shade higher than in 1983. The figures for other countries show no great changes either.

And yet the American figures are distorted by two phenomena: the aging of the baby-boomer generation, born between 1946–64, who account for 47% of the workforce and have now reached an age when most of them do not want to move; and the increase in mothers returning to permanent jobs.

Some parts of the workforce display unmistakable signs of change. Job tenure for men aged 35 and over has decreased since 1983. And the average 32-year-old in America has already worked for nine different firms. There has also been a sharp increase in job insecurity, a measure distinct from, but related to, job stability. Most polls show that Americans—particularly older male workers with long tenure—are more frightened than ever of losing their jobs.

Most important of all, there are solid reasons why careers should change, probably at an increasing rate. Ken Goldstein, an economist at the Conference Board, a business-research group, points to the switch of jobs from big manufacturing firms to small, service ones. Companies with fewer than 100 workers account for half the American workforce and are responsible for two out of three new jobs. Even the biggest manufacturers, such as General Electric, try to act "small" by organizing their operations into a network of autonomous units.

This means that the old model of a career, in which an employee worked his way up the ladder in a single company, is becoming rarer. Small service firms seldom have more than three layers; and even big companies, which still possess more of a hierarchy, tend to promote people in jumps. There is also a much higher chance of being ousted. Although the United States has been creating more than 100,000 net new jobs a month, it is also true that over the past two years some 300,000 people have been filing first-time claims for unemployment each week, indicating that many must endure the stressful experience of losing their jobs before finding another one.

With the life-cycle of products shrinking, and competition coming from unexpected corners of the globe, companies have to be more nimble than ever. This uncertainty helps some workers: if a firm has no idea from which direction the next competitive threat will come, one of its few sensible strategies is to amass good people to prepare for as many contingencies as possible. But it also increases the pressure on companies to contract out their "non-core" activities to (often smaller) specialized companies or to use more temporary workers than in the past (as four in five American firms now do).

This has threatened in all sorts of ways the type of career which Organisation Man once assumed was a birthright. About one in ten American workers, or 12.5 million people, are either independent contractors or on some sort of temporary contract. Around 10 million people work outside

their corporate office at least three days a month (double the proportion in 1993).

One hunch is that the biggest changes in work patterns are occurring at the top and bottom of the income scale. One good place to test this thesis is California's Silicon Valley, the home of the most innovative and fastest-changing industry in America.

• •

THE VIEW FROM PALO ALTO

It is hard not to feel optimistic about the future of work sitting down to lunch with four students of Stanford Business School. The conversation drifts from potential careers to the enormous amounts of money being made around Silicon Valley. The four lunchers are not typical of the American workforce, but not too strange a mix by Californian standards—a Midwesterner, a Chilean, a woman from Northern Ireland and a Californian educated at Eton, Britain's most elite private school. They have already crammed what many people would regard as a career's worth of achievement into their short working lives. They have held jobs as management consultants and investment bankers (or both); one worked down a mine, another restructured a succession of companies.

The four are quietly confident that their success will continue: "Stanford provides you with your global driver's license," says one. But they also recognize that they will have to be nimble. They discuss a Stanford alumnus who graduated in 1994 and is already on his sixth start-up firm. One remarks that business school helps to improve your most important asset—your Rolodex—before adding that one of his first jobs as a young investment banker was to sell the company that makes the device.

The students come from diverse backgrounds, but their attitude is quintessentially Californian. The state has created jobs faster than the rest of the United States, but its labor market is also more volatile. The median job tenure for Californian workers is only three years. Almost half of them have been with their current employers for two years or less, and only a fifth have been with their employer for more than ten years (compared with a national average of a third). A sixth of the state's adults report either losing their job in the past three years or moving to a new job because they thought they were about to lose their existing one.

The fastest-growing part of California's economy is the temp business: it has added as many jobs as the software and electronic-equipment industries combined. Now the Internet seems to be having much the same effect on "job trading" in the state as it has already had on share trading. Career sites such as Monster.com, which advertises 140,000 jobs at a time, offer an easy chance to almost everyone to indulge the whim to "see how much I am really worth."

In Silicon Valley the turnover of employees is close to 20% a year—a number that skyrockets if companies miss profit targets and imperil option packages. "Retaining good people is paramount," says Bob Spinner, the chief executive of Extensity, a software maker. Like everybody else in the valley, he treats the globe as his recruiting ground—a fifth of Extensity's 150 workers were born abroad—and he views age as less significant than talent. He reckons that most of his employees work 60 hours a week. Extensity tries to recompense them for long hours with perks as well as money, such as a company cabin in the mountains or, for those with "alternative lifestyles," the extension of health-care coverage to same-sex partners.

Extensity is a client of Icarian, another Silicon Valley firm which applies "just-in-time" manufacturing techniques to employment. In hours, claims Doug Merritt, Icarian's boss, he can summon not just secretaries and assistants but freelance engineers (for $90–$200 an hour), technical writers ($75–$150), marketing directors ($200–$500), and chief executives ($300–$800), although all these figures are before negotiations about equity stakes. Mr. Merritt says that business people are becoming ever more like film actors, with talent agents who offer package deals for their "stars." One famous team of Silicon Valley bankers has changed employers four times in the past decade, increasing their "brand value" each time.

Yet even in Silicon Valley there is another side to this story. According to Joint Venture: Silicon Valley Network, a consultancy, the poorest fifth of the valley's households saw their real income fall by 8% between 1991 and 1997 (income for the richest fifth rose by 19%). There are plenty of secretaries on low pay with not much more to show for their long hours than a fistful of worthless stock options.

● ● ● ● ● ● ● ● ● ● ● ● ● ● ● ● ● ●

A DIFFERENT PLACE

Will Silicon Valley's experience be replicated elsewhere? Probably not exactly. Silicon Valley's concentration of fast-growing high-tech firms is unusual by any standards. And yet in the long term, the same forces that have reshaped work habits there are likely to have similar effects in many other places. The information technology industry in America is growing more than twice as fast as the economy as a whole—and in every state it is producing more job changes. In one recent study of American lay-offs in 1993–98 by Challenger, Gray & Christmas, a Chicago consultancy, the computer industry was the third-largest downsizer, and telecoms the fourth.

Other industries are beginning to display a similar pattern. Icarian also sells its just-in-time jobs to the drug and finance businesses: in both industries it claims that, as in Silicon Valley, career volatility is highest for "strong-brand" people at the top but also for "no-brand" people at the bottom. Signs of the same pattern are emerging even in Japan, where the annual number of requests for temporary workers has soared from 100,000 a decade ago to 1 million today.

So careers may not be "over," but they are becoming a bit more flexible, and are likely to become ever more so. Is this revolution welcome? Optimists claim that a flexible workforce is basically a happier workforce. One recent survey of work trends by researchers at Rutgers University and the University of Connecticut found that 91% of Americans said that they liked their jobs.

Even job-churning has a liberating side. *US News & World Report* reckons that 17 million Americans will have voluntarily quit their job for another post in 1999, compared with only 6 million five years before. Many of the jobs that have been phased out have been fairly brutal, tedious ones (unless you think that coal mining is a noble art). And even fairly mundane factory jobs now give workers more variety and responsibility (through self-governing teams and the like).

But there are worries. To begin with, there is overwork. On average, Americans work 1,957 hours a year, more than those in other rich countries. According to the Economic Policy Institute, a think-tank, the average middle-income married couple with children now works a combined 3,335 hours a year, eight work-weeks more than in 1979. Much of this increase has come from middle-class mothers going to work instead of staying at home.

Cell-phones and beepers act like electronic leashes, keeping people perpetually tied to their job. One study by the Families and Work Institute, a New York–based charity, showed that about 75% of college-educated 25- to 32-year-olds in Manhattan work more than 40 hours a week; in 1977 only 55% did. In Silicon Valley people talk about "sleep camels" (those who store up

sleep at weekends). The average mother and father spends 22 hours less every week with their children than parents did in 1969.

Many people want their lives to have some predictability. But the fashion for flattening hierarchies makes it more difficult to plan their careers. A few make spectacular leaps. Most stay at the same level for years, insecure and frustrated.

The drawbacks of the new American workplace for the educated are nothing compared with the drawbacks for the uneducated. Even a full-time contingent worker typically is paid only 80% of a regular full-time employee—and the benefits are often minimal. When people talk about basic jobs becoming more interesting, they are usually describing jobs in manufacturing. Many service-sector jobs offer little variety. Ask any pizza-delivery man.

There is also the continuing problem of inequality. In 1979, the average American college graduate earned 38% more than the average high-school graduate; now the gap is 71%. This is a guilty concern for the students at Stanford Business School. The young woman from Northern Ireland wants to save enough by the age of 40 to move into the voluntary sector. The Midwesterner starts out by saying that "in the axis of opportunism to loyalty, I'm on the opportunist end of the spectrum," but later admits that he hopes for a second career as a teacher.

The full benefits and losses of more flexible, insecure careers will become evident only when the American economy slows down. But for most, the lesson is stark: educate yourself, and then reeducate yourself. In the 1950s, when three out of five American workers were "unskilled," education was considered a bonus; now the one in five workers who is unskilled is at a big disadvantage. The need for continual reeducation extends even into the later stages of most working lives. Few can any longer afford to rest on their laurels, or to rely on experience that rapidly becomes obsolete because of technological change.

The new job market presents almost as many challenges to companies as to workers. The most talented and hard-working people are unlikely to go to firms that Jeffrey Pfeffer, a professor at Stanford, dubs "toxic workplaces." Focusing on core competencies might mean outsourcing peripheral employees, but it also means creating a core group of loyal employees who have worked for the company for years; who have absorbed, or helped to create, its ethos; and who are committed enough to transmit that ethos to future employees. As with Extensity, the focus is increasingly on finding nonfinancial carrots to retain these "core" employees (if the only reason why an employee stays with any particular firm is money, then he or she is much easier to poach).

Efforts to hold back these changes with laws guaranteeing workers job protection are growing ever costlier. Just compare the high unemployment rates in Europe, where it is more difficult both to hire and to fire workers, with the low rate in the United States. The exigencies of the new-style labor market will put increasing pressure on governments not only to dismantle obsolete labor regulations, but to adapt to the growing need of both employers and workers for more flexible pensions, training and—in the United States—health care. Even as the old social contract between employers and workers fades, the new one is still unclear. The students at Stanford Business School and the job-hopping members of the Five O'Clock Club might have a clear idea of the bargain they strike with employers. But many other workers do not. Some American employers are offering an implicit (and sometimes explicit) deal to their employees: accept that we may have to sack you and, in exchange, we will make sure that you have the marketable skills needed to find another job.

But many firms and workers still find this idea unsettling. Establishing a new understanding between the two looks like being one of the great social, political, and economic challenges of the next few decades. Until that happens, like most other workers, high or low, you are on your own. It may be time to start building your "brand" and getting out there to network, network, network.

VIII-4: A Lifetime of Generous Company: An Interview with Warren Bennis

KIMBERLY HOPKINS PERTTULA

Warren Bennis, one of the world's foremost thinkers on leadership, is a Distinguished Professor of Business Administration and founding chairman of The Leadership Institute at the University of Southern California. A prolific writer, he has authored more than 1,500 articles and 25 books on man-

Reprinted from the *Journal of Management Inquiry* 9 (4): 353–360.

agement and leadership, including *Leaders: The Strategies for Taking Charge, On Becoming a Leader, Why Leaders Can't Lead,* and *Organizing Genius.*

After earning a Ph.D. in economics and social sciences at the Massachusetts Institute of Technology, Dr. Bennis served on the faculties of M.I.T., Boston University, and Harvard University. His long and fruitful career has also included appointments as provost at the State University of New York (Buffalo) in 1967 and, later, president of the University of Cincinnati. In 1980 he came to the University of Southern California where he continues to teach, write, research, and consult with corporate and political leaders.

In 2000 we celebrate Warren Bennis' 75th birthday and his 50 years as a student of organizations and leadership. As Warren himself noted in the preface to *An Invented Life,* a collection of essays published in 1993[1], "I've been thinking about leadership almost as long as I have been thinking." In May 2000, the Department of Management and Organization at USC hosted a Festschrift[2] to celebrate the life and career of Dr. Bennis. As part of this celebration, a conference was held in Warren's honor on the theme of "Emerging Issues for Developing the Next Generation of Leaders." In this interview, I asked Warren to reflect on his life experiences and offer his insights on the future of leadership in this new millennium.

HOPKINS: What would you say is the essence of effective leadership?

BENNIS: The enduring quality of leadership is *managing relationships.* I was just on the phone with a reporter from *Fortune* magazine who was asking, "Why all the recent interest in executive coaching?" Basically, coaching is getting people to hold up a mirror to themselves to provide "reflective backtalk." Because if there is one thing that leadership is all about, it is that there has to be willing and inspired followers. If you really reduce leadership to its essence, it would be a person with a certain goal and the relationships to get people fully aligned and committed to achieving that goal. The leader would fully deploy his or her own talents in a collaborative way to reach their goal.

Even with all the changes taking place in the workplace, I don't think that the importance of managing relationships will change at all. In fact, I was just talking to a 28-year-old multimillionaire who lives in Santa Barbara but has an e-commerce business in Silicon Valley and flies his own airplane back and forth. I asked, "How long do you think you will be doing this?" And he said, "Oh, maybe three or four years." I replied, "So then what?" And he said, "Oh, I don't know, sell it or start another one." In the new e-world, *there is no long term,* but even so, what he has got to do, in a very short period of time, is to animate and energize his people. Currently, there are only 250 people in his company, but he has to worry about their involvement, their commitment, and their empowerment. He needs to work at getting people behind him and enrolled in his vision. I think if you take a look at the career of Steve Jobs and look at the difference between Steve Jobs now and Steve Jobs 10 years ago, I think he has learned just that. It is not just because he developed tangerine and purple colors for his iMac; it's because he's developed new colors for himself.

Change is in the air—changes in the concept of time, changes in the concept of success, changes with regard to life-long learning. Any kind of professional will be in graduate school of one kind or another. Not necessarily for a Ph.D. but rather to keep learning. And jobs are going to be like serial monogamy. Moving from job to job to job. But with all of those changes, the affairs of the human heart don't change. Managing relationships, emotional intelligence, trust, meaning, direction, and vision—those ideas have no shelf life.

HOPKINS: Is the way that leaders manage and develop relationships changing in today's frenetic, fast-paced world?

BENNIS: The new forms of organizations are already beginning to resemble the Hollywood model where you come together for a distinct and finite period of time—thus today's leader is going to be much like an executive producer in a film. Consider 28-year-old Winona Ryder. I haven't seen her movie, *Girl Interrupted*, but what is interesting is that she was the executive producer of her own film. She was also the lead. She had to get all of the people involved in the film to rally around her vision, to really *understand* what that movie was all about. While being the executive producer and the star, she had to abandon her own ego for the talents of other people. Winona Ryder had to bring together all of these people—a reluctant director whom she had to enroll and a cast of people to do the filming—in a very short period of time. She created and incarnated a dream (the movie) and then it dissolved and broke apart (e.g., "dissipative structures"). And that's what more and more organizations are going to be like. That means we will have to be much better and much quicker at developing relationships and then letting go.

The implications of this issue are profound. I talk about this in the book *Temporary Society*—the difficulty of being able to connect quickly with people and then break apart. How do you create commitment, trust, and love quickly and then dissolve? There are some people who have a knack for being immediate. Take a look at Bill Clinton versus Bill Bradley. Bradley is somewhat remote. He is not immediate. With Clinton you get an immediate connection.

But perhaps the connection doesn't have to be like romance and love. It can just be that we are working together on this terrific task. We are going to finish the film, the book, the project, the research. We are going to spend six months together having a terrific time and then we are going to break apart and move on to something else. There doesn't have to be such pain involved. Maybe the task and excitement will keep people together.

HOPKINS: What is the role of leadership in these new forms of organizations? Is it different than in more traditional organizations?

BENNIS: Think of 28-year-old Marc Andreessen, founder of Netscape, who quit after AOL acquired it because he figured AOL has an "old" culture. The average age of employees at AOL was 42 or 43 years old and he was only 28. He then started his own incubator and venture capital firm.

But it is not just that the new leaders dress differently, talk differently, and lack MBAs (although many of them soon will have MBAs given that 30–40% of the graduating class of almost any first rate business school is going into e-commerce or some type of Internet business.) Take a look at people like Eckhardt Pfeiffer who comes out of that old model and who just couldn't make it at Compaq. He just wasn't surfing his competitors' web pages and was almost eaten alive by Dell and Gateway because he was still operating out of older models of leadership. I think we are right at a terribly important inflection point, one of Stephen Jay Gould's "punctuated equilibria."

My next book is going to be about leaders 30 years and younger and leaders 70 years and older. *Geeks and Geezers* is the working title. I have already started my interviews with leaders 30 years and younger and it's fascinating because they *are* different. First, what is it like to grow up digital (i.e., in a virtual and visual culture)? What is it like to have seven or eight different careers and be active until you're 80 and 90? As a matter of fact, a recent research finding of Aeon Research Institute showed that the average American will have had nine different jobs by the time they are in their 30s. And what is it like to have a much different concept of time? I recently interviewed the head of a large automobile company in Europe and he was saying it was going to take him 36 months for a new model of car to come out. But that is way too long. If you talk to some of the younger people at the same company they say, "Are you kidding?" "Three years! Way too long!" The concept of time is going to be totally different.

HOPKINS: Interviewing both younger and older leaders is a wonderful new direction. Do you have any preliminary insights?

BENNIS: One difference is becoming clear. It seems that the really young group, the 25 year olds, have a bigger sense of wanting to give back to society. This is not to say that at this point the 70 year olds aren't feeling this way. But I do think that the 70 year olds were just thinking about surviving when they were "making it." The two groups have grown up in totally different macro environments. Think of the Depression and World War II. These experiential chasms can't help but have an effect on the 70 plus group and their outlook in life and sense of career. For example, even though many people in the older group have had different careers, I don't think they felt at the age of 30 that they weren't sure what they would be doing three years from now.

But I also suspect that the younger and older leaders are going to be alike in many ways. After all, we are choosing really interesting people. Take Arthur Levitt, Frank Gehry, John Gardner, George Shultz, and Bob Galvin. These are people in their 70s and early 80s who really have kept reinventing themselves. I think there are going to be incredibly interesting similarities between the two groups because all the individuals are really learners. When I was in Las Vegas a few weeks ago I saw a casino called Circus Circus. I had this fantasy of a new casino that I was going to call Learning Learning. Think about that phrase—Learning Learning. What if you had a casino with slot machines but the whole idea of the casino was about learning? I really think this is what the younger and older groups will have in common—they have both learned learning. However, their concepts of career, time, and success are going to be different.

HOPKINS: The recent mergers of entertainment and technology organizations seem to pose a special leadership challenge. Managing relationships will be important but this may not yield to the impatience and project type emphasis of today's young leaders. Do you have any insights on these types of developments?

BENNIS: As I mentioned before, the affairs of the human heart will never be obsolete. Whether you are a dot.com or a more conventional business like a GM, I don't think that managing relationships will be different. But I do believe that the question of time will be different. More than ever, speed is incredibly important in this world.

I don't think the Internet is any more profound than electricity or turbine engines. They are all incredibly seminal, tectonic changes in how we do work and how we do life. Look at electricity, for example. Electricity has turned us all into workaholics. But it is the increasing rapidity with which these changes affect segments and systems of society that is so amazing. In the year 1900 there were 10 miles of paved roads. The freeway system did not come into existence until Eisenhower's term. How many years did that take—50 years? In contrast, the Internet just hit a few years ago. Three years ago, no one was ordering electronically and AOL wasn't a household word. The speed with which change is happening is much greater today than ever before. I think this is going to make a huge difference in new organizations.

HOPKINS: Given the new generation of workers we read so much about, what do today's leaders need to do to attract and retain the very best people?

BENNIS: I don't think people are going to be happy working for any organization where they can't deploy their full talents. I am going to give you a very real case study. We can call him Joe. Joe has been the protégé of a widely respected CEO at Company X, a major industrial company in the Northeast. But Joe has just recently left Company X to work for Jeff Bezos at Amazon.com. And when I asked him why he was making that change he answered, "Because I want to make more money and I want to make history and I can't do that at Company X." Now I just happened to be with the CEO of Company X a little while ago. Knowing about this guy leaving but not wanting to bring it up directly, I asked him, "How do you keep your terrific young people?" The CEO looked crestfallen and said, "I don't know."

Now what could have the CEO done to keep this young, gifted, 32 year old at Company X? I think he could have done something. I am consulting with a company right now where there is an executive who has a terrific idea for a new business. He has plans to leave but I have been urging the CEO to create an incubator within the company so this guy could be given money and support and the company could have equity in the business. We are going to have to figure out how to unleash intellectual capital, the human imagination. The issue today for any leader is, "How do we incubate the human imagination? How do we develop future leaders?"

Another thing is that I don't think people today are as interested in leading or managing as they are in doing exciting things at work. I want to give you an example. There is a research institute that has had 40 years of leadership problems. The issue is that the scientists don't (a) understand what leadership is about, and (b) don't want to do it, whatever they think it is. What they want to do is science, not manage *or* lead. And when I went to this Blue ribbon, global financial services company recently, none of them wanted to do leadership or management. They want to do mergers and acquisitions, they want to trade equities, and they want to issue bonds. They couldn't care less about managing other people. So the issue for this company is how do they get someone to manage their Asia business?

The research institute I mentioned earlier recruited a distinguished scientist, a member of the National Academy of Sciences. His contract read, "You must spend 80% of your time leading and managing the institute and 20% in your lab." It turns out that he is spending 80% of his time in his lab and 20% of his time doing what he thinks is managing. And what *he* thinks is managing is writing E-mails and allocating office space. It reminds me of the E.M. Forster line in *Passage to India,* "The main job of the English civil servant was telegrams and anger." So, as we are moving more and more towards organizations that are based solely on human imagination and intellectual capital, and where the fun is going to be producing ideas, teaching, and the research and developing of software architecture, why should anyone want to lead?

There is going to be a tremendous dearth of people who are going to be willing to do it. My answer to that is it is going to have to become a civic or civil responsibility of people in organizations. Such that for three years, the Gretchen Spreitzers and Julia Liebeskinds are going to be asked to lead our department whether they like it or not. And then we will give them a sabbatical their fourth year so they can return to their main love. And who knows: some of them may even like it and want to make a career of academic leadership. Worst things can befall them.

HOPKINS: Given that many people today, like you, have careers spanning up to 50 years, in what ways can they recreate themselves in new ways to stay fresh and in tune with a changing environment? What are your lessons of experience?

BENNIS: How people keep reinventing themselves is the other part of my book. As I mentioned before, I am studying leaders 30 years and younger and leaders 70 years and older. I do not fully understanding this yet. I think if I could understand why people get *stuck,* I would also understand more about the people who keep learning and growing, who keep their eyebrows continually raised in wonder and innocence. When I talk to Norman Lear, for example, who is now 80, he seems as young as most people in my department in terms of his being vibrant, questioning, curious and wide-eyed

with wonder and innocence. It was once said by Berlioz, a nineteenth-century composer, as he was talking about Saint-Säens whom he didn't particularly like and whose music he didn't approve of, "Saint-Säens? He knows everything. All he lacks is inexperience." I also think of Rudolf Serkin, the pianist, who at the age of 80 changed his whole classical repertoire into the new music. He was famous for his classical repertoire but at the age of 80, he began learning a completely new, contemporary body of work. Or my wife, Grace, who retired as a physician and has redirected her passion to the fiddle. I envy her passion.

There is something about why some people get so bound in the past that they really can't think anew. Is unlearning that difficult? Are some people so frightened by transition and change that their self-esteem is always akimbo?

For me, now being more personal about it, teaching bright undergraduates is absolutely essential. Here I am teaching students this year who were born after the Vietnam War, who were born after the Civil Rights Movement, who were born after the women's movement, after the Kennedy and Martin Luther King Jr. assassinations, who were born after Watergate, who were born after everything! How do you connect? How do you manage to get inside their heads? But I think the beauty of being a professor is that I have the opportunity to interact with those who are young enough to be my grandchildren. And I keep in touch with a lot of young people. Not just Ph.D. candidates but also undergraduate students.

I also am able to stay fresh by making friends totally outside of my own discipline. My closest friends are not only in the School of Business. They are writers and artists, filmmakers, editors, businesspersons, and people in media. An ethnic and disciplinary cocktail of friends. And I try very hard to stay up with popular culture; I mean movies, novels, art, and theater.

HOPKINS: It seems that the reinvention of self would help leaders be responsive to the changes that are happening around them. But if leaders keep reinventing themselves, do they become a puzzle to those around them? Do they outgrow their team?

BENNIS: Take leaders like Michael Armstrong or Jack Welch who have both reinvented themselves. Macro changes helped them to evolve and behave differently. Welch made it very clear that if he was going to take an organization like GE into the twenty-first century—an organization with a bloated bureaucracy, 425,000 people, and businesses they should not be in—he was going to have to do some very serious downsizing. Here is a guy who really thought he was "Empowerment Jack" suddenly becoming "Neutron Jack." This nickname was like a shot to his gut. It was the same with Michael Armstrong of AT&T. The environment changed drastically. He took over a giant company and then realized that he might be out of business because of Baby Bell competition in the long distance market. So he moved to betting the company on cablevision.

HOPKINS: But isn't today's Warren Bennis the same Warren Bennis from whenever he gained consciousness?

BENNIS: The core of me remains the same. I know I have changed a lot over the years but it has been very much like my handwriting. Take for instance my signature from my very first passport in 1951. I came upon it not too long ago and the signature is very like my present signature. There are subtle changes in it but the core is still there. Reinventing yourself doesn't mean you become a different person. It just means that we evolve. We all do that. It's subtle—just like you don't notice it yourself when you are gaining or losing weight but other people will if they haven't seen you in six months. I don't think Jack Welch is a totally different person in 2000—he is still a tough Irishman brought up in a working-class suburb in Boston. He is not the same Jack Welch but he sure is Jack Welch.

HOPKINS: In your writings you have noted the importance of place and time in one's intellectual and personal development—that great leaders often emerge as a result of being in stimulating environments. Do you think this is a requirement for greatness?

BENNIS: I think history and geography have really favored my career. Consider Alan Kay. He is considered the inventor of the first PC. How did he and others know to go out to the University of Utah? There was a whole group of people who just gravitated there, and there was a whole group of people who went to M.I.T. to work. A group of the newly emerging mathematical economists just "smelled" that it was an exciting place to be. It's got to do with what Michael Porter talks about in his book on international competitive strategy—the Seventh Avenue Syndrome. There is something about the density or critical mass of a certain number of people doing similar things that creates that excitement, that competitiveness, which is both threatening and competitive, but so exciting. It was like the story of Freud when he met fellow Viennese Stefan Zweig in London and asked him how he liked London. Zweig's scornful response was, "London, London, how can you mention London and Vienna in the same breath! In Vienna, there was sperm in the air!"

Look at what is happening here in L.A. in the media industry. Everybody is listening to each other, competing with each other, trying to outdo each other. It is ultra competitive and spirited and lively. You are always on the edge. You are always being challenged. It is no accident that all the nuclear physicists in the 1920s congregated at the University of Göttingen in Germany—all the people who created the foundations of nuclear physics. There is something about the density and intensity of community. There is an African saying: I AM BECAUSE WE ARE.

HOPKINS: Given your many accomplishments and contributions, what is the one thing that you would like to be most remembered for?

BENNIS: That's easy. To be thought of as "generous company."

Notes

1. Warren G. Bennis, *An Invented Life: Reflections on Leadership and Change,* (Reading, Mass.: Addison-Wesley Publishing Co., 1993).
2. Fest·schrift *(fest shrift) n.* A volume of learned articles, essays, and the like, contributed by colleagues and admirers as a tribute, especially to a scholar. (It's Old German and means a Festival of Writing—*fest,* festival and *schrift,* writing. Over the years it's taken on a slightly different meaning, really a celebration of the writings of an admired colleague.)

VIII-5: Managing a Virtual Workplace

WAYNE F. CASCIO

EXECUTIVE OVERVIEW

Virtual workplaces, in which employees operate remotely from each other and from managers, are a reality, and will become even more common in the future. There are sound business reasons for establishing virtual workplaces, but their advantages may be offset by such factors as setup and maintenance costs, loss of cost efficiencies, cultural clashes, isolation, and lack of trust. Virtual teams and telework are examples of such arrangements, but they are not appropriate for all jobs, all employees, or all managers. To be most effective in these environments, managers need to do two things well: Shift from a focus on time to a focus on results; and recognize that virtual workplaces, instead of needing fewer managers, require better supervisory skills among existing managers. Taking these steps can lead to stunning improvements in productivity, profits, and customer service.

The virtual workplace, in which employees operate remotely from each other and from managers, is a reality for many employers now, and all indications are that it will become even more prevalent in the future. Virtual organizations are multisite, multiorganizational, and dynamic.[1] At a macro level, a virtual organization consists of a grouping of businesses, consultants, and contractors that have joined in an alliance to exploit complementary skills in pursuing common strategic objectives.[2] The objectives often focus on a specific project.[3] In and of itself, this grouping represents a dramatic change in how we work, and it presents two new challenges for managers. The challenges stem from the physical separa-

Reprinted from *Academy of Management Executive* 14 (3) (2000): 81–90.

tion of workers and managers wrought by such information-age arrangements as tele-work and virtual teams. "How can I manage them if I can't see them?" is a question that many managers are now asking. It defines the first managerial challenge of the virtual workplace: making the transition from man-aging time (activity-based) to managing projects (results-based).

The second managerial challenge of the virtual workplace is to overcome uncer-tainty about whether managers will still be valued by their companies if they are man-aging employees who are not physically present. In one case, a first-level manager recalled his boss coming out of his office, looking at the empty cubicles around him, and saying, "What do I need you for?"[4] As we shall see in this article, the need is not for fewer managers, but for better supervisory skills among existing managers.

This article identifies the business rea-sons for, as well as some potential argu-ments against, virtual workplaces; examines alternative forms of virtual workplaces, along with the advantages and disadvan-tages of each; and provides tools and infor-mation to managers of virtual work-places, based on advances in research on this topic.

. . . .

BUSINESS REASONS FOR VIRTUAL WORKPLACES

Many companies have instituted virtual workplaces, and have reaped the following benefits:

- **Reduced real estate expenses.** IBM saves 40 to 60 percent per site annually by elimi-nating offices for all employees except those who truly need them.[5] Northern Tele-com estimates the savings gained from not having to house an employee in a typical 64-square-foot space, considering only rent and annual operating costs, at $2,000 per person per year.[6] Others estimate the sav-ings at $2 for every $1 invested.[7]

- **Increased productivity.** Internal IBM stud-ies show gains of 15 to 40 percent. USWest reported that the productivity of its tele-working employees increased, some by as much as 40 percent.[8]

- **Higher profits.** Hewlett-Packard doubled revenue per salesperson after moving its sales people to virtual workplace arrange-ments.[9]

- **Improved customer service.** Andersen Con-sulting found that its consultants spent 25 per-cent more time face-to-face with customers when they did not have permanent offices.[10]

- **Access to global markets.** John Brown Engineers & Constructors Ltd., a member of the engineering division of Trafalgar House, the world's third largest engineering and construction organization, with 21,000 employees around the globe, was able to access local pharmaceutical engineering tal-ent at a project site in India. Using virtual work arrangements, the firm was able to traverse national boundaries, enabling it to work with and present a local face to its global clients. This enhanced its global com-petitiveness.[11]

- **Environmental benefits.** At Georgia Power, 150 people, or 13 percent of the workers at headquarters, are teleworkers. This has reduced annual commuting mileage by 993,000 miles, and automobile emissions by almost 35,000 pounds.[12] A U. S. government study showed that if 20,000 federal workers could telecommute just one day a week, they would save over two million commut-ing miles, 102,000 gallons of gasoline, and 81,600 pounds of carbon dioxide emissions each week. The emissions savings for one week under this arrangement are equiva-lent to the amount of carbon dioxide pro-duced by the average car over 9.3 years.[13]

. . . .

POTENTIAL DISADVANTAGES OF VIRTUAL WORKPLACES

Offsetting these advantages, however, are some potentially serious disadvantages that managers should consider carefully before institutionalizing virtual-work arrangements:

- **Setup and maintenance costs.** For individual employees, the additional cost required to equip a mobile or home office varies from roughly $3,000 to $5,000, plus about $1,000 in upgrades and supplies every year thereafter.[14] In addition, to be viable, virtual offices require online materials that can be downloaded and printed; databases on products and customers that are accessible from remote locations; well-indexed, automated, central files that are accessible from remote locations; and a way to track the location of mobile workers. Technology is the remote worker's lifeline. In the absence of the administrative and technical support that one might find at the home office, the technology must work flawlessly, and technical support should be available 24 hours a day, seven days a week. (Or at least a help desk should be staffed from 8 A.M. to midnight.) Decision makers need to consider the incremental costs associated with setting up and maintaining virtual workplaces.

- **Loss of cost efficiencies.** When expensive equipment or services are concentrated in one location, multiple users can access them. When the same equipment or services are distributed across locations, cost efficiencies may be lost. For example, in the securities industry, certain real-time information sources are necessary. Most stock quotes are available on the Internet on a 15-minute delay, which is adequate for most people's needs. However, for brokers and traders quoting prices to customers, it is imperative that quotes be up-to-the-second. Companies such as Bloomberg, Bridge Financial System, Reuters Quotron, and ILX Systems provide this real-time service. Each is willing to install its system at the customer's place of choice. Typical costs are about $1,200 per month for the first installation of such a system, and about $200 per month to install each additional system in the same location. When a securities firm needs this information for 50 brokers, along with related services (e.g., CDA Spectrum,

Multex.com's Market Guide, and First Call/Thomson Financial), it is more cost-effective to have all employees at one location, rather than working at many different locations.[15]

- **Cultural issues.** Virtual organizations operating in the global arena often have to transfer their business policies and cultures to work with dispersed business teams across collaborating organizations, geography, and cultures. This can lead to potential clashes of business and national cultures, which, in turn, can undermine the entire alliance.[16] If the members of a virtual organization or a virtual team are not empowered to make decisions, the technology that enables their collaboration will add little value, and the competitive advantage associated with rapid responses to demands in the marketplace will be lost.

- **Feelings of isolation.** Some level of social interaction with supervisors and coworkers is essential in almost all jobs. Without it, workers feel isolated and out of the loop with respect to crucial communications and contact with decision makers who can make or break their careers.

- **Lack of trust.** A key ingredient to the success of virtual work arrangements is trust that one's coworkers will fulfill their obligations and behave predictably. Lack of trust can undermine every other precaution taken to ensure successful virtual work arrangements, such as careful selection of employees to work in the virtual environment, thorough training of managers and employees, and ongoing performance management.

WHEN VIRTUAL WORK ARRANGEMENTS ARE APPROPRIATE

Virtual workplaces are not appropriate for all jobs. In fact, an organization must first understand the parameters of each job it considers for a virtual work environment. To do so, it must determine what function the job serves; if the work is performed over the phone, in person, via computer, or in some combination; how much time the employee spends in direct contact with other employees, customers, and business contacts; if the location of the office is critical to performance; whether the hours have to be 9 to 5; and whether the employee must be reachable immediately.[17]

Jobs in sales, marketing, project engineering, and consulting seem to be best suited for virtual workplaces because individuals in these jobs already work with their clients by phone or at the clients' premises. Such jobs are service- and knowledge-oriented, dynamic, and evolve according to customer requirements.[18] Even in these jobs, however, virtual work arrangements are not recommended for new employees or those who are new to a position. Newcomers require a period of socialization during which they learn to adapt to their new company, new environment, and new managers and coworkers. They need time to learn business skills, how and why things are done in the new company or new position, and the dos and taboos of the company's culture.

For employees whose jobs are appropriate for virtual work arrangements, and who are internally motivated self-starters who know their jobs well and are technically self-sufficient, the key is to work with them well ahead of planned transitions. Firms such as Lotus, IBM, and Hewlett-Packard have written guidelines, training, and networks of peers to facilitate the transition. For example, Hewlett-Packard's guidelines for virtual workplaces address topics such as who can participate, family and household issues, remote office setup, and administrative processes.

Just as not all employees are suited to work away from their primary business locations during scheduled work hours, not all managers are suited to manage employees with virtual-work arrangements. Those who are seem to have the following characteristics:

- An open, positive attitude that focuses on solutions to issues rather than on reasons to discontinue virtual-work arrangements.
- A results-oriented management style. Those who need structure and control are unlikely to be effective managers in virtual-work environments.
- Effective communications skills, both formal and informal, with employees working remotely and at the primary business location.
- An ability to delegate effectively, and to follow up to ensure that work is accomplished.

While these characteristics apply to progressive managers in conventional as well as virtual-work environments, the need is greater in virtual environments that lack the attributes of traditional social contexts, such as physical proximity, verbal and non-verbal cues, norms of behavior, and, in the case of teams, a sense of cohort.

VIRTUAL TEAMS

In a virtual team, members are dispersed geographically or organizationally. Their primary interaction is through some combination of electronic communication systems. They may never meet in the traditional sense. Further, team membership is often fluid, evolving according to changing task requirements.[19] Such an arrangement provides several advantages:

- It saves time, travel expenses, and provides access to experts.
- Teams can be organized whether or not members are in proximity to one another.
- Firms can use outside consultants without incurring expenses for travel, lodging, and downtime.
- Virtual teams allow firms to expand their potential labor markets, enabling them to hire and retain the best people regardless of their physical location, or, in the case of workers with disabilities, whether or not they are able to commute to work.

- Employees can more easily accommodate both personal and professional lives.
- Dynamic team membership allows people to move from one project to another.
- Employees can be assigned to multiple, concurrent teams.
- Team communications and work reports are available online to facilitate swift responses to the demands of a global market. For example, Veriphone uses a so-called relay race to develop software products faster than its competitors. Software engineers at the firm's Dallas headquarters work a full day on a project, then put their work product online on the company's intranet. Veriphone engineers in Honolulu take up the project, then post it for their counterparts in Bombay. As the Bombay software engineers leave work, they transmit their work product electronically back to headquarters in Dallas, where the originators are arriving for the next day's work. Electronic communications media make the relay race possible. Clients benefit from the firm's speedy response to their needs.

DISADVANTAGES OF VIRTUAL TEAMS

The major disadvantages of virtual teams are the lack of physical interaction—with its associated verbal and nonverbal cues—and the synergies that often accompany face-to-face communication. These deficiencies raise issues of trust. Trust is critical in a virtual team because traditional social control based on authority gives way to self-direction and self-control. Members of virtual teams need to be sure that all others will fulfill their obligations and behave in a consistent, predictable manner.

An empirical analysis of the development of trust in 29 global virtual teams that communicated strictly by E-mail over a six-week period found that teams with the highest levels of trust tended to share three traits. First, they began their interactions with a series of social messages—introducing themselves and providing some personal background—before focusing on the work at hand. Second, they set clear roles for each team member, thus enabling all team members to identify with one another. Third, all team members demonstrated positive attitudes. Team members consistently displayed eagerness, enthusiasm, and an intense action orientation in all of their messages.[20] The lessons from this research are that first impressions are critical, and that especially in virtual-work environments, initial messages need to be handled well. Keep the tone of all messages upbeat and action-oriented. One pessimist in the group has the potential to undermine trust in the entire virtual team, and lack of trust affects overall group productivity. Not surprisingly, low-trust teams were less productive than high-trust ones.

TRAINING MEMBERS AND MANAGERS OF VIRTUAL TEAMS

Because virtual teams are growing in popularity, it is important to address the issue of how best to train members and managers of virtual teams. A majority of U. S. corporations use some form of team structure in their organizations.[21] Virtual teams add another layer of complexity to any team-work situation. They have created a rich training agenda, for example:

- How to use the software to enhance team performance.
- How to manage the anonymous environment, and when to use it.
- How to provide anonymous participation and feedback when ideas or criticism need to be brought out. This is particularly important since the traditional cues of social interaction—body language and hand gestures—may not be available.
- Social protocol for virtual teams.

- Since changes in team membership must occur with seamless continuity, it is important to teach common cultural values.

These issues imply that managers should think carefully about the kinds of behaviors that are most likely to enhance a virtual team's ability to function effectively. Empirical findings with global virtual teams suggest that these behaviors fall into three key areas: virtual-collaborative skills, virtual-socialization skills, and virtual-communication skills.[22]

Key virtual-collaboration behaviors include the ability to exchange ideas without criticism, develop a working document in which team members' ideas are summarized, exchange it among team members for editing, track member comments in a working document with initials, agree on activities, and meet deadlines.

Key virtual-socialization behaviors include the ability to communicate with other team members immediately, solicit team members' feedback on the process the team is using to accomplish its tasks, disclose appropriate personal information, express appreciation for ideas and completed tasks, apologize for mistakes, volunteer for roles, and acknowledge role assignments.

Key virtual-communication behaviors include the ability to obtain local translator help when language skills are insufficient to be understood, rephrase unclear sentences so that all team members understand what is being said, use E-mail typography to communicate emotion, acknowledge the receipt of messages, and respond within one business day.

There is also much to learn from other research on teams in general, especially with respect to self-limiting behaviors by team members.[23] Team members may limit their involvement for any one of the following reasons: the presence of someone with expertise; the presentation of a compelling argument; lack of confidence in one's ability to contribute; an unimportant or meaning-less decision; pressures from others to conform to the team's decision; or a dysfunctional decision-making climate in which members become frustrated, indifferent, unorganized, or unwilling to commit to making an effective decision.

To avoid these problems, managers should choose team members carefully and give each member a good reason for being on the team. They should also frame the team's decision task appropriately, emphasizing clear, well-defined goals and the consequences of the team's decision. The first team meeting is crucial and will establish lasting precedents for the team. Managers should set productive team norms, for example, and clarify whether decisions will be made by consensus and whether all team members will share responsibility for implementing the final decision. Managers should also monitor the team's process. If this proves difficult, they should include a team-development specialist to serve as a resource to the team, assisting it with technical problems, and facilitating their interaction when necessary.[24] Finally, they should provide honest feedback to group members about their individual behaviors and the final outcome of the team's work. Doing so may uncover unproductive behaviors that will enable group members to work better the next time around.

TELEWORKING

Telework is work carried out in a location remote from central offices or production facilities, where the worker has no personal contact with coworkers, but is able to communicate with them electronically.[25] Teleworking is a popular and rapidly growing alternative to the traditional, office-bound work style. Two of every three *Fortune* 500 companies employ teleworkers. Forty million employees telework on a global basis, and by 2003 more than 137 million workers worldwide are expected to telework at least on a part-time basis.[26] Survey results indicate that employees want more opportunities for telework, and that their top priority is to gain the flexibility to control their own time.[27] Some companies are actively encouraging the trend. In February, 2000, both Ford Motor Company and Delta Air Lines announced that they are giving employees personal computers for home use.[28]

Telework may also assume other forms:

- **Hoteling:** Ernst & Young workers in Washington, D. C., use workstations and meeting rooms in nearby hotels. The firm has hoteled eight offices and is converting seven more, and has found that workers focus less on the office and more on the customer.[29]
- **Hot desking:** About 20,000 IBM employees, primarily those in sales and service, share offices with four other people, on average. Cisco Systems, a technology firm in San Jose, California, has several thousand people sharing a variety of spaces around the world. As noted earlier, however, hoteling and hot desking are not for everyone.[30]
- **Telework centers:** Corporate office environments in miniature, offering more technology than an employee has at home, may be located in residential neighborhoods. Small groups of employees who live nearby work in these centers, rather than commute. For example, the Ontario Telebusiness Work Center near Los Angeles offers electronically equipped suites to companies.[31] The suburban location minimizes commuting time, while maximizing productive time.

TELEWORK AND THE BALANCE BETWEEN WORK AND FAMILY

Although there is little empirical research on the effect of telework on work-family relations, a recent study in three Canadian organizations revealed that teleworkers had significantly lower levels of interference from work to family, significantly lower levels of interference from family to work, and significantly fewer problems managing their family time than they did before teleworking.[32] These data support the positive view of telework and suggest that working from home helps employed parents balance work and family demands.[33]

IMPLICATIONS OF TELEWORK RESEARCH FOR DECISION MAKERS

Decision makers should be skeptical of claims about the effects of telework that are not grounded in rigorous empirical research. For example, several studies have suggested that the level of teleworking participation will have a negative impact on visibility, and, therefore on career advancement.[34] But empirical research has not addressed this out-of-sight, out-of-mind argument. Before drawing conclusions about telework and framing organizational policy on this issue, decision makers should also consider the extent to which research findings might apply to their own industries and organizational cultures, and to employees at different stages of their careers.

TRAINING MANAGERS AND EMPLOYEES FOR TELEWORK

In a telework relationship, time is not important. This is one of the harder lessons for managers of teleworkers to learn, and many have to rethink completely how they view supervision. They need to understand that managing employees they can't see differs considerably from walking around offices to see that employees are at their desks. Learning to make the transition from managing time to managing projects is critical and will determine the success of an organization's telework program.[35]

Before a telework arrangement is finalized at Merrill Lynch, process consultants study how employees in a given area communicate and do business, and identify what the barriers to teleworking will be. This alleviates managers' concerns and focuses attention on areas that need to be addressed. Formalized training for telework is divided into teleworker training, supervisor and manager training, and team training, in which teleworkers and their managers come together to discuss issues that affect their relationship. Some organizations also set aside time to train and educate the entire staff, from the mail room to the board room.[36]

In teleworking arrangements, cultural, managerial, and interpersonal implications also need to be addressed. Training for workers and managers should begin together so they hear the same message, and understand the business case for implementing telework arrangements. Both groups address such issues as the lack of face-to-face time (which may create resentment among workers who remain in the office), potential losses in creativity from lack of personal interaction with coworkers and managers, and potential losses in productivity from absence from the office. Employees and managers who already have experience with telework arrangements should make presentations. Both groups should be encouraged to begin measuring productivity through assignments and projects, rather than hours spent in the office.[37]

Project management is especially important in instances where teleworkers or virtual members are not part of the same organization. Each person is hired to accomplish a specific task, and that person often has no vested interest in monitoring the end result. If a manager does not actively monitor the progress of the overall project and the usefulness of the final product, the team's productivity will never result in improved profitability.

The time frame for completion can cause problems for some managers who are new at managing teleworkers or virtual teams. Most managers establish completion dates, which are necessary. However, completion of a project may be delayed if managers do not establish milestone activities, critical completion points within the overall duration of a project. Through the use of milestones, a manager can see early in a project's life cycle whether or not the necessary pieces are progressing satisfactorily. This allows corrections and changes during the project that ensure timely completion, or at least forewarn of problems.[38] The principles of effective project management are not new, and they do not change in virtual work environments. They simply become more important.

Managers and workers should be wary of naive expectations about what working away from the office is really like. To provide a realistic preview for prospective teleworkers, Merrill Lynch uses a simulation lab, a large room with work stations where employees work for two weeks without face-to-face contact with their managers. After the two-week trial, some employees decide that telework is not for them.[39] While some firms use short, self-scored surveys to help workers identify how likely they are to succeed as teleworkers, there is really no substitute for a job tryout, such as a simulation lab provides.

A final component of telework training is to bring managers into the evaluation process about six months after the implementation of the telework program, using productivity measurements as the basis for a business case analysis. Examining the impact of telework on productivity, cost, and customer satisfaction allows for adjustments or enhancements to the program, or to its cancellation.

● ● ● ● ● ● ● ● ● ● ● ● ● ● ●
VIRTUAL OFFICE CHALLENGES FOR MANAGERS

It is important at the outset to ensure that all departments that will interact with members of virtual teams or teleworkers accept and support the concept of the virtual-work arrangement. If they do not, it will fail.[40] As the vice chairman of American Express noted: "It's important to have a multifunction team of senior managers promoting and supporting a virtual-office initiative from the start. We had three departments involved in our effort: HR, technology, and real estate. The individuals must be enthusiastic and not unnecessarily fettered by traditional approaches. And they must be made knowledgeable about all the key issues.[41]

Broad support alone is not enough to guarantee the success of virtual workplaces. Managers also must set and enforce ground rules for communication, and institute a comprehensive process of performance management.

COMMUNICATION

Communication is a major challenge for managers implementing a virtual-work environment. Many managers have to learn new communication skills to prevent team members from feeling isolated and not part of a larger group. It is important not to rely solely on E-mail, which is one-way communication. Managers should learn how to conduct effective audio meetings, and to balance E-mail, voice mail, video conferencing, and face-to-face communications.

Begin with some ground rules so that all team members understand the method of communication and what is expected during those communication sessions. For example, use E-mail for reports, and the computer-based chat room to discuss project issues. In addition, all team members should be available by phone between certain hours.[42]

Scheduled virtual meetings are essential and attendance must be enforced strictly to ensure that all team members participate. Face-to-face meetings on a regular basis, if at all possible, allow team members to put faces to E-mail. Forging personal relationships among team members contributes to successful implementation. Since facial expressions and body language cues are not available in the virtual work environment, teleworkers must compensate with other forms of communication in order to understand each other fully. This generally means asking more questions and conversing more frequently. The manager or team leader should communicate with all team members, not just a few, and include all team members on distribution lists. This ensures that all members are accounted for and are equal contributors to the team. Regular updates and status reports are necessary to replace hallway conversations, networking, and the daily stimulation of a traditional office environment.

When team members do not work at the same time, or in the same location, members themselves must make exceptional efforts to ensure accurate, timely communications. Some virtual teams must contend with different time zones. Others must disseminate detailed information, perhaps on spreadsheets or by using computer-aided design (CAD) software. Managers can provide guidance and coaching on how to improve communications, but team members themselves have to shoulder responsibility for providing accurate, timely information.

PERFORMANCE MANAGEMENT

By far the biggest challenge is performance management, which requires that managers do three things well: define, facilitate, and encourage performance.[43] While these principles are important to follow in conventional working environments, they are even more imperative in virtual working environments.

DEFINE PERFORMANCE

On a virtual team, a fundamental requirement is that all team members understand their responsibilities.[44] A manager trying to define performance might ask the following questions to help clarify these responsibilities:

- What is the team's overall objective?
- Do you expect each team member to fulfill more than one role on the team?
- Which responsibilities will team members share (e.g., selecting new members, rating one another's performance)?
- Will the team elect a leader? What responsibilities will this person have?
- Who is responsible for disciplinary action if the need arises?
- How will the team make decisions (e.g., by consensus, or by majority-rule)?
- Which decisions does the team have the authority to make?

The next step is to develop specific, challenging goals, measures of the extent to which goals have been accomplished, and assessment mechanisms so that workers and managers can stay focused on what really counts. To be useful, the measures should be linked to the strategic direction, business objectives, and customer requirements for the company.[45] For a cable-television company, a major strategic thrust might be to increase the number of new subscribers, or the number of current subscribers who pay for premium channels. For a firm that provides outsourcing services in information technology, major customer requirements might be timeliness of response to inquiries, and cost savings relative to in-house capability.

In defining performance, regular assessment of progress toward goals focuses the attention and efforts of an employee or team. A manager who identifies measurable goals, but then fails to assess progress towards them, is asking for trouble.

The overall objective of goals, measures, and assessment is to leave no doubt in the minds of remote workers what is expected of them, how it will be measured, and where they stand at any given point in time. The need for such ground rules is even more pressing in a virtual work environment. There should be no surprises in the performance management process, and regular feedback to remote employees helps ensure that there won't be.

FACILITATE PERFORMANCE

Managers who are committed to managing remote workers effectively recognize that two of their major responsibilities are to eliminate roadblocks to successful performance and to provide adequate resources to get a job done right and on time.

Obstacles that can inhibit maximum performance include outdated equipment or technology, delays in receiving critical information, and inefficient design of work processes. Employees are well aware of these, and are usually willing to identify them when managers ask for their input. Then it is the manager's job to eliminate these obstacles.

Adequate capital resources, material resources, and human resources are necessary if remote workers or members of virtual teams are to reach the challenging goals they have set. In the words of one observer, "It's immoral not to give people tools to meet tough goals."[46] Conversely, employees really appreciate their employer's providing everything they need to perform well. Not surprisingly, they usually do perform well under those circumstances.

ENCOURAGE PERFORMANCE

To encourage performance, especially repeated good performance, it is important to provide sufficient rewards that employees really value, in a timely and fair manner.

Begin by asking remote workers what's most important to them. For example, is it pay, benefits, free time, technology upgrades, or opportunities for professional development? Then consider tailoring your awards program so that remote workers or teams can choose from a menu of similarly valued options.

Next, provide rewards in a timely manner, soon after major accomplishments. For example, North American Tool & Die, a metal-stamping plant in San Leandro, California, provides monthly cash awards for creativity. This is important, for an excessive delay between effective performance and receipt of the reward may mean the reward loses its potential to motivate subsequent high performance.

Finally, provide rewards in a manner that employees consider fair. Procedures are fair to the extent that they are consistent across persons and over time, free from bias, based on accurate information, correctable, and based on prevailing moral and ethical standards.[47] Not surprisingly, employees often behave very responsibly when they are asked in advance for their opinions about what is fair. Indeed, it seems only fair to ask them.

IMPLICATIONS FOR MANAGERS

New business realities, coupled with demands by workers for more flexibility and empowerment, suggest that virtual workplaces are here to stay. The challenges of managing a virtual workplace will escalate in scope. The use of new technology and tools only enables competitive advantage. Realizing competitive advantage requires effective management coupled with new ways of doing business. Organizations in which virtual-work arrangements thrive will be flatter than they are today. Knowledge workers within these environments will have more autonomy and responsibility than in traditional organizations, yet lines of authority, roles, and responsibilities will still need to be defined clearly. New ways of

communicating and interacting among workers in virtual environments will need to be developed and implemented, yet face-to-face communications will remain essential ingredients of successful workplaces. Heavy emphasis will be placed on establishing and maintaining the technical tools that are the lifeblood of workers in virtual environments. Workers as well as managers will need continual training in both new tools and new processes to operate effectively in these environments.

Managers who are committed to virtual-work environments will understand that basic principles of management are not different in virtual-work environments, but that the principles need to be followed more closely than ever. They understand that better, not fewer, management skills and managers will be needed.

To be a beneficiary, rather than a victim, of emerging virtual-workplace trends, institute the performance-management systems, information-access capabilities, and training systems to develop skills that will be important in the future. Always look ahead; learn from the past, but don't live in it. By embracing these emerging changes in the world of work, proactive managers can lead change, not just react to it.

Endnotes

1. Snow, C. C., Lipnack, J., & Stamps, J. 1999. The virtual organization: Promises and payoffs, large and small. In C. L. Cooper & D. M. Rousseau (Eds.), *The virtual organization:* 15–30. New York: Wiley.
2. Dess, G. G., Rasheed, A. M. A., McLaughlin, K. J., & Priem, R. L. 1995. The new corporate architecture. *The Academy of Management Executive,* 9(3):7–18.
3. M. Igbaria & M. Tan (Eds.). 1998. *The virtual workplace.* Hershey, PA: Idea Group Publishing.
4. Grensing-Pophal, L. 1999. Training supervisors to manage teleworkers. *HR Magazine,* January, 67:72.

5. O'Connell, S. E. 1996. The virtual workplace moves at warp speed. *HRMagazine,* March 51:77. See also *Business Week,* 1996. The new workplace. April 29:105–113.

6. Cooper, R. C. 1997. Telecommuting: The good, the bad, and the particulars. *Supervision,* 57(2):10–12.

7. McCune, J. C. 1998. Telecommuting revisited. *Management Review,* 87:10–16.

8. Matthes, K. 1992. Telecommuting: Balancing business and employee needs. *HR Focus,* 69(3)December: 3.

9. O'Connell, op. cit.

10. Ibid.

11. Grimshaw, D. J., & Kwok, F. T. S. 1998. The business benefits of the virtual organization. In Igbaria & Tan (Eds.), op. cit., 45–70.

12. McCune, op. cit.

13. The Green Commuter. *http://libertynet.org/cleanair/green /summer98/greentext8-98.html.*

14. Clark, K. 1997. Home is where the work is. *Fortune.* November 24:219–221.

15. Arko, D. et al. 1999. Virtual teams. Unpublished manuscript. University of Colorado Executive MBA Program, Denver.

16. Serapio, M. G., Jr., & Cascio, W. F. 1996. End-games in international alliances. *The Academy of Management Executive,* 10(1):62–73. See also Cascio, W. F., & Serapio, M. G. Jr. 1991. Human resource systems in an international alliance: The undoing of a done deal? *Organizational Dynamics,* Winter:63–74.

17. Apgar, M., IV. 1998. The alternative workplace: Changing where and how people work. *Harvard Business Review,* May–June:121–136.

18. Townsend, A. M., DeMarie, S. M., & Hendrickson, A. R. 1998. Virtual teams: Technology and the workplace of the future. *The Academy of Management Executive,* 12(3):17–29.

19. Ibid.

20. Coutu, D. 1998. Trust in virtual teams. *Harvard Business Review,* May–June:20–21. See also Jarvenpaa, S. L., Knoll, K., & Leidner, D. E. 1998. Is anybody out there? Antecedents of trust in global virtual teams. *Journal of Management Information Systems,* 14(4):29–64.

21. Townsend et al., op. cit.

22. Knoll, K., & Jarvenpaa, S. L. 1998. Working together in global virtual teams. In Igbaria & Tan (Eds.), op. cit.:2–23.

23. Mulvey, P. W., Velga, J. F., & Elsass, P. M. 1996. When teammates raise a white flag. *The Academy of Management Executive,* 10(1):40–49.

24. Townsend et al., op. cit.

25. Gupta, Y., Karimi, J., & Somers, T. M. 1995. Telecommuting: Problems associated with communications technologies and their capabilities. *IEEE Transactions on Engineering Management,* 42(4):305–318.

26. Anderson, C., Girard, J., Payne, S., Pultz, J., Zboray, M., & Smith, C. 1998. *Implementing a successful remote access project: From technology to management.* New York: Gartner Group, Report R-06-6639, Nov. 18.

27. The new world of work: Flexibility is the watchword, 2000. *Business Week,* January 10:36. See also Conlin, M. 1999. 9 to 5 isn't working anymore. *Business Week,* September 20:94–98.

28. Rivenbark, L. 2000. Employees want more opportunities to telecommute, report reveals. *HR News.* April:14–16.

29. *Business Week.* 1996. op. cit.

30. "Office Hoteling" isn't as inn as futurists once thought. 1997. *The Wall Street Journal.* September 2:A1.

31. O'Connell, S. E., op. cit.

32. Duxbury, L., Higgins, C., & Neufeld, D. 1998. *Telework and the balance between work and family: Is telework part of the problem or part of the solution?* In Igbaria & Tan (Eds.) op. cit.: 218–255.

33. Ibid.

34. Austin, J. 1993. Telecommuting success depends on reengineering the work processes. *Computing Canada,* 19:37–38. See also DuBrin, A. J., & Barnard, J. C. 1993. What telecommuters like and dislike about their jobs. *Business Forum,* 18:13–17. See also Dutton, G. 1994. Can California change its corporate culture? *Management Review,* 83:49–54.

35. Grensing-Pophal, op. cit.

36. Ibid.

37. Grensing-Pophal, L. 1998. Training employees to telecommute: A recipe for success. *HRMagazine,* Dec:76–82.

38. Arko et al., op. cit.
39. Grensing-Pophal, op. cit.
40. Anderson, C. 1998. *The top 10 non-technical reasons telecommuting programs fail.* New York: Gartner Group, Report COM-04-0431, March 25.
41. Apgar, op. cit.:125.
42. Telecommuting: Practical option or management nightmare? *http://www.eeicom/eye/telecomm.html.*
43. Cascio, W. F. 1998. *Managing human resources: Productivity, quality of work life, profits* (5th ed.). Burr Ridge, IL: Irwin/McGraw-Hill. See also Cascio, W. F.

1996. Managing for maximum performance. *HR Monthly* (Australia), September:10–13.
44. Townsend et al., op. cit.
45. Moravec, M. 1996. Bringing performance management out of the stone age. *Management Review,* February:38–42.
46. Kerr, S. in Sherman, S. 1995. Stretch goals: The dark side of asking for miracles. *Fortune.* November 13:31.
47. Greenberg, J. 1987. Reactions to procedural justice in payment distributions: Do the means justify the ends? *Journal of Applied Psychology,* 72:55–61.

VIII-6: Congress Urged to Move on Genetics Legislation

THERESA MINTON-EVERSOLE

The issue of genetic discrimination in the workplace was addressed in testimony given July 20 during a hearing conducted by the U.S. Senate Committee on Health, Education, Labor, and Pensions.

While decoding the human genome is certainly exciting, knowledge of our genes could be used against us, said committee Chairman Sen. James M. Jeffords (R-Vermont). But, achieving consensus on how to address the use or abuse of genetic information within the workplace in a legal framework will take time, he added. At issue is whether potential forms of genetic discrimination in the workplace are covered under current legislation, such as the Americans with Disabilities Act (ADA) and the Health Insurance Portability and Accountability Act (HIPPA), or whether additional federal policy or laws are needed to regulate the treatment of genetic information.

Among the panelists testifying that clear legislation is needed to ensure that

genetic information is not used to make employment decisions or withhold health insurance were Dr. Francis S. Collins, director of the National Human Genome Research Institute, and Paul Steven Miller, commissioner of the Equal Employment Opportunity Commission (EEOC).

"While genetic information and genetic technology hold great promise for improving human health, they also can be used in ways that are fundamentally unjust," said Collins. "The misuse of genetic information has the potential to be a very serious problem, both in terms of people's access to employment and health insurance and the continued ability to undertake important genetic research."

Miller noted that employers could misinterpret and misuse genetic test results to weed out persons according to their health risks rather than to hire them based solely on their ability to perform the job. He said the EEOC currently interprets the ADA as covering bias based on genetic information under a clause that prohibits employers from discriminating against workers

Reprinted from *HR News* 19 (9).

"regarded as" disabled, but the law "does not explicitly address the issue and its protections are limited and uncertain."

Therefore, he said, "it is imperative that we have safeguards in place to protect workers as technology develops."

"Many people are scared that genetics tests will be used against them," agreed Ronald Weich, a legislative consultant to the American Civil Liberties Union (ACLU). "No one should lose a job or insurance policy because of a genetic predisposition. Americans should be judged on their actual abilities, not their potential disabilities," he added.

Senate Democratic leader Thomas A. Daschle, D-South Dakota, who also provided testimony, said the Genetic Nondiscrimination in Insurance and Employment Act legislation proposed by him and Sen. Ted Kennedy, D-Massachusetts, would provide those safeguards.

"[S. 1322] bars insurance companies from raising premiums or denying patients health care coverage based on the results of genetic tests," Daschle said. "It prohibits employers from using predictive genetic information to make decisions about hiring, advancement, salary, or other workplace rights and privileges, and it says a person's genetic information cannot be disclosed without his or her consent. Finally, it gives victims of genetic discrimination the right to seek justice in court."

But some members of the business community believe more legislation could be overkill. Susan Meisinger, SPHR, chief operating officer of the Society for Human Resource Management, in her testimony cautioned Congress not to quickly adopt "preventive legislation."

"While some recent reports suggest employers regularly use such information, it has not been our experience," Meisinger said. "Indeed, we believe such practices are rare, if they occur at all."

Other critics contend that a prohibition against discrimination based on genetic information is already embedded in the Americans with Disabilities Act. Meisinger noted the following in her testimony:

"In 1995 the EEOC adopted the view that the ADA prohibits discrimination against workers based on their genetic makeup. This view was contained in EEOC's Definition of Disability policy guidance. The policy explicitly states that discrimination on the basis of genetic information is covered by the ADA under the third part of the statutory definition of the term 'disability,' which covers individuals 'regarded as' having impairments that substantially limit one or more major life activities.

"This prong of the ADA is designed to protect against myths, fears, and stereotypes about disability and reflects a recognition by Congress that the reactions of others to an impairment or a perceived impairment can be just as disabling as the limitations caused by an actual impairment," Meisinger said. "In my opinion, genetic predisposition discrimination is exactly the kind of fact scenario Congress intended to be covered by the 'regarded as' prong."

Furthermore, Meisinger said there is still a significant amount of confusion over what constitutes genetic testing, genetic information, and genetic monitoring that "highlights the need for caution in any legislative endeavor in this arena."

Still, House Democrats on June 21 launched a discharge petition drive to bring their version of the Genetic Nondiscrimination in Insurance and Employment Act (H.R. 2457) directly to a vote on the House floor.

"We want to protect genetic privacy of Americans against loss of insurance and protect their employment," said bill sponsor Rep. Louise Slaughter, D-New York. "If brought up for a vote, I know it would pass."

Both bills were introduced in July 1999. No hearings have been held on H.R. 2457 thus far.

VIII-7: Illegal Child Labor Comes Back

BRIAN DUMAINE

Like tuberculosis and measles, child labor is making a comeback in the United States. From New York to California, employers are breaking the law by hiring children of 7 to 17 who put in long, hard hours and often work in dangerous conditions. Some examples:

- In many states, small fly-by-night candy distributors are hiring young children to sell boxes of chocolates door-to-door, late at night, and unsupervised, in strange neighborhoods. In Washington State, one 11-year-old girl selling candy alone at 10 P.M. on a school night, 160 miles from home, was struck and killed by a passing car.

- In New York City and Los Angeles, immigrant children who should be in school work in garment industry sweatshops that are dirty, crowded, and often contain hazards like locked fire doors.

- In the Southeast, the Labor Department is investigating Food Lion, the fast-growing supermarket chain, for hundreds of possible labor violations, most of them safety related. Underage children allegedly used meat-cutting machines and paper-box bailers—machines that compact and crush cardboard cartons and are known to kill.

- In California and Texas—along the Mexican border—and in south Florida, young children still work beside their parents for up to 12 hours a day as migrant farmers. As a 13-year-old, Mexican-American Augustino Nieves started picking olives and strawberries in California. He missed months of school that year, working from 6:30 A.M. until 8 P.M., with a 20-minute lunch break, six days a week, at less than the minimum wage.

- In Miami, the Labor Department last December fined Burger King $500,000—the largest child labor penalty in history—for letting 14- and 15-year-olds work late into

the night on school days. The Fair Labor Standards Act of 1938 prohibits kids that age from being on the job later than 7 P.M.

Over the past ten years, U.S. government statistics show a marked rise in child labor violations. In 1992 the Labor Department logged 19,443 such offenses, about twice the 1980 level. Most involved kids working too late on school nights in grocery stores and fast-food restaurants or using hazardous equipment like meat saws and slicers. Says California state labor commissioner Victoria Bradshaw: "You have a lot of kids in the workforce, and they don't know they're entitled to certain rights."

Why is this problem growing again? Peter Rachleff, an associate professor at Minnesota's Macalester College and a specialist in the history of child labor, links its reappearance to "the overall deterioration of working-class life in America." More middle-class families, feeling the jobs pinch, are encouraging their kids to work to supplement family income. Child labor also tends to increase during periods of heavy immigration. In the past decade the number of immigrants—both legal and illegal—has surged. To scrape by, many ask even very young children to help out. Says New York State labor commissioner John Hudacs: "Whenever you have immigrants who don't speak the language and need to make ends meet, employers will take advantage of them."

Under federal law it is illegal for anyone under 18 to work in manufacturing or construction or to operate most kinds of power tools. With a few exceptions, like paper routes, acting, and family farm work, it is illegal for anyone under 14 to be employed, period. On school days, 14- and 15-year-olds can't work before 7 A.M. or after 7 P.M.

Child labor laws, however, rarely are enforced. In 1980 the U.S. Labor Department

Reprinted from *Fortune* (April 5, 1993): 86–88, 92–94.

had 1,059 investigators. Today, after several budget cuts, it deploys only 833 agents to enforce not only the child labor laws but a dozen other major regulations, among them minimum wage laws. According to the National Safe Workplace Institute, a Chicago nonprofit group funded by foundations and corporations, a business can expect a visit by a federal labor inspector once every 50 years.

On the state level, the situation isn't much better. New York, Washington, Maine, and California have passed laws that further restrict the hours teens can work during the school year or ban certain employment such as hospital jobs that might expose kids to dangerous medical waste. But three states—Colorado, Kansas, and Mississippi—have no state child labor laws at all. Maryland has a set of progressive child labor laws on the books but was forced by budget problems to fire all its investigators 18 months ago.

For middle-class suburban families the most serious child labor problem in America may be excessive hours in the fast-food industry. Says William Brooks, a former Assistant Secretary of Labor who is now a GM executive: "The fast-food joints are the coal mines of the 1990s." Though some work after school is laudable, too many kids get carried away and shortchange what should be their first priority—getting the best education. The Japanese, who outscore American teens on standardized math and science tests—and who are no slouches when it comes to working hard as adults—take a completely different approach. While many American teens work during the school year, very few Japanese kids do.

But as an immediate threat to a child's safety and well-being, fast-food work is a far less pressing concern. What is rising rapidly to the top of the list in New York, California, Washington, Texas, and other states is a new kind of child labor abuse—door-to-door candy selling. Says Bob Smith, chief state labor investigator for northern California: "We have nine investigations going

in my region, and we haven't even scratched the surface."

Don't confuse these operations with selling Girl Scout cookies. Girl Scouts sell in their own neighborhoods, to people they know, and get driven around by parents. But in the typical candy-selling scam, vans operated by a host of small, shady operators pick up children, some as young as 7, after school and drive them to strange neighborhoods and distant towns to sell their wares until late at night. Some are not ideal employers. Gerald Winters, also known as the Candy King, is serving a 34-year sentence in federal prison for, among other things, beating one rival with a baseball bat and having another's van set on fire.

Brandy Woodrow, 13, of Vallejo, California, who recently stopped door-to-door selling, describes the work in two words: "Real scary." A confident and sassy girl with a beehive hairdo, jeans, lots of jewelry, and a bright maroon and green jacket—in other words a typical teen—Brandy started selling candy when she was 11. She recounts her experience:

> "We used to sell every day. The van would pick me up at 3:30 and I'd work until 10 P.M. on weekdays and until midnight on weekends. The driver would have 20 kids in his van. We'd usually sit on the floor; there were no seat belts. First we'd sell in Vallejo, and then we went all over. One time we were in Livermore, 50 miles away, and the van broke down. I didn't get home until 3:30 in the morning.
>
> I sold the candy for $5 a box and kept $1 for myself. On a good night I could sell 10 boxes. Sometimes the kids drank in the van or used drugs. One kid stole some tools from a house and sold them to the driver. One time the driver left a boy in Napa, and he had to walk 15 miles home at night. The driver just forgot him. Another night I waited for two hours on the corner to get picked up. I'd like to sell candy again, but only if it were safer."

"These candy companies," says officer Mary Pedretti of the Vallejo police department, "break just about every child labor law on the books." They start by hiring underage kids, who are then allowed to work the streets alone, when by California law they have to work in pairs. Usually the children are taught to lie. Youngsters selling in New York City's Rockefeller Center claim to be raising money for a charity, when they're not. In California the line is they're selling to help inner-city kids escape drugs and crime. For example, John, 13, a door-to-door seller in California, told FORTUNE that he was raising money for his school baseball team, when in fact he was selling for a local business. Says William Moffett, a retired career counselor for the Vallejo school system who's now dedicating much of his time to shutting down the candy sellers: "The lesson the kids learn about work is, the better you lie, the more money you make."

Rising immigration may be fueling an increase in child labor abuse in a more traditional problem area—garment industry sweatshops. In the 1980s most major American apparel manufacturers shifted work to the Third World, chasing dollars-a-day wages. To stay competitive, some small U.S. operators started hiring immigrant children at below the minimum wage. Says Tom Glubiak, head of New York State's garment industry task force, which is responsible for investigating child labor abuses: "These employers love kids because they tend to be willing workers. They don't complain, and they think they're making a lot of money when they're not."

For every offending employer who is discovered, doubtless scores more go undetected. On a recent Tuesday, FORTUNE, accompanying a team of state labor inspectors, found three minors working illegally in garment factories in Manhattan. In one sweatshop in Chinatown, Gao and Ying, two girls fresh off the boat from Fukien, China, and speaking no English, worked the sewing machines. The factory, in a ramshackle building, was hot and crowded, with garbage on the floor and old electrical wires hanging from the ceiling. One of the proprietors, reacting to this raid like Bruce Lee on angel dust, claimed the girls were 20 and then paced up and down the floor, screaming at the inspectors, "I'll kill you, I'll kill you."

Under New York law, the owner had 10 days to supply proof of age or stop employing the girls. Andy Chan, one of the investigators, believes the girls were no more than 14 or 15 and says the business never got back to him with the proper documentation. The girls have disappeared, probably to another of the 1,500 sweatshops in the city.

At another clothing factory, in midtown Manhattan, a shy Mexican girl named Faviola Flores, with black hair and a puffy white blouse, was hiding from investigators in a clothes rack. Though the seamstress claimed she was 20, investigators assume she wasn't much more than 15. Faviola lives in New York City with her three sisters and sends money back to her brother in Mexico. When asked whether she would rather be at the factory than in school, she replied poignantly, "I don't like working here, but I have no choice."

Children also continue to labor illegally on farms in Texas, California, and Florida. Among migrant families, it's still natural to pull young teenagers out of school to lend a hand during harvest. And since most families lack any kind of affordable day care, they sometimes bring even very young children to the fields. Migrant farm workers are paid by the box—be it carrots, grapes, or cherries—so every little hand helps.

While this kind of exploitation of young kids should certainly be stopped, sometimes enforcement of the child labor laws governing agriculture can seem capricious, especially when it involves older teens. In California's Imperial Valley, a rich farmland just north of the Mexican border, FORTUNE tagged along as state and federal inspectors found three 17-year-old boys picking cauliflower—a backbreaking task. They would typically start at 7 A.M. and work until dusk, bending over and over again, cutting the cauliflower with a sharp knife and dropping it in a box on a moving tractor. Their only respite: three 10-minute breaks a day.

Under California law, the three were working illegally because they didn't have a work permit from a school. But in a Kafkaesque twist, what these teenagers were doing was perfectly legal under federal law, which stops policing teens once they're 16. While the California inspector was telling the employer he had to fire the kids, the federal inspector merely stood by and cracked, "The state is doing nothing more than harassing these boys." He had a point. One, Eduardo Cardenas, was a strong, strapping fellow, who had left 11 siblings behind in Mexico to come to the United States to improve his lot in life. The other, Ivan Flores, was married and had a young daughter. "So I can't work now?" he asked angrily. "That can't help anything."

The National Safe Workplace Institute estimates that 300 children are killed and 70,000 injured every year on the job. One of the most dangerous areas for minors is construction, where it's illegal for anyone under 18 to work. In the Bronx last year, two 14-year-old boys, employed by a contractor to paint the inside of a huge storage tank, were overcome by solvent fumes and suffered permanent brain damage. In California a boy, 13, working for a Santa Barbara builder was doing chin-ups on a steel boom that rested precariously on a pile of wood. The boom fell over, crushing and killing him.

Danger lurks in the service trades as well. In 1991, Charles Kenney, 16 at the time, was working for an ice cream distributor in New York City. While climbing a 12-foot-high pile of boxes in a freezer—a prohibited area for minors—he slipped, caught his ring on the edge of a shelf, and lost his finger. In 1988, Michael Hucorne, then 17, was working at a Weis supermarket in Pennsylvania. He tried to reach into a bailer—a machine

that crushes and binds paper boxes and cartons and is, again, off-limits for minors—to free some jammed material and got caught. The machine crushed his body for at least 30 minutes before he suffocated. In its defense, Weis Markets says that no one ever proved in court that Michael was killed "in the act of doing his job."

Currently the Labor Department is investigating a huge case involving the Food Lion supermarket chain, headquartered in Salisbury, North Carolina. The potential violation: Hundreds of teens employed by Food Lion may have used meat-cutting saws as well as paper-box bailers—both of which are prohibited by federal law for kids under 18. As far as anyone knows, no one at Food Lion has yet been hurt by these machines. The company claims that the government's charges involve technical violations. For instance, it insists that teenage workers simply threw cardboard boxes into bailers that weren't operating and they were therefore in no danger. But some adult Food Lion employees, both past and present, insist that it was common practice for minors to operate bailers and use meat saws.

True, the employees who make these charges are all also party to a lawsuit against the supermarket chain for not paying them adequate overtime. But while one might be dubious about the testimony of an ex-employee suing his former company, FORTUNE spoke with six former or current employees—all of whom said they often observed underage workers violating the safety laws.

As these people tell it, Food Lion routinely broke child labor laws to save money. The company, for example, limited the number of hours its meat cutters could work per week to avoid paying overtime. Meat cutters usually left the market by 6 P.M., so if a customer wanted a cut of meat, the store manager would sometimes tell his 16- and 17-year-old grocery baggers to prepare the order. Says Kim Caudill, a meat cutter at

Food Lion for six years before he quit last January: "It was common as dirt for kids to use the meat-slicing equipment. If the customer asked for a certain cut of meat and a bagger was around, they would use whatever equipment was necessary, despite signs prohibiting children under the age of 18 from going anywhere near the machines." The company denies using minors to cut meat.

Joe Baker, who is still a market manager at a Food Lion store in Hickory, North Carolina, claims that until Labor Department investigators began looking into child labor violations last fall, it was quite common for 16- and 17-year-old bag boys to use the paper-box bailer in his store. Baker's sister-in-law, Lisa Baker, 22, who in 1987 also worked at the Hickory Food Lion, says that when she was 16, some managers told her it was part of her duty to put paper boxes into a bailer, and she did so daily, in clear violation of the rules. "I got in trouble," she says, "if I *didn't* do it."

What can be done to stem this new tide of child labor violations? The last thing most businesses want, and rightly so, is a new army of investigators harassing law-abiding employers. Besides, in an era of limited budgets, that's unlikely anyway.

Smarter enforcement offers a better alternative. Working with the states, Washington could, for instance, create task forces that concentrate on specific areas where abuses are known to be most egregious. One model might be New York State's garment industry task force, whose 24 investigators root out violators in New York City sweatshops. California, with its new TIPP program, is taking a cross-agency approach, using state tax filings and business licensing and registration records to pinpoint employers with a history of skirting the rules. These companies, state officials have found, are the most likely child labor lawbreakers.

Education helps too. Parents, teachers, employers, and children need to be made better aware of the child labor laws. High-profile cases like those the Labor Department has brought against nationally known companies such as Burger King go a long way in sending a message to all employers to obey the law. Above all, in today's global economy no wealthy nation can expect to remain well-off unless it keeps stressing to all its children that ultimately how well you prepare yourself for tomorrow's workplace matters more than how much you work while doing so.

VIII-8: The Monster under the Bed
How Business Is Mastering the Opportunity of Knowledge for Profit

STAN DAVIS AND JIM BOTKIN

THE SEVEN WAYS

First, business is coming to bear the major responsibility for the kind of education that

Reprinted from *The Monster Under the Bed: How Business Is Mastering the Opportunity of Knowledge for Profit*, Stan Davis and Jim Botkin (New York, Simon & Schuster, 1994).

is necessary for any country to remain competitive in the new economy.

Second, the marketplace for learning is being redefined dramatically from K-12 to K-80, or lifelong learning, whose major segments are customers, employees, and students, in that order.

Third, any business can become a knowledge business by putting data and information to productive use, creating knowledge-based products and services that make its customers smarter.

Fourth, a new generation of smart and humanized technologies will revolutionize learning by employees and customers in business before it affects students and teachers in schools.

Fifth, business-driven learning will be organized according to the values of today's information age: service, productivity, cus-tomization, networking, and the need to be fast, flexible, and global.

Sixth, schools will embrace businesslike practices to improve their own perfor-mance. The three R's will be complemented by the new six R's: risks, results, rewards, relationships, research, and rivalry.

Seventh, the revolution in the way we learn will worsen the already grave division between social classes, requiring us to redress human and social inequities.

VIII-9: The Quest for Lifetime Employability

JEANNE C. MEISTER

As companies face rapidly changing tech-nologies, increased customer expectations, and escalating competitive pressures, the workplace is becoming a dynamic, interde-pendent one, where thinking and acting must be done by all employees. The increase of knowledge workers pervades our workplace. While many jobs may still entail manual skills, they now also require theoretical knowledge that must be refreshed on a con-tinuous basis. In fact, Peter Drucker esti-mates that knowledge workers will comprise two-thirds of the workforce by the end of this century.

Across industries and occupations, the chief concern for knowledge workers is the shortened shelf life of the knowledge they possess, hence the need to constantly retool their skills. In other words, what we know today will not add value tomorrow unless we have the ability to learn new skills and broader roles. These new skills run the gamut from enhanced technical abilities to creative problem-solving and leadership develop-ment. The key goal for an organization is to provide its workers with the ability to contin-ually retool their skills and knowledge. . . .

Reprinted from the *Journal of Business Strategy* (May/June 1998): 25–28.

CAREER SELF-MANAGEMENT

[C]areer self-management [corresponds] to the responsibility all employees have to manage their own careers. You can think of this competency as the skill possessed by individuals who are self-starters. Perhaps the need for this competency is best described by Peter DiToro, a 45-year-old middle man-ager who has survived a half-dozen rounds of layoffs at Computervision, a Bedford, Massachusetts–based computer company. In a *New York Times* interview DiToro dis-cussed the importance of self-management: "Job security is gone forever. I expect a revo-lution in my career every five to seven years. So, I now believe I am the corporation and it's my responsibility to manage my career."

This focus on career self-management comes at a time when corporate America is just recovering from severe job losses. In early 1996 the *New York Times* did a seven-part series on corporate downsizing. . . . According to the series, lifetime employa-bility is replacing lifetime employment and the new social contract in American busi-ness. Michael Weiss, vice chairman of The Limited, put the employer's side of this social contract in the simplest of terms: "We show you that we value you by helping you develop your career."

Hence, career self-management is becoming an important competency emphasized at a number of corporate universities. Career self-management is the ability to keep pace with the speed at which change occurs within the organization and the industry and to prepare for the future. It signifies a recognition on the part of the individual employee to keep learning because jobs that are held today may evolve into something else tomorrow, or simply disappear entirely. Career self-management also involves learning to identify and obtain new skills and competencies that allow the employee to move to a new position, either inside or outside of the organization.

A company that supports and encourages career self-management may ultimately have more highly skilled and flexible employees, because employees understand the need to continuously refresh and update their skills. One effective way to nurture and support career self-management is to create a career center within the corporate university. This career center becomes a visible sign of the company's commitment to employee development, allows employees to assess their skills and benchmark them against company and industry standards, and cultivate skills that will help them succeed better in both their current and future jobs.

In the *Annual Survey of Corporate University Future Directions* we found that of the 100 corporate university deans surveyed, 43 percent currently have a career development center and another 15 percent are contemplating creating one. By far the most important function of the career development center is to be the resource center for assisting employees in self-assessment of their skills and advising them on the range of new skills, knowledge, and competencies needed to successfully compete in the global marketplace.

The emphasis today is on promoting career self-management. Often there is no longer a clearly marked career path for employees because the nature of the business changes so fast. An individual who wants to move within a company where the traditional career path no longer exists must know how to manage his or her career. Hence, making career information accessible, providing assessment instruments and benchmarking tools, as well as opportunities to talk with experts are the first steps in creating a workforce that is aware, motivated, and career-resilient. However, creating a culture that encourages and sustains career self-management while maintaining employee loyalty is a challenge. It requires commitment to the idea of employee self-development on the part of managers, a workplace culture where employees recognize the need for continuous learning, and an organization that develops self-development programs for both the employee and the manager.

Raychem in Menlo Park, California has developed an innovative approach to institutionalizing a culture of career self-management. Raychem, with 1996 sales of $1.67 billion and a 1996 net income of $148 million, launched a career development center in 1994. The former CEO, Bob Saldich, made learning and self-development a visible part of the culture; employees were taught to think of themselves as self-employed and encouraged to explore many career options.

Raychem, under new CEO Richard Kashnow, is building upon this culture of employee self-development by making people development a key competency for Raychem managers, along with such performance targets as 15 percent annual growth in earnings per share. The Raychem human resources department recently launched a program called HR Review in which an annual strategic plan for people development is created and Raychem managers are rated on their ability to develop their employees.

This People Development Strategic Plan covers how employees should be coached and cultivated, the specific competencies needed for their success, and the employee development initiatives that will be undertaken by employees. "The HR Review process, along with management accountability for employee development, and the emphasis on feedback, will drive the movement toward supporting employee development," says HR Manager Suzanne Edises, who is responsible for people development at Raychem.

A critical component of this people development initiative at Raychem Career Development Center is currently housed in Raychem's corporate library. The Career Development Center is outsourced to Career Action Center, a local nonprofit agency with expertise in the development and delivery of career management services. The Raychem Career Development Center provides employees with self-assessments, career workshops, and referrals to career resources. Raychem is now exploring the idea of putting some self-assessment materials on-line and making them accessible to employees throughout the world.

An important function of the Raychem Career Development Center is to guide employees in developing a list of competencies they need for their current job or will need in the future. By providing resources on industry skill standards, and sometimes suggesting companies to benchmark, Raychem Career Development Center helps employees see where their skill level is in relationship to what the market demands or will demand in the future. Employees can then chart their own development plan, which may include taking advantage of Raychem's tuition reimbursement program, participating in formal training programs at Raychem University, requesting developmental assignments, or seeking masters or mentors to role model on the job.

"We are looking at a variety of options," says Edises. "We want to provide development opportunities for our employees and we are seeking out the most efficient and effective ways to accomplish this. In the future, much of what we currently do may be done on-line so that we can serve our growing global population of employees."

The types of career self-management tools developed by the Raychem Career Development Center ultimately create what Robert Waterman calls a career-resilient workforce, defined in the *Harvard Business Review* [July/August 1994] as: "A group of employees who not only are dedicated to the idea of continuous learning but also stand ready to reinforce themselves to keep pace with change, take responsibility for their own career management, and last but not least, are committed to the company's success. The result is a group of self-resilient workers and a company that can thrive in an era where the skills needed to remain competitive are changing at a dizzying pace."

Many companies profiled here have taken a firm stand on the importance of having employees understand that it is their responsibility to manage their own development. The assumption made by these companies is that once the company sets the direction and defines the core workplace competencies, each employee must assess if he or she has these competencies and, if not, how they can be developed.

● ● ● ● ● ● ● ● ●

EMPLOYEE SELF-DEVELOPMENT LINKED TO COMPENSATION

As more companies focus on creating a culture of career self-management and employee self-development, many are going one step further by tying completion of learning plans to compensation. Together the employee and the employer develop learning goals for the year. Saturn comes to the forefront as a leader in developing an innovative approach to link learning to compensation. Gary High, director of Human Resources Development, defines the Saturn learning culture as:

- Every team member has his or her training and development plan.
- Training has a demonstrated impact on job performance.
- Training is an investment, not a cost.
- Training is driven by the needs of the organization.
- A high percentage of Saturn team members are involved in providing training.

Central to Saturn's learning culture is the partnership Saturn builds with each individual team member. Training requirements lead to higher and higher levels of professional competence. This partnership is formalized in an agreement known as the individual training plan (ITPs) where Saturn team members and their leaders outline the specific training and development activities that each team member will undertake in a given year. These activities, outlined in ITPs, range from taking Saturn-specific formal training programs, teaching a class, cross-training a team member, reading a book, completing a computer-based training program, or taking a university course. Once a team member successfully completes this combination of learning activities on the plan, he or she will have achieved the 5 percent or 92 hours learning goal. Importantly, this partnership stresses team member professional development so that each Saturn team member learns new skills to improve his or her performance on the job, not merely to complete a required number of training hours. In this way learning becomes the goal rather than simply using training to fulfill a human resources policy.

This partnership agreement does something else—it links Saturn's commitment to training to the team member compensation system. According to the partnership agreement developed between Saturn management and the representatives of the United Auto Workers union, 12 percent of each Saturn employee's base compensation is at risk, pending meeting specific goals. Interestingly, as this "risk percentage" has increased from 5 percent in 1995 to the current level of 12 percent, the reward has also increased to its maximum of $12,500 per person, but what is critical here is how Saturn defines this risk/reward formula. Five percent of base compensation at risk is directly tied to completion of one's training plan objectives, 5 percent at risk relates to meeting product quality goals, and 2 percent relates to how well Saturn self-managed teams are able to demonstrate their effectiveness in working together in teams. The reward portion of the compensation gives additional compensation up to $12,500 over the base salary. It is tied to quality and productivity results that exceed the industry standard and to the achievement of financial goals for the year. Tim Epps, vice president of People Systems at Saturn, comments on the benefits of this compensation system when he says, "Doing the right training, in the right way, at the right time really can leverage the company's ability to build better, and more cars and, in the end, increase every team member's salary level."

Linking attainment of training goals to compensation has become an increasingly important factor in ensuring that training is linked to a performance management system. According to Gary High, "As the risk percentage has increased over time at Saturn, so have our team member's salary levels. In essence, this has motivated us to achieve higher levels of performance by taking the ambiguity out of one's job and putting a spotlight on the important deliverables needed for the team to be successful. We believe one of our critical success factors in creating this culture of continuous learning is to clearly define the risk and reward formula to our workforce and to provide them with the opportunity for achieving their learning goals as well as other performance goals." Saturn's use of an incentive-based professional development plan reflects the company's belief that success at Saturn is dependent upon everyone making a commitment to life-long learning.

●●●●●●●●●●●●●●●●●●
THEMES OF FORMAL AND INFORMAL LEARNING PROGRAMS

More and more companies realize that workers at the turn of the century will be much more involved in coaching, teaching, and motivating teammates than just execut-

ing the technical aspects of their jobs. The companies profiled here have understood the growing complexity of jobs at every level of the organization. They have observed that work is becoming less task-oriented and more people-oriented, requiring workers who can think critically, make decisions, solve problems, effectively communicate with co-workers and customers, and see the business as an integrated whole. The university model for training has become their means of "upskilling" their workforces to meet these new demands. They provide an important example for other companies to follow.

VIII-10: Reconstructing Management Education as Lifelong Learning

RICHARD E. BOYATZIS AND KATHY E. KRAM

The landscape of work is changing dramatically and rapidly. Individuals can step into management roles at many points in their lives, not just following early career periods of five to seven years. Additionally, those entering the workforce today can expect to have as many as four to six careers during their lifetimes.[1] Simple career models that trace progress through several defined stages are not sufficient to provide insight into the complexity of paths through multiple careers.[2] Indeed, the authors of such models have begun to reverse their perspectives on careers to suggest a more protean approach, with individuals seen as continuously developing new competencies and regularly changing jobs and organizations.[3] Management development is thus needed at several points during the course of one's working life (for example, at the start of a new career).

Such development can also serve as a stimulus to making a career change.

In the past, when a person joined a company at the start of a career and then moved ahead in the organization, career and life-transition issues were dealt with outside of work. The current modes of multiple careers, combinations of part-time work into one job, and movement into and out of the full-time workforce (for either personal or organizational reasons) make job and organizational choices a way of resolving transition issues.

In hierarchical systems, characteristic of past decades and larger organizations, a manager is expected to direct and motivate workers. Such systems breed paternalism and represent an outside-in interpretation of life and work: that is, it is assumed that if direction and motivation do not come from outside the individual, he or she will not work efficiently and effectively. There has, however, been an increasing shift to the opposite view, with a career seen as being in the individual's

Reprinted from Selections (Autumn/Winter) 2000: 17–27.

charge. A worker walks out the door at the end of the workday and, typically, returns the next morning—but may not.

The need to manage one's own development in an environment of greater uncertainty and turbulence makes relational learning more important than ever before.[4] In today's context, individuals of every age, organizational tenure, and career stage find themselves to be novices. A worker may have to learn a radically new job, acquire new technical skills, or begin working with people of very different backgrounds and worldviews. Relationships are a critical resource for learning in these instances; without them, a sense of isolation and despair is all too likely.[5] Workers would be wise to actively build developmental alliances with senior colleagues, peers, and subordinates, as well as with individuals outside the organization.

People need to develop the requisite skills to make connections with various others. Such skills as self-reflection, self-disclosure, active listening, giving and receiving feedback, and collaboration are becoming recognized as core managerial–relational competencies.[6] These same skills are also essential for effective teamwork, suggesting a new area of content and process learning in management education.

Currently, most management school offerings related to lifelong learning are available only in executive education programs. The executive MBA degree is the most recent exception to this pattern. EMBA programs are viewed as being just as important to the school's mission as the historically mainstream programs, with senior faculty expected to teach in them as part of their regular workloads.

• •

THE INFLUENCE OF LIFE AND CAREER STAGES

It is estimated that in 2000, approximately one-third of the workforce in the United States will be in their forties or fifties—the time of life that inspired the term "mid-life crisis." Whatever term one uses, this time in a life and career can today be a time of change in the direction of one's career path. The seventy-six million baby boomers in this country are reframing the views of many of life's traditional transition points, bringing their needs and interests, as well as their more self-directed approach, into their organizations. Having lived through the deterioration of the career-long psychological contract between individuals and their work organizations, they do not expect organizations to help them throughout their careers and lives.[7]

In contemplating career-long or lifelong growth, we are drawn to models in which growth is a function of experience and time. The more experience someone has, the more developed we believe that person to be. Unfortunately, experience does not automatically imply learning. Unrecognized transitions often result in misplaced effort and increasing frustration. Today's leaner, flatter, more flexible organizations depend on their leaders for creative and effective thought and action. No manager can competently fulfill that charge without also considering his or her life and career changes. Awareness of and attention to one's own transitions are essential. Although there is no statistical evidence that a specific percentage of poor business decisions is caused by life and career transitions, the examples reported by organizational consultants and board members are too numerous to be dismissed as unique events.

It is equally important to consider how group memberships shape individual experiences of transitions. There is now a wealth of evidence to suggest that not only is each stage of both life and career experienced differently by men and women, but also that the texture of experiences at successive stages is shaped by race, ethnicity, and social class.[8] At every career stage, personal efforts to develop become increasingly complex when combined with any of the following:

- Concerns related to the integration of work and family roles

- The need to reconcile with the dominant culture of the organization, which is most often based on values and perceptions about work and the world from a white, male perspective (especially in North America and Europe)

- The necessity of forming effective developmental relationships with individuals of the opposite gender or of different racial backgrounds

From stage to stage in one's life or career, the predominant concerns affecting motivation, style, and attitudes shift. In the past, each stage of a career encompassed roughly five to nine years. The rapidly increased pace of change in the occupational landscape has led to dramatic changes in the duration and frequency of these stages.[9] Often, the stages themselves are shorter, while the periods of transition between them are longer. Uncertainty and instability in the workplace and changing social attitudes toward marriage, family, and geographic mobility have added confusion to these periods of transition. While older models may still portray the lives and careers of some people, we cannot adhere strictly to outdated models that do not address the majority of the current workforce. We must instead be flexible, adapting a pluralism of models.

The transitions between stages are often more evident than the stages themselves. As life and career issues arise, a number of responses are seen. Some people choose to ignore these transition issues; on the surface, at least, they find this solution easier than attempting to deal with the transitions. Many who do pursue resolution do so only in light of personal concerns, with less concern about the consequences to the organization than might have been the case in past decades. Some adopt a self-serving posture and claim that anything that maximizes their personal productivity will benefit the organization, even if that includes their leaving the firm.

Various theories describe the progression through life and career.[10] Each is characterized by a somewhat different view of the world, of the nature of work, and of what people want from life and from a job. People may want to learn about management and leadership in any of these stages. While the tasks, functions, and competencies needed in order to be a superior performing manager or leader may remain the same, the individual's values, goals, and attitudes may be different. To be responsive and engaging, management education and development must address this pluralism of needs and desires.

THE NEW CHARGE FOR MANAGEMENT EDUCATION

On the whole, management education is designed for undergraduates or MBAs, then extended to managers and executives. Many executive education courses use the same cases, and in the same ways, as MBA and undergraduate classes. It seems self-evident that not all of these students will gain equally from the same materials and methods. The rapid expansion of the training and consulting industry in the last 25 years is, in part, evidence of the need for teaching methods, styles, and materials that are different from those used in schools of management. In addition, outcome studies of student change often suggest that undergraduates and MBAs are not retaining knowledge and skills at the level we have believed them to be.[11] Various reviews of management education have been critical of schools' lack of response to the needs and desires of employers.[12]

The following principles of lifelong learning or growth serve as a beginning to the reconceptualization of management education as a lifelong process:

1. A person's needs and interests change during his or her life.
2. An organization's needs for contributions from its people and from any particular job will change over time.
3. A person's durable learning should be respected and built upon in further training, education, and development.
4. Since experience does not equal learning, past experiences are not as important to development as is *learning* from those experiences.
5. People change themselves; people must want to change; people decide what they will learn.
6. Self-directed change involves a change in one's image of self or in one's image of the ideal.
7. Self-directed learning includes self-directed change, an awareness of the change, and an understanding of how the change occurred.
8. A person chooses to change according to his or her personal vision, specific values, philosophy, interests, and life and career stage cycle.[13]

An example of the application of these self-directed learning principles to an executive education program is the Professional Fellows Program at the Weatherhead School of Management, Case Western Reserve University.[14] The yearlong program begins with a three-day residency in late summer, followed by two four-month sessions involving one evening a week and one Saturday a month. A second three-day residency completes the program.

Successful participants receive a certificate and are inducted into the Fellows Society. This group creates monthly or quarterly developmental events on various topics, with faculty assisting in finding appropriate resource people to lead or facilitate the events and provide the settings.

This degree of self-directed choice begins during the program. The Monday night seminars are focused on current topics in management (in particular, the management of professionals and professional service firms). Faculty select the topics for the first four sessions, after which students select the topics. In the spring, participants form teams and identify projects for continued in-depth study.

At Boston University School of Management's Executive Leadership Center, high-potential executives come to campus for both open-enrollment and customized programs. Action learning and self-directed learning are essential components of the educational experience. Programs place strong emphasis on self-assessment and goal-setting activities along with exposure to the latest management theories, perspectives, and practices. Students are expected to bring a major strategic challenge to the program, to implement action plans after returning to work, and to reflect on their experiences with implementation during follow-up sessions on campus or consultations with a peer coach.

Pluralism regarding developmental modes can be designed into the process. Assessments of student progress might involve any of several methods, with the particular method used chosen by the learner according to his or her own growth mode.[15] Those in the Performance (Mastery) Mode may appreciate a grade, or they might prefer descriptive feedback comparing their performances in using material to those who effectively use such material in actual management jobs. Students in the Learning (Novelty) Mode may appreciate qualitative feedback referenced against other material that has been learned or used; or, these students may want to be given other ideas to consider in exploring the material further. Those in the Development (Meaning) Mode may appreciate assessment in the form of questions as to the implications or value (i.e., meaning) of the topics.

One of the leadership courses in the Weatherhead School's Executive Doctorate in Management Program provides an example of the usefulness of different assessment processes. The average age of participants in this program is 47; students have considerable management experience, often gained in top executive positions. It is thus appropriate to assume that within a class there are people in each of the modes of growth described above. In this particular leadership course, assignments include writing a series of papers that involve conducting many interviews concerning a particular leader. The interviews, conducted not only with the individual but also with a variety of other people important to the leader's career and life, lead to an analysis of the person based on the topics covered in class.

Students in the Performance Mode want to study an effective leader in order to benchmark what effective leadership really is. Those in the Learning Mode prefer to examine themselves as leaders. Those in the Development Mode have various wishes: some want to examine themselves in order to get back in touch with their core values and goals in life, while others want to study thought leaders or leaders of not-for-profit organizations to examine issues beyond the maximizing of organizational performance.

The course has been restructured to accommodate varying preferences by allowing each participant to choose the subject for the papers. This has required the rewriting of assignments and the creation of comparable workload expectations, with faculty members given sufficient material to evaluate each participant's work.

Traditional assessment practices carry assumptions that must be challenged, and possibly changed. For example, grades are used to judge the individual's performance against criteria established by the instructor or against the performances of other students. Neither of these techniques would likely be adequately engaging to or appropriate for learners in anything but the Performance Mode.

In the past, learning was frequently viewed as an individual activity. However, much of the material to be learned in preparation for management or leadership positions requires a social context for application, experimentation, and testing of concepts, ideas, principles, and skills. Team-oriented learning activities are also a more appropriate mirror of most organizations. To be effective, team-learning activities require more than merely having students complete an individual assignment within a group. Instructors need to assist with the group process and construct group-oriented rewards.

At Boston University, student teams in both undergraduate and graduate management programs are an integral part of core courses and are supported by the Center for Team Learning. In the university's EMBA program, participants work in teams during the first two-thirds of the program. During the last third, they form new teams based on industry interests and complete a capstone team project. At this stage, participants are expected to demonstrate a strong mastery of team leadership and membership skills. Team activities are supported by a faculty coordinator and a 17-month course entitled Team Learning, which is integrated into the entire curriculum.

INSIDE-OUT DEVELOPMENT

Students' expectations and desired outcomes derive from their own implicit theories about both management and learning. The challenge is to have students articulate those theories so that, as David Hunt has put it, the developmental event becomes an inside-out rather than an outside-in process.[16] Through essays, group discussions, or exercises, students could answer such questions as why they want to be managers in the first place.

Further, because students have a variety of learning styles, multiple approaches should be built into the materials and the design. For example, using Kolb's experiential learning theory, we could design alternative approaches to the introduction of material to address accommodative (concrete and active), divergent (concrete and reflective), assimilative (reflective and abstract), or convergent (abstract and active) learning styles.[17] Many executive education programs use a diagnostic instrument to assess learning styles early on to help participants become more aware of their optimal learning styles.

At Case Western Reserve, additional assessments are used later in the programs to examine learning flexibilities (and inflexibilities). The process and structure design of both the overall program and each class is most effective when all elements of the learning cycle are addressed.

Boston University's EMBA program participants are expected to keep journals tailored to each learning unit. The journals provide a structure for reflection, goal setting, and action planning to assist students in connecting what they have learned to their own experience, development, needs, and work context. Thus, the same content is applied uniquely in as many ways as there are individual students.

One way to address multiple learning styles is through the use of action learning projects. An example is the capstone project in Boston's EMBA program. This team project requires the integration of technical and functional knowledge and skills, managerial perspectives, and team learning. Each team is expected to develop a plan for doing business in a country that is either a major trading partner of the United States or a developing economy in transition. Following completion of the project, students travel to that country to assess the accuracy and feasibility of their business plans. The final assignment requires students to iden-tify what they have learned about doing global business in their respective industries.

The design of management development can also be approached from a life-stage perspective.

- *In the late twenties (or after five to seven years of work):* The individual should learn any management basics that have not yet been covered on the job or in earlier preparation. If study is undertaken in addition to full-time work, this learning might take about a year.

- *In the late thirties:* Developmental learning should focus on examining values, life purpose, and goals and should provide an opportunity for the students to examine each of their lives as a whole. Additional learning units should be added to help students proceed with their learning plans for the next era of life.

- *In the late forties:* Learning units should explore a variety of nonoccupational aspects of life, including community and volunteer work. Planning for the next era should also incorporate thoughtful consideration of the nature of retirement and identification of desired and meaningful activities.

An example of how courses may differ for participants at various life stages can be seen in the design and delivery of the self-directed learning assessment and development courses at the Weatherhead School. For MBAs, who enter at an average age of 28, the focus is on management development. While students examine their values and vision, they also develop a learning agenda (i.e., Learning Plan) during the first semester, based upon a future ideal. Students can then develop or enhance their knowledge, abilities, and perspectives, as well as maintain their strengths in these areas.

For the EMBAs, who enter at an average age of 38, the focus is on executive management and leadership. Students examine their life and career stages as well as their personal visions, values, philosophies, and future aspirations. Since EMBA students are often prepared to make dramatic shifts in their current careers and organizations or to move into new industries or careers, the self-assessment and development course is taken in the last semester. Assessment activities involve many of the same ones used with MBAs, with the addition of a "360-degree" assessment: questionnaires are collected from each participant's boss, spouse, various peers, and even clients, if the participant is in a service industry or profession.

Participants in the Professional Fellows and Executive Doctorate in Management programs enter at an average age of 47. For these two groups, the focus is on personal growth or leadership. Students spend a great deal more time than MBA or EMBA students examining their values and philosophies and discussing these issues with spouses, significant others, or close friends. The learning agenda in these programs is developed from a picture of the life the participant wants to be living, and how she or he expects to be contributing to the community, profession, or industry and possibly, addressing global issues.

Professional Fellows engage in this activity throughout the program. In the Executive Doctorate in Management Program, participants engage in aspects of this examination early on and return to it later in the program.

The assessment activities in both programs are as comprehensive as those used by the EMBAs. Most of these participants are either at the beginning or in the midst of a major career or life transition. Some participants develop a learning agenda, including occupational or professional development activities (e.g., students in the Performance Mode), while others pursue development related to non-work-related aspects of their lives, such as artistic expressiveness (e.g., students in the Development Mode).

RELATIONAL LEARNING IN MANAGEMENT EDUCATION

Relational learning occurs when individuals acquire skills, competencies, and perspectives in dialogue and connection with others.[18] There is already considerable evidence regarding the potency of this kind of learning in relationships at work through mentoring, coaching, and dialogue groups.[19] Individuals find guidance and support through these relationships for addressing concerns about their identity and values, and for developing the new skills and competencies they need to tackle new task-related challenges.[20] Although most schools use electronic means to facilitate communication through E-mail, bulletin boards, and coursework, an increasing number of schools are attempting to use groupware to facilitate project and team work. This application of distance learning is intended not only to eliminate some of the obstacles of geographic distance, but also to make use of the distinctive attributes of electronic interaction to enhance the development of teams, relationships, and innovative ways of working together.

Relational models of growth and development, derived from studies of women's development, conceptualize learning as movement through increasingly complex states of interdependence rather than as a process of increasing individuation. Thus, development is viewed less as a process of differentiating oneself from others than as one of understanding oneself as increasingly connected to others.[21] The assumption here is that participants will benefit most from interactions with their colleagues in school when relationships both inside and outside the classroom are characterized by interdependence, mutuality, and reciprocity. This means that participants enter relationships assuming that both parties will learn, even if one or the other party is at a more advanced life or career stage. Another assumption is that through self-disclosure, active listening, reflection, and empathy, both parties will develop a greater understanding of themselves and of the organizational environment.

With an infrastructure for relational learning, we can expect benefits to accrue to participants in every stage of life and career. Such an infrastructure should include opportunities to work in teams and to develop the requisite interpersonal skills, with the expectation that participants will actively learn in teams and in peer-coaching relationships. Since students vary in their willingness to see relationships as sources of personal growth and learning and in their capacities to build developmental relationships, the infrastructure must be sufficiently flexible to accommodate this pluralism of needs and skill levels.

Boston University's Center for Team Learning is a vehicle for designing a structure and a process into the various program experiences to make group projects more than an administrative convenience to faculty. Many of the courses in the undergraduate, MBA, and EMBA programs require team learning. The Team Learning Lab helps participants learn new process and team-membership skills along with content. Students can later practice these skills as they participate in various team projects. The lab provides observed and/or recorded team experiences as a basis for structured peer feedback. This feedback is both developmental, in that it identifies strengths and weaknesses as well as ways to improve team skills, and evaluative, in that it partially determines course grades based on peer perceptions of participation and contributions.

In the EMBA program, the Team Learning curriculum has evolved to include an emphasis on peer coaching. Each student is matched early in the program with a peer from another team, with the two expected to support each other's learning throughout the program. Ideally, members of a pair are at similar or complementary stages in their careers.

In addition, teams are regularly asked to help their members interpret evaluative feedback from the class assessment of students' contributions to class learning. Students participate in several classes devoted to the development of coaching skills and to reflection on their experiences in coaching pairs and in teams.

When participants are assessed and recognized on the basis of their contributions to the learning of others, relational learning is encouraged. For example, a structured process that enables students to give and receive feedback to one another fosters personal learning, develops essential interpersonal skills, and prepares participants to build and manage high-performance teams.

Informal study groups have been used for years in many professional schools as a means for students to assist one another. By making peer learning a formal component of the educational process, we can expand the learning output beyond content to include process and skills. If participants have a clear set of expectations about how they will support one another's learning both during the unit and afterward, they have the opportunity to develop critical relational skills.[22]

The regular reflection and dialogue that take place with relational learning are added benefits. These two processes are now often framed as meta-competencies that individuals need in order to navigate in an increasingly turbulent and complex organizational world.[23]

A typical question concerning the relational learning infrastructure is that of cost. How can a school obtain sufficient resources for such a venture? In the traditional view of both higher education and business, with faculty or human resource personnel designing specific classes that people can take to address any learning need, the costs would be prohibitive and the system unmanageable. There is, however, another way to look at the challenge.

If students are assisted in identifying learning agendas and planning ways to work toward their learning goals, they can learn not only through structured or corporate activities, but also through day-to-day experiences and personal time. If they have a focus, an agenda, and a clear idea of how to explore, students are able to obtain more learning from their experiences.

Further, creative design of classes or other learning experiences can accommodate many variations in people's learning styles, life and career stages, and other important individual differences. The design task is more complex. The challenge is not to assume that covering the same material in the same way, with many people responding in prestructured ways, is the only way to achieve economies of scale. The challenge is to create a design and a process that will address the needs and desires of those seeking management education while embracing and incorporating the diversity of individual issues. What was once a two-year management major or MBA experience can thus become a truly lifelong learning process.

Notes

1. D.T. Hall, ed., *The Career Is Dead—Long Live the Career* (San Francisco: Jossey-Bass, 1996).
2. G. Dalton and P. Thompson, *Novations: Strategies for Career Development* (Glenview, Ill: Scott, Foresman, 1986); E.H. Schein, *Career Dynamics: Matching Individual and Organization Needs* (Reading, Mass.: Addison-Wesley, 1978); D.T. Hall, *Careers in Organizations* (Glenview Ill.: Scott, Foresman, 1976).
3. D.T. Hall, J.P. Briscoe, and K.E. Kram, "Identity, Values and the Protean Career," in C. Cooper and S. Jackson, eds., *Handbook of Organizational Behavior* (New York: John Wiley, forthcoming).
4. K.E. Kram, "A Relational Approach to Careers," in D.T. Hall, ed., *The Career Is Dead—Long Live the Career*, 132–157; K.E. Kram and D.T. Hall, "Mentoring in a Context of Diversity and Turbulence," in E. Kosseck and S. Lobel, eds., *Human Resource Strategies for Managing Diversity* (Blackwell Publishers, 1996), 108–136.
5. K.E. Kram, "A Relational Approach to Careers," in D.T. Hall, ed., *The Career Is Dead—Long Live the Career*, 132–157.
6. Ibid.
7. R.E. Boyatzis and F. Skelly, "The Impact of Changing Values in Organizational Life," in J.S. Osland, D.A. Kolb, and I.M. Rubin, eds., *The Organizational Behavior Reader*, 6th ed. (Engelwood Cliffs, N.J.: Prentice Hall, 1996).
8. J.V. Gallos, "Exploring Women's Development: Implications for Career Theory, Practice, and Research," in M.B. Arthur, D.T. Hall, and B.S. Lawrence, *Handbook of Career Theory* (New York: Cambridge University Press, 1989); D.J. Levinson, with C.N. Darrow, E.B. Klein, M.H. Levinson, and B. McKee, *The Seasons of a Man's Life* (New York: Knopf, 1978); D.J. Levinson in collaboration with Judy D. Levinson, *The Seasons of a Woman's Life* (New York: Knopf, 1996); D.A. Thomas and C.P. Alderfer, "The Influence of Race on Career Dynamics: Theory and Research on Minority Experiences," in M.B. Arthur, D.T. Hall, and B.S. Lawrence, *Handbook of Career Theory*; D.T. Thomas, "Racial Dynamics in Cross-Race Developmental Relationships," *Administrative Sciences Quarterly* 38(3): 169–194.
9. G. Sheehy, *New Passages: Mapping Your Life Across Time* (New York: Random House, 1995).
10. D.J. Levinson et al., *The Seasons of a Man's Life*: E. Erickson, *The Life Cycle Completed: A Review* (New York: W.W. Norton and Company, 1982, 1985); R.E. Boyatzis, "Performance, Learning, and Development as Modes of Growth and Adaptation," in M.A. Peiperl and M.B. Arthur, eds., *Career Frontiers: New Conceptions of Working Lives* (London: Oxford University Press, 1999), 76–98; see also reference 2.

11. R.E. Boyatzis and M. Sokol, *A Pilot Project to Assess Characteristics of Students in Collegiate Business Programs* (St. Louis, Mo.: American Association of Collegiate Schools of Business, 1982); Development Dimensions International, *Final Report: Phase III* (St. Louis, Mo.: American Association of Collegiate Schools of Business, 1985); D.G. Winter, D.C. McClelland, and A.J. Stewart, *A New Case for the Liberal Arts: Assessing Institutional Goals and Student Development* (San Francisco: Jossey-Bass, 1981); L. Specht and P. Sandlin, "The Differential Effects of Experiential Learning Activities and Traditional Lecture Classes in Accounting," *Simulations and Gaming* 22(2) (1991): 196–210; E.T. Pascarella and P.T. Terenzini, *How College Affects Students: Findings and Insights from twenty Years of Research* (San Francisco: Jossey-Bass, 1991); A.W. Astin, *What Matters in College: Four Critical Years Revised* (San Francisco: Jossey-Bass, 1992); R.E. Boyatzis, S.C. Cowen, and D.A. Kolb, *Innovation in Professional Education: Steps on a Journey from Teaching to Learning* (San Francisco: Jossey-Bass, 1995).

12. L. Porter and L. McKibbin, *Management Education and development: Drift or Thrust into the 21st Century?* (New York: McGraw-Hill, 1982); H.J. Muller, J.L. Porter, and R.R. Rehder, "Have the Business Schools Let Down U.S. Corporations?" *Management Review* 77(10) (October 1988); G. Fuchsberg, "Business School Gets Bad Grades," *Wall Street Journal*, 6 June 1990, B1–B2; M.R. Lewis, "The Gap in Management Education," *Selections* 6(3) (1990): 1–12.

13. R.E. Boyatzis, S.S. Cowen, and D.A. Kolb, "A Learning Perspective on Executive Education," *Selections* 11(3) (1995): 47–55.

14. Ibid; R. Ballou, D. Bowers, R.E. Boyatzis, and D.A. Kolb, "Fellowship in Lifelong Learning: An Executive Development Program for Advanced Professionals," *Journal of Management Education* 23(4) (1999): 338–354.

15. Boyatzis and Kolb, "Performance, Learning, and Development as Models of Growth and Adaptation" (see reference 10).

16. D.E. Hunt, *Beginning with Ourselves: In Practice, Theory, and Human Affairs* (Cambridge, Mass.: Brookline Books, 1987).

17. D.A. Kolb, *Experiential Learning: Experience as the Source of Learning and Development* (Englewood Cliffs, N.J.: Prentice Hall, 1984).

18. W.N. Isaacs, "Taking Flight: Dialogue, Collective Thinking, and Organizational Learning," *Organizational Dynamics*, 1993, 24–39. Jean Baker Miller, "The Development of Women's Sense of Self," in J.V. Jordan, A.G. Kaplan, J. Baker-Miller, I.P. Striver, and J.L. Surrey, eds., *Women's Growth in Connection* (New York: Guilford Press, 1991); P.M. Senge, *The Fifth Discipline: The Art and Practice of the Learning Organization* (New York: Doubleday, 1990); E. Schein, "On Dialogue, Culture, and Organizational Learning," *Organizational Dynamics*, 1993, 40–51.

19. Cf.M.W. McCall Jr., M.M. Lombardo, and A.M. Morrison, *The Lessons of Experience* (Lexington, Mass.: Lexington Press, 1988).

20. See reference 4.

21. Jean Baker Miller, *The New Psychology of Women* (Boston: Beacon Press, 1986); J. Fletcher, "A Relational Approach to the New Protean Worker," in D.T. Hall, ed., *The Career Is Dead—Long Live the Career*, 105–131; J.V. Jordan et al., *Women's Growth in Connection*.

22. C. McCauley and D.P. Young, "Creating Developmental Relationships: Rules and Strategies," *Human Resources Management Review* 3(3) (1993): 219–230; M.N. Ruderman, P.J. Ohlott, and C.D. McCauley, "Assessing Opportunities for Leadership Development," in K.E. Clark and M.B. Clark, eds., *Measures of Leadership* (West Orange, N.J.: Leadership Library of America, 1990).

23. K. Seibert, "Experience Is the Best Teacher If You Can Learn from It," in D.T. Hall, ed., *The Career Is Dead—Long Live the Career*, 246–264.